OFFICE PROCEDURES FOR THE LEGAL PROFESSIONAL

DELMAR CENGAGE Learning

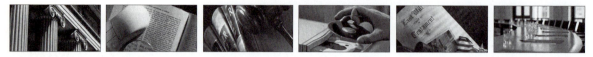

Options.

Over 300 products in every area of the law: textbooks, online courses, CD-ROMs, reference books, companion web-sites, and more – helping you succeed in the classroom and on the job.

Support.

We offer unparalleled, practical support: robust instructor and student supplements to ensure the best learning experience, custom publishing to meet your unique needs, and other benefits such as Delmar Cengage Learning's Student Achievement Award. And our sales representatives are always ready to provide you with dependable service.

Feedback.

As always, we want to hear from you! Your feedback is our best resource for improving the quality of our products. Contact your sales representative or write us at the address below if you have any comments about our materials or if you have a product proposal.

Accounting and Financials for the Law Office • Administrative Law • Alternative Dispute Resolution • Bankruptcy Business Organizations/Corporations • Careers and Employment • Civil Litigation and Procedure • CLA Exam Preparation • Computer Applications in the Law Office • Constitutional Law • Contract Law • Court Reporting Criminal Law and Procedure • Document Preparation • Elder Law • Employment Law • Environmental Law • Ethics Evidence Law • Family Law • Health Care Law • Immigration Law • Intellectual Property • Internships Interviewing and Investigation • Introduction to Law • Introduction to Paralegalism • Juvenile Law • Law Office Management • Law Office Procedures • Legal Nurse Consulting • Legal Research, Writing, and Analysis • Legal Terminology • Legal Transcription • Media and Entertainment Law • Medical Malpractice Law Product Liability • Real Estate Law • Reference Materials • Social Security • Sports Law • Torts and Personal Injury Law • Wills, Trusts, and Estate Administration • Workers' Compensation Law

---

DELMAR CENGAGE Learning
5 Maxwell Drive
Clifton Park, New York 12065-2919

For additional information, find us online at:
www.delmar.cengage.com

OFFICE PROCEDURES FOR THE LEGAL PROFESSIONAL

Judy A. Long

DELMAR
CENGAGE Learning

Australia • Brazil • Japan • Korea • Mexico • Singapore • Spain • United Kingdom • United States

DELMAR
CENGAGE Learning™

Office Precedures for the Legal Professional
Judy A. Long

Vice President: Dawn Gerrain

Director of Editorial: Sherry Gomoll

Editorial Assistant: Sarah Duncan

Director of Production: Wendy A. Troeger

Production Manager: Carolyn Miller

Production Editor: Betty L. Dickson

Director of Marketing: Wendy Mapstone

Cover Design: Dutton and Sherman Design

For product information and technology assistance, contact us at
Cengage Learning Customer & Sales Support, 1-800-354-9706
For permission to use material from this text or product,
submit all requests online at **www.cengage.com/permissions**
Further permissions questions can be emailed to
permissionrequest@cengage.com

Library of Congress Cataloging-in-Publication Data: 2004043921

ISBN-13: 978-1-4018-4083-9

ISBN-10: 1-4018-4083-3

Delmar
Executive Woods
5 Maxwell Drive
Clifton Park, NY 12065
USA

Cengage Learning is a leading provider of customized learning solutions with office locations around the globe, including Singapore, the United Kingdom, Australia, Mexico, Brazil, and Japan. Locate your local office at **international.cengage.com/region**

Cengage Learning products are represented in Canada by Nelson Education, Ltd.

For your course and learning solutions, visit **delmar.cengage.com**

Visit our corporate website at **www.cengage.com**

Notice to the Reader

Publisher does not warrant or guarantee any of the products described herein or perform any independent analysis in connection with any of the product information contained herein. Publisher does not assume, and expressly disclaims, any obligation to obtain and include information other than that provided to it by the manufacturer. The reader is expressly warned to consider and adopt all safety precautions that might be indicated by the activities described herein and to avoid all potential hazards. By following the instructions contained herein, the reader willingly assumes all risks in connection with such instructions. The publisher makes no representations or warranties of any kind, including but not limited to, the warranties of fitness for particular purpose or merchantability, nor are any such representations implied with respect to the material set forth herein, and the publisher takes no responsibility with respect to such material. The publisher shall not be liable for any special, consequential, or exemplary damages resulting, in whole or part, from the reader's use of, or reliance upon, this material.

Printed in the United States of America
4 5 6 7 11 10 09 08

DEDICATION

To Michael

BRIEF CONTENTS

CONTENTS

Many different employees comprise the law office team. The goal of this text is to present an overview of the structure and functions of the law office while providing the student with an opportunity to learn about different responsibilities of various law office employees. Different specialty areas of law are explored in depth from the perspective of one who is preparing the paperwork and documents for these practice areas. Practical problems such as one would encounter in a law office are presented.

The book may be used by students learning to become legal administrators, legal assistants, paralegals, or other types of law office professional. The material presented is beneficial for any law office employee. Thus, the text may be used as a research tool for individuals employed in law offices.

Several trends are evident in the law office setting. Large law firms employ paralegals and legal assistants in many different specialty areas. Smaller law firms may employ one individual who performs the function of the paralegal and legal assistant in one or more specialty area. This book serves the need of both communities in that it is divided into chapters emphasizing the different practice areas. The student will find it useful to take the book with them when they pursue their legal careers. It will provide an excellent research tool for various practice areas as well as the administrative functions required in the law office.

Organization of Text

The text begins with a very basic explanation of the various types of law office structure and the different employee functions. It explains the different types of law offices, including private law firms, public firms, government office, and the courts. A chapter is set aside for the organization of the courts, including state and federal.

An in-depth study is provided into the administrative responsibilities of a law office employee. The duties covered consist of preparing calendars, billing, timekeeping, making travel arrangement, preparing legal correspondence and documents, and using the computer and the Internet.

The procedures used at trial are discussed, including the civil and the criminal trial. Explanations are given for trial book preparation and the compilation of evidence for trial. The sequence of the trial and appellate procedures are explained.

Individual chapters cover the different legal specialty areas of criminal law, civil litigation, estate planning, probate, family law, business organizations, bankruptcy, real property, and contracts. The last chapter is devoted to the process of obtaining employment as a legal assistant or paralegal, including the job search, preparing resumes and cover letters, interviews, and follow-up letters.

Project Notebooks

 Students should be required to prepare a reference notebook that will be useful both during this course and later on the job. A notebook logo beside documents and projects in the text indicates that they should be placed in the notebook. To prepare the notebook, the student will need a three-ring binder with dividers and tabs. Each section in the notebook should coincide with a chapter in the text. The student should be required to prepare the "skeleton" notebook before beginning the textbook assignments.

As each chapter is studied, documents or forms with the notebook logo should be added to the notebook along with instructions given in the text for preparing the document. Whenever the instructor gives the student specific instructions on the manner in which a document is prepared, served, or filed, these directions should be added to the notebook along with a sample of the document. All checklists in the text should be included in the notebook under the appropriate subject heading. Each chapter concludes with projects that require the student to work with documents and forms in the chapter. After the projects are graded, they should be put into the notebook. At the end of the course, the instructor should again check the notebook to be sure that all required items are included.

The student should be encouraged to add to the notebook as he takes more courses in the program. Some of the material encountered in subsequent courses will fit under the headings established for this course. In some cases, new headings will be added as the student progresses through the course of study.

The notebook will prove valuable after graduation from the program. Most employers require a writing sample to be submitted with the employment application. The assignments in the notebook can be used for this purpose. The notebook also assists in teaching organizational skills and provides models to use when similar documents are prepared on the job. Since documents prepared in law offices tend to be repetitive in nature; the student may follow the format of a document in the notebook and simply fill in the names and other new information.

Each time the student prepares something new "on the job" or in another class, it should be included in the notebook. The student should add to the notebook throughout her legal career. Former students have agreed with the benefits of keeping a notebook even after several years in the legal profession. Instructors are encouraged to use this "notebook" approach throughout the course of study in the paralegal or legal assistant programs.

Special Features ✦

- **State Specific Information** boxes are included in each chapter. These boxes provide space for students to write down information on rules and procedures specific to their own state.

- **Key Terms** are printed in bold type and are defined in the margin where they first appear within the chapter.

- **Chapter Summaries** at the end of each chapter provide a brief review of the main concepts covered.

- **Self Tests** at the end of each chapter help students to review the main concepts discussed. Answers to the self-test questions are included in the Appendix to enable students to identify any areas that they may not have addressed thoroughly.

- **Review Questions** in short-answer format also appear at the end of each chapter to provoke an additional review of chapter concepts.

- **Notebook Projects** at the end of each chapter provide students with practical experience in performing the tasks of legal assistants and paralegals, including proofreading, drafting and preparing documents, and filling out forms.

- **Notebook Logos** precede those projects that students should place in their Notebooks.

- **Notebooks** must be prepared by all students and are explained in the Organization of Text section of this Preface. Pages from the text should be placed in the notebooks if the notebook logo appears therein.

Supplementary Materials ✦

This text is accompanied by support material that will aid instructors in teaching and students in learning. The following supplements accompany the text:

- **Resource Book** This supplementary book includes forms for documents and pleadings that are prepared in the law office. In most cases, the student may "fill in the blanks" to use these forms.

- **Instructor's Manual** This supplement is designed for instructors to assist in presenting text material in an organized and comprehensive manner. The manual includes a detailed summary of each chapter, lesson plans (including suggestions for speakers and field trips), answers to the Review Questions, and suggestions for additional projects. A comprehensive test bank contains more than 200 objective test questions and answers. Transparency masters are provided for use in lectures.

- **CD-ROM** A CD-ROM is provided with selected documents and helpful hints in Word format. The CD-ROM may be used to complete certain end-of-chapter projects that have the CD-ROM logo.

The CD-ROM will also include templates of documents that will be commonly used in the law office as well as a selection of forms that students will need to complete assignments from the text.

- **Web Pages** Come visit our Web site at **www.paralegal.delmar. cengage.com** where you will find valuable information such as sample materials to download, as well as other West Legal Studies products.

- **Westlaw®** West's online computerized legal research system offers students "hands-on" experience with a system commonly used in law offices. Qualified adopters can receive ten free hours of Westlaw. Westlaw can be accessed with Macintosh, IBM PC, and other compatible computers. A modem is required.

- **Survival Guide for Paralegal Students** A pamphlet by Kathleen Mercer Reed and Bradene Moore covers practical and basic information to help students make the most of their paralegal courses. Topics covered include choosing courses of study and note-taking skills.

- **West's Paralegal Video Library** West Legal Studies is pleased to offer the following videos at no charge to qualified adopters:

  - *The Drama of the Law II: Paralegal Issues Video* ISBN 0-314-07088-5

  - *The Making of a Case Video* ISBN 0-314-07300-0

  - *ABA Mock Trial Video—Product Liability* ISBN 0-314-07342-6

  - *Arguments to the United States Supreme Court Video* ISBN 0-314-07070-2

- Court TV Videos West Legal Studies is pleased to offer the following videos from Court TV for a minimal fee while supplies last:

  - *New York v. Ferguson—Murder on the 5:33: The Trial of Colin Ferguson* ISBN 0-7668-0198-4

  - *Ohio v. Alfieri* ISBN 0-7668-1099-2

  - *Flynn v. Goldman Sachs—Fired in Wall Street: A Case of Sex Discrimination?* ISBN 0-7668-1096-8

  - *Dodd v. Dodd—Religion and Child Custody in Conflict* ISBN 0-7668-1094-1

  - *In Re Custody of Baby Girl Clausen—Child of Mine: The Fight for Baby Jessica* ISBN 0-7668-1097-6

  - *Fentress v. Eli Lilly & Co., et al—Prozac on Trial* ISBN 0-7668-1095-X

  - *Garcia v. Garcia—Fighting over Jerry's Money* ISBN 0-7668-0264-7

  - *Hall v. Hall—Irretrievably Broken A Divorce Lawyer Goes to Court* ISBN 0-7668-0196-9

  - *Maglica v. Maglica—Broken Hearts, Broken Communications* ISBN 0-7668-0867-X

  - *Northside Partners v. Page and New Kids on the Block—New Kids in Court: Is Their Hit Song a Copy?* ISBN 0-7668-9426-7

About the Author ✦

Judy Long is a retired attorney and college professor. She taught at a community college for 25 years and developed a paralegal program that was approved by the American Bar Association. Prior to teaching, she spent twelve years working as a legal assistant in private law offices and corporate law departments. Her first legal position was as a part-time legal assistant in a small private law firm while she was in high school. She has written several legal textbooks, including:

1. *Basic Business Law* (co-author 2d edition), Prentice-Hall, 1994
2. *Law Office Procedures*, Delmar Cengage Learning, 1997
3. *Legal Research Using the Internet*, Delmar Cengage Learning, 2000
4. *California Legal Directory*, Delmar Cengage Learning, 2000
5. *Computer Aided Legal Research*, Delmar Cengage Learning, 2003
6. *Legal Research Using Westlaw*, Delmar Cengage Learning, 2001
7. *California Supplement to Civil Litigation*, Delmar Cengage Learning, 1995

Acknowledgments ✦

Many individuals provided valuable assistance in the preparation of this textbook.

First and foremost, I would like to thank my editor, Pam Fuller, and editorial assistant, Sarah Duncan, for their numerous suggestions and considerable assistance.

The following individuals provided very valuable suggestions and recommendations in their reviews of the text:

Linda DeLorme
Olympic College

Lucille Flores
Briarwood College

Susann Shanahan
Central Technology Center

Marilyn Wudarcki
North Idaho College

I sincerely appreciate the considerable support I received from the following individuals, who provided suggestions and materials for use in this text:

John Callinan for his material and charts on the California court structure.

Sheila Cantrell for her information and materials on expense accounts and preparation of time sheets.

Dave Scott for the real estate materials.

Rachel Sotelo for her landlord/tenant materials.

Finally, I would like to thank all the other people whose names have been inadvertently omitted.

Feedback

The user may contact the author through, e-mail at **Jaler@aol.com** with questions, suggestions, or comments about the text or supplements.

Judy A. Long, J.D.

Please note that the Internet resources are of a time-sensitive nature and URL addresses may often change or be deleted.

Contact us at paralegal.delmar@cengage.com

ORGANIZATION OF THE LAW OFFICE

CHAPTER OUTCOMES

As a result of studying this chapter, the student will learn:

- The similarities and differences of the basic structures of private and public law offices

- Why corporate law departments work differently from law firms

- To distinguish government law offices that operate on federal, state, county, and local levels

- The legal specialty areas in private and public law offices

LAW OFFICE STRUCTURE

Law offices are structured based on whether they are public or private, and many are also defined by their legal specialty. Individual law firms may be organized as individual proprietorships, partnerships, or professional corporations, as will be described more fully in Chapter 11. However, all law offices employ much the same personnel. This section describes the many different individuals who comprise the law office team. The chart in Exhibit 1-1 on page 2 shows the organization of a typical law office.

Lawyers/Attorneys

The terms *lawyer* and *attorney* are used interchangeably and have the same meaning. In order to use either the title of lawyer or **attorney**, a person must graduate from law school, pass the state bar examination for the state in which the individual intends to practice, and be formally admitted to that state's bar organization. To practice in another state, one must pass the bar examination for that state and be admitted to practice there. Typically, one must first obtain an undergraduate degree to become eligible for law school. Law school usually consists of approximately three years of classes. Upon graduation, the person becomes eligible to take the bar examination in that state.

Large law firms may have attorneys at several different levels, including senior partners, partners, junior partners, senior associates, associates, and junior associates. In general, the larger the law firm, the more levels of titles its attorneys will have.

attorney lawyer; a person licensed to practice law.

EXHIBIT 1-1 Law Office Organization Chart

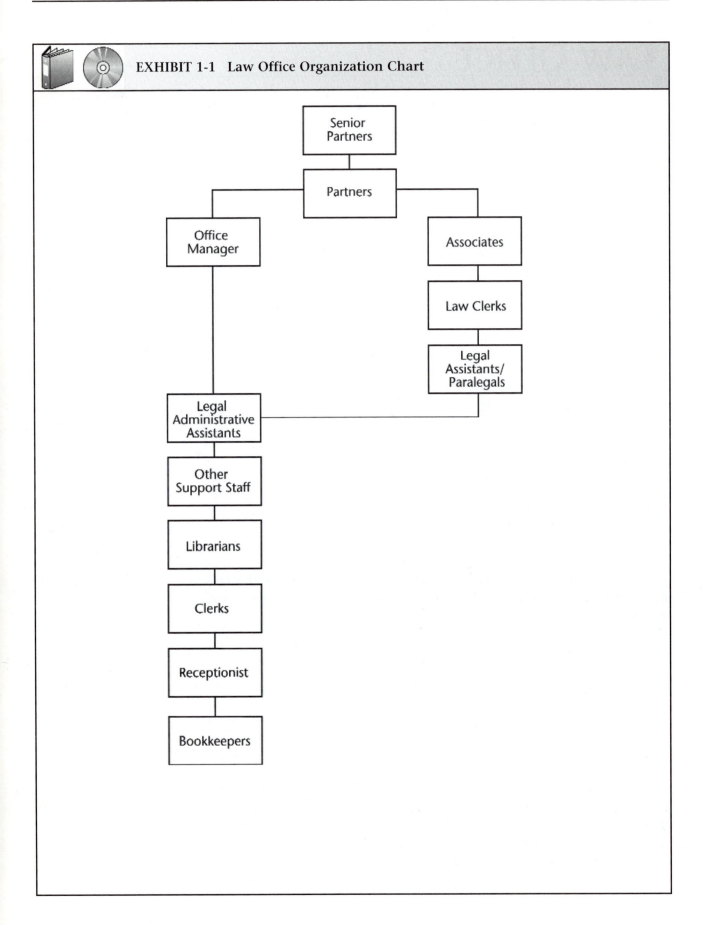

Government law offices may have different titles for their attorneys, such as district attorney, prosecutor, public defender, advocate, and so on. Corporate law departments may also have varied titles for their attorneys, such as general counsel, general attorney, or some other title depending on the nature of the company. Regardless of the title, the individual must have passed the state bar examination in the state in which he practices in order to hold one of these positions. No one may practice law without a state license to do so.

Partners are the actual owners of the firm and receive a percentage of its profits. Senior partners generally have a greater ownership interest than other partners and are often the founders of the law firm. Associates are paid a salary and are not allocated an ownership interest in the law firm. Neither do they share in the profits. New associates are called junior associates in some large law offices.

Attorneys with the title "Of Counsel" act in an advisory capacity to the firm, often in a given specialty area. They generally do not have an ownership interest in the firm and do not share in the profits.

Law Clerk

A large percentage of law students who wish to obtain practical training will seek employment in law firms on a part-time basis. Some of these students work for judges in the courts. In general, these students have completed at least two years of law school. Their responsibilities include legal research, document preparation, case investigation, and drafting pleadings. Some law clerks file documents with the courts and do errands for the attorneys. Their duties vary with the size and type of law firm. Many of these part-time law clerk positions will enable the student to obtain a position at the firm as an attorney upon completing law school and passing the bar exam.

Managing Attorney

Managing attorneys are responsible for the day-to-day legal operations of the law firm. They may review cases handled by other attorneys and hold weekly progress meetings. They may also be responsible for dividing the case load among the attorneys. If the firm does not employ an administrative manager, the managing attorney may be responsible for the administrative functions of the firm.

Law Office Manager

The law office manager is responsible for administering the business, management, and office operations of the firm. Depending on the size of the firm, this individual may also manage other administrators in the firm, including the human relations manager, file manager, librarian, accounting officer, paralegals, and other administrative staff. Although the paralegals will be assigned to do work for specified attorneys, the law office manager will be responsible for distributing the workload and making sure that rush projects are distributed in a timely manner.

The law office manager may be a senior paralegal with management training, an attorney, or an individual with a degree in business who has had law firm experience. This person is responsible for all of the administrative and support functions of the law office, including general administration, human resources, employee benefits, file room, duplicating services, library, equipment, and purchasing. The position carries a tremendous amount of responsibility and requires talent in a broad range of administrative functions.

Law Librarian

Law librarians are employed in large firms and should have training in one of the computerized legal research systems, such as Westlaw® or Lexis®. Their responsibilities include computerized legal research, general legal research, keeping track of volumes, ordering books, updating volumes, and generally maintaining the library. Usually a law librarian has a degree in library science, legal training, or both.

Legal Assistant/Legal Administrative Assistant

In smaller law firms, the legal assistant may also be assigned paralegal responsibilities. However, in larger firms, the two positions have distinctly different tasks. Well-trained and efficient legal assistants represent a tremendous asset to a law firm.

The **legal assistant** may work for one or several attorneys, depending on the work load. Responsibilities include calendaring, answering the telephone, taking messages, handling mail, docket control, scheduling appointments, travel arrangements, filing, and typing correspondence and documents. The Internet is an invaluable tool for the legal assistant for doing research, making travel arrangements, and providing routes and maps to distant or local sites.

Most legal assistants are trained in legal assistant programs in community colleges, adult education, or proprietary schools. Computer training is essential, especially in the many software packages available for the legal profession.

Paralegal/Legal Assistant

paralegal/legal assistant individual who does law-related work for attorneys, government agencies, and corporations; must work under attorney supervision.

Although some firms use the terms paralegal and legal assistant interchangeably, most of the larger firms have two distinct levels for these positions. In firms with two different positions, the paralegal generally has additional responsibilities. In smaller firms with a combination paralegal and legal assistant, the individual has paralegal and administrative duties combined.

Paralegals may assist lawyers in several different areas, including drafting documents, discovery, interviewing clients and witnesses, and doing legal research and investigation. Depending on the attorney's specialty, the paralegal may also be involved in other activities.

In general, paralegals are trained professionals with either a four year bachelor's degree and a paralegal certificate or a two-year associate's degree in paralegal studies.

Receptionist

The first contact a client has with a law firm is through the receptionist; hence, this is considered to be one of the most critical positions in the office. Encountering a rude receptionist may set the tone for a difficult meeting between the attorney and the client. On the other hand, if the receptionist is cordial and friendly, the client will be in a better mood for the meeting with the attorney. The receptionist should be trained in how to handle difficult clients and situations, and be computer literate and have good keyboarding skills.

Accounting/Payroll Clerk

While many firms employ an outside service to manage their accounting and payroll functions, some larger firms have separate accounting and/or payroll departments for this purpose. This department or firm keeps the books of the firm, prepares the payroll, pays the firm's bills, and sends out monthly statements to individual clients after compiling the data from the attorney and paralegal timesheets.

THE LEGAL PROFESSIONAL AND THE CLIENT ✦

It is important to remember that the primary role of all members of the law firm is to help solve a client's problem. Be sure to maintain a professional atmosphere and attitude in all contacts with clients. Remember that all information obtained from the client is confidential and should not be divulged to anyone except the attorney working on the case. A more detailed analysis of the ethical codes for confidentiality will be discussed in Chapter 3.

There will be times when you have six different projects on your desk at once, one of which has an impossible deadline, and a client calls you on the telephone for what you think is an unreasonable request. Remember that the client is not aware of your other projects, and, in fact, most clients want to be treated as if they are the firm's only clients. Be polite, keep a smile in your voice, and offer to call the client back after you obtain the information. If the client has an e-mail address, offer to send an e-mail after you research the question.

THE LEGAL PROFESSIONAL AND THE ATTORNEY ✦

Working as a legal professional can be a very stressful position because of the many deadlines with which you are faced. The attorney is often under a degree of stress as well and may have different expectations of your abilities.

One of the most important rules to remember when working with an attorney is that your primary job is to save time for the lawyer so that he or she is free to perform other tasks. You must accomplish all tasks accurately and in a timely fashion. If it is impossible to finish a job on time, tell the attorney or office manager before the deadline so that help can be obtained. The following is a partial list of expectations an attorney has of a legal assistant:

1. *Receive instructions for an assignment.* Remember that attorneys are often very busy and may assume that you understand the instructions when you are unclear. Never start an assignment until you know exactly what is expected. You may take several hours to complete what you think the attorney wants, only to find that what he really wanted would have taken a much shorter period of time. Your most important question about any assignment is, "When is it due to be completed?" It is helpful to receive the client's file at the same time as you receive the assignment so that you can look up names, spellings, and other key information you might need for the assignment.

2. *Communicate your limitations.* If you are given an assignment that you are not capable of completing, be sure to indicate this to the attorney at the outset. Particularly with new legal assistants, the attorney may not be familiar with your capabilities. However, if instructions on how to complete the assignment can be obtained by doing a minimal amount of research, try to accomplish the task before admitting defeat. Remember that the attorney may become impatient when the assistant makes the same mistakes over and over again, so check your work carefully.

3. *Be willing to accept responsibility.* Approach new tasks with a smile and enthusiastically. Be ready to accept added responsibility. Do not grudgingly accept a new assignment with a scowl or you may be relegated to the more mundane tasks, which can make your job very boring.

4. *Take notes.* Never enter the attorney's office without a pen and notebook in your hand. Expect instructions each time you see the attorney and don't expect to remember them. Write everything down. Keep your notebook even after the assignment is completed. Date your notebook at the beginning of each day so that you know when the assignment was given. Also note its due date.

5. *Listen carefully.* One of the major causes of errors is not listening carefully. Listen to every word the attorney says and take good notes. Do not expect to remember instructions you were given without writing them down. If you do not understand the instructions, ask questions.

6. *Record instructions for later use.* If you are doing a particular type of assignment for the first time, type up the instructions and put

them in your Notebook of Projects Completed for future reference. Then, when the attorney has a similar assignment for you, find the instructions in your Notebook.

7. *Review the files.* If time permits, review the client's file to obtain background information on the assignment. If you are completing a project that you have never done before, ask the attorney if you can obtain a sample from another client's file. Make copies of each sample for your Notebook.

8. *Review the assignment.* Read through the instructions before starting the assignment to determine whether you are clear on what has to be done. If you have further questions, make a list and ask the attorney when he has free time. Never ask several different questions at different times when you can ask them all at the same time.

9. *Do the work in a timely fashion.* Keep in mind the assignment's deadline. Work efficiently and accurately. Check and recheck your work. Remember that using spell check is not enough because you may write the wrong word that will not be noted because it is an actual word. For instance, writing "council" for "counsel" would not be noted by spell check.

10. *Prioritize projects.* Prioritizing projects is particularly important when you work for more than one attorney. You must know which job is the most important and should be completed first. If you are not sure, ask both attorneys or the office manager.

11. *Assemble the finished product neatly.* Complete the project accurately and be sure there are no smudges on the document. Staple multiple pages in the upper left corner. Reread the document one last time to be sure there are no errors. Depending on the attorney's preference, you may put the finished paperwork in a folder, in an "in box," or another place preferred by that particular attorney. If the project requires the attorney's signature, be sure that he will be in the office on the date the job is completed.

THE LEGAL PROFESSIONAL AND OTHER EMPLOYEES

Maintain the same positive attitude when dealing with all employees of the law firm. Remember that individuals will protect their territories and domains, so always follow proper procedures when taking books from the library, taking files from the file room, or removing any materials that are supervised by another individual.

Be helpful if another assistant is doing a rush job and you have some free time and can help. You might be in the same position another day and need their help.

Do not take part in office gossip. This is particularly essential in the law office environment because of the confidentiality issue. Sometimes you will have an interesting case and be tempted to discuss it with other employees. This is not appropriate unless the person is working on the case with you and knows all of the same details of the case. In some situations, another assistant might be involved in another aspect of a large case and not be familiar with your part of it. In that instance, it would not be appropriate to discuss the case with him.

PRIVATE LAW FIRMS ✦

Private law firms may consist of one attorney and one combination legal assistant/paralegal. In their largest form, they may be composed of several attorneys, paralegals, assistants, and all of the other employees discussed above. The larger the law firm, the more specialized the duties of the staff members.

Therefore, you may expect to assume the responsibilities of many of the employees previously mentioned if you work for a small law firm. If you are working for a large firm, you will likely work for one attorney who is in a specialized practice area. Of course, there are many different sizes of law firms between the sole practitioner and the large mega firm. You will find that if you like many diverse duties in a smaller less formal office, you may prefer working for a sole practitioner. On the other hand, if you enjoy a more formal atmosphere where you have very specific duties and responsibilities, employment in a large firm will probably be your preference.

CORPORATE LAW DEPARTMENTS ✦

Most large corporations have their own law departments. Attorneys in these departments are called in-house counsel. A corporate law department employs paralegals and legal assistants, librarians, file clerks, and other legal support personnel. However, it does not include accounting or other administrative personnel because they are available in other departments of the corporation. For instance, the corporation may have its own Human Resources and Payroll Departments, which will perform those functions for the law department.

Employment responsibilities in a corporate law department are as diverse as the corporation's products or services. Listed below are some of the specialty areas of the corporate law department:

- Workers compensation
- Contracts
- Real estate
- Patents
- Industrial relations
- Insurance
- Environmental law

- Taxes
- Finance
- Stock operations

In most cases, the corporate law department's only client is the corporation itself. Therefore, client contacts are limited to contacts with other employees of the corporation. The pace of a corporate law department may be less hectic than that of a private law firm because the paralegal or legal assistant has only one client.

Other departments of the corporation lend support to the law department related to their own specialties. For instance, accounting reports are available from the Accounting Department. Information on personnel is available from the Human Resources Department. Experts are found in each department based on their area of specialty.

GOVERNMENT LAW OFFICES

A large number of government agencies employ paralegals and legal assistants in various capacities. Many job opportunities exist in criminal law from prosecution to defense. Positions also exist in family law, consumer law, and probate. County governments have domestic violence programs that utilize paralegals and legal assistants, under attorney supervision, to assist victims in obtaining restraining orders. The probate department of the county court employs paralegals and legal assistants.

Government agencies provide regular hours, excellent benefit packages, and regular salary reviews and opportunities for advancement. Duties and responsibilities tend to be as varied as the area of government in which the paralegal is employed.

The Federal Government

The United States Department of Justice, with branches in most major cities, is one of the largest employers of paralegals and legal assistants in the country. Agencies within the Justice Department, with which you might obtain employment, include the Drug Enforcement Administration, the Office of the Solicitor General, and the Office of Personnel Management. Other federal departments employing paralegals and legal assistants include the military branches, Civil Rights Commission, Equal Employment Opportunity Commission (EEOC), Transportation Department, Postal Service, Federal Deposit Insurance Corporation (FDIC), Commerce Department, Labor Department, and the Securities and Exchange Commission (SEC), to name only a few.

Paralegals and legal assistants may be involved in investigating cases, examining case files, preparing documents and correspondence, doing legal research, reading and analyzing statutes, interviewing witnesses, making travel arrangements, developing and studying evidence, gathering documents, and compiling information for trials. Cases may be as diverse as prosecution of drug dealers, court martials, stock fraud, or employment discrimination.

State and County Governments

A large number of legal assistants and paralegals are employed by the state and county in criminal law, both for the prosecution and the defense. They help prepare cases for trial, do legal research, find and prepare witnesses for trial, prepare documents and correspondence, make travel arrangements, and investigate cases. When working for the defense, or public defender, time may be spent interviewing persons accused of crimes and investigating their backgrounds. When working for the prosecutorial side, or district attorney, time may be spent investigating prior convictions, doing legal research, preparing cases for trial, preparing correspondence and documents, making travel arrangements, and compiling information for a trial book.

County government departments employ paralegals and legal assistants in consumer protection agencies, to assist county counsel, in environmental protection agencies, and in many other areas of the county where legal assistance is required. Local governments are increasingly becoming involved with environmental matters. Some government agencies prosecute individuals and businesses that violate the laws related to air and water pollution. Individuals interested in environmental law should contact their county and local governments to learn what positions may be available in these areas.

NATIONAL PROFESSIONAL ORGANIZATIONS ✦

Membership in a legal professional organizations is beneficial not only for future employment but also for keeping abreast of the latest developments within the profession. It is important for legal secretaries and paralegals to join the appropriate organization for their particular profession. Most organizations offer less expensive student memberships that provide the opportunity for students to attend meetings, meet individuals already employed in the profession, and network for future employment. The following are the specific organizations for these professions:

- National Association of Legal Professionals, formerly National Association of Legal Secretaries, (NALS)
- National Association of Legal Assistants (NALA)
- National Federation of Paralegal Associations (NFPA)

National Association of Legal Professionals (NALS)

This organization's main office is located in Tulsa, Oklahoma and has been the major association for legal professionals for nearly 75 years. Most large metropolitan areas have branches of NALS. Their Web site, located at **www.nals.org**, has links to many other interesting sites, including legal news, education, careers, on-line learning, ethical codes, certification, and membership. Information about their professional certification is also available on their Web site.

National Association of Legal Assistants (NALA)

NALA is a leading professional organization for paralegals and provides continuing education and professional development programs. It is comprised of over 18,000 paralegals, including individual members of 90 state and local affiliated associations. Their Web site, **www.nala.org**, describes the organization and their education programs, as well as providing general information about the paralegal profession and paralegal careers.

National Federation of Paralegal Associations (NFPA)

NFPA is a leading organization of paralegals that is national in scope. Their Web site, located at **www.paralegals.org**, describes the organization and provides links to other legal resources, career opportunities, industry resources, membership, their certification program–PACE, continuing education, professional development, and their own publication entitled the *National Paralegal Reporter*.

Local Organizations

Many other local professional organizations exist in the larger metropolitan areas. A good place to find these associations is to start with a search of the local or county bar association in your city. Several bar

EXHIBIT 1-2 National Professional Organizations

NALS - National Association of Legal Professionals
314 East 3d Street, Suite 210
Tulsa, OK 74120
Phone: (918) 582-5188
E-mail: info@nals.org

NALA - National Association of Legal Assistants
1514 S. Boston, Suite 200
Tulsa, OK 74119
Phone: (918) 587-6828
E-mail: nalanet@nala.org

NFPA - National Federation of Paralegal Associations
PO Box 33108
Kansas City, MO 64114
Phone: (816) 941-4000
E-mail: info@paralegals.org

associations also enable students to join for a lower fee. Many localities have local branches of the national organizations listed above.

CHAPTER SUMMARY
✦

Private and public law offices may have different basic structures, but their employees all consist of attorneys, paralegals, legal assistants, and other support personnel. Corporate law departments work differently from law firms in that their only client is the corporation.

Government law offices operate on the federal, state, county, and local levels. Specialty areas in government include criminal, consumer protection, environmental law, and litigation, to name a few. Legal specialty areas include civil litigation, criminal, family, corporate, and real property law.

ETHICS and ETIQUETTE

The most important aspect of ethical considerations in the law office is the practice of attorney-client privileged communication. The law protects disclosure of privileged statements made to the attorney by the client. The law also applies to the attorney's employees who are working on a particular client's case. The basic rule to follow is: when in doubt about whether a communication is privileged, do not disclose any part of it to anyone except the attorney.

The law protects the revealing of privileged information relating to a client under any circumstances. For instance, if you are subpoenaed in a court proceeding and asked to reveal privileged communications received from the client, you are protected by the law so that you do not have to reveal this information.

The privilege of attorney-client confidentiality is so inclusive that it protects all information received from the client from being revealed at any time or place. Exceptions to this rule include the situation in which a client reveals that he is about to cause bodily harm to himself or another person, that he is about to commit a crime, or if he is about to commit a fraudulent act. In those cases, the attorney may be obligated to report the information. The exception also applies if the client is seeking the assistance of the attorney in these endeavors. Since there is a considerable amount of controversy surrounding several aspects of this ethical rule, it is advisable for the paralegal or legal secretary to not reveal the information unless directed to do so by the attorney or unless she has first received the attorney's approval. Realistically, it is highly unlikely that the client would tell the paralegal or legal secretary any of this information. In most cases, he would tell the attorney.

The client's confidential information in the law office should not be compromised accidentally. For instance, never answer questions on the telephone or give information about a client's case unless you are certain the person calling is the client. Someone may call you pretending to be the client and ask for confidential information. If you are not sure the person is the client, ask her to send you a letter or stop into the office so that you can be sure of the caller's identity.

Be careful about speaking on the telephone about one client's case when another client can listen. In fact, if one client asks you if another individual is a client of your firm, you may not reveal that fact or anything about the case. For instance, suppose there are two different clients waiting in your office to see the attorney. If one of them asks you the nature of the other's visit, you may not divulge this information. You may say, "I'm sorry, but I cannot reveal any information about a case or a client."

However, suppose one client proceeds to discuss her case with the other client in the office. In that case, the client herself is revealing the information. Only the client may reveal the information to a third party, as the privilege belongs to the client. You should never reveal information received from the client unless directed to do so by the attorney.

Solicitation of clients on behalf of the attorney is also forbidden. Although the attorney is allowed to advertise to the public at large, directly seeking a prospective client's business is prohibited. Therefore, the law office may not employ individuals who directly solicit business from clients. These people are called "cappers" and may operate near unemployment offices, hospitals, ambulances, and anywhere else where potential clients exist. In some cases, they use radios with police bands which enable them to know when ambulances have been dispatched. They are the modern-day "ambulance chasers."

If an attorney-employer tells you she will give you a monetary sum for getting clients for the attorney, this is solicitation and it is forbidden by the ethical codes and also by statutes in some states. You are not precluded from recommending your attorney-employer if a friend asks you for a reference, but at no time may you take money from the attorney for this recommendation.

The courts have held that attorneys may not pay their employees for bringing business to the firm. However, the end-of-the-year bonus given by most firms to their employees has been upheld by the courts as not qualifying under the solicitation provision even though this bonus is usually related to the firm's profits for the previous year.

The major difference lies in the direct solicitation of clients, either in person or by telephone. The exception to the rule is in class action litigation where contact may be made with those who are potential plaintiffs in the lawsuit in most states. However, some jurisdictions forbid this practice. However, it is important to know the rules for your own state in these situations.

✦ KEY TERMS

attorney   paralegal/legal assistant

✦ SELF TEST

Match the lettered positions with their numbered functions.

____ a. paralegal	1. drafts documents
____ b. legal administrative assistant	2. manages administration
____ c. law office manager	3. maintains library
____ d. law librarian	4. schedules meetings
____ e. bookkeeper	5. pays bills
____ f. lawyer	6. advises clients

Indicate whether the following statements are true (T) or false (F).

____ 1. Corporate law departments have many more clients than private law firms.

____ 2. The professional organization for paralegals is NALS.

____ 3. The professional organization for legal administrative assistants is NALA.

____ 4. The attorney who prosecutes defendants is called the district attorney.

Fill-in-the-blanks.

1. The managing attorney performs the administrative functions of the _____ in the law firm.

2. In order to call himself an attorney, a person must have passed the _____ for the state in which he practices.

3. The person who greets the clients as they arrive at the law office is called the

   _____.

4. A professional organization for legal secretaries is _____.

Return to the positions listed on the left in the matching section. Indicate which position is responsible for each of the following functions. Positions may be used more than once.

____ 1. updating books in the library

____ 2. running errands for the attorney

____ 3. sending bills to clients

____ 4. typing documents

____ 5. drafting documents

____ 6. negotiating settlements with insurance companies

____ 7. hiring paralegals

____ 8. appearing in court on behalf of the client

____ 9. giving the client legal advice

____ 10. answering the firm's telephone

____ 11. finding new offices for the firm

✦ REVIEW QUESTIONS

1. List four departments of the federal government that employ legal secretaries and paralegals.

2. Describe the functions of a legal assistant or paralegal.

3. What is the difference between a partner and an associate in a law firm?

4. Explain the differences between a private law firm and a corporate law department.

✦ NOTEBOOK PROJECTS

 1. Is there a federal Office of Personnel Management in your city? If not, where is the closest office?

 2. Does your locality have local chapters of any of the legal secretary or paralegal professional organizations? List their names and addresses, as well as the dates of their meetings.

CHAPTER 2

ORGANIZATION OF THE COURTS

CHAPTER OUTCOMES

As a result of studying this chapter, the student will learn:

- To distinguish between state and federal courts
- Where to obtain information about the makeup of state and federal courts, as well as filing procedures, court rules, and other information
- To recognize statutes of limitations that set time limits within which cases must be filed
- To distinguish the various state and federal administrative agencies that are important at all levels of government

UNITED STATES COURT SYSTEMS

Fifty-one court systems comprise the courts of the United States. One court system exists for each state, as well as one system for the federal structure. In order to serve the needs of the law office, legal assistants and paralegals must be familiar with the federal, state, and local rules applicable in each location, as well as the statutes that indicate the time limits within which materials must be filed with the courts. Time constraints are critical when filing documents with the proper court. If a deadline is missed, the client may be precluded from filing the case later. Missed deadlines are a major reason for malpractice suits against attorneys. Therefore, a good office calendaring system, which may be prepared on the computer, is essential when dealing with court deadlines.

One of the best ways to gain knowledge of a particular court's procedures is to attend a trial. Most courtrooms are open to the public. You can go to the courtroom and observe the trial while studying the procedures. Before attending a trial, it may be beneficial to study the state and federal codes and practice manuals on the local court's rules. This chapter provides an overview of a "typical" state court system and the federal court system, as well as the people who work in these courts. Before studying the court systems, however, it is necessary to understand two important concepts related to the judicial system: jurisdiction and venue.

JURISDICTION

Jurisdiction is the power of a particular court to hear a case brought before it. Courts of original jurisdiction are the trial courts where an action is initiated. Jurisdictions vary from state to state; therefore, you should check the statutes (laws) of your own state to learn the jurisdiction of its various courts. Federal court rules for jurisdiction should also be studied.

Courts of appellate jurisdiction are those to which a case is appealed from the trial court. Some appellate courts are required to hear all cases appealed. Others have the option of hearing a case or refusing it. You should check your state's statutes for the applicable appellate procedures, as well as the federal appellate rules if dealing with a case before the federal appellate courts.

Subject Matter Jurisdiction

Subject matter jurisdiction relates to the type of case being heard in the court. The case must be the kind of case this particular court hears in order for the court to have subject matter jurisdiction over this particular case.

State courts with **general jurisdiction** in civil actions may hear any kind of case brought before it except for those cases that must be brought in federal court. They may be called superior courts, circuit courts, or county courts. Most states also have trial courts of **limited jurisdiction** that have the authority to hear certain types of cases. For instance, some courts have the authority to hear only family matters, probate matters, or cases where there is a limited amount of money in dispute. They may be called municipal, justice, or district courts.

Personal Jurisdiction

The court may also be required to have **personal jurisdiction** over these parties. This means that the court has the power or authority over the individuals in the case, and particularly the defendant. This is also called **in personam jurisdiction**. In some cases, the court may lack personal jurisdiction over the parties but have either **in rem jurisdiction** or **quasi in rem jurisdiction** over the property that is the subject of the lawsuit. **In rem jurisdiction** means that property that is the subject of the lawsuit is located in that state. **Quasi in rem jurisdiction** may be possible if the defendant owns property in that state, even if the property is not the subject of the lawsuit. However, in that case, the judgment must be collected from the property in the state.

Courts must have subject matter jurisdiction over all cases. They must also have either personal, in rem, or quasi in rem jurisdiction in the case.

---

jurisdiction the geographical area within which a court or a public official has the right and power to operate. Also, the power of a particular court to hear a case.

subject matter jurisdiction the case must be the kind of case this particular court hears in order for the court to have subject matter jurisdiction over this particular case.

general jurisdiction court that may hear any kind of case brought before it except for those cases that must be brought in federal court. They may be called superior courts, circuit courts, or county courts.

limited jurisdiction courts that have the authority to hear certain types of cases. For instance, some courts have the authority to hear only family matters, probate matters, or cases where there is a limited amount of money in dispute.

personal jurisdiction (in personam jurisdiction) means personal jurisdiction over these particular parties. This means that the court has the power or authority over the individuals in the case, and particularly the defendant.

in rem jurisdiction jurisdiction is obtained over property that is the subject of the lawsuit and is located in that state.

quasi in rem jurisdiction jurisdiction is obtained if the defendant owns property in that state, even if the property is not the subject of the lawsuit. However, in that case, the judgment must be collected from the property in the state.

VENUE ✦

Proper venue for the specific court should not be confused with the concept of jurisdiction. **Venue** refers to the appropriate geographic area in which a case should be heard, usually where the defendant resides or where the incident occurred. Sometimes an attorney will file a Motion for a Change of Venue, listing reasons why the location of the trial should be moved to another district. The most common reason for requesting a change of venue is pretrial publicity about the case that may prevent the defendant from getting a fair trial because potential jurors may have been influenced by reports they have heard. The judge will consider the defendant's ability to get a fair trial in that particular location when deciding whether to change the venue.

Courts of Law and Equity

Under the English common law system, which is the source of our court system, two separate courts existed. One set of courts heard common law (legal) cases, while the other heard cases in equity that were based on equitable issues. In our country, these courts have been merged into one system. Civil actions, where the plaintiff is asking for money damages, are known as actions at law. For example, an automobile accident that causes personal injuries and damage to the car may lead to a civil lawsuit for money damages for injuries and repairs. In a suit in equity, the plaintiff is generally asking for restitution or attempting to force the defendant to do or stop doing an act. Typical examples are a suit for an **injunction** to stop a chemical plant from dumping pollutants into a stream or a suit for a restraining order to prevent an abusive spouse from approaching the victim. Equitable actions also include those cases where a specific law does not cover the situation, but the plaintiff is asking the court to "do justice" for fairness purposes.

Some cases involve both legal and equitable issues and are held at the same time. For example, a client may wish to sue for damages as a result of being beaten and may request a restraining order against the defendant at the same time.

venue the local area where a case may be tried. A court system may have jurisdiction to take a case in a wide geographical area, but the proper venue for the case may be one place within that area for the convenience of the parties.

injunction a judge's order to a person to do or to refrain from doing a particular thing.

STATE COURT SYSTEM ✦

Each state has its own court structure. However, since the majority of the states have similar systems, a typical state structure will be described here. The specific structure of your own state may be found in the court clerk's office or the local law library.

Trial Courts

Since trial courts are the originating level of courts in the state structure, they are called "courts of original jurisdiction." The court that hears the case initially is its court of original jurisdiction. The two most common levels of state trial courts are municipal (district or justice) and superior (county or circuit) courts. The municipal court is a lower-level court that hears misdemeanor criminal cases and civil cases up to a certain dollar amount ($25,000 in California.) Superior courts hear felony criminal cases and civil cases over a specified dollar amount. Most states also have small claims courts within the municipal court system that hear simple civil cases between litigants without the expense of an attorney. The dollar amounts in small claims court vary by state.

Appeals from the court of original jurisdiction are heard in the next higher court. For example, appeals from small claims court or municipal court would be heard in the appellate department of the superior court.

The chart in Exhibit 2-1 shows the structure of the California court system. You should obtain a copy of your own state court's structure and include it in the State Specific Information box on page 21.

State Court Web Pages

Many state courts have their own Web pages. If you are not able to find your own state courts' Web page, the following is a list of links to state sources:

http://www.lawsonline.com/

http://www.findlaw.com/

http://law.house.gov/17.htm

To conduct a search for your own state courts' Web page, use the following key words for conducting the search:

{name of state} state courts

For example, California provides a considerable amount of information about their state courts on the following Web page:

http://www.courtinfo.ca.gov/

Information may be obtained at this site regarding state court opinions, judicial council forms, court rules, information concerning branch courts, structure of the California judicial system, and an on-line guide to the California courts with information about family, juvenile, criminal, small claims, and traffic courts, as well as alternative dispute resources, jury duty, and legal resource links.

State Appellate Courts

In order to have a case appealed to a higher court, that court must have the power to review the decision of the court of original jurisdiction that originally heard the case. The appellate court hearing the case may make the following rulings:

EXHIBIT 2-1 The California Court System

Courtesy: Reprinted from Luten, *California Civil Litigation 3rd Edition*, Thomson Delmar Learning

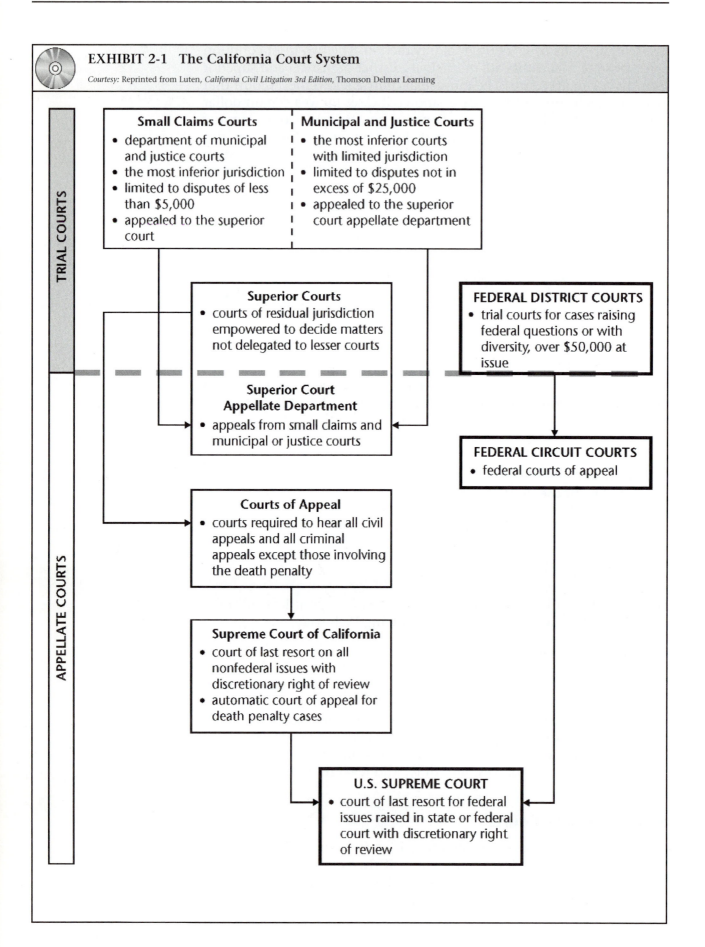

STATE OF _____ COURT STRUCTURE
AND JURISDICTION

1. Affirm the decision of the lower court

2. Reverse the decision of the lower court

3. Reverse the lower court's decision and remand the case back to the trial court for another trial (called reverse and remand).

The appellate court will not retry the case, but it may return the case to the lower court to have another trial there. Courts of appeal on the state level include the state court of appeals, the state supreme court, and the United States Supreme Court. In some cases, the lower trial court's cases (such as municipal or county court) would be appealed to the higher trial court's (such as superior court) appellate department.

An appellate court hearing is different from a trial. Each attorney will have already submitted her materials to the appellate court, which will also receive a transcript of the trial. At the hearing, each lawyer will have the opportunity to argue her side of the case to the justices. (Note that judges are called justices on the appellate and supreme court levels.) The decision will be rendered at a later date.

Cases are appealed from the trial court based on errors made at the trial court that were so egregious that they affected the outcome of the case. No new facts may be introduced at the appellate court level. The attorneys will have prepared appellate court briefs that attempt to persuade the court to rule in their client's favor. Briefs must include all the case precedents and statutes that support the client, as well as the attorney's most compelling arguments. Pertinent quotations from the cases and statutes are included and called Points and Authorities (or P&As.)

Paralegals may perform legal research for the preparation of the appellate court brief. They may also be asked to update ("**Shepardize**") cases and statutes, find code sections, or actually draft portions of the brief. The legal assistants will compile the information that is prepared by the attorney and/or paralegal into the finished product. It is important to check with the appellate courts in your own state to determine its particular rules for the preparation of the appellate brief. Some courts require that they be of a certain color, print size, binding, or have other conditions.

State Supreme Courts

The highest court in each state is usually called the supreme court, although some states use other names for their highest court. In New York and Maryland, the highest court is called the court of appeals. A few states have more than one supreme court. In Texas and Oklahoma, for example, the supreme court is the highest court for civil cases, whereas the court of criminal appeals is the highest court for criminal cases.

Hearings in the supreme court are conducted similarly to those in the appellate court. Briefs are presented to the supreme court as they are in the appellate court. A hearing is held in which both attorneys have a specified period of time to present oral arguments, after which

Shepardize use a Shepard's case citator to trace the history of a case after it is decided.

the justices may ask questions. The justices then consider their arguments and render a decision at a later date.

Not all cases can be appealed to the state supreme court. Generally, death penalty cases (in those states that have death penalties) are automatically reviewed. In all other instances, the state supreme court will hear appeals on a discretionary basis.

THE FEDERAL COURT SYSTEM ──────────── ✦

The only court established in the United States Constitution, Article III, is the United States Supreme Court. Under Article III, however, Congress was given the power to establish inferior courts as it sees fit:

> The judicial power of the United States shall be vested in one supreme court, and in such inferior courts as the Congress may from time to time establish.

Like state courts, the federal courts are structured in three tiers: trial courts, appellate courts, and the Supreme Court. See Exhibit 2-2.

Federal District Courts

The general trial courts in the federal system are known as the federal district courts. Various specialized trial courts also exist under this system, including the court of claims, tax court, and court of international trade. The court of claims handles civil cases against the United States government where the plaintiff is seeking money damages, except for tort claims, which are heard in the district courts.

There are 94 federal judicial districts, with at least one district located in each state. Larger and more heavily populated states, such as New York and California, have several districts. Most cases heard in a district court involve questions of federal law, such as federal statutes, treaties, or the United States Constitution. If an offense is a crime violating a federal statute, the district court will hear the case.

Diversity of citizenship cases are also heard in the federal district court. Thus, if the plaintiff and defendant reside in different states and the amount in controversy is greater than $50,000, the case may be heard in federal court. In general, under diversity of citizenship cases, the court applies the laws of the state in which the case is being heard. These cases usually involve concurrent jurisdiction of the federal and state courts. That is, the action could be filed by the plaintiff in either state or federal court. If the case is filed in state court, usually the defendant will have the right to have the case transferred to a federal court. The defendant must file a Notice of Removal, a document that requests the court to have the case removed from state court and transferred to federal district court. Cases may also involve concurrent jurisdiction when the controversy is between two or more states.

The larger district courts have several judges. Trials are conducted in a manner similar to those on the state level. Either party may request a jury trial in civil actions if money damages are sought.

EXHIBIT 2-2 The Federal Court System

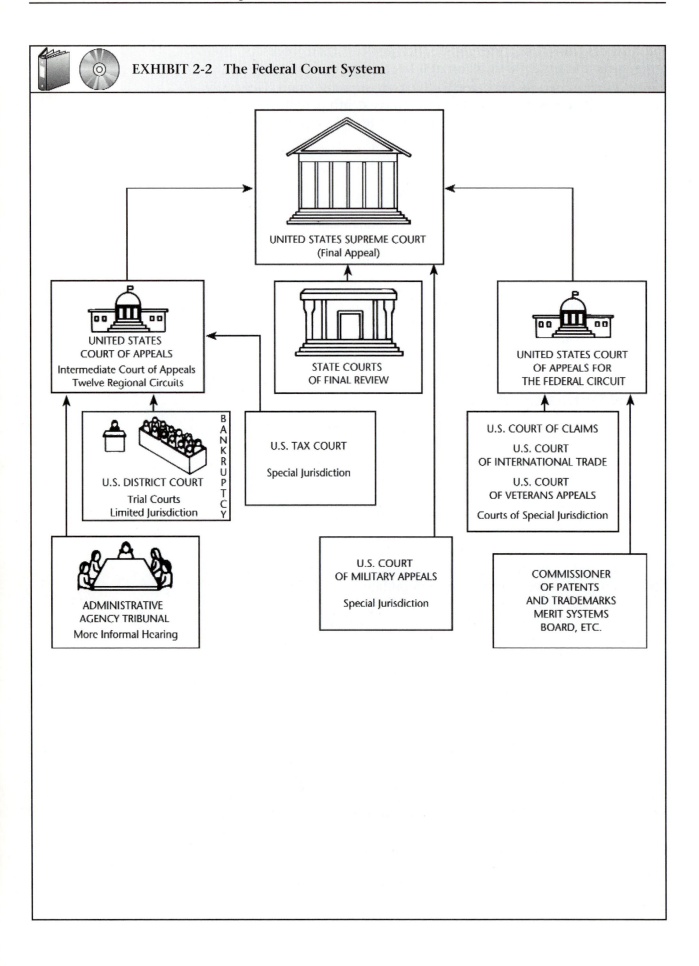

Specialized Federal Trial Courts

As mentioned above, the specialized courts in the federal system hear special types of cases. The bankruptcy court of each district is a part of the federal district court and hears all bankruptcy cases. Customs and international trade disputes are handled by the court of international trade. The tax court conducts cases between the Internal Revenue Service and taxpayers.

Circuit Courts of Appeal

Cases appealed from the district courts are heard in the thirteen federal circuit courts of appeal. Each circuit includes several states. The number of justices in each circuit depends on the size of the court and the number of cases being heard. Each individual case is heard before a panel of three justices. No trial is presented, but the attorneys file appellate briefs and present their oral arguments at the hearing.

United States Supreme Court

The highest federal court is the United States Supreme Court in Washington, D.C. Nine justices sit on this court, one of whom is the chief justice who presides over the court. All decisions of the federal circuit courts of appeal may be appealed to the Supreme Court. It may also hear cases where the highest state court has issued a decision that challenges the validity of a federal law.

Appeals to the Supreme Court begin with the appellant (the person bringing the appeal) petitioning the court for a **writ of certiorari**. This writ asks the court to hear the case; if four of the justices agree, the court will hear the proceeding. Generally, the court only hears cases that raise significant constitutional issues. Most cases referred to it are rejected.

Once the court agrees to hear the appeal, the clerk schedules the case for a hearing. Each side must then submit briefs to the Court. Like other appellate briefs, these are persuasive documents that attempt to convince the court to rule in the client's favor.

During the hearing before the full court, the attorneys present their oral arguments to convince the court to rule in their favor. The justices have the opportunity to question the attorneys at this time. The court will hand down a written decision at a later date, usually within three to six months.

Federal Court Web Sites

Many Web sites are available for finding information about federal laws and federal courts. Some of the more frequently used sites will be discussed here.

United States Supreme Court.   Web sites that exist for different areas of the Supreme Court follow:

writ of certiorari a writ from the higher court asking the lower court for the record of the case; similar to an appeal but one which the higher court is not required to take for decision.

1. Current court calendar—
   http://supct.law.cornell.edu/supct/calendar.htm
2. Oral arguments—
   http://supct.law.cornell.edu/supct/argcal97.html
3. Case name search—
   http://www.fedworld.gov/supcourt.csearch.htm
4. FindLaw page for Supreme Court cases and United States Code
   http://www.findlaw.com/casecode/supreme.html
5. Cases from 1967–present—**http://www.ijextra.com/cgi-bin/ussc**
6. Supreme Court cases—**http://www.usscplus.com/research.**
7. Supreme Court rules—
   http://www.law.cornell.edu/rules/supct/overview.html

The Federal Legal Information Through Electronics (FLITE) database includes over 7,000 Supreme Court cases from 1937 to 1975. Volumes 300–422 of the *United States Reports* are included in this database. If the case in which you are interested was decided during that time period and you know the name and citation number, you may access the following Web site to find the case:

> **http://www.fedworld/gov/supcourt/index.htm**

If you would like to do a key word search and do not know the name or citation number of the case, use the following Web site:

> **http://www.fedworld.gov/supcourt/fsearch.htm**

Be aware that Web sites change their addresses or are sometimes deleted. Therefore, if you cannot find the information you want on one of these pages, either do a key word search or look on another of the enumerated pages.

Circuit Courts of Appeal. A web page that includes general sources for all circuits includes federal court opinions, Supreme Court rules, appeals court rules, and rules from some state and federal agencies. It is located at:

> **http://www.law.vill.edu/Fed-Ct/fedcourt.html**

COURT PERSONNEL ✦

As we have seen, the state and federal courts are organized in much the same way. Not surprisingly, then, the two court systems employ many of the same kinds of personnel who perform similar functions.

Judges

A judge presides over a trial court. Appellate and supreme court judges are known as justices. Thus, Justice Warner presides over an appellate or supreme court, while Judge Kwan presides over a trial court. It is important to address these individuals properly, in both written and oral communication.

In many states, judges are political appointees. In order to be a judge, however, an individual must have been an attorney who has practiced law for a set number of years. Some states also appoint commissioners who may be elevated to a judge's position when one becomes available. Commissioners must also be attorneys but may have practiced law for fewer years in some states.

Court Clerk

There are two different types of court clerks, and their functions should not be confused. One court clerk works in the courtroom and assists the judge. This clerk's duties include keeping a record of the day's proceedings, administering oaths to witnesses, and recording and storing exhibits to be introduced at trial. When evidence is presented, the clerk is responsible for preserving it. The clerk is also responsible for noting exhibit numbers as the exhibits are introduced into evidence. Unless paralegals or legal administrative assistants attend a trial, they will have very little contact with this clerk.

The other type of court clerk works in the clerk's office, which is located in the courthouse. Here one can purchase court forms, file documents, or obtain information about cases that have been filed in that court. Paralegals and legal administrative assistants often have contact with clerks in the clerk's office. Each courthouse will have one or more clerks available. It is important to remember that clerks are not attorneys and may not give legal advice.

Filing in the Clerk's Office. All cases must be filed in the appropriate clerk's office, that is, the clerk's office of the court having jurisdiction in the case. When documents are filed, it is imperative that all exhibits and filing fees accompany them. Specific filing fee schedules may be obtained from the clerk's office. Filing procedures can be found in the court rules and/or the codes or statutes for your state or for the federal courts.

Some courts allow documents to be filed by fax machine to the clerk's office. When a fax filing is made, an original, signed copy must also be filed within a designated period to be determined by the individual court. Be sure to check each time a case is filed with a different court to determine their specific filing rules.

Bailiff

The bailiff, generally a sheriff or marshal, is responsible for assisting the judge, taking care of the jury's needs, and maintaining order and decorum in the courtroom. The bailiff also escorts the jury and guards defendants in criminal trials.

Training for bailiffs is usually conducted at a police academy or training facility. Their instruction includes both physical training and legal education. Some bailiffs started as police officers and transferred to the courts.

Court Reporter

Court reporters record all testimony presented at the trial. Once the testimony is recorded, the reporter manually transcribes it into a transcript. Recently, some courts have been experimenting with automatic recording of trial testimony with the use of specialized computers. Once this system is perfected, it may be appropriate for use in a civil trial; however, face-to-face reporting is required in a criminal trial.

If the attorneys request daily transcripts of the trial, two reporters will alternate in recording the testimony. One will record for a time; then the other will record while the first reporter transcribes the recorded portion; then they switch places. Whenever you attend a trial and notice that the reporters keep switching, it is probably because an attorney has requested a daily transcript.

The Jury

One of the basic precepts of our legal system is the right to a trial by jury. Jurors are among the most crucial persons at a trial, for they decide the fate of the accused or the judgment in a civil trial. Although the right to trial by jury is guaranteed by the United States Constitution, a criminal defendant may waive this right and choose to have the case tried by a judge. In civil cases, where money damages are sought, either party may request a trial by jury; the case will be tried by a judge if both parties agree and do not insist on their right to a jury trial. In cases of equity, however, such as those where a restraining order or injunction is sought, there is no right to a jury trial and the case will be heard by a judge.

Prospective jurors are usually drawn from voter registration rolls or from driver's license records. Jurors are chosen from a pool of potential jurors who have been summoned to appear by the court. Jury selection, which is known as voir dire, consists of a process whereby the judge calls prospective jurors by number. These individuals are questioned as a group and then individually by the judge and the attorneys. An unlimited number of jurors may be excused "for cause," generally bias or prejudice. In addition, each attorney has several peremptory challenges that can be used to excuse prospective jurors without cause; that is, the attorney can excuse a juror whom he thinks may be likely to vote against his client without having to demonstrate that the juror is actually prejudiced against the client. The number of peremptory challenges available varies depending on the nature of the case.

Most juries consist of twelve individuals, although a few states allow as few as five jurors in some cases. In Virginia, for instance, civil cases involving $5,000 or less are heard by five-person juries, and cases where the amount in controversy is more than $5,000 are heard by seven persons.

The jury's responsibility is to decide issues of fact in the case. The judge will instruct them on the applicable law. The decision of the jury is called a verdict, whereas a judge's decision is called a judgment. If the judge feels that the jury has not properly applied the law to the facts of the case, then he may set aside the verdict and render a judgment in the case, known as judgment n.o.v. (judgment notwithstanding the verdict.) Such judgments are rare.

In civil actions in most states, 75 percent of the jury must find for the plaintiff if the plaintiff is to prevail. In other words, if nine jurors on a twelve-person jury vote for the plaintiff, then the plaintiff will win the suit against the defendant.

Jury verdicts in criminal cases must generally be unanimous; that is, all members of the jury must vote for the defendant's guilt for her to be found guilty. If all jurors cannot agree, a "hung jury" results. The prosecutor will then decide whether to try the case again with a new jury. In recent years, however, a few states have enabled nine or ten of the twelve jurors to establish the defendant's guilt.

If the jury finds the defendant guilty, then the sentence, or penalty, is imposed on the defendant. Usually, the sentence is imposed at a later time during what is called the penalty phase of the trial. Most states require that the judge render the sentence. However, a few states (including Virginia and Kentucky) allow the jury to make the sentencing decision.

Check the rules for juries in your own state and add the information in the State Specific Information box.

STATE SPECIFIC INFORMATION

Rules for juries in the state of _____:

1. Civil cases: _____-person juries; _____ must vote for plaintiff to prevail.

2. Criminal cases: _____-person juries; _____ must vote for guilt.

Special state rules:

_____

_____

_____

STATUTE OF LIMITATIONS ✦

Every case filed, except for murder, has a statute of limitations that indicates the time limit within which the action must be filed with the proper court or administrative agency. The court will dismiss the case if it is not filed within the statute of limitations, regardless of the case's merits.

Some statutes are difficult to determine, such as for actions where personal injury results. In those cases, the statute begins to run from the time the plaintiff knew or should have known of her injuries. Sometimes this date is difficult to determine, especially in actions such as medical malpractice or fraud. The court must determine whether the plaintiff should have known of the malpractice at the time of the treatment, or whether he should have known at a later date. Proving when the plaintiff knew of the injury, or when he should have known of the misconduct, becomes a major part of the trial process.

The federal statute for actions against the United States requires that civil actions are barred unless the complaint is filed within six years after the right of action first exists. Exceptions include those cases provided in the Contract Disputes Act of 1978, actions of a person under legal disability or, actions of a person out of the country at the time the action occurs. When dealing with a federal statute of limitations, be sure to check the United States Codes under Section 28 USC S.2401.

If an attorney files an action after the statute has run, the client will usually be unable to file the action at a later date. The client's recourse would then be to sue the attorney for malpractice if the client presented the case to the attorney in a timely manner.

In some cases, the statutes may be "tolled" (suspended or stopped temporarily), such as during the defendant's absence from the jurisdiction and during the plaintiff's minority (that is, before the plaintiff reaches the age of majority.)

Some of the more common statutes are listed in Exhibit 2-3.

ADMINISTRATIVE AGENCIES ✦

A large number of administrative agencies exist on the federal, state, county, and local level. Although they are not courts of law, they do hold hearings and reach decisions that can have important consequences for clients.

Federal Administrative Agencies

The following are some examples of federal administrative agencies:

1. *Social Security Administration (SSA)* This agency oversees the Social Security system and makes decisions on such matters as eligibility for benefits. Their Web site provides the ability to access your own personal earnings and future benefits estimates. Information is provided about Social Security benefits and Medicare. Explanations are provided for the system's regulations. The site is available at

   http://www.ssa.gov/SSA_Home.html.

EXHIBIT 2-3 Common Statutes of	
Tort actions	One year after injury
Oral contracts	Two years after breach
Written contracts	Four years after breach
Criminal acts	Varies by crime
Murder	No statute of limitations

2. *Federal Aviation Administration (FAA)* This agency regulates and oversees the nation's airlines. It is responsible for the safety of civil aviation and has the following functions:

  a. Regulating civil aviation to promote safety

  b. Encouraging the development of air commerce and civil aeronautics

  c. Developing and operating air traffic control and navigation systems for both civil and military aircraft

  d. Developing and executing programs to control aircraft noise and other environmental effects of civil aviation

  e. Regulating commercial space transportation

  A considerable amount of information about this agency is available on their Web site at **http://www.faa.gov/**.

3. *Immigration and Naturalization Service (INS)* This agency, under the Department of Justice, is responsible for the admission, naturalization, stopping illegal entry, and deportation of foreign nationals. Its appeals board hears appeals to deportation orders. The Web site includes the latest rules and regulations, as well as forms that are used in this specialty area. It may be found at **http://www.ins.usdoj.gov**.

4. *Department of Justice (DOJ)* This department manages the legal business of the United States. All federal law enforcement agencies are within the DOJ. It represents the United States in civil and criminal cases, runs the federal prison system, and has departments responsible for immigration (INS), antitrust laws, civil rights laws, the FBI, the Drug Enforcement Administration (DEA), and a number of other agencies. It is headed by the Attorney General of the United States. Its Web site is located at **http://www.usdoj.gov** and includes information on the various agencies in the department, recent case decisions involving the department, and other information related to the United States legal community.

For a comprehensive listing of government sources on the Internet, contact the Government Sources of Business and Economic Information at:

http://www.lib.umich.edu/00/inetdirrstacks/govdocs:tsangaustin

State Agencies

One of the most important agencies at the state level is the Workers' Compensation Board. Cases before this board relate to injuries sustained by workers while on the job. Many law offices specialize in workers' compensation cases and may employ a considerable number of paralegals and legal administrative assistants to handle the large volume of required paperwork to get the cases settled. In some states, paralegals are allowed to represent a client before the Board.

ETHICS and ETIQUETTE

In some cases, the paralegal or legal assistant may be required to attend a court proceeding with the attorney. In those situations, proper courtroom decorum must be practiced. Most courts do not allow talking, chewing gum, or cell phones. The paralegal or legal assistant should maintain a professional appearance at all times. Instead of whispering to the attorney during the proceedings, write a legible note and unobtrusively place it next to him. Listen carefully during the court proceeding and take notes for the attorney. In some cases, a laptop computer will be used for this purpose. Avoid fidgeting, excessive moving that is noisy, and any other movements or gestures that might be distracting to the court.

It is important to remember that an individual who is not an attorney may not represent a client in a court proceeding. However, there are certain administrative agencies that allow representation of clients by nonlawyers. Some state agencies allow nonlawyers to represent individuals before them. The procedure varies from one state to another. For instance, some states allow nonlawyer representation before the Department of Workers' Compensation, while others do not. It is advisable to check the rules of the particular agency as well as state laws to determine whether this practice is allowed before attempting the representation of a client before a governmental agency.

Federal government agency rules related to nonlawyer representation of clients are also varied and periodically change. Therefore, it is also imperative for the paralegal to determine the rules of each agency prior to attempting representation before it. In most cases, the attorney will know the current rules. However, a telephone call to the appropriate individual at the agency in question will be able to give you the information.

A number of freelance paralegal services provide assistance to the general public for completing forms and/or documents in different types of cases. Ethical considerations in these areas relate to whether or not the paralegal is just providing the forms and typing them for the client or is actually telling the client what information to put into the forms. The latter situation involves the unauthorized practice of law and is not allowed.

On the county and local levels, consumer protection agencies, planning commissions, and zoning boards are among the most well known agencies for employment of legal professionals.

Each one of these agencies has its own rules for filing documents and conducting hearings. You must consult the rules of the particular agency before filing a case. The rules and regulations usually are available in the law office if the attorneys regularly practice before that agency. Most state, county, and local government agencies have Web pages. Sometimes the appropriate forms for filing cases may be downloaded from their Web pages.

Paralegals may sometimes represent clients before administrative agencies. Paralegals employed by legal aid or legal service organizations represent clients before administrative agencies, such as Social Security or the state Workers' Compensation Board. Check your own state's rules and regulations and complete the State Specific Information box relating to whether paralegals may represent clients before administrative agencies in your state.

STATE SPECIFIC INFORMATION

In the state of _____, paralegals may represent clients before these administrative agencies:

_____

but not before these administrative agencies:

_____.

CHAPTER SUMMARY ✦

State and federal courts have similar structures. At the lowest level is the trial courts with the appellate and supreme courts at the top. Although the various state systems differ slightly, they share several general features. Generally, a state has two levels of trial courts, one for the lesser crimes and minor civil cases and a higher-level court for major crimes and major civil cases. Above the trial courts are the appellate courts, which review decisions reached by the trial courts.

The federal system has one level of trial court, the federal district courts, as well as several specialty courts, such as the tax court and court of claims. Cases may be appealed to the circuit courts of appeal and then to the United States Supreme Court.

Many state and federal courts have their own Web pages where information may be obtained about the makeup of the court as well as filing procedures, court rules, and other information. Similar personnel are found in both court systems. A court will ordinarily have a judge, a court clerk, a bailiff, a court reporter, and in trial courts, a jury.

All types of cases have statutes of limitations that set time limits within which cases must be filed. Therefore, it is imperative that the paralegal and legal assistant keep track of the statutes so that the client will be able to file a suit in a timely fashion.

Administrative agencies are becoming more important at all levels of government. Many of them have their own Web pages. The Social Security Administration, Workers' Compensation Board, and planning commissions are all examples of administrative agencies at different levels.

✦ KEY TERMS

general jurisdiction	quasi in rem jurisdiction
injunction	Shepardize
in rem jurisdiction	subject matter jurisdiction
jurisdiction	venue
limited jurisdiction	writ of certiorari
personal jurisdiction (in personam jurisdiction)	

✦ SELF TEST

Indicate whether the following statements are true (T) or false (F).

_____ 1. The United States has fifty different court systems.

_____ 2. You may never file a document late with the court.

_____ 3. Jurisdiction refers to the proper geographic area in which to file a case.

_____ 4. Most state trial courts are municipal and superior courts.

_____ 5. Small claims court allows litigants to represent themselves.

Circle the correct answer to the following uestions:

1. A major reason for malpractice suits against attorneys is
   a. missed deadlines.
   b. failure to sign documents.
   c. failure to return telephone calls.
   d. failure to show up for interviews.

2. The best method of keeping track of court deadlines is
   a. reminder slips.
   b. message forms.
   c. an office calendaring system.
   d. none of the above.

3. Under the English common law system, two different courts heard cases related to
   a. law.
   b. legal and equitable issues.
   c. statutes.
   d. civil cases.

4. Civil actions where the plaintiff is asking for money damages are actions
   a. at law.
   b. in equity.
   c. for compensation.
   d. by statutes.

5. Small claims courts allow litigants to appear
   a. with an attorney.
   b. with a paralegal.
   c. without an attorney.
   d. all of the above.

Fill-in-the-blanks.

1. The United States has _____ different court systems.

2. _____ refers to the proper geographical area in which a case should be heard.

3. The power of a court to hear a case is called _____.

4. State trial courts are usually called _____ and _____ courts.

5. Small Claims Court is part of the _____ court.

✦ REVIEW QUESTIONS

1. Describe the functions the following individuals perform in the courtroom:
   a. Judge
   b. Bailiff
   c. Juror
   d. Court Clerk

2. The highest court in the state is the _____ court. How are cases appealed to this court?

3. Define the following:
   a. Federal District Court
   b. Circuit Court of Appeals
   c. United States Supreme Court

✦ NOTEBOOK PROJECTS

 1. Describe how the state and federal courts are organized, including the number of judges/justices on each. Discuss the types of cases that are heard by each of these courts.

 2. Prepare a diagram of your state's court system.

 3. Find your state's statute of limitations for the following actions, and write them in the spaces provided:

Tort actions: _____

Oral contracts: _____

Personal injury: _____

Written contracts: _____

ADMINISTRATIVE RESPONSIBILITIES

CHAPTER OUTCOMES

As a result of studying this chapter, the student will learn:

- The difference between giving information and giving legal advice
- The importance of calendaring
- How to communicate effectively over the telephone and by e-mail
- How to record all time spent working on a case
- Where to find resources to arrange travel
- How to properly prepare legal correspondence

CONFIDENTIALITY

Attorneys are governed by strict rules related to attorney/client privilege, which is the privilege that attorneys must adhere to in their dealings with clients. All information divulged by a client is deemed to be confidential and must not be revealed to anyone outside the law office. Even those who are employed by the law firm but not working on the client's case should not be privy to the information. Ultimately, it is the attorney who is responsible for actions of her employees that breach the attorney/client privilege. Therefore, it is imperative that all employees of the law office maintain the utmost degree of propriety and **confidentiality** when dealing with clients and client information.

Regulations for this purpose are administered by the state bar of each state and the **American Bar Association**, who writes codes and guidelines for attorneys on confidentiality. The state, usually through its state bar association, will maintain jurisdiction over attorneys who practice within the state regarding their relationships with their clients. Power to regulate attorneys resides in the state judicial system, either through a system of state bar courts or the state court system. The highest court of each state, generally the supreme court, has the final authority for judgments on violations of confidentiality by attorneys.

confidentiality the requirement that a lawyer, or anyone working for a lawyer, not disclose information received from a client.

American Bar Association the largest voluntary organization of lawyers in the country.

Complaints about attorney wrongdoing may be made to the complaint department of the state bar association. While each state has its own system, most states will have forms that complainants must complete and submit to the state bar. A team of investigators will read and investigate all complaints and determine whether the complaint has any merit, whether more information is required, and/or whether the attorney should be reprimanded, suspended, or disbarred. In some cases, clients might complain about a problem with an attorney that is not actionable. In other cases, several individuals may complain about the same attorney, causing the investigators to look at the case more closely.

Attorneys are required to take an ethical examination, called the Professional Responsibility Exam, as part of their state's bar exam. It is a test of the ethical guidelines for attorneys and is generally given after the student completes the ethics course in law school. In most states, an attorney cannot be admitted to practice law in that state until the exam is passed.

Although attorneys are required to be members of their state bar in order to practice law in the state, membership in the American Bar Association (ABA) is voluntary. However, the ABA provides model rules that the states use as models to establish their own ethical rules.

The American Bar Association maintains a Web site at

http://www.abanet.org/

Information about the organization may be found at this site, as well as the following information:

1. Membership information
2. Publications
3. Continuing legal education issues
4. The *ABA Journal*
5. Links to other law-related sites
6. Public information about the legal profession
7. Specialty sections and news about their events
8. Paralegal information.

Most state bar associations also maintain Web sites. To find your own state bar's Web site, you should do a key word search, using the name of your state, and "state bar organization." Write the address of the Web site in the State Specific Information box.

STATE SPECIFIC INFORMATION

The Web site for the State Bar of _____ is located at:

_____.

Information versus Advice

Only attorneys are allowed to give legal **advice**. Sometimes a very fine line exists between the dissemination of information and actually giving advice. When in doubt, refer the client to the attorney to obtain the needed information. If the sentence starts with "I advise you to…" then you are probably giving legal advice.

CALENDARS AND SCHEDULES ✦

Keeping track of deadlines and appointments is an important part of the paralegal's and legal assistant's responsibilities. Many offices have computers with the capability of performing this function. For a computer system to operate properly, however, someone has to key in the correct information, such as dates, times, and names. Generally, the legal assistant will keep the attorney's calendar. The paralegal should keep her own calendar of appointments and due dates.

Each piece of mail that comes into the law office should be read and logged into a mail log. Any required action should also be noted. The date a response is due should be indicated on the calendar, using either a manual or a computer system. A notation about two weeks ahead of the due date should also be made on the calendar, another should be made one week ahead, and another three days ahead. In this manner, you can avoid the "last minute crunch" of having to prepare documents and/or correspondence on the anticipated due date. Usually, the product is better if sufficient time is allowed to prepare it properly. Calendaring items properly will help to avoid any malpractice suits against the attorney for missed deadlines.

A good tool for keeping the attorney "on track" is the daily schedule. The legal assistant should prepare a daily schedule each morning of appointments for that day and items that are coming due within the next week. This schedule can be printed and given to the attorney with the mail each morning so that the day can be planned efficiently. Paralegals and legal assistants should develop a procedure for using their own computers for making daily schedules. With the systems now available, the day's activities can be called up on the computer screen at the beginning of each day by using a simple code. Then, as more items come into the office and additional cases are filed, the schedule can be updated.

Whenever a document is served on a client through the law office, the paralegal and legal assistant should note on the calendar when an answering document is due. Again, make a note of the event two weeks ahead, one week ahead, three days ahead, and one day ahead. Many documents require further research before they can be prepared. Therefore, the paralegal should plan the amount of time needed for doing the research and preparing the document. A date for preparation before the due date should be noted on the calendar. Many law offices call this procedure a tickler system.

For those individuals who do not feel comfortable using a computer calendaring system, numerous manual systems are available. A desk

advice an opinion given to clients by their lawyers and meant to assist in determining correct action or conduct.

calendar and/or diary may be used. A card file with months and dates may be set up. Booklets with separate headings for months and dates are also readily available.

Court Dockets

Scheduled court dates are listed on the office's court **docket** list, which also includes the time of the court appearance, case name and number, and names of the attorneys who will make an appearance on the case. The list is particularly useful for large law firms where many attorneys are appearing in different courts. These firms may have a docket control clerk who prepares and verifies the dockets.

Exhibit 3-1 shows a sample docket slip for the fictional firm of Weiss & Richardson, which includes ten attorneys.

EXHIBIT 3-1   A Sample Court Docket

SUPERIOR COURT DOCKET SLIP

Weiss & Richardson

June 23, 200x

Time	Case	Courtroom	Attorney
9:00 a.m.	Wilson v. Beck	B22, North Superior Court	Evans
9:00 a.m.	Sanchez v. Johns	D44, Hadley Municipal	Richardson
2:00 p.m.	Alter v. Rio	B25, North Superior Court	Michaels
3:00 p.m.	Stand v. Ross	C44, North Superior Court	Richardson

Computerized Docketing/Calendaring Programs

Many law firms use computerized docket control programs that are specifically developed to help track important deadlines and dates. These programs are useful for keeping track of court appearances and filing deadlines, as well as client appointments and firm meetings.

Many paralegals and legal assistants use docket control programs for self-imposed deadlines. For instance, suppose a paralegal has been asked to draft a complaint. Although the final draft may not be due for three weeks, the paralegal might set a personal deadline of one week in which to complete the first draft of the complaint. This self-imposed deadline can be entered into the computer along with the other dates.

docket a list of cases, usually with file numbers, scheduled for trial in a court; a list of specific actions taken in a court.

EXHIBIT 3-2 Sample Screen From Calendaring Program

Courtesy: Reprinted by permission of Abacus Data Systems

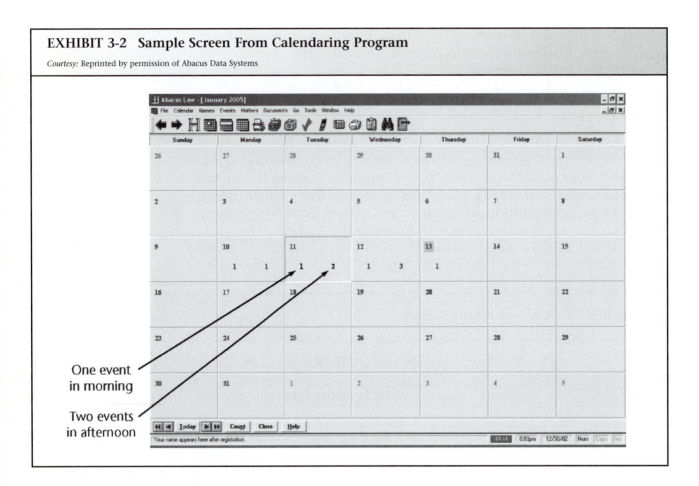

Most computer docket control programs have a built-in reminder ("tickler") system to provide advance notice of an approaching deadline or appointment. For instance, look at Exhibit 3-2, which shows a sample monthly display screen from a calendaring program. The identifier at the top of the screen indicates that this is the January 2003 schedule for an individual with the initials "RSS." Now look at the square for January 18, 2003. The screen shows three numbers: 1, 2, and 3. This means that RSS has one appointment, one critical deadline, and one self-imposed deadline. For specific information on these deadlines, the user would position the cursor on the square for January 18 and press the Enter key. A more detailed summary then appears at the bottom of the screen.

Docket control programs also allow users to print a variety of reports. For example, a list of events for a particular day or a list of all deadlines related to a specific client's case may be printed. Exhibit 3-3 is a sample printout of a weekly calendar for Courtney C. Richards. Note that on Tuesday, March 19, the second entry has an asterisk next to it. The asterisk indicates that this entry is a reminder of a future deadline or appointment, which in this case is a trial date.

tickler file a reminder system to keep track of deadlines; similar to a calendar, with notations each day about what needs to be done that day.

Tickler Files

The same computer-generated calendar may also be used to maintain a **tickler file**, or reminder of what must be done on a given day. Title

EXHIBIT 3-3   A Sample Printout of a Weekly Calendar

COMPULAW, LTD.
WEEK AT A GLANCE   Page 1

Report for Courtney C. Richards
For the week beginning March 18, 2005

Monday 18	Tuesday 19	Wednesday 20	Thursday 21	Friday 22
9:00 a.m. Case Tools Corporation CTC v. Bren Industries, Inc. 10056.003 Hearing Los Angeles Superior Court Defendant's motions to dismiss. 1:00 p.m. to 4:00 p.m. Apex Construction Company v. Jones APEX-001 Meeting: Client Office Discuss settlement offer.	9:30 a.m. to 12:00 p.m. Apex Construction Company v. Jones APEX-001 Deposition Office Depo of Lawrence G. Smith at the offices of West & Rains, 1400 West North Street, 21st floor. *Due on 05/28/2005 No Time Acme Refrigeration Acme vs. The March Group ACME-001 Trial and Pretrial Dates Santa Monica Superior Court THE DATE THAT THIS CASE IS SET FOR JURY OR NONJURY TRIAL.	No Time Precision Parts, Inc. v. United Systems, Inc. PREC-001 Discovery Office LAST COURT DAY FOR RESPONSE TO INTERROGATORIES TO BE SERVED. See Document #11. 10:00 a.m. Precision Parts, Inc. v. United Systems, Inc. PREC-001 Deposition Opposing counsel's office Depo. of Lois West at the offices of Smith, Jones, Adams & Johnson, 21st floor. 5:00 p.m. Acme Refrigeration Acme v. The March Group| ACME-001 Discovery Santa Monica Superior Court LAST COURT DAY TO SERVE (BY MAIL) REQUESTS FOR THE PRODUCTION OF DOCUMENTS. *** BE SURE TO ALLOW ENOUGH TIME TO MAKE A MOTION TO COMPEL.	No Time Apex Construction Company v. Jones APEX-001 Discovery Office LAST COURT DAY FOR RESPONSE TO INTERROGATORIES TO BE SERVED. 12:00 p.m. Case Tools Corporation CTC v. Bren Industries, Inc. 10056.003 Meeting: Client Restaurant: Business Lunch with Howard Jones of CTC. Wong Chu Chinese Restaurant, 444 East April Lane. 5:00 p.m. Bell Computer Products Bell v. Delta Chips of GA 100092.001 Last day to file this action Los Angeles Superior Court Last court day to apply for correction of award. CCP 1284.	8:30 a.m. to 10:00 a.m. Office Administration Meetings 0000-001 Meeting: Office Related Office Meeting to discuss the great new features of our calendar program. The new WEEK AT A GLANCE report can be printed in land-scape format. We have the option to print the TRI-CAL on top or bottom. Quick review should make it very easy for attorneys to look at their schedules. 5:00 p.m. Acme Refrigeration Acme v. The March Group ACME-001 Trial and Pretrial Dates Santa Monica Superior Court LAST COURT DAY TO FILE AND SERVE (BY HAND) NOTICE OF MOTION FOR SUMMARY JUDGMENT. *** CHECK CURRENT LAW AND MOTION CALENDAR TO ASSURE AVAILABILITY OF HEARING DATE.

the calendar entry *tickler file* and key in the material that has to be prepared that day instead of the appointments. Alternatively, the space at the bottom of the calendar page can be used for reminders of items that must be completed on a given day.

TIME MANAGEMENT ✦

The ability to manage your time effectively is imperative in the legal profession. Each day provides a different challenge in keeping track of deadlines and being sure that all items are prepared before their due dates. Good calendaring and tickler systems enable the individual to manage his time efficiently and thus do a good job.

Of particular concern is the preparation of written documents and reports, which often have to be revised several times before producing a finished product. Good writing quality in a written document takes time. Therefore, it is imperative that the paralegal and legal assistant allow enough time to complete the writing project in a timely fashion. Always record the deadline for written material on a date that is far enough ahead of the due date to enable you to prepare a polished final document.

STRESS MANAGEMENT ✦

Legal positions are often very stressful because of the many deadlines the paralegal and legal assistant must face. Good time management also assists in alleviating much of the stress associated with a law office. If written materials are prepared ahead of time instead of waiting for the "last minute rush," much of the stress for the paralegal and legal assistant will disappear.

Taking frequent short breaks when completing a large project is beneficial in easing stress. Sitting at one's desk for several hours can be very taxing. Soft background music is very relaxing. If the law office policy allows you to have music playing in your office, be sure it is at a low volume and not annoying to others. Always check with the law office administrator to determine whether the playing of music is allowed.

TELEPHONE TECHNIQUES ✦

A prospective client's first impression of the law office comes from the voice on the other end of the telephone. Answering the telephone represents an opportunity for you to make the client feel exceptional. Make a special effort to be friendly, professional, and courteous each time you answer the telephone. Even when you are preparing a rush job and the telephone has been ringing all day, you should try to keep a "smile in your voice." Your voice will either encourage or discourage prospective clients from employing the law firm. You must convey through your voice that you and the firm are friendly, helpful, professional, and responsive to the caller's needs. Remember that you are representing the attorney each time you communicate on the telephone.

Incoming Calls

Incoming calls should be answered by the third ring. If you are the first person to answer the call, you should identify the name of the firm and your name:

> "Good afternoon, Jefferson and Sells, Ms. Rodriquez speaking."

If someone else has answered the incoming call and transferred it to your office, you should identify yourself:

> "Ms. Daniela's office, Mr. Michaels speaking"
> or
> "Mr. Michaels speaking."

Voice Mail

In most offices, voice mail enables you to be away from your desk while your calls are answered automatically. You should leave a brief, courteous message on your voice mail. If you will be away from the office for an extended period of time, let the caller know. In most cases, someone else will be assigned to handle your calls in case of a long absence. Identify the substitute for the caller. The following are some examples of voice mail messages:

> You have reached the office of Marie Maris, Mr. Jeffries's legal assistant. I am away from my office at the moment but will return by 2:00 p.m. Please leave a message at the tone and I will return your call upon my return.

> You have reached the office of Marie Maris, Mr. Jeffries's paralegal. I will be away from the office until January 15. My calls are being handled by Selena Rogers, who may be reached at Extension 4333. Please dial 6-4333 on your telephone to reach Ms. Rogers.

Your voice mail messages should be changed frequently so that callers will know the approximate time of your return.

Telephone Conversations

Listening carefully is the key to good communications. Although you may be involved in several projects when the telephone rings, pay attention to what the caller has to say. Concentrate on that caller as though you had nothing else to do. Try to listen without interrupting.

Ask appropriate questions to obtain correct information. Address the caller by name.

If you have a smile on your face, the client will recognize the smile in your speaking voice. However, remember that some clients will call the office in a distressed state. They will often need empathy more than a cheerful voice.

Write down any notes of your telephone conversations as soon after hanging up the telephone as possible. In some cases, you may want to take notes during the telephone call. If the individual is giving you information, be sure to note their name and location or telephone number.

Sometimes clients call frequently for what you may think are unimportant reasons. It is important to be courteous to these individuals. If the conversation becomes too lengthy, you may need to find a polite way to end it. Each individual has her own style of ending a call. Be sure that you are not abrupt or rude. For example, you may tell the client that you have another call or that you will get the information he requested and return the call.

Copies of messages should go in the client's file, as well as the time (or times) you called them or attempted to return their calls. Any specific information received should also be noted.

Telephone Tag

With the increased use of voice mail, many of us spend a considerable amount of time playing "telephone tag." You call his voice mail; he calls your voice mail back; you call his voice mail back. This may continue for several days before you reach the person.

To alleviate the problem, establish a specific time of day to return the call. Leave a message stating when you will be in your office and indicate that if the person is not available at that time, you will call him at a specified time. You might leave one of the following messages:

I will be in and out of the office all afternoon. I will call you back between 4 and 5 p.m. this afternoon.

I will be in my office from 1 to 4 p.m. today for your return call. Otherwise, you may reach me tomorrow between 9 and 11 a.m.

Returning Calls

Many clients complain that their attorneys do not return their telephone calls. If the attorney is involved in a long trial or several meetings, the telephone messages can pile up quickly. Some attorneys devote a certain time each day for client calls. Others ask their paralegals or legal secretaries to handle certain calls for them. Many situations that arise can be handled by the paralegal or legal assistant as long as she does not give legal advice to the client. Any time the paralegal or assistant finds himself saying, "I would advise you to …," legal advice is being disseminated; and this is not allowed.

E-Mail

Many people use e-mail as a substitute for returning telephone calls when the purpose of the call is to disseminate information. It is often faster to compose an **e-mail** at the computer letting the client know the required information instead of calling back and forth playing telephone tag.

One of the questions to ask at the initial client interview is the client's e-mail address. E-mail is becoming so popular that many businesses and law firms list their e-mail address on their business cards. It is a considerably more efficient method of communication.

You must be careful regarding confidential communications sent in e-mails. Many firms have programs on their computers to protect the release of confidential information via e-mail. Encoding programs are also available to protect against e-mail "theft." Investigate to determine whether your firm has any protections for confidential e-mail communications. If none is in place, consider examining what programs are available for this purpose.

Handling Client Calls

Each client believes that her problem is the most important case in your office. When the client calls the attorney and the assistant tells her that the attorney is with another client, she may wish to interrupt the attorney to take her call. It is better to tell the client that the attorney is in a meeting or out of the office. Do not give information on the telephone about the attorney's whereabouts unless you know the situation is a genuine emergency or unless you have received prior authorization from the attorney.

Sometimes the attorney may decide to have a luncheon meeting with a client or another attorney. If the attorney is not back in the office by 3 p.m., it is not appropriate to tell the client that the attorney is "still out to lunch." Similarly, if the attorney took the afternoon off to play golf or attend to personal business, you should not tell the caller that the attorney "took the afternoon off." You should say the attorney is "out of the office" or "away at a meeting" or cite a similar justification for his absence.

Messages

A telephone message pad should always be kept next to your telephone. If you are taking a message for someone else, be sure that you spell the caller's name correctly. Spell the name back to the caller if you have any question about the spelling. Note the time and the date

e-mail electronic mail.

of the call. Ask for the area code and telephone number, along with a brief message. If the individual wants to be called back, ask the time when he will be at that number. Be sure to repeat the telephone number back to be certain that you have recorded it correctly. If the caller says the call is urgent, ask the nature of the urgency.

Take a detailed message for the person being called. Keep a copy for the file. In the case of a long, detailed message, write a memorandum indicating the essence of the message and put the memorandum in the appropriate client file. A copy of the memorandum should be given to the attorney.

Appointments

If you set up an appointment with the client over the telephone or in person, be sure to write a letter of confirmation indicating the date, time, and place of the meeting. If it is an initial consultation, the prospective client should be informed about whether or not the consultation is free. Appointments should not be scheduled back to back in the event that one takes longer than expected. In your confirmation letter, indicate the purpose of the meeting and list any materials that the individual should bring to the meeting. To save time, you can compose form letters on your computer for this particular type letter, which will be written each time you schedule an appointment. A sample form letter is shown in Exhibit 3-4.

Telephone Numbers

Various methods may be used to keep track of frequently called telephone numbers. You may use a card file, a rotary file, or the computer for this purpose. The following information should appear for each individual in the directory:

1. Name
2. Title/Position
3. Address with zip code
4. Telephone number with area code
5. Fax number
6. E-mail address
7. Time zone (if the person or firm is in another part of the country, e.g., EST +2 would indicate that the person or firm is in the Eastern Standard Time zone and the time in that zone is two hours later than in your city).

Directories of court personnel and attorneys, if they are available for your state, should be kept on your desk. Some of these directories are available on diskette or CD-ROM so that you may keep the file in your computer.

EXHIBIT 3-4   Form Letter—Confirming Appointment

FIRM LETTERHEAD

Date

Name
Address
City, State zip code

Dear Mr. [name]:

You are scheduled for an initial consultation with Mr. Jeffries on Monday, December 30, at 2:00 p.m. Please plan to arrive at the office approximately fifteen minutes early, at 1:45 p.m., to complete the preliminary paperwork. Please bring the following items to the meeting with you:

1. [name of item]
2. [name of item]

We look forward to seeing you on December 30.

Very truly yours,

Marie Daniels
Legal Assistant

Searching for Web Sites

Many law firms have Web sites and links to their e-mail addresses. If you would like to send an e-mail but do not know the address, do a search on the name of the law firm. Access the Internet and key the name of the firm into the "search" box, generally located at the top of the screen. If the firm has a Web page, the name will become visible in the list of items that will appear after the search is completed. This method is also useful if you are trying to find a company or business.

In Chapter 1, the Web sites for various professional organizations were discussed. Chapter 2 disclosed many of the government and court Web addresses. These Web sites will prove useful if you are trying to contact that particular organization. Most Web sites have a box for "contact us" that may be used to send the organization an e-mail. A more comprehensive description of using the Internet will be discussed under "Using the Internet" later in this chapter.

TIMEKEEPING AND BILLING ✦

Although most law firms require their paralegals to keep track of the amount of time they spend on each client's case, legal secretaries are generally not required to record their time spent on each individual item.

In most law offices, time spent working on a project is recorded on a **time sheet** such as the one shown in Exhibit 3-5. Usually, the name of the client, the amount of time spent, and the task performed are recorded on the time sheet. Firms using this system require that their attorneys and paralegals keep track of their **billable hours** so the client can be billed for their time. Usually, a firm requires its attorneys and paralegals to generate a minimum number of billable hours per year. Some firms use the number of billable hours spent by a given paralegal when computing bonuses and/or salary increases.

Exhibit 3-6 on page 50 shows a timesheet for recording time entries manually. However, most firms use a computer program to track attorney time. Attorneys input their own time directly into the computer on the appropriate form.

Nonbillable hours are the hours spent working in the law office that cannot be billed directly to a client. For instance, the paralegal may be asked to perform legal research in the law library to determine what additional volumes should be purchased. This time is billed under a special administrative code.

It is important to keep track of all time spent working on each client's case. Sometimes paralegals are reluctant to complete a timesheet for a ten-minute telephone call. But if you spend a lot of time on the telephone, you may come up very short on billable hours if all calls are not noted and billed. Consider that six ten-minute calls in a day equal one hour that should be billed to clients. New paralegals are often reluctant to note the actual time spent preparing a document for the first time because they are concerned that the attorney will think they spent too long on that project. Obviously, preparing a given type of document for the first time will take longer than preparing it for the tenth time. The attorney is aware of this, and the firm may reduce the amount of time charged to the client. Therefore, all time spent on each client's case should always be noted on the timesheet.

Hours are recorded on the timesheet in tenths; that is, every six minutes equals .1 hour. Thus, if the paralegal spends an hour interviewing a client, it is recorded as 1.0 hour. If the paralegal spends six minutes talking on the telephone with a client, that time is billed as .1 hour. Uneven amounts are rounded up to the next tenth. Therefore, if fifteen minutes are spent on a project, the time is billed as .3 hour. If the paralegal is performing a function that is not billable to the client, then a special code will be used for that purpose.

Attorney Fees

The most commonly used types of attorney fees are hourly fees, contingency fees, and fees by the particular project. Some firms use a combination of these methods. To avoid fee disputes with the client, all fee

time sheet a system to keep track of the time spent working on each case; used to bill clients.

billable hours those hours spent working on a client's case that will be billed to the client.

nonbillable hours those hours spent working in the law office that cannot be billed directly to the client.

arrangements should be in writing and signed by both the attorney and the client at the initial client interview. Some states *require* that all fee arrangements with clients be written and signed by the attorney and the client.

Hourly Fees. If the firm bills the client hourly, the attorney will charge an **hourly fee**, which is a specified amount for each hour

hourly fees   a set amount per hour that the attorney who works on a case charges the client.

EXHIBIT 3-5   Sample Time Sheet

Time Record

Name: <u>Jane Martinez, Paralegal</u>   Date: <u>October 25, 2006</u>

Client Number	Client/Case	File Number	Description of Services	Time	
				Hours	Tenths
PI99544	J. Roberts Personal injury	45678	Draft Interrogatories	1	3
PV4444	M. Martinson Probate matter	19999	Draft Petition to Distribute	2	2
YV23458	S. Stanford Contract	15876	Draft Contract	2	2
PI3333	L. Lawson Auto accident Lawson v. Stanford	45777	Summarize Deposition	2	4
			Total time:	8	1

EXHIBIT 3-6 A Sample Time Sheet

Courtesy: Reprinted by permission of Sheila Cantrell, Sheppard, Mullin, Richter, and Hampton

TIMESHEET

NONCHARGEABLE CATAGORIES

Client/File No.	Description	Client/File No.	Description
001-00001*	Public and Alumni Activities	00A-00008	Billings and Collections
002-00002*	Recruiting	00B-00009*	Department/Practice Group/ Firm Meetings
003-00003*	Client Development	00C-00010*	Firm Committee Work
004-00004*	Professional Activities	00D-00011*	Internal Education
005-00005	Travel Branch	00E-00012*	Firm's Own Account
006-00006	Sick Day	00F-00013	Other Office Time
007-00007	Vacation Day	00G-90061*	MCLE
009-nnnn*	Pro Bono	00H-00014*	Zero Hour Weekend Time

* First File Number in a Series — Additional File Numbers also exist.

GLOSSARY LIST — CHARGEABLE AND NONCHARGEABLE

aa	– Acquisition Agreement	ea	– Employment Agreement	pf	– Prepared for
af	– Arranged for	ep	– Estate Plan	pld	– pleadings
ag	– Agreement	exh	– exhibits	r	– Reviewed
arb	– Arbitration	fi	– file	ri	– Response to Interrogatories
att	– Attended	fin	– finalized	rr	– Reviewed and revised
az	– Analyzed	hea	– hearing	rs	– Researched
c	– Court	int	– Interrogatories	rv	– Revised
cd	– Closing Documents	ld	– Loan Documents	sa	– Security Agreement
ch	– Charter Documents	loi	– Letter of Intent	sag	– Settlement Agreement
clo	– Closing	m	– meeting	sl	– Sick time
cor	– Corresponded with	md	– motion documents	t	– Trial
cr	– Conferred re	mem	– memorandum	tcr	– Telephone conference re
cw	– Conferred with	n	– negotiated	tcw	– Telephone conference with
dep	– deposition	neg	– negotiations	tra	– Transcripts
doc	– documents	p	– Prepared	va	– Vacation time
drf	– Drafted	pd	– Prepared documents	wk	– Weekend
				wo	– Worked on

WORK LOCATION CODES:

LA – Los Angeles   SD – San Diego   OT – Other
OC – Orange County   SF – San Francisco

PAGE _____ OF _____ PAGES

SORT CODES:

PRET – Pre-Trial		TRIAL – Trial
DIS – Discovery	DOC – Documents	SETT – Settlements
CLOSE – Closing	MEET – Meetings	OTH – Other

NO.	NAME:				DATE:			

CLIENT #	FILE #	CLIENT/MATTER NAME	TIME H	TIME T	CITY CODE	SORT CODES	WORK CODE	FUNCTION CODE	CON-TIN

spent working on the client's case. Generally, a lower hourly fee is charged for paralegal time than for attorney time. In most states, secretarial time is not billed directly to the client unless the secretary is performing paralegal tasks. In firms that charge hourly fees, the paralegal must keep track of all billable hours so that the client may be charged appropriately.

Contingency Fees. Contingency fees are used when a client, the plaintiff, sues another individual or company, the defendant, for money damages. These cases typically involve personal injury and/or property damage, such as automobile accidents. The attorney's fee is a percentage of the award that the client receives from the defendant. For example, if the attorney charges the client a 40 percent contingency fee and the client receives an award of $40,000, the attorney would receive $16,000 and the client would receive $24,000. Contingency fees are not allowed in divorce, dissolution, or criminal actions.

Project Fees.   Many law offices charge their clients a flat fee based on the project to be undertaken. For example, the attorney may charge a **project fee** for preparing a simple will, establishing a living trust, or setting up a corporation.

Retainer Fees.   Some attorneys charge special fees that are payable at the outset of the case or at the time the client retains the attorney to work on her case. These fees, called **retainer fees**, may be in addition to the other fees charged and are used to reserve the attorney's time to perform work on the case. They are deposited into the client trust account and drawn on, as needed, as the attorney works on the case. For instance, if the attorney charged the client a $3,000 retainer fee and performed $2,000 worth of work on the case, he could draw the $2,000 from the client trust account, leaving $1,000 in the account for future work. As the retainer fee is used, the attorney will bill the client for additional fees. These fees are usually used in hourly fee arrangements, but some attorneys also use retainers in contingency fee cases.

Statutory Fees

Some attorney fees are set by state statute, such as those used in probate and workers' compensation cases. These state established fees are called **statutory fees**. In probate, they are based on the size of the estate and represent a percentage of its assets. In unusual situations that take extraordinary amounts of time, the attorney may petition the court to obtain fees greater than those set by statute in probate cases. Recent cases have allowed attorneys to ask the court for extraordinary fees for paralegal and other lay personnel time when these individuals performed work on the probate.

TRAVEL   ◆

The attorney will often be required to travel to other locations, either local or long distance. A number of sites are available on the Internet

contingency fees
a percentage of the award received in a civil case that is paid to the attorney for his or her fee.

project fees   attorney's fees that are set based on the work the attorney performs, such as writing a will or preparing a trust agreement.

retainer fees   fees paid at the outset of the case by the client for use only in that particular case.

statutory fees   attorney fees set by statute, such as for the probate of an estate.

for making travel arrangements, as well as arranging maps for local travel. If the attorney is traveling to a different courthouse, be sure to get directions and/or make a map. Reconfirm the location if you make a map from one of the sites on the Internet, as they are not always completely accurate. This may often be accomplished by an e-mail to the individual's office that the attorney is planning to visit. In some cases, it may be advantageous to set up a meeting in a private chat room instead of requiring all participants to physically travel to a meeting place.

Local Travel

A number of sites are available on the Internet to obtain maps when the attorney is traveling locally. Always confirm the address of the location. Be aware of traffic patterns at certain times of the day to allow the attorney enough time to reach the appointment on time. Try to avoid meetings on the other side of a large city during "rush hours," which typically occur between 8 a.m. and 10:00 a.m. and in the afternoon after 3:00 or 4:00 p.m.

Listed below are some of the sites that are sources for maps and directions, both local and long distance

http://www.mapquest.com

http://www.mapblast.com

http://www.mapsonus.com.

In order to get driving directions from one location to another, you merely key in the starting location and the ending location and click on the "driving locations" icon on the Web page. You will then receive detailed driving directions, a map, and the mileage and estimated driving time. Bear in mind that this driving time does not take traffic conditions into account, so you will often have to adjust the time based on the time of the day the attorney will be traveling.

Some larger metropolitan areas have Web sites devoted to the traffic in those particular areas. A search for the appropriate Web site will often yield one dedicated to traffic conditions. You may discover these locations by accessing the Federal Highway Administration's site for national traffic and road closure information. Links are provided for each state, as well as for distinctive traffic sites. This Web page may be found at

http://fhwa.dot.gov/trafficinfo/.

Once you have accessed the site for your particular state or area, be sure to bookmark it or deposit it in your "Favorite Places" so that you can return to it each time you are interested in learning about traffic conditions.

Long Distance Travel

For those cases where the attorney is required to travel to remote locations, the Internet provides a considerable amount of information, including travel reservations, weather, hotels, cities, and maps. Some travel agencies specialize in on-line reservations.

Most airlines have their own Web sites where reservations may be made and e-tickets obtained. E-tickets consist of e-mails with confirmation numbers and avoid the necessity of actual tickets. Some airlines have imposed an extra charge on travelers who require actual tickets instead of the e-ticket confirmation.

One comprehensive site that provides a considerable amount of travel information is located at

http://www.cheaptickets.com

This site enables you to make plane, hotel, and car reservations. It has the ability to track a flight in progress once it leaves its origination point. Once a plane reservation is made, you may have three people notified automatically by e-mail when the flight arrives at its destination. This may prove valuable in cases where people are arriving from different cities to attend a meeting.

The Expedia Web site provides a special corporate section for business travel. It is located at

http://www.expedia.com

For a small fee, a business may become a member of their Corporate Travel Group and receive reduced fares as well as trip assistance en route.

In order to assist travelers who prefer to stay at hotels that have an in-room computer with Internet access, *Forbes* magazine has developed "Rooms with a Clue" at

http://www.forbes.com/tool/toolbox/clue/

The site provides rate and contact information, and displays the hotel's telephone jack type, power plug type, and whether the telephone system is digital or analog.

Travel Abroad

The State Department's home page provides information about obtaining passports and is found at

http://www.state.gov/index.html

The State Department also provides a page where individuals may check to determine what countries had travel warnings issued concerning them. These warnings are issued when the State Department decides to recommend that Americans avoid travel to a particular country. Public announcements disseminate information about terrorist threats and other conditions posing significant risks to the security of American travelers. Such warnings are issued when there is a perceived threat that will include Americans as a target group. Some examples of these announcements include short-term coups, bomb threats to airlines, violence by terrorists, and anniversary dates of specific terrorist events. This information is available at

http://www.travel.state.gov/travel_warnings.html

General information about Europe's large cities may be found in a multimedia presentation of tours of these cities. The site includes films, photographs, audio, and virtual reality experiences. This site is found at

http://www.lion.com/cineworld/index.html

On-Line Meetings

Internet providers have the capability of establishing "chat rooms" for meetings and conferences. Private meetings may be set up in private chat rooms by law firms, corporations, or any individuals who wish to meet in a concealed setting. The subscriber may set up a private chat room and invite those individuals he wishes to participate in the meeting.

In many cases, considerable expense of traveling to remote locations may be avoided by this type of setup. For instance, a lawyer in Canada may speak online to a client in New York without incurring long distance telephone charges or travel fees by setting up a chat room for this meeting. A lawyer in a New York law firm may set up a meeting with members of the same firm located in Los Angeles. A judge at the World Court in New York may set up a room to meet with opposing lawyers from two countries in a lawsuit to discuss fishing rights. Staff meetings may be conducted with branch offices in other parts of the country or in other countries as well. Endless possibilities exist for the constructive use of chat rooms in conducting business.

Airline Web Sites

All major airlines have their own Web sites as well as the capability of allowing you to make reservations online. Some of the sites will even permit you to make hotel and car reservations at their Web site. Listed below are a few of the major airlines' Web sites. A quick search by the airline's name will allow you to find others.

American Airlines	**http://www.aa.com**
British Airways	**http://www.britishairways.com**
Continental Airlines	**http://www.continental.com**
Delta Airlines	**http://www.delta.com**
Northwest Airlines	**http://www.nwa.com**
Southwest Airlines	**http://www.swa.com**
United Airlines	**http://www.ual.com**

As you can readily see, most of the airlines' Web sites are either the name of the airline or their initials. If you would like to gain access to a different airline's Web site, you may conduct a search using the airline's name. If there is one particular airline that is used most often by the members of your law firm or company, bookmark their Web site for faster retrieval.

Many of the airlines also allow you to obtain not only your reservations and e-tickets online, but also to book your seat assignment as well. Some sites have information about different cities being visited. Others allow you to track the airplane from departure to arrival. Most airlines also have weekly newsletters that can be sent to you regarding any special fares they might have that particular week or about exceptional sales on tickets.

Expense Accounts

When an employee returns from a trip, the law firm will require the preparation of an expense report so that the individual may be reimbursed for the expenses. Exhibit 3-7 on page 56 shows an example of an expense summary to request reimbursement of costs incurred by the attorney on behalf of the law firm. Most firms require receipts for all expenditures. Other items required are the date of the expense, the location of the activity, a description of the expense, the business purpose of the expense, other persons involved as well as their business relationship, the amount paid, and the client account number. This particular firm has many locations and many practice areas; thus, they also require that the individual note the location of the office as well as the practice group involved.

PREPARING LEGAL CORRESPONDENCE ✦

Paralegals and legal secretaries prepare much of the correspondence in a law office. Some items are different from the ordinary business letter. Exhibit 3-8 on page 57 shows a typical letter format, and the next paragraphs explain each part of the letter. You should check the files in your own office to determine whether it uses a different format.

Letterhead

All law offices have letterhead paper for preparing correspondence. The letterhead includes the name, address, telephone number, and fax number of the law firm. Some firms list all partners of the firm, while others list all attorneys employed by the firm. Paralegals may be listed, but must be identified by title so that no one reading the letterhead will infer that a paralegal is an attorney because no title is given. Various state bar associations have said that paralegals may be listed on a firm's letterhead as long as their title appears after their name.

EXHIBIT 3-7 Expense Summary

Courtesy: Reprinted by permission of Sheila Cantrell, Sheppard, Mullin, Richter, and Hampton

EXPENSE SUMMARY

☐ Administration (07)

Office

☐ Los Angeles (01) ☐ West Los Angeles (10)
☐ Orange County (03) ☐ Santa Barbara (04)
☐ San Francisco (05) ☐ Del Mar Heights (06)
☐ San Diego (08) ☐ Central Services (07)

Practice Group

☐ Antitrust & Trade Reg. (11) ☐ Corporate (10) ☐ Labor & Employment (04)
☐ Business Crimes (16) ☐ Financial Institutions (13) ☐ R.E., Environ. & Construction (12)
☐ Finance & Bankruptcy (03) ☐ Gov't. Contracts & Regulated Indus. (15) ☐ R.E./LUNR/Environment (02)
☐ Business Trial Practice (14) ☐ Intellectual Property (08) ☐ Tax/Emp. Benefits/Trusts & Estates (05)

Date: _____   Attorney Billing Number or Employee I.D.: _____   Name: _____

*Receipt No.	Date Expense Incurred or Travel Dates	Location of Activity or Travel Itinerary	Description of Expense	Business Purpose (for business meals and entertainment, state nature of business discussion or activity)	Persons other than you involved and business relationships	Amount Paid Personally to be Reimbursed or Reported	Client Matter Number or G/L Account Number (see reverse)

Total: $ _____
Less Advances: $ _____
Amount Due (firm/me): $ _____

X _____

By submitting the foregoing expense summary, I certify that the amounts claimed were actually incurred in connection with Sheppard Mullin business and are reimbursable under the Firm's reimbursement guidelines.

_____
Executive Director Approval or Designee

Page _____ of _____

Notes:

In all cases, list amounts spent on food or beverages separately from other amounts such as hotel room charges.

By submitting this form, you verify your presence when food or beverages were served for which you seek reimbursement as a "business meal" whether or not the expenditure is chargeable to a client.

* Receipts: The I.R.S. requires that all items of $25.00 or more have a receipt attached. Every effort should be made, however, to provide receipts for all expenses, regardless of the amount. Attach "original" receipts. To ensure receipts are "contemporaneous," notations should be made on the receipts themselves as to persons entertained, business purpose, etc.

EXHIBIT 3-8   Sample Legal Correspondence

[FIRM LETTERHEAD]

{Today's Date}

Ms. Selena A. Daniella
Attorney at Law
433 East Fourth Street
Scottsdale, AZ 85060

RE: Format for Legal Correspondence

Dear Ms. Daniella:

Here is an example of the manner in which we prepare legal correspondence using the block format. Other offices use the modified block format, where the paragraphs start with a five-space indention from the left margin and the date and signature block are at the center of the page.
Reference initials are used and include the writer's and typist's initials. Enclosures and copies are noted. If you do not want the recipient of the letter to know who receives the copies, then "bcc" should be typed on the copies only. An ordinary copy is noted on the original.

Very truly yours,
LONG AND GALLO

Judy A. Long

cc: Jeffrey W. Daniels

Date

The current date must be included on the letter. Be sure the year is correct, particularly at the beginning of the year when many people tend to use the previous year's date.

Inside Address

The name, title, and full address of the recipient should be included; the address should include the proper state abbreviation and zip code. Attorneys may be referred to as "Carl H. Jensen, Esq." or in tow lines as "Mr. Carl H. Hansen, Attorney at Law." Never refer to an attorney as "Mr." and "Esq." at the same time. A judge of a trial court is addressed as "Judge Juan Carrera," while a justice of an appellate court is addressed as "Justice Anna Romero." Try to limit the inside address to four lines if possible.

Re (Subject) Line

In legal offices, the subject line is called the "RE line." This line usually includes the name of the case or client and the case number. However, if a different topic is the subject of the letter, that information is used instead.

Salutation

The salutation should use the same form of address used in everyday conversation. Therefore, if you usually address Mr. Jensen as Carl, the salutation would be "Dear Carl." However, if you do not address Mr. Jensen by his first name in conversation, the proper salutation would be "Dear Mr. Jensen." The following are other appropriate forms of address:

Dear Judge Parker:

Dear Justice Madrid:

Dear Doctor Rodriquez:

Body

The body of the letter should be as brief as possible. The recipient may not read an inordinately long letter. If a request is being made, the due date should be included in the last paragraph of the letter. As in any other writing, the following format should be used:

1. Introduction
2. Body
3. Conclusion or request.

Closing

Most law offices use "Very truly yours" as the closing. However, if you are writing to a friend who is also an associate or colleague, "Sincerely yours" would be appropriate. Again, consult the office files to determine the closing used in your firm.

Signature Line

The name of the law firm is used in the signature line, as well as your name and title. The following are typical signature lines for a paralegal and a legal assistant:

Very truly yours,
LONG AND MARIN

JANET R. KIEFER
Paralegal

Very truly yours,
LONG AND MARIN

JOHN R. MARTIN
Legal Assistant to Judy A. Long

Multipage Letters

Although letterhead is used for the first page of a letter, most firms use plain paper for the second and subsequent pages. Some firms have a shortened form of their letterhead that is used for the second page.

Two styles are used for the heading for the second and subsequent pages of letters. They are shown below.

Ms. Selena Daniella   -2-   June 27, 2003

Ms. Selena Daniella
Page 2
June 27, 2003

Since the standard page numbering for a document in a word processing program generally numbers pages sequentially at the top or bottom of the page, you may have to code the letter by using the Headers/Footers feature of your software.

File Numbers

Some firms require a coded file number to appear on each piece of correspondence at the bottom of the letter after the signature line. This code may refer to the writer, client, and/or file number. It enables the legal assistant to find the information more quickly in electronic storage.

Macros

If the paralegal or legal assistant is called upon to prepare the same type of letter many times, then a form letter should be created on the computer by using a macro. A macro may be created for each individual form letter by following the instructions in your word processing program. You may record and play back a macro to perform tasks, which may range from simple to complex. Be sure to name each macro to reflect its purpose. For example, if the same letter is sent to clients notifying them of their court dates, a macro may be created with the title "client court date."

Macros may be created for mouse selections and key strokes, type text, or insert macro commands. You could record a macro that inserts the closing portion of a letter or a standard phrase used in a pleading. Any time you find yourself doing repetitive key strokes, consider recording a macro for those keystrokes and giving it an appropriate name.

Internal Correspondence

Interoffice memorandum forms are used for correspondence within the office, company, or law firm. Several different formats are used, the most common of which will be explained here. However, to find the proper format for your particular law office, look in the files for prior memoranda or consult the office's style manual if one exists.

Some memoranda are typed using forms that are available in a software package on your computer. For instance, if you are using Microsoft® Word, you may choose one of their memorandum forms by opening the Templates. Choose "Memos" and then "Professional Memo." If you are using Word's XP version, you would perform the following steps:

1. Choose File
2. Click on "New"
3. Click "Memos"
4. Click "Professional Memo"

If you are using another version of Word, or another word processing program, consult their Help file to determine the method for choosing these formats.

Parts of the Memorandum

The parts of the memorandum are explained here:

DATE: The date the memorandum is sent

MEMORANDUM TO: This is the recipient of the memorandum

FROM: Your name (sender)

RE: Case name and number or other subject

The body of the memorandum is similar to that of a letter but is generally more informal since it is being sent within the firm. Be sure to include a "Confidential" stamp if the memorandum contains privileged information.

Envelopes

Envelopes for external correspondence have return addresses similar to the office letterhead. Use the template for envelopes and key in the recipient's name and address, or use the "copy and paste" function to take the name and address from the letter itself and copy it into the envelope template.

Envelopes for internal correspondence are generally of a different quality and type and require only the recipient's name and location. They may be addressed by hand or on the computer.

Answering Correspondence

Most attorneys require their paralegals or legal assistants to answer routine correspondence. If the attorney for whom you work asks you to answer his routine correspondence, a letter to the attorney arrives in the mail, and you have the information to answer it, draft a letter for the attorney's signature and attach it to the incoming letter before giving it to the attorney. This saves the attorney considerable time in reading the letter when it arrives, drafting a reply, and giving it to a secretary to be typed. However, this correspondence must be answered in a timely manner.

If you are asked to draft a letter over your own signature, you may use the law firm letterhead and the same format as you would use for the attorney. Under the closing and signature line, use the following:

Very truly yours,

ADAMS AND BACON

JANET R. EVANS

Legal Assistant to Mr. Adams

If you have the recipient's e-mail address, it is often faster and easier to draft a quick e-mail when answering correspondence. Be sure that there is no breach of confidentiality and that the e-mail address is correct. There have been cases where the e-mail address is mistyped and the wrong person gets a confidential communication that was meant for a client.

Faxes

A large number of firms and individuals use faxes to send material instantaneously. It is very important to key in the correct number when sending a fax. The author often receives faxes meant for other recipients because the sender has keyed in the wrong fax number. If you receive a fax meant for someone else, you may return it to the sender or call the sender to tell her you have received their fax in error.

Faxes containing confidential information must include a "Confidential" designation or stamp. Some offices have their own forms of coding to protect against faxes being routed to the wrong individuals. In one case, several different fax numbers were on an office's speed dialing. The legal assistant inadvertently sent a confidential communication meant for the client to the opposing counsel. Particular care should be taken when dialing fax numbers or using your speed dial to prevent such incidents from occurring.

The Microsoft Office Template "Wizard" may be used to create for formats for faxes. Follow the instructions on the form itself for composing faxes.

E-mail

Most law offices, government offices, and corporate law departments have access to the Internet and thus have their own electronic mail (e-mail) addresses. Therefore, it is often more expedient to send someone an e-mail than to call on the telephone, write a letter, or send a fax. An e-mail may be composed, sent from your computer keyboard, and received almost instantaneously.

Although the format for e-mails is more informal than for the formal letter, it is appropriate to use the individual's name in the e-mail itself, similar to a salutation. If the e-mail is being sent internally within the law firm or company, or to a personal friend, then no salutation is necessary. Be sure to type the person's screen name exactly, using proper spelling, or the recipient will not receive it. E-mails that are not addressed properly may be returned or may be routed to another individual with the screen name you mistyped. Be especially careful when sending sensitive or confidential information via e-mail, as some individuals may be able to gain access to others' e-mail if they are adept at "hacking." Some firms have coding systems for use when sending e-mail. When sending privileged or confidential communications via e-mail, include the appropriate designation at the bottom of the message.

Although e-mail is more informal than the written letter, be sure to check for spelling and grammatical errors. Some programs have an automatic spell check. Some Internet providers have a method for an individual to check to see whether the recipient received the e-mail.

With some programs, other material may be imported into the e-mail, such as reports, exhibits, graphics, or other documents.

E-mail can be sent outside the office via the Internet or internally via an intranet. That is, within an organization a network is often set up to send and receive e-mails within the company or building. Sometimes internal networks are set up for law firms with offices in different locations or cities. A directory of all employees' e-mail addresses is often included in the e-mail address book.

FORMAT FOR LEGAL DOCUMENTS

Law offices use similar basic formats for their legal pleadings and documents. Check your office files to find the appropriate heading for your state. Using legal pleading paper, called "legal cap," certain items are put on the numbered lines as is shown in Exhibit 3-9. Some law firms have pleading paper letterhead with the name and telephone number of the law firm imprinted in the upper left corner, starting on line 1. A few states have this letterhead in the lower part of the page. Always refer to your own state's guidelines to determine the proper format.

Using Microsoft® Word, a component of Microsoft Office®, the legal pleading paper may be accessed by using the template for "Pleading Wizard." The "wizard" will enable you to complete the document by keying in the appropriate information from questions asked in the program. Once the basic information has been typed into the template, you can save it to use it on future documents as a macro.

In most states, the name and address of the law firm should appear on Lines 1–4. On Line 8, the name of the court and its address should be centered in all capital letters. The case caption begins on Line 11; it includes the name of the parties, case number, and document name. An example is shown in Exhibit 3-9.

Pleading Captions

Most cases involve one plaintiff in opposition to one defendant and use the caption found in Exhibit 3-9. However, there are other specialized cases that use different type captions, which are shown as follows:

1. Minors

PATRICIA ZARKON, as Guardian
ad litem for RAY ZARKON, a
Minor,
Plaintiff,

v.

JAMES RICHARDSON,
Defendant.

EXHIBIT 3-9 Sample Pleading

1	JACKSON CASE
2	2433 Poplar Avenue
3	Memphis, Tennessee 23456
4	Telephone: (901) 555-9876
5	
6	Attorney for Plaintiff
7	
8	Superior Court of Shelby County
9	State of Tennessee
10	
11	JANE MARRI,) Case No.: No. 12-3-456789-1
12	)
13	Plaintiff,) COMPLAINT FOR DAMAGES
14	)
15	vs.)
16	JOHN DEFENSE,)
17	Defendant)
18	_____)
19	[Pleading goes here.]
20	
21	Dated this 1st day of April, 2004
22	_____
23	JACKSON CASE
24	
25	
26	
27	
28	

2. Class Action Suits

JOHN KELLY, on behalf of
himself and all Plaintiffs
similarly situated,
Plaintiffs,
v.
DELANEY CORPORATION,
Defendants.

3. Executor of an Estate

JANE JONES, Executor of the
Estate of MARY JONES,
Plaintiff,
v.
JOHN ROBERTSON,
Defendant.

Finding State Forms and Documents On-line

Several Web sites are available for finding the appropriate forms and documents to use in the various states. West Legal Studies, an imprint of Delmar Cengage Learning, provides downloadable forms from its Web site at

http://www.paralegal.delmar.cengage.com

The different state court Web pages also provide forms that may be copied for that particular state.

California, New York, and a few other states utilize court forms for many documents so that the attorney's office is not required to prepare a separate pleading each time a particular purpose must be achieved. For example, California has a packet of forms that are used in all probates in the state, whereas some other states require that the law offices have typed documents for this purpose.

Pleadings

The complaint and answer or answering documents in a civil case are called pleadings. Pleadings introduce the case and define the character and scope of the matters being litigated by narrowing disputed issues.

The complaint notifies the defendant of the claims asserted by the plaintiff and petitions the court for jurisdiction of the matter. To establish a cause of action, the attorney must first determine which court has jurisdiction, whether the plaintiff has in fact raised valid contentions, and what issues are being litigated. All pleadings must be prepared on ruled and numbered pleading paper, unless the state has court forms for this purpose.

Z-Rulings or Slash Marks

Signature lines for pleadings or other legally-binding documents may not be typed on a separate page from the document itself. At least two lines of the document should be placed on the same page as the signature line.

Pleading paper contains 28 numbered lines. If you find your document ending on line 26, stop typing the document on line 24 and include the last two lines on the following page, along with the signature lines. Three slash marks should be typed on each numbered line below line 24 down to and including line 28.

If the document ends several lines earlier, however, and the signature line does not fit on that page, some law offices prefer the use of "Z-rules" from the last line of the text to the end of that page. Two examples follow:

25	///
26	///
27	///
28	///

23

24

25

26

27

Multiparty Actions

In cases where there are several plaintiffs and/or several defendants, all of their names must be mentioned on the first pleading filed with the court. Thereafter, most courts allow the use of the term *et al.,* which means "and others." Check with the court in which you are filing the document to be certain of their procedures. You may also use the term when you are writing a letter or memorandum about the case. When you are including the name of a case within a letter or document, it should always be underlined. Here is an example of a case name with multiple parties written within a document

<u>John A. Remington, et al. v. Alexander J. Garcia, et al., Case No. PI-23995</u>

Signature Lines

Two types of signature lines may be found on legal documents and pleadings. The first is used by a sole practitioner and the second by a member of a law firm, government agency, or corporation. The signature line begins in the middle of the page and continues to the right margin as follows:

1. Sole practitioner

_____

DANIELLE ALICE MICHAELS
Attorney for Plaintiff

2. Law firm

JEFFRIES AND WILLIAMS

By: _____
SCOTT W. JEFFRIES
Attorney for Defendant

Proofreading

All documents that are filed with the court must be accurate or they may be rejected. Be sure to proofread all correspondence and documents for accuracy and spelling. Remember that even though you use spell check on the computer, if the word you wish to use is spelled incorrectly but is an actual word, it will not be corrected by spell check. After typing a letter or document, reread it twice, once for spelling and the second for accuracy. Listed below are items that you should check carefully:

- *Names and addresses.* Be sure all names and addresses are spelled correctly. Check the numbers on addresses to be sure they are typed accurately.
- *Capitalization.* If a word is capitalized at the beginning of the letter or document, be consistent in capitalizing it throughout the writing.
- *Check the caption* of a pleading carefully to be sure that all parties' names are spelled correctly and their designations are correct. Legal names should always be used. If one of the parties is a corporation, its legal name may be obtained from the office of the

Secretary of State in the state in which the corporation is registered. The corporation's official reports, such as its annual report, are also good sources for this information.

- *Check the case number* on all correspondence and documents to be sure it is correct.
- *Recheck any citations* to cases for accuracy. It has been determined that judges will ignore case information if the case citation is not exact.
- *Review the file* for accuracy of names, spellings, and addresses.

ETHICS and ETIQUETTE

Confidentiality of client communications is especially critical in the administrative area. Be sure the attorney is aware of all appointments, meetings, and court dates. Special care should be taken when due dates arise in court proceedings so that all documents required are prepared on time. One of the major reasons attorneys are sued for malpractice is because of missed deadlines. Be especially conscious of deadlines and remind the attorney what is due and when.

If you are required to complete a timesheet of all client matters worked on during the day, report the time accurately. If you spend five minutes on a telephone call with the client, record it as .1 hour. If you spend a half hour on the telephone talking to a friend, which is not allowed in most offices, then do not charge the client for this time on your time sheet. In a controversy in court over attorney fees, these time sheets will be available to the court.

When you are preparing legal correspondence that is of a confidential nature, do not leave your desk with the material on your screen, particularly if you do not have a private office. Save the item first, whether it is a letter, memorandum, report, or fax. Be especially careful when sending a confidential fax that you send it to the correct fax number. In one case, the legal assistant sent a confidential fax intended for the client to the opposing counsel in a case, which caused considerable problems in the case. If you have speed-dialing for faxes, check the number before sending the fax. Transposing numbers is easy to do but can be disastrous. I have personally received many faxes intended for other recipients, and I have sent them back to the sender.

In today's legal community, as in the business world in general, much business is conducted by e-mail. However, good screening devices must be in place on the computers in your firm to assure that these e-mails are not accessible to hackers. Most law offices realize this problem and install the best technological equipment to avoid this problem. If there is a doubt about the privacy of your e-mail system, do not send confidential communications via e-mail. If the material in the e-mail is particularly sensitive to the case, obtain permission from the client before sending it. Many law offices have encryption devices for e-mail in these situations.

Mobile telephones are used extensively in today's society. However, these communications may not be confidential if someone overhears the conversation or if the call is intercepted by a listening device. Use caution in discussing cases on a mobile phone.

Setting legal fees is another area reserved for the attorney only. The paralegal, or legal assistant, may not set the fees to be charged to the client. There may be occasions when the attorney instructs the paralegal, or legal assistant, to tell the client that the fee is a certain amount. Repeating this information is allowed because the attorney is setting the fee.

CHAPTER SUMMARY

One of the most important tasks of the paralegal and legal assistant is calendaring. Since a majority of situations in the law office require deadlines, it is imperative that items be noted on the calendar and/or tickler file.

Billable hours are the hours charged to the client. The paralegal must record all time spent working on a case so the client can be billed properly. Various billing methods are used, including hourly fees, contingency fees, statutory fees, and project fees.

The attorney spends a considerable amount of time traveling, both locally and out of town. The legal assistant has several options open for making travel arrangements on the Internet.

Legal correspondence and documents follow certain formats that are different from the ordinary business office. Several different formats have been provided in this chapter.

✦ KEY TERMS

advice	hourly fees
American Bar Association	nonbillable hours
billable hours	project fees
confidentiality	retainer fees
contingency fees	statutory fees
docket	tickler file
e-mail	time sheet

✦ SELF TEST

Indicate whether the following statements are true (T) or false (F).

____ 1. Contingency fees are charged in divorce cases.

____ 2. Billable hours represent the total hours to be billed to an individual client.

_____ 3. Attorneys do not bill clients for telephone calls.

_____ 4. Attorney fees in probate are hourly.

_____ 5. The caption of a pleading includes the signature line.

Circle the correct answer to the following questions.

1. Contingency fees represent
   a. an hourly amount.
   b. a percentage of the award received from the defendant.
   c. a percentage of the deceased's estate.
   d. none of the above.

2. Fees used to bill clients include
   a. contingency fees.
   b. hourly fees.
   c. statutory fees.
   d. all of the above.

3. Attorneys are reprimanded or sanctioned by
   a. the ABA.
   b. their state bar.
   c. the federal government.
   d. none of the above.

4. "Et al" means
   a. and the following.
   b. and others.
   c. out of court.
   d. from a contract.

Fill-in-the-blanks

1. The paper used for the preparation of legal documents and pleadings is known as

   _____.

2. A set fee charged to a client based on the job to be undertaken is called

   _____.

3. List the Web page for one of the sources on the Internet for driving directions and/or maps. _____

4. The subject line in legal correspondence is called the _____ line.

5. The caption on a legal document includes the following items: _____
   _____
   _____.

✦ NOTEBOOK PROJECTS

1. James Rodriquez is suing Sally Lopez for damages for personal injuries sustained in an automobile accident. Prepare a caption for use on a complaint in your state. The case number is not yet known, so leave that portion blank. (The court will fill it in when the complaint is filed.) Place the caption in your Notebook after it is graded by the instructor.

2. Discuss the manner in which you would address the following telephone calls to your firm.

    a. Mrs. Debbon is calling for the fifth time today. The attorney has told you that he does not wish to talk to her if she calls again.

    b. The attorney has taken the afternoon off to play golf. His client, Mr. Roberts, calls and wants to know his whereabouts.

    c. A client, Mr. Ross, calls to speak to the attorney. She has left the office and has not told you where she is going or when she will return.

    d. Mr. Allen, a client, wants to make an appointment with the legal assistant handling his case.

3. Prepare a time sheet of your own activities for one day this week. List all activities in which you are engaged and the amount of time spent on each, in tenths of an hour. Use the form provided in Exhibit 3-10 on page 72.

4. Research and review two computerized docket control programs and compare their features, convenience and ease of use, and cost. Write a memorandum to your instructor discussing your findings.

5. Research three timekeeping and billing software programs. Prepare a comparison summary in memo format.

6. Prepare a letter to the client, Mrs. Rose Aaronson, 422 East Broad Street, your town, your state, informing her that she is scheduled for an appointment with the attorney, Mr. Danielson, at 10:00 a.m. next Monday. Provide the date and address of your office. Prepare your own letterhead using your word processing program. See Exhibit 3-11 on page 73.

7. Review, via the Internet, an article or case relating to cyberlaw. Summarize the article and discuss the issues that relate to confidentiality and security of electronic communications.

EXHIBIT 3-10　Time Sheet for Use with Projects

Time Record

Name: _____　　　Date: _____

Client Number	Client/Case	File Number	Description of Services	Time	
				Hours	Tenths

EXHIBIT 3-11   Letterhead

Jeffrey W. Danielson

Attorney at Law

1122 Main Street

Providence, RI 22222

USING COMPUTERS

CHAPTER OUTCOMES

- As a result of studying this chapter, the student will learn:
- To describe many different uses of computers in the law office
- Where to find resources on the Internet for specialized research purposes
- To use Mail Merge for the preparation of mailing lists, form letters, and faxes

INTRODUCTION

Since the law office is required to maintain and retain a considerable amount of information, the computer is used extensively. The law office compiles data about clients, cases, evidence, financial reports, and employee materials. A significant amount of legal research is done on the computer via the Internet or software packages from legal publishers. Since much of the information used in documents is repetitive, the computer is ideal for compiling forms and macros for these items. For example, many software packages exist for probating an estate, preparing a dissolution, writing a will, establishing a corporation, handling a bankruptcy, and managing any other proceeding that requires the same type documents.

Document (word) processing programs allow the legal assistant or paralegal to assist in writing, editing, revising, and printing pleadings, legal documents, correspondence, and research memoranda. More of this material may be created in a timely manner by using the computer.

Software packages are available that execute complicated financial computations used in probate, dissolution, tax, real estate, and litigation cases. Once a system is set up on the computer, it may be used over and over again with the substitution of different calculations. Not only is this method faster than performing the operations by hand, but it is more accurate as well.

DOCUMENT PROCESSING

Word processing, also known as document processing, enables you to use the computer to support the preparation of correspondence and

document (word) processing programs
programs that allow the legal assistant or paralegal to assist in writing, editing, revising, and printing pleadings, legal documents, correspondence, and research memoranda.

word processing (document processing)
program that enables you to use the computer to support the preparation of correspondence and documents.

documents. Documents prepared using word processing programs may be either originals or those that utilize the standardized macros set up within the program. For example, Microsoft® Word provides a "wizard" for legal pleadings that enables you to make a standard form for your pleadings and that can be accessed each time you write a new document. In this manner, only the changes to the pleading must be retyped, which eliminates repetitive key strokes during document preparation. A considerable amount of preparation time is saved using this method of document production.

New pleadings, correspondence, and documents may be created by using a document from a prior case and making appropriate changes. The original version of the text may be accessed, changes made, and the document name changed for the new case. By saving the new document with a different name, both documents will be available for use.

Document assembly programs are obtainable for large cases with multiple parties and many documents. It is possible for a complex case to have a roomful of files that must be accessible. Only with the use of a computer program designed for this purpose are these documents easily accessible when needed.

Court Forms

Some states, such as California and New York, use forms for many of the documents that are filed with the courts. Software packages of all **court forms** are available that allow the user to key the information into the form on the computer and print out the completed form. This alleviates the necessity of preparing these forms on a typewriter keyboard and typing directly onto the form itself.

The forms may also be downloaded from the Internet via the legal Web sites discussed in the following secton. Many forms and legal pleadings are also available at

http://www.paralegal.delmar.cengage.com

Federal and state court forms and pleadings are available on this site.

USING THE INTERNET

Most material that was previously available only in book form is now obtainable on the Internet. A vast number of Web sites are available that specialize in the legal profession. Previously, the use of e-mail for communications was discussed. Travel arrangements and the Web sites available for this purpose were also explained. This section will be devoted to the specialized use of the Internet for the law office. Additional information about Web sites will be discussed under the various specialty chapters commencing with Chapter 4.

One of the most common uses of the Internet in the law office is legal research. In addition to subscription legal research services, such as Westlaw, many other sources are accessible for legal research.

court forms forms used for some of the documents that are filed with the courts; generally published by the courts and available on their Web pages.

The Library of Congress maintains a Web page that provides a catalog of all available publications. You can search for any book that has been published and has an ISBN. Searches may be undertaken by title, key words, or author. The site for the Library of Congress is located at

http://lcweb.loc.gov/

One of the more comprehensive Web pages for finding information about different areas of law is available at

http://www.amicus.ca/links.html

This site provides information on specific practice areas along with background information on law-related topics. It is particularly useful for finding resources in a practice area with which you are unfamiliar or where more information is required than can be found under the federal or state links. In addition to a large number of specialty sources, information is obtainable on the growing body of law governing Internet use, as well as additional links connected to this topic. General links are provided to hardware and software information along with leads to conducting searches.

The FindLaw site has been touted as being the best site to find legal resources. This Web page is available at

http://ww.findlaw.com/

Some links available on this site include:

- Consumer law
- United States Supreme court cases
- State cases and laws
- Law schools
- Legal subject indexes
- State law resources
- Foreign and international resources
- Law firms
- Legal organizations
- Government directories
- Legal practice materials

If you are looking for a site on a law subject and do not know the Web address, it is often easier to find the site on FindLaw than to do a search on your own. It is especially valuable if you are not sure exactly what topic under which to conduct your key word search. A copy of the FindLaw Web page may be found at Exhibit 4.1.

EXHIBIT 4-1 Findlaw Home Page

Courtesy: Reprinted by permission of www.FindLaw.com

The American Bar Association maintains a Legal Research Law Link that has links to all branches of government as well as the courts, Judicial Council, court home pages, law school libraries, and a number of other legal reference resources. It is located at

http://www.abanet.org/lawlink/home.html

Customized legal documents are provided at

http://www.legaldocs.com/

and at

http://www.LegalLawForms.com

A copy of the Web page may be found at Exhibit 4-2.

These Web pages enable the user to prepare customized documents online from given templates. Some of these documents are free, and others require a small payment. Available documents include wills, trusts, leases, partnership agreements, business forms, and real estate forms.

Westlaw® and Lexis®

Computerized legal research systems are accessible on the Internet for a fee. The most widely used systems are Westlaw and Lexis. You must first establish an account with their organization. You will then obtain a password to gain access to their databases. Your time using the database is computed automatically and charged to the attorney's account. These sites may be found at

http://www.westlaw.com

and

http://www.lexis.com

Many research sources are found on these Web sites, including cases, courts, law reviews, newspaper articles, and statutes on both the federal and state level. Westlaw also provides a legal directory of attorneys called *West's Legal Directory of Attorneys*.

Law Schools and Their Law Libraries

Most law schools have Web sites for both the school itself and the library, that include the various legal research sources available. The law school sites provide particular information about the individual law schools, such as academic services, faculty, placement activities, courses offered, and admissions requirements. Individual law school sites will provide links to their libraries. Please note that Web sites sometimes change, and any of the sites listed here may have a different address by the time this text is published. If you wish to find a

EXHIBIT 4-2   Legal Law Forms Home Page

Courtesy: Reprinted by permission of www.LegalLawForms.com

www.LegalLawForms.com

Real Legal Forms Drafted By Real Attorneys!
Your Complete Legal Form Resource Site!

Easy to use...You just fill in the blanks in the legal form with your personal information, print & sign. You can even edit the legal forms as you like! Fast downloads. Receive your attorney drafted agreement now!

DOWNLOAD THESE LEGAL FORMS NOW to save you time and money!
Clear and easy to use attorney drafted legal forms for your needs.

ALL FORMS DRAFTED
AND REVIEWED BY
ATTORNEYS

HOME

ORDER
FORMS NOW!

ABOUT US

LAW CHAT
ROOM

INFORMATION
AND HELP

VIEW A
SAMPLE FORM

NEW FORMS
ADDED MONTHLY

FORMS USABLE IN
ALL 50 STATES

Live, real time chat on legal subjects. Join the chat forum nightly at 7:00 PM EST.

• Get the same forms the attorneys use!

• Penetrate the secrets of the law!

• Save hundreds of dollars in legal fees!

• The power of our documents will please you!

Most Popular Forms:
1. Power of Attorney
2. Partnership Agreement
3. Promissory Note
4. Leases
5. Option Agreement To Purchase Business
6. Non-Disclosure Agreement
7. Premarital Agreement

Categories:
Bills of Sale Forms
Business Agreements
Contract Forms
Corporation Documents
Credit & Collection Forms
Distributor Agreements
Employment Agreements
Intellectual Property & Inventions Forms
Internet - Website Agreements
Leases - Landlord & Tenant Documents
Limited Liability Corporation Documents
Limited Partnership Documents
Marriage & Divorce Documents
Miscellaneous Forms
Notes, Guarantees & Loan Documents
Partnerships & Joint Ventures
Power Of Attorney Forms
Real Estate Documents
Sale/Purchase of Business Documents

Click on any category at left to browse for Forms

FREE newsletter on the law and contracts. Insert your email address below:

[ ] Go!

Did you know...
A contract written on a coconut shell is legal.

A contract written on a napkin is enforceable.

Searching for a specific form? Enter
Keyword or Form Name: [ ]
Go!

Go to entire legal form library!
These attorney drafted legal forms provide an easy solution to your legal form needs.

continued

Exhibit 4-2 *continued*

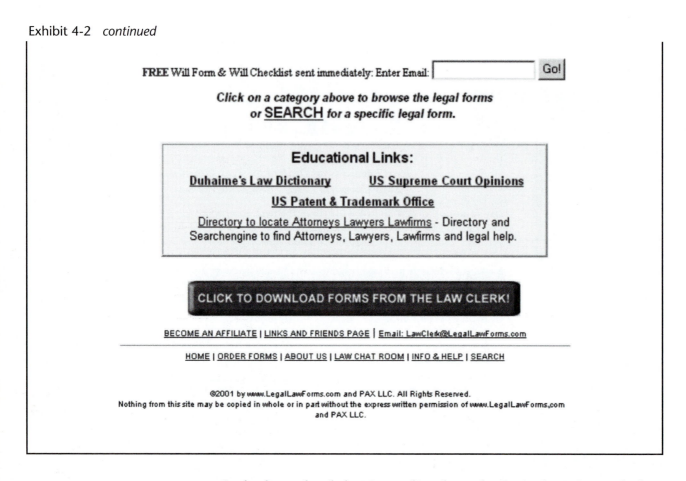

particular law school that is not listed or whose site has changed, do a search on the name of the law school.

Case Western Reserve University—Ohio

Both the law school and its library are available online. To go directly to the law school, find

http://lawwww.cwru.edu/

and to go directly to the library, find

http://lawwww.cwru.edu/cwrulaw/library/libinfo.html

In addition to general information about the law school itself, the law school site provides links to other legal reference materials, as well as publications and research by the law school students and professors.

The library page provides a guide to Case Western's law library as well as online catalogs of library materials, links to other law school libraries, and the location of their basic legal research information.

Kent College of Law/Library—Chicago

This law school and library offers one of the best sites for finding links and information about any of the law libraries available online.

In addition to providing information about its own law school, links to various court departments are included. Their law review is available online, and decisions of the Illinois Human Rights Commission are provided.

The law school is available at

http://www.kentlaw.edu/

and the law library at

http://www.infoctr.edu/lawlib/

Cornell University—Law School/Library

Perhaps the largest provider of links to applicable legal research sites, Cornell provides their law school Web page as well as sites for the law library and the Legal Information Institute. Their addresses are:

Law school: **http://www.law.cornell/edu/admit/admit.htm**

Law library: **http://www.law.cornell.edu/library/default.html**

Legal Information Institute:

http://www.law.cornell.edu:80/lii.table.html

The law school provides a great deal of information about the school as well as law reviews and studies undertaken at the law school. The law library's page supplies an extensive legal research encyclopedia, a Global Legal Information Network dealing with international law sources, research guides, and law journals.

The Legal Information Institute provides links to various government agency Web pages and has one of the largest number of legal research. Access to the Supreme Court's most recent decisions is also available at this site. The decisions may be accessed through five search methods:

1. The full citation
2. A topical index
3. A key word search
4. Indices of the names of parties by the year of the decision
5. By date of decision (for the most recent term only).

A gallery of the Supreme Court Justices is provided, with biographical information and pictures of all the justices, along with links to the opinions written by each justice, including concurring and dissenting opinions.

Emory University—Law School/Library

This site provides access to links to many federal circuit court decisions and other documents available on the Web. It also provides information on legal materials in Georgia and a research aid as well.

The law school may be found at

http://www.olaw.emory.edu/

and the library at

http://www.law.emory.edu/LAW/law.html

Information about a subscription to Westlaw may be obtained at

http://www.westlaw.com

which is the official site for Westlaw. You may also access Westlaw from this site if you have an existing account.

Legal Search Engines

In order to find a site that provides a number of different search engines to other legal information, go to

http://www.dreamscape.com/frankvad/search.legal.html

Law-Related LISTSERVS

As discussed earlier, listservs represent a means for an individual to subscribe to a discussion group that sends e-mail out to a number of people about different topics. Once you have subscribed to the listserv, your e-mail address becomes part of the listserv's database. When someone sends out an e-mail to the list, all members receive a copy. If you wish to respond to an e-mail, a reply is sent to the group. Often valuable information may be obtained about legal issues.

For instance, when the author was writing this textbook, she asked the members of the paralegal educator's listserv about legal links they may have used and found to be valuable in their teaching of legal research. Many of these suggestions are included here.

One particularly valuable listserv actually contains lists of other list-servs, journels, law firms on the net, and bulletin boards that might be of interest to the legal profession. One may join this listserv by sending an e-mail with the following information:

TO: **listserv@justice.eliot.me.us**
FROM: <your screen name>
SUBJECT: legal list
BODY: Subscribe LEGAL_LIST <your screen name>

Once you join any listserv, you will continue getting all e-mail distributed on the listserv until you unsubscribe. After you join, an e-mail will be sent to you with information on how to post messages and how to unsubscribe. Be sure to keep this e-mail in your files in the event you decide at some future time that you are no longer interested in receiving e-mail from the list.

An excellent source for obtaining lists of all accessible legal listservs is available at

http://www.kentlaw.edu/lawlinks/listservs.html

This site provides information about over 400 legal lists that you may join as well as a number of different newsgroups on legal topics.

One particularly valuable list is aimed at the exchange of information about law-related Internet resources. Subscribing to this list will assure the receipt of every announcement of new or updated law-related resources. Discussions are also provided on the merits of various sites and questions asked and answered about how to find a particular topic. If you do a considerable amount of legal research on the Internet and wish to keep abreast of all the latest developments on new sites, it would be beneficial to join the list. The following e-mail will enter a subscription to this list:

TO: **Listserv@listserv.law.cornell.edu**
FROM: <your screen name>
SUBJECT: list <or any other topic>
BODY: Subscribe LAWSRC-L <your screen name>

One relatively new list that is comprised primarily of attorneys who are new to using the Internet for legal research is called NET-LAWYERS. Individuals share their discoveries of new sites and critique various sites. People ask and answer questions about where to find certain items. Although the site is largely made by and for attorneys, it is valuable to anyone who does legal research on the Internet and may be joined by sending the following e-mail:

TO: **net-lawyers-request@webcom.com**
FROM: <your screen name>
BODY: Subscribe <your screen name>

MAIL MERGE

"**Mail Merge**" is an element of most word processing programs and enables the user to generate form letters, envelopes, mailing labels, registers, and mass e-mail and fax circulation. In order to understand this feature, it is first necessary to learn some of the basic terminology associated with mail merge. The program used in this description is Microsoft® Word; however, the process would be similar for other word processing programs. If you are using a different program, consult the program's Help file for a detailed description of that program's system.

mail merge an element of most word processing programs that enables the user to generate form letters, envelopes, mailing labels, registers, and mass e-mail and fax circulation.

The main document contains the text that is being used for all versions of the document being merged. For instance, if you are creating a form letter, the main document might contain the return address and closing. It might also contain the same body with portions left out, such as dates and times, if you are developing a form letter to use for making appointments. The data source consists of a file that includes the material that is being merged into the document or letter. It may contain a list of names and addresses of the recipients of the letter you are using as the main document. The "merge" field is inserted in the main document where you wish to place information such as the address of the recipient. For instance, if you were to insert the merge field <<Address>> in the main document, the address stored in the address data field would be added at that point in your document.

The steps used to create form letters and mass mailings using the mail feature follow:

1. Construct a main document to use. This document will be sent to all addresses in the data source.

2. Open or create a data source. This source may be an address list previously created in your word processing program.

3. If appropriate, add a merge field. For instance, if you are inviting individuals to attend conferences in several different cities, then you would insert <<City>> where you wanted the individual cities to appear.

4. Merge the information from the data source into the main document so that you have a new document that includes the merged information.

In Microsoft® Word, the wizard will guide you through the various steps to perform a mail merge. Instructions will be provided.

If you want to create an address list to use for mail merge, the Mail Merge wizard will instruct you, step-by-step, through the process of making this list. In order to send a letter to all addressees in a certain city, you must select only those individuals.

Data Source

The data source is a separate file that contains information that looks like a table with several columns. Each of the columns represents a data field that is a separate grouping of information such as name, address, and zip code. The heading on each column indicates the related data that is included in that column. For instance, the names of recipients will be listed under the column entitled "Names."

Envelopes for Mass Mailings

Envelopes may be created using the Mail Merge wizard for letters that are being sent to many individuals. The instructions are as follow:

1. Go to the <u>Tools</u> menu and point to <u>Letters and Mailings</u>; click <u>Mail Merge Wizard</u>.
2. Click <u>Envelopes</u> under <u>Select document type</u>.
3. Click <u>Next: starting document</u>.
4. The wizard will then guide you through the process, which differs depending on whether you are creating a new envelope or are starting with an existing envelope.

Labels for Mass Mailings

In some cases you might have other documents being sent with the letters and need to have labels typed to place on larger envelopes. The steps for creating labels using the mail merge feature are as follow:

1. Go to the <u>Tools</u> menu and point to <u>Letters and Mailings</u>.
2. Click the <u>Mail Merge Wizard</u>.
3. Under the heading <u>Select document type</u>, click <u>Labels</u>.
4. Click <u>Next: starting document</u>.

The wizard will guide you through the remainder of the process depending on whether you are creating a new sheet of labels or using an existing sheet of labels. Be sure to have a sheet of blank labels in your printer when you are ready for copying.

Faxes

If your computer has the appropriate software installed, you can use the Mail Merge wizard for creating a fax to be sent to a group. A fax modem must also be installed in your computer. The steps for creating a fax in this manner are listed below.

1. If you are including a cover sheet, turn on that option in your fax software.
2. Point to <u>Letters and Mailings</u> in the <u>Tools</u> menu.
3. Click <u>Faxes</u> under <u>Select document type</u>.
4. Click <u>Next: starting document</u>.

The wizard will guide you through the rest of the process. More detailed information will be shown in your word processing Help file.

CHAPTER SUMMARY ♦

In this chapter, you learned the many different uses of computers in the law office. A number of different sites on the Internet were addressed for specialized research purposes.

The Internet provides a wealth of information for the legal researcher. Formats for pleadings and documents may be found and utilized. Computerized legal research systems, such as Westlaw and Lexis, are available for a fee.

Most word processing programs offer a mail merge element, which enables legal professionals to generate form letters, envelopes, mailing labels, registers, and mass e-mail and fax circulation.

ETHICS and ETIQUETTE

Protecting the privacy of confidential material is the key to using the computer and the Internet. Many legal research resources are available on the Internet; however, it is imperative that these sources be checked for accuracy, particularly if you are using a site that you have not used in the past. Remember that anyone with the ability may develop a Web page that looks official. Some of these sites are questionable when it comes to accuracy of information.

Official government sites, and the more well-known sites discussed in this text, are generally both reliable and safe. However, any site is only as safe as the program you have on your own computer for protecting its safety. As discussed in the previous chapter, be sure your law firm has an appropriate "fire wall" as well as the virus protection and privacy protection programs on the firm's computers. It is also advisable to have your own computer "password protected." That is, prior to being able to get into any of the information on an individual's computer, the proper password must be entered. Do not keep your password in plain view on your desk or taped to your computer. Memorize the password. Try to use something unique that no one else would be able to determine. For instance, don't use your birthday, name, address, or telephone number, because someone who wanted to "break into" your computer would likely try those passwords first.

✦ KEY TERMS

court forms

document (word)
   processing programs

Mail Merge

word processing
   (document processing)

✦ SELF TEST

Indicate whether the following statements are true (T) or false (F).

____ 1. The most commonly used word processing program in the law office is Excel.

____ 2. *West's Legal Directory of Attorneys* may be found in Westlaw.

____ 3. The *Encyclopedia Britannica* is found on the University of Chicago Web site.

____ 4. The American Bar Association maintains a Legal Research Law Link that has links to all branches of government.

Circle the correct answer to the following questions.

1. The leading computerized legal research systems are:
   a. Westlaw.
   b. Lexis.
   c. Nexis.
   d. a and b.
   e. all of the above.

2. The Legal Information Institute enables you to find the most Supreme Court decisions by using the following search method(s):
   a. Citation
   b. Topical index
   c. Key word
   d. Date of decision
   e. All of the above

3. An encyclopedia that is not a legal encyclopedia but contains many sources of interest is called
   a. The *World Book*.
   b. Eblast.
   c. *Encyclopedia Britannica*.
   d. Westlaw.
   e. none of the above.

4. A service available for Westlaw subscribers that enables users to discuss pertinent issues and items related to the Westlaw data base is known as a
   a. chat room.
   b. listserv.
   c. news group.
   d. user group.

5. Books may be found on the Library of Congress Web site by
   a. title.
   b. key word.
   c. author.
   d. ISBN.
   e. all of the above.

✦ NOTEBOOK PROJECTS

1. Using your word processing pleading wizard or legal pleadings feature, prepare a macro for a caption for use in your state for a complaint. Leave the case number blank since it will be filled in when the document is filed with the court.

2. Write a letter to Westlaw inquiring about their system, pricing, and requesting brochures about Westlaw.

3. Go to one of the Web sites where legal documents are available and download one that is free. Adapt it for use in your own state.

4. Prepare a form letter for notifying clients that appointments have been set for them. Use a short address list that includes the following clients:

Mr. Kenneth Calvert
1188 River Road
Your town, Your state zip code   Appointment: July 31, 2004 at 10:00 a.m.

Ms. Maria Cerva
522 San Miguel Road
Your town, your state zip code   Appointment: July 30, 2004 at 9:30 a.m.

Mr. John Brown
1122 East Main Street
Your town, your state zip code   Appointment: July 30, 2004 at 11:00 a.m.

Ms. Joan Adams
855 Brickdale Drive
Your town, your state zip code   Appointment: July 31, 2004 at 9:00 a.m.

TRIAL PROCEDURES

CHAPTER OUTCOMES

As a result of studying this chapter, the student will learn:

- How to prepare a Trial Book for a civil or criminal trial
- To distinguish and identify different types of evidence
- The sequence of a trial

PREPARING FOR TRIAL

Trials occur in both the criminal and the civil arenas. The paralegal and the legal assistant play important roles in the pretrial process, in the trial itself, and in posttrial procedures such as appeals. The preparations for the trial include preparing the Trial Book, helping witnesses get ready to testify, and gathering evidence.

Preparation of the Trial Book

At the beginning of the case, the paralegal and legal assistant initiate the preparation of the Trial Book. The Trial Book is a notebook that organizes everything that the attorney needs at trial so items can be retrieved quickly when needed. Usually, the Trial Book is a three-ring binder with a series of tab dividers that help to index and organize the various documents included in the notebook. Exhibit 5-1 shows a typical Trial Book for a civil lawsuit.

The content and organization of the Trial Book will be determined by the supervising attorney and may vary depending on the case. The following are some typical items that may be included in a Trial Book:

- Copies of the complaints and answers of the parties
- Copies of all motions and pleadings filed in the case
- Answers to written interrogatories
- Deposition transcripts and/or summaries
- Notes on any discrepancies between the interrogatories and depositions in a particular witness's testimony. These notes are usually arranged in the order in which the witnesses will appear at trial.

EXHIBIT 5-1   Typical Trial Notebook for a Civil Case

Courtesy: Reprinted with permission. LawFiles Trial Notebook, Courtesy of Bindertek, Sausalito, California

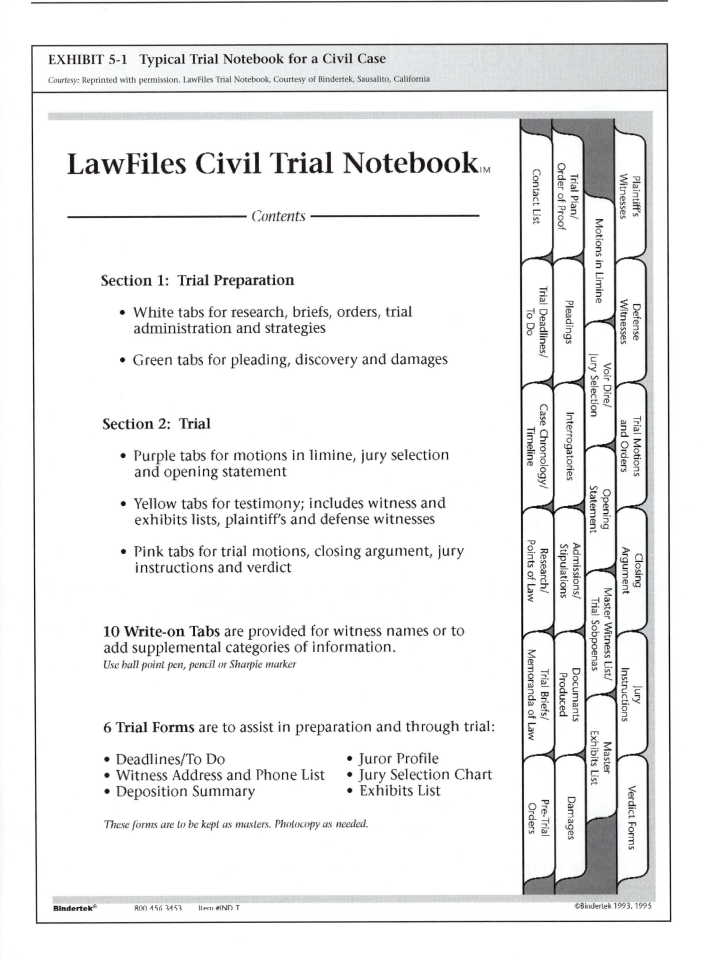

LawFiles Civil Trial Notebook™

———— *Contents* ————

Section 1: Trial Preparation

- White tabs for research, briefs, orders, trial administration and strategies

- Green tabs for pleading, discovery and damages

Section 2: Trial

- Purple tabs for motions in limine, jury selection and opening statement

- Yellow tabs for testimony; includes witness and exhibits lists, plaintiff's and defense witnesses

- Pink tabs for trial motions, closing argument, jury instructions and verdict

10 Write-on Tabs are provided for witness names or to add supplemental categories of information.
Use ball point pen, pencil or Sharpie marker

6 Trial Forms are to assist in preparation and through trial:

- Deadlines/To Do
- Witness Address and Phone List
- Deposition Summary
- Juror Profile
- Jury Selection Chart
- Exhibits List

These forms are to be kept as masters. Photocopy as needed.

Tabs (right side):
- Contact List
- Trial Plan/Order of Proof
- Motions in Limine
- Plaintiff's Witnesses
- Trial Deadlines/To Do
- Pleadings
- Voir Dire/Jury Selection
- Defense Witnesses
- Case Chronology/Timeline
- Interrogatories
- Opening Statement
- Trial Motions and Orders
- Research/Points of Law
- Admissions/Stipulations
- Master Witness List/Trial Subpoenas
- Closing Argument
- Trial Briefs/Memoranda of Law
- Documents Produced
- Master Exhibits List
- Jury Instructions
- Pre-Trial Orders
- Damages
- Verdict Forms

Bindertek®   800 456 3453   Item #IND T   ©Bindertek 1993, 1995

- An outline of the issues to be raised in the case
- Copies of exhibits to be introduced at trial
- An index of the exhibits
- A chronological list of events in the lawsuit
- A copy of the Trial Brief, which most attorneys prepare to describe the issues being decided in the case
- Copies of jury instructions
- A schedule of witnesses. This schedule should include the names of the witnesses and the approximate dates when they will appear at the trial, as well as notes on any discrepancies in previous statements made by each witness. In most states, the parties exchange witness lists so that there will be no surprises at the trial. The paralegal is often responsible for investigating the statements made by the adverse party's witnesses to learn the substance of their testimony and identify any discrepancies in their previous statements.
- A possible list of questions for each witness or perhaps an outline of information that should be explored

Another item that might be included in the Trial Book is a chart of the jury box for the jury selection process. The chart would include a seating chart with the names of prospective jurors and where they are seated. Post-It™ Notes are excellent for this chart because they are easy to remove. One Post-It™ Note is prepared for each prospective juror; the note includes the person's name and any comments by the attorney or paralegal. If an individual is challenged and removed, then the note with the juror's name is replaced with a note for a new prospective juror. This method is used until all twelve jurors are chosen. Exhibit 5-2 shows an example of a jury selection chart.

Witness Preparation

Before the trial the paralegal may be responsible for helping the witnesses prepare to testify. Although the paralegal may not tell a witness what to say, it is appropriate to describe the general types of questions that will be asked. Preparing the witness for **cross-examination** by the adverse party's attorney may also be the responsibility of the paralegal. The witness should be provided with a copy of any previous statements, such as depositions or other sworn statements. Discrepancies should be noted and discussed with the witness so that she will be prepared to explain the discrepancies if asked about them at trial. If the attorney plans to introduce any exhibits into evidence when the witness testifies, the paralegal should familiarize the witness with the exhibits.

Ask the witness if she would like to talk further about the appearance. If the witness is nervous about testifying, you might suggest that she visit a trial in progress before testifying. Make sure the witness

cross-examination the questioning of a witness by the opposing attorney.

EXHIBIT 5-2 Sample Jury Chart (Police Brutality Case)

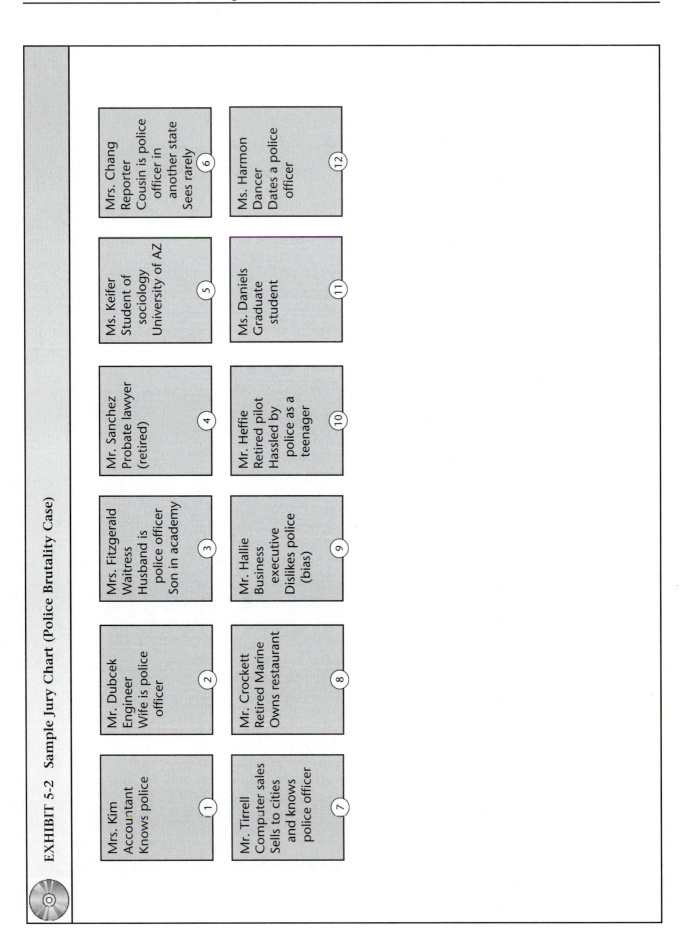

Mrs. Kim
Accountant
Knows police
1

Mr. Dubcek
Engineer
Wife is police
officer
2

Mrs. Fitzgerald
Waitress
Husband is
police officer
Son in academy
3

Mr. Sanchez
Probate lawyer
(retired)
4

Ms. Keifer
Student of
sociology
University of AZ
5

Mrs. Chang
Reporter
Cousin is police
officer in
another state
Sees rarely
6

Mr. Tirrell
Computer sales
Sells to cities
and knows
police officer
7

Mr. Crockett
Retired Marine
Owns restaurant
8

Mr. Hallie
Business
executive
Dislikes police
(bias)
9

Mr. Heffie
Retired pilot
Hassled by
police as a
teenager
10

Ms. Daniels
Graduate
student
11

Ms. Harmon
Dancer
Dates a police
officer
12

understands courtroom etiquette, including proper dress. The witness should dress conservatively and professionally.

It may be necessary to serve some witnesses with a subpoena to ensure their appearance at the trial. Try to call or write to the witness before issuing the subpoena to let her know it will be coming, explain why her testimony is important, and stress that you will try to minimize the time she must spend in the courtroom.

When the trial begins, you should have the original subpoenas along with the proof of service with you in the courtroom so that you will have proof that the individual witnesses were actually served. If a witness who has been served with a subpoena fails to appear at the scheduled time, she may be held in contempt of court for violating a court order.

The legal secretary should retain a copy of the witness schedule. It should include each witness's name and telephone number. If a particular witness's testimony will be postponed, the paralegal should call the witness or the legal secretary from the court. If the court adjourns early one day, all subsequent witnesses may have to be contacted and told to appear on a later date. In addition to the copy of the witness list in the Trial Book, the paralegal should also keep a copy.

During the trial, the paralegal and/or legal secretary should keep in touch with the witnesses. Those who are nervous about testifying may need more reassurance.

Evidence

The paralegal and/or legal secretary may be asked to gather and/or prepare evidence for the trial. This may include taking pictures, drawing charts, or preparing other demonstrative evidence. The paralegal or legal secretary may be asked to gather evidence from other sources as well. Whenever evidence comes from outside the firm, its source should be noted.

All evidence that will be introduced at the trial must be authenticated; that is, the custodian, writer, or preparer must state that the evidence is what it purports to be. This **authentication** may be accomplished by a sworn statement or testimony at trial or by a certified copy of the document. When gathering the evidence, the paralegal or legal secretary must check to be sure all documents have been authenticated and all other evidence has been preserved properly. Under the **Best Evidence Rule**, an attorney introducing records, letters, or reports into evidence must either use the original or show why it was not available for introduction. The paralegal should therefore check to make sure that originals are on hand or, if that is impossible, that their absence can be explained.

All evidence should be logged in the Trial Book. A chronological record should be maintained showing the time the evidence will be introduced at the trial. To ensure that the evidence will be safe until the trial, all items should be kept in a locked file drawer. Papers should be placed in sealed envelopes with their authentication. Lists should be kept with notations on the location and authentication of all evidence.

authentication a formal act that certifies that a document is correct so that it may be admitted into evidence; evidence proving a document is what it purports to be.

Best Evidence Rule a rule that requires that when a document is admitted into evidence at trial, either the original must be used or the attorney must show why it is not available.

THE TRIAL ✦

We have previously discussed one of the main differences between civil and criminal trials. Civil suits are generally brought by private persons or entities against other private persons or entities, although the government or one of its agencies can also be the plaintiff or defendant. In contrast, in a criminal case, the plaintiff is always the people or the state (not the individual victim) represented by the prosecuting attorney.

The other major difference between civil and criminal trials is the burden of proof required for the jury to reach its decision. Juries in civil trials must reach a decision by the **preponderance of the evidence**, which means that the event is more likely than not to have happened in that manner. In many states, only three-fourths of the jurors must find for the plaintiff for the plaintiff to prevail.

In a criminal trial, the standard for finding the defendant guilty is **beyond a reasonable doubt**, which is a very high standard. Many articles and books have been written about the meaning of this standard. Although "beyond a reasonable doubt" does not mean that the jury has no doubt that the defendant is guilty, it does mean that the jury has no *reasonable* doubt, bearing in mind that there will always be a slight doubt even with considerable evidence.

Aside from these differences in the parties and the burden of proof, civil and criminal trials are very similar. Both proceed through the same steps and follow similar procedures.

The Paralegal at Trial

Today, more than ever, paralegals are attending trials to assist their attorney employers. Paralegals may help in picking the jury, gathering evidence, and preparing witnesses. They may watch the witnesses testifying to assess their credibility based on their body language and nonverbal communication, as well as on their answers to the attorney's questions. Paralegals also keep the Trial Book and prompt the attorney on events as they occur.

Conducting the Trial

preponderance of the evidence the burden of proof in civil suits. It means that the event in question is more likely than not to have happened in that manner.

beyond a reasonable doubt the standard of proof in criminal cases; a higher standard than the preponderance of the evidence standard used in civil cases.

A trial generally proceeds through the following sequence:

1. Voir dire (picking the jury)
2. Opening statements
3. Direct examination of witnesses
4. Cross-examination of witnesses
5. Closing arguments
6. Jury instructions
7. Jury deliberations
8. Judgment or verdict

Each will be discussed in this section.

Voir Dire. During the **voir dire** (literally "to speak the truth") the attorneys and the judge conduct the preliminary examination of the prospective jurors. The paralegal should observe the proceedings carefully so he can help the attorney select the best possible jury. You should watch the facial expressions, gestures, and body languages of the jurors as well as listen to their answers to questions. Watch for signs that a juror may have negative feelings toward the client or the attorney.

Keep a chart as shown in Exhibit 5-2 for the attorney and make notes on each person as appropriate. When a juror is excused, remove that note from the chart and replace it with a new one with the new name. The attorney may ask your opinion on individual jurors. Be honest about whether you think the juror should be kept or rejected. Give the attorney your reasons. Your contributions can help the attorney select the best jury for the client.

Attorneys have an unlimited number of **challenges for cause**. A challenge for cause allows an attorney to dismiss a juror if the attorney can show bias or prejudice by the prospective juror. Each attorney also has a limited number of **peremptory challenges**; the number varies depending on the nature of the case. No reason is required to dismiss a juror with a peremptory challenge. However, peremptory challenges cannot be used to exclude potential jurors based solely on race or ethnic background. The attorney should be careful not to use up his peremptory challenges too soon, or he may be unable to dismiss a later juror whom he does not want.

Opening Statements. Once the jury is selected, the attorneys present their **opening statements**. The plaintiff's attorney speaks first, followed by the defendant's attorney. These statements provide a brief introduction to the facts of the case from the perspective of the respective parties. This is the first opportunity that the attorneys have to make a good impression on the jury. Each attorney instructs the jury on what they should note in the evidence and stresses the facts in his client's favor. The attorneys may not use the opening statement to present an argument; this is reserved for closing arguments.

During the opening statements, the paralegal should watch the jury carefully to determine how they are reacting to the attorney. Does their body language show belief or disbelief? Are they listening to the attorney? The attorney should be made aware of any potential problems.

Examination of Witnesses. After the opening statements, the attorneys present their cases by calling witnesses to the stand to answer questions. Evidence is also introduced and marked as exhibits. The plaintiff's attorney begins the process with the **direct examination** of the witnesses for his party. After the plaintiff's attorney questions each of his witnesses, the defense may cross-examine that witness. The defense attorney may only cross-examine the witness about information brought out during direct examination, however. Then the

voir dire the process in which the judge and attorneys select a jury.

challenges for cause dismissal of prospective jurors where bias or prejudice can be shown.

peremptory challenges dismissal of prospective jurors without having to give a reason; may not be used to exclude jurors solely on the basis of race or ethnic background.

opening statement the introduction to the facts of the case each attorney presents to the jury at the beginning of the trial.

direct examination the questioning of a witness by the attorney who called that witness.

plaintiff's attorney may institute redirect examination (questioning the witness again), but only on information brought out on cross-examination. Occasionally, the defense may institute re-cross-examination (questioning the witness a second time), but only on information brought out during redirect examination. Thinking of the examination process as a series of boxes within boxes as in Exhibit 5-3 will help make this concept clearer. Notice that the boxes become smaller, reflecting the scope of the questioning, as the examination process continues. The testimony of the plaintiff's witnesses represents the plaintiff's case in chief. At the end of all testimony by the witnesses, the plaintiff's attorney rests his case.

At this point, the defense attorney presents her case in the same manner as the plaintiff's attorney did. Witnesses are called and examined and evidence introduced. The plaintiff cross-examines the witnesses, the defense redirects; the plaintiff may re-cross-examine. Then the defense attorney rests her case.

During witness examination, the paralegal should watch the jury as well as the witnesses. Determine if the jury is paying attention. If a juror is sleeping, a pencil discreetly dropped on the floor may awaken him. Watch the impression each witness is making on the jury by observing his or her body language. Watch the reaction of the jury members to each attorney's presentation.

You may also be asked to gather your side's witnesses. Be sure they are in court at the scheduled time. You may have to sit with them in the corridor while they are waiting to testify. In this event, you obviously

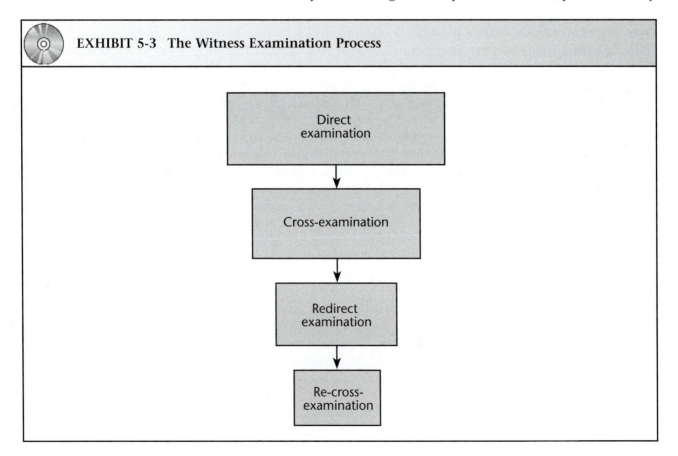

EXHIBIT 5-3   The Witness Examination Process

will not be able to observe the witnesses' testimony or the impression the attorney is making on the jury.

Closing Arguments.   Once both sides have presented their respective cases, the attorneys present their **closing arguments**. Again, the plaintiff's attorney goes first. He presents a summary of the evidence and the witnesses' testimony from the plaintiff's perspective. Then the defense attorney presents her closing arguments. In many states, the plaintiff's attorney is allowed to make a rebuttal argument.

The closing arguments are the last opportunity the attorneys have to talk to the jury. They want to present the best possible summation of the case from their own client's perspective. Some attorneys believe the closing argument is the most critical phase of the trial because it is the last statement the jury will hear from the attorneys before deliberations begin.

The paralegal should watch the jury carefully during closing arguments to determine their reactions to the attorney. Their body language may suggest belief or disbelief. It may also show their favorable or unfavorable impression of the attorney.

Jury Instructions.   Paralegals may assist in the preparation of **jury instructions**, which are typed by the legal assistant. Books in the law library will provide sample instructions for different legal issues. Both attorneys may submit jury instructions to the judge to be read to the jury. The judge also has her own instructions for the jury. If there is no jury, the attorneys present their instructions to the judge. After the judge reads the instructions to the jury, they go into the jury room to deliberate. The deliberations may take a few hours or several days.

Jury Deliberations.   When the jury enters the jury room, they elect a foreman or forewoman, who becomes the spokesperson for the group. After discussing the case and the evidence, the jury votes on the guilt or liability of the defendant. The foreman or forewoman then collects the votes and reads the verdict to the court.

Judgment or Verdict.   Civil juries render a **judgment**. If the plaintiff is suing for money damages, the judgment includes the amount of the damages awarded.

Criminal juries render a **verdict**—guilty or not guilty. If the verdict is guilty, the judge sentences the defendant. In Virginia and Kentucky, the jury is allowed to sentence the defendant. In some states the sentence is imposed in a separate proceeding, called the sentencing phase of the trial.

AFTER THE TRIAL

Contacting the Jurors

Once the jury reaches its decision and is dismissed by the judge, most jurisdictions allow attorneys to contact individual jurors. They are an excellent source of information about the impression the attorney and

closing argument
the summary of the case each attorney presents to the jury at the end of the trial.

jury instructions   the instructions the judge gives to the jury before deliberations to explain the law the jury should apply.

judgment   the decision in a civil case; may include money damages.

verdict   the decision reached by a jury in a criminal case as to whether the defendant is guilty or not guilty; must be unanimous in most states.

the witnesses make. The jurors' impressions of various evidence introduced at the trial may also be useful. For instance, they may point out that a chart you made to show the sequence of events was unclear. Information of this type may be extremely valuable for the subsequent trials.

The attorney may ask the paralegal or legal assistant to contact the jurors, who may or may not be eager to speak with you. An informal telephone call explaining your function and the reason for the call may be a first step to a later interview. Always ask if this is a good time to call or whether another time might be more convenient. Explain the reason for your call. Try to arrange a private interview with the juror at his convenience. If coming to your office would be inconvenient, arrange to meet at the juror's home.

Contact the jurors as soon after the trial ends as possible. Information will be fresh in their minds and therefore more valuable to you.

Enforcing Civil Judgments

Sometimes the jury in a civil case awards the plaintiff a substantial judgment against the defendant, but the defendant fails to pay the amount due. In that case, the attorney will have to institute further proceedings to force payment.

The first step in this process is a supplementary proceeding known as an **Examination of Judgment Debtor**. This proceeding is a court hearing where the defendant appears and testifies about her assets. The format for this procedure varies from state to state, so you should check the local court rules on the proper documents to prepare.

After the hearing, you may file a **writ of execution** (see Exhibit 5-4) against the defendant's assets. This document tells the defendant that unless she pays the judgment within a certain time, the sheriff or marshal will take possession of the property and sell it at a public sale. The proceeds from the sale will be used to pay the judgment. Any money left over will be returned to the defendant. A writ of execution may be filed against either real or personal property (real property is land and other real estate; personal property is all other property). Forms are available in the court clerk's office for this purpose. Some states refer to these documents as **writs of attachment**.

If the defendant has no property, or the property is insufficient to pay the judgment, the plaintiff may file a **garnishment** against the defendant's wages. A certain percentage of the wages will be paid to the plaintiff each pay period until the judgment has been satisfied.

Judgments are usually valid for eight to ten years. Therefore, if the defendant has insufficient assets to satisfy the judgment today, you may still collect on the judgment for the next eight to ten years. At the end of that time, some states allow the plaintiff to file an order to renew the judgment.

Appeals

The losing party in a civil suit may decide to appeal the decision to a higher court, as may a defendant who has been found guilty in a

---

Examination of Judgment Debtor   a formal court hearing where the defendant appears to answer questions about her assets.

writ of execution   a writ filed against assets of the debtor to enable a creditor to satisfy a judgment. The assets may be sold to pay the debt.

writ of attachment   a writ of execution.

garnishment   a procedure that enables a creditor to obtain a percentage of the defendant's wages for payment of debt owed.

EXHIBIT 5-4 Writ of Execution

Courtesy: Reprinted from *West's California Judicial Council Forms 2003*, with permission of West, a Thomson business. For more information about this publication please visit http://west.thomson.com.

ATTORNEY OR PARTY WITHOUT ATTORNEY (Name and Address):   TELEPHONE NO:

[XX] Recording requested by and return to:

Jeffrey M. Williams
Michaels & Williams
1122 Main Street, Seal Beach, California 99999

[X] ATTORNEY FOR   [X] JUDGMENT CREDITOR   [ ] ASSIGNEE OF RECORD

FOR RECORDER'S USE ONLY

NAME OF COURT: Orange County Superior Court
STREET ADDRESS: 224 Civic Center Drive
MAILING ADDRESS:
CITY AND ZIP CODE: PO Box 11122
BRANCH NAME: Santa Ana, California 99999

PLAINTIFF: Richard L. Danielson

DEFENDANT: Joanne V. Peterson

WRIT OF
[X] EXECUTION (Money Judgment)
[ ] POSSESSION OF   [ ] Personal Property
[ ] Real Property
[ ] SALE

CASE NUMBER:
C-444555

FOR COURT USE ONLY

1. **To the Sheriff or any Marshal or Constable of the County of:**
Orange
You are directed to enforce the judgment described below with daily interest and your costs as provided by the law.
2. **To any registered process server:** You are authorized to serve this writ only in accord with CCP 699.080 or CCP 715.040.
3. *(Name):* Richard L. Danielson
is the [X] judgement creditor [ ] assignee of record
whose address is shown on this form above the court's name.
4. **Judgment debtor** *(name and last known address):*

Joanne V. Peterson
529 Beach Drive
Newtown, California

[ ] additional judgment debtors on reverse
5. **Judgement entered** on *(date):* May 9, 1995
6. [ ] Judgment renewed on *(dates):*

7. **Notice of sale** under this writ
a. [ ] has not been requested.
b. [X] has been requested *(see reverse):*
8. [ ] Joint debtor information on reverse.

9. [ ] See reverse for information on real or personal property to be delivered under a writ of possession or sold under a writ of sale.
10. [ ] This writ is issued on sister-state judgment.
11. Total judgment .... $ 55,499
12. Costs after judgment (per filed order or memo CCP 685.090) .... $ 200
13. Subtotal *(add 11 and 12)*........... $ 55,699
14. Credits......................... $
15. Subtotal *(subtract 14 from 13)* .... $ 55,699
16. Interest after judgment (per filed affidavit CCP 685.050).............. $ 101
17. Fee for issuance of writ .... $ 50
18. **Total** *(add 15, 16, and 17)*.......... $ 55,850
19. Levying officer: Add daily interest from date of writ *(at the legal rate on 15)* of .... $ 22.00
20. [ ] The amounts called for in items 11-19 are different for each debtor. These amounts are stated for each debtor on Attachment 20.

(SEAL)

Issued on *(date):* May 15, 2005

Clerk, by _____ , Deputy

— **NOTICE TO PERSON SERVED: SEE REVERSE FOR IMPORTANT INFORMATION** —
(Continued on reverse)

Form Approved by the Judicial Council of California

WRIT OF EXECUTION

Code of Civil Procedure, §§ 699.520, 712.010, 715.010

continued

Exhibit 5-4 *continued*

SHORT TITLE: Danielson v. Peterson	CASE NUMBER: C-444555

Items continued from the first page:

4. ☐ **Additional judgment debtor** *(name and last known address):*

7. ☐ **Notice of sale** has been requested by *(name and address):*

8. ☐ **Joint debtor** was declared bound by the judgment (CCP 989-994)
   a. on *(date):*
   b. name and address of joint debtor:

   a. on *(date):*
   b. name and address of joint debtor:

9. ☒ *(Writ of Possession or Writ of Sale)* **Judgment** was entered for the following:
   a. ☐ Possession of real property: The complaint was filed on *(date):*   *(Check (1) or (2)):*
      (1) ☐ The Prejudgment Claim of Right to Possession was served in compliance with CCP 415.46.
   the judgment included all tenants, subtenants, named claimants, and other occupants of the premises.
      (2) ☐ The Prejudgment Claim of Right to Possession was NOT served in compliance with CCP 415.46.
          (a) $ was the daily rental value on the date the complaint was filed.
          (b) The court will hear objections to enforcement of the judgment under CCP 1174.3 on the following dates *(specify):*
   b. ☒ Possession of personal property
      ☒ If delivery cannot be had, then for the value (itemize in 9e) specified in the judgment or supplemental order.
   c. ☒ Sale of personal property
   d. ☐ Sale of real property
   e. Description of property:
      1995 Porsche Carrerra automobile, estimated value $65,000.00

— NOTICE TO PERSON SERVED —

WRIT OF EXECUTION OR SALE. Your rights and duties are indicated on the accompanying Notice of Levy.
WRIT OF POSSESSION OF PERSONAL PROPERTY. if the levying officer is not able to take custody of the property, the levying officer will make a demand upon you for the property. If custody is not obtained following demand, the judgment may be enforced as a money judgment for the value of the property specified in the judgment or in a supplemental order.
WRIT OF POSSESSION OF REAL PROPERTY. If the premises are not vacated within five days after the date of service on the occupant or, if service is by posting, within five days after service on you, the levying officer will remove th occupants from the real property and place the judgment creditor in possession of the property. personal property remaining on the premises will be sold or otherwise disposed of in accordance with CCP 1174 unless you or the owner of the property pays the judgement creditor the reasonable cost of storage and takes possession of the personal property not later than 15 days after the time the judgment creditor takes possession of the premises.
► A Claim of Right to possession from accompanies this writ (unless the Summons was served in compliance with CCP 415.46)

* NOTE: Continued use of form EJ-130 (Rev. Jan. 1, 1989) is authorized until June 30, 1992, *except* if used as a Writ of Possession of Real Property

EJ-130 (Rev. September 30, 1991*)   **WRIT OF EXECUTION**   Page two

criminal case. If a defendant is found not guilty, the prosecution may not appeal the verdict. The party who appeals the case is known as the **appellant**. The opposing party is called the **appellee**. Appeals may be taken based on an error made at the trial that deprived the appellant of a fair trial. The error must have been so critical that it could affect the outcome of the case. Errors that do not affect the outcome are known as "harmless errors" and do not provide grounds for an appeal.

The time to appeal a case varies among the states but is usually between thirty and sixty days from the date of the final judgment. The Notice of Appeal must be filed in the trial court that heard the case initially. A copy must be served on the adverse party. In the federal courts, the appeal must be filed with the original trial court within thirty days from the entry of judgment. A sample Notice of Appeal is shown in Exhibit 5-5.

Appellate Court Briefs. Although the format for the appellate court brief varies from state to state, many states follow the federal rules. A federal appellant's brief should include the following:

1. A table of contents, which includes a table of cases, authorities, and statutes

2. A statement of the subject matter and appellate jurisdiction

3. A statement of the issues that are being reviewed

4. A statement of the nature of the case and its disposition in the lower court. This should include a statement of the relevant facts with reference to the trial court record.

5. The argument of the issues presented along with the reason the appellate court should reverse the trial court. This section must include citations to the authorities used.

6. A conclusion that includes the relief sought.

The appellee is allowed an opportunity to respond to the appellant's brief; the appellee's brief should include the same sections as the appellant's brief except that the statement of jurisdiction and the statement of the issues of the case are not required unless the appellee is dissatisfied with those presented by the appellant. The appellant then has the opportunity to present a reply brief.

Technical Requirements. The federal appellant's and appellee's briefs must also satisfy certain technical requirements. The briefs must be no more than fifty pages in length, and the reply brief is limited to twenty-five pages. The appellant's brief must be filed within forty days after the record is filed. The appellee's brief is due within thirty days of the date the appellant's brief is served.

The federal court requires that twenty-five copies of the brief be filed and that two copies be served on each party. If the appellant fails to file the brief within the allotted time, the appellee may move for dismissal of the appeal. If the appellee fails to file within the time

appellant the individual or entity that appeals a case.

appellee the individual or entity against whom the appellant appeals; the opposing party to the appeal.

EXHIBIT 5-5   Notice of Appeal

1 | Patricia Barraganto

2 | Attorney at Law

3 | 12222 Ocean Avenue

4 | Long Beach, FL 20008

5 | Telephone: (999) 123-4567

6 | Attorney for Defendant

7 |

8 | NOTICE OF APPEAL TO A COURT OF APPEALS FROM

9 | A JUDGMENT OF A FEDERAL DISTRICT COURT

10 |

11 |

12 | UNITED STATES DISTRICT COURT FOR THE

13 | SOUTHERN DISTRICT OF FLORIDA

14 |

15 | DANIELSON DELIVERY SERVICE,   )

16 | Plaintiff,   )

17 | v.   )   Notice of Appeal

18 | PETERSON PLUMBING COMPANY,   )   Case No. WP-22233

19 | Defendant.   )

20 |

21 | Notice is hereby given that PETERSON PLUMBING COMPANY, defendant above named,

22 | hereby appeals to the United States Court of Appeals for the Ninth Circuit from the

23 | final judgment entered in this action on the 20th day of October, 2005.

24 | _____

25 | PATRICIA BARRAGANTO

26 | Attorney for PETERSON PLUMBING COMPANY

27 | 12222 Ocean Avenue

28 | Long Beach, FL 20008

allotted, he will not be allowed to present oral arguments unless special permission is obtained from the court.

Under Rule 32 of the Federal Rules of Civil Procedure, federal briefs must also meet the following requirements:

1. The briefs must be typed or printed.

2. At least 11-point type must be used.

3. The briefs should be on opaque unglazed paper.

4. If typed, the briefs should be bound in volumes. The pages should be 6⅛ by 9¼ inches with the typing occupying an area 4⅙ by 7⅙ inches.

5. If another process, such as printing, is used, the bound pages must not exceed 8½ by 11 inches, and the typing must not exceed 6½ by 9½ inches.

6. The text must be double-spaced

7. The cover should be blue for the appellant's brief and red for the appellee's brief.

The paralegal and legal assistant should be extremely careful to follow all of the requirements of the court. Check with your own state court to determine their technical and formatting requirements. Since most briefs are printed, you should proofread the galleys very carefully. Once the brief is returned from the printer, "Shepardize" all of the cases cited to be sure they are still "good law." Shepardizing means looking up all citations included in the brief in *Shepard's Case Citations* to be sure none of the cases have been overruled. If so, the attorney should be informed.

During a field trip to the Supreme Court of California with a paralegal class the author observed an attorney citing a case in support of his position. One of the justices asked if he had Shepardized the case and

ETHICS and ETIQUETTE

The paralegal or legal assistant is prevented from revealing any information learned from the client in a court proceeding. The paralegal or legal assistant may not testify in court about confidential communications received from the client.

The paralegal or legal assistant may assist the attorney in preparing for a trial. Duties might include the preparation of the Trial Book discussed in the chapter. You may be required to prepare the witnesses for trial by explaining courtroom decorum and appropriate demeanor. However, under no circumstances will you be able to represent the client in a court proceeding. Only an attorney may appear in court to represent the client. You may go to the trial and sit at the attorney's table in the courtroom to render your

> assistance, but at no time may you actually question a witness, plead a motion, or speak on behalf of the client before the court in any proceeding.
>
> As discussed previously, however, it may be possible in certain states for the paralegal to represent the client before certain administrative agencies. Individual state laws and agency regulations must be reviewed to determine whether this is feasible.
>
> In some states, nonlawyers are allowed to assist prison inmates in handling their own proceedings when the inmates are representing themselves *pro per* or *pro se*. Again, the rules vary considerably from one state to the other, and it is imperative that you check the rules for your own state before proceeding to represent a client in this manner.

said that if he had, he would have known the case had been overruled by a subsequent decision of the same court. This experience taught the students a valuable lesson on the importance of Shepardizing.

CHAPTER SUMMARY ✦

This chapter takes the student through the complete trial process. In preparation for trial, a Trial Book is compiled to assist the attorney during the court proceeding. The trial begins with the selection of the jury (voir dire) by the attorneys. Once the jury is selected, the attorneys for both sides make their opening statements. Next, each side, beginning with the plaintiff, presents its case by calling witnesses and presenting evidence. Direct examination of each witness by the plaintiff's attorney is followed by cross-examination by the defendant's attorney. After the plaintiff's case is presented, the defense begins. The defense attorney questions each witness (direct examination); the plaintiff's attorney then cross-examines the witness. When the cases have been presented, closing arguments are given by both attorneys, after which the judge gives the jury instructions indicating the law they should follow during their deliberations.

If the plaintiff receives a favorable decision in a civil trial, the defendant may be required to pay money damages to the plaintiff. Various methods of collection are available if the defendant does not pay voluntarily.

Either party in a civil case may appeal an adverse judgment to the next higher court, as may a defendant who is found guilty in a criminal case. Appellate court briefs must be prepared carefully to meet the requirements of the particular court.

✦ KEY TERMS

appellant

appellee

authentication

Best Evidence Rule

beyond a reasonable doubt	jury instructions
challenges for cause	opening statement
closing argument	peremptory challenges
cross examination	preponderance of the evidence
direct examination	verdict
Examination of Judgment Debtor	voir dire
garnishment	writ of attachment
judgment	writ of execution

✦ SELF TEST

Indicate whether the following statements are true (T) or false (F).

_____ 1. A chronological list of the events in the suit is included in the Trial Book.

_____ 2. Witness schedules include only the witnesses' names and the dates they will appear in court.

_____ 3. Only the attorney may prepare the witnesses to testify at the trial.

_____ 4. Witnesses should dress conservatively for the trial.

_____ 5. To ensure that the witness will appear at the trial, a complaint may be served on the witness.

Circle the correct answer to the following questions.

1. Before evidence is introduced at the trial, it must be
   a. demonstrated.
   b. published.
   c. authenticated.
   d. shown to the jury.

2. The rule that requires an attorney to introduce the original of any records, letters, or reports into evidence or show why the original was not available is called the
   a. Best Evidence Rule.
   b. Records Evidence Rule.
   c. Authentic Records Rule.
   d. Trial Book Rule.

3. The burden of proof required for the jury to reach a verdict in a criminal trial is
   a. a preponderance of the evidence.
   b. beyond a doubt.
   c. beyond any doubt.
   d. beyond a reasonable doubt.

4. Voir dire refers to the
   a. opening of statements.
   b. cross-examination of witnesses.
   c. jury selection process.
   d. jury instructions.
   e. closing arguments

5. Which of the following occur during the trial?
    a. Voir dire
    b. Opening statements
    c. Jury instructions
    d. a and b only
    e. a, b, and c

Fill-in-the-blanks.

1. The preliminary examination of the prospective jurors is called
   _____.

2. The _____ attorney is the first to give an opening statement.

3. After the defense presents its closing arguments, the plaintiff is allowed to make a
   _____ argument.

4. Civil juries render a _____ while criminal juries render a _____
   _____.

5. In most states, a jury in a criminal case must return a guilty verdict unanimously, but
   generally a plaintiff in a civil case can prevail if _____ of the jury
   members vote for the defendant's liability.

✦ REVIEW QUESTIONS

1. Discuss the stages of the trial and how the paralegal, legal assistant, or legal secretary
   assists at each stage.

2. Explain the differences between a trial in a civil case and trial in a criminal case.

3. What does "beyond a reasonable doubt" mean?

4. Explain the difference between "beyond a reasonable doubt" and a "preponderance of the
   evidence."

5. What is the purpose of a Trial Book? List five items that would be included in the Trial Book.

✦ NOTEBOOK PROJECTS

1. Review the discussion of the Trial Book at the beginning of the chapter.
   Prepare a list of items you would include in a Trial Book for the following
   cases:
   a. Client Paul Stevens is suing defendant Robert Beckman for injuries sus-
      tained in an automobile accident.
   b. Client Susan Beck is suing the Local Groceries Company for injuries sus-
      tained when she slipped on a banana peel in the produce department.

2. Prepare a blank chart for jury selection.

3. Prepare a Notice of Appeal from an adverse judgment received on December 26,
   200x. Use Exhibit 5-5 as a model. Our client is Ms. Emily Azpeitia, the plaintiff;
   her address is 128 Alabaster Court, Your Town, Your State. The defendant is

Jonathan Rasmussen; his address is 999 Winding Brook Lane, Your Town, Your State.

4. Our client, Mrs. Betty Jo Maldonado, was involved in an automobile accident on May 5, 200x, at 3:00 p.m. at the corner of Main and Broad Streets in Your Town. She alleges that the defendant, Joseph Pacheco, ran the red light and hit her car on the driver's side. She was driving a 2004 Lexus four-door LS400. The defendant was driving a 2002 Chevrolet pickup truck. Attorney Williams has asked you to draft some questions to ask the following witnesses:

   • Witness 1: Ms. Joan Maldonado was a passenger in her mother's automobile at the time of the accident and was injured. She is our witness.

   • Witness 2: Joanne Pacheco, the defendant's wife, was a passenger in his truck at the time of the collision. She is a witness for the defense. Mr. Williams has asked you to draft questions to ask Mrs. Pacheco on cross-examination. She is expected to say that the light was green and that our client ran the red light.

5. Attorney Jeffrey Williams has asked you to meet with a client, Ms. Kitzman, to discuss her appearance at an upcoming trial. She is suing the defendant for personal injuries sustained in an automobile accident. Prepare a list of items that should be addressed during your discussion with her, including how she should dress for the trial, the types of questions she may be asked, and any other information you feel is appropriate.

6. Assume the client in Project 5 is not able to visit the office. Draft a letter to her from Mr. Williams addressing the key points that should be discussed and explained to her about her testimony at the upcoming trial.

CHAPTER

6

CRIMINAL LAW PRACTICE

CHAPTER OUTCOMES

As a result of studying this chapter, the student will learn:

- The differences between criminal and civil law
- The elements and basic categories of crimes
- The definitions of the most common crimes
- The basic procedures followed from arrest through trial and sentencing

CRIMINAL AND CIVIL LAW

Thus far we have discussed civil law, which deals with the rights and responsibilities of individuals. As we have seen, in a civil lawsuit, a private individual or entity brings a suit against another individual or entity: private attorneys represent both the plaintiff and the defendant. In contrast, criminal law deals with wrongful acts against society. In a criminal action, the plaintiff is the state or society as a whole, not the individual victim of the criminal act. Criminal offenders are prosecuted by attorneys who represent the government of the prosecuting state. Private attorneys or public defenders represent the defendant.

Different objectives exist for criminal law. Its purposes are to prevent behavior that society has determined is unacceptable and to punish those individuals who commit these unacceptable acts (crimes). However, the objective of civil law is to compensate those individuals who are injured by another's wrongful act.

CRIMINAL LAW AND CRIMINAL PROCEDURE

Each area of law separates the substantive law from the procedural aspects. *Criminal law* defines the crime and determines what acts are prohibited and what the punishment is for committing those acts. It also establishes the degree of intent required for criminal liability. *Criminal procedure* defines the procedures used to bring defendants to justice. It commences with the police investigation of the criminal act and continues throughout the justice process of arrest, arraignment, preliminary hearing, trial, and sentencing.

PUNISHMENT

Violators of criminal law are ultimately brought to trial, found guilty, and sentenced to prison or county jail, depending on the nature of the crime. The purpose of incarceration has been debated for some time. Several theories emerge, including the deterrence of the commitment of future crimes by the individual; that is, if one commits a crime and is sent to prison, he will be less likely to commit another crime when he gets out of prison for fear he will be put in prison again. Another theory involves the fact that while the individual is incarcerated, he is not capable of committing other crimes. A third theory relates to rehabilitation of the person who committed the crime so that, if the individual is subjected to various training and educational programs and receives professional counseling, his behavior may be changed and he may become a useful member of society. While many of these theories sound feasible, it should be noted that the rate of **recidivism**, the relapse into criminal behavior, in the prison population, is great. A large portion of those people in prison have committed other crimes.

ELEMENTS AND CATEGORIES OF CRIMES

The states and the federal government pass criminal laws to punish individuals who commit acts that are objectionable in a civilized society. When individuals are found guilty of crimes, they may be sent to prison to deter them from committing further crimes and to set an example in the hope that others will also be deterred from committing crimes. Sometimes prisons attempt to rehabilitate the inmates as well as incarcerate them by providing educational facilities and work opportunities. In this section we will examine the nature of the criminal acts for which people may be sent to prison and will also discuss the various categories of crime.

Criminal Acts and Their Elements

Criminal acts can be divided into felonies and misdemeanors based on how serious they are. A **felony** is a serious crime that exposes the defendant to imprisonment for more than one year. Most persons convicted of felonies are incarcerated in state prisons, but some offenses, such as drug trafficking, violate federal laws and can lead to incarceration in federal prison. Murder, manslaughter, kidnapping, robbery, arson, rape, and burglary are all felonies. A **misdemeanor** is a less serious crime that is punishable by incarceration in the county jail for up to one year. Petty theft, drunk driving, malicious mischief, and simple assault are examples of misdemeanors.

Most crimes have two elements—the criminal intent and the committing of the criminal act. For instance, you may have the desire to kill someone, but if you never commit the act, there is no murder. On the other hand, if you kill someone accidentally and do not have the

recidivism the return to prison of an individual who was previously incarcerated; individual sometimes known as habitual offender.

felony a serious crime punishable by incarceration in a state prison for more than one year.

misdemeanor a minor crime punishable by incarceration in a county jail for up to one year.

intent to kill, as in an automobile accident, no murder has been committed. In some crimes, such as the rape of a minor (**statutory rape**), simply carrying out the act implies intent. Other crimes that do not require specific intent include strict liability crimes.

Not all offenses are crimes. An **infraction** is an offense that does not constitute a crime and is punishable by a fine. Many traffic violations are infractions. For instance, if you park your car in a "no parking" zone, you may get a ticket and pay a fine, but you will not go to jail unless you fail to pay the fines to the point that a warrant is issued for your arrest.

Categories of Crime

Based on the person or entity at which they are directed, crimes can be categorized as crimes against the person, crimes against the public, or crimes against property.

Crimes against the Person. Crimes that are directed against an individual are known as crimes against the person. They include the following:

1. *Homicide.* **Homicide** is the unlawful killing of another without justification. It can be broken down further into first-degree murder, second-degree murder, and manslaughter. First-degree murder is an intentional killing or a death under the **Felony Murder Rule** doctrine. Under this rule, if a death occurs during the commission of a serious felony, all defendants involved in the felony may be found guilty of first-degree murder, regardless of which of them caused the death. Premeditated murder, poisoning, and murder by torture are also examples of first-degree murder. Second-degree murder includes any intentional killing not classified as first-degree murder. Manslaughter generally involves killing someone without actual criminal intent, such as during a fight or during the "heat of passion."

Many states have adopted the Felony Murder Rule, but differ on the enumerated felonies; most include kidnapping, torture, and robbery, however. Some states also have adopted a **Special Circumstances Rule** for capital punishment (the death penalty). Under this rule, if the victim died during the commission of a kidnapping, torture, or other felonies enumerated in the state's statutes, the defendant may receive capital punishment if he committed the crime in question, if he **aided and abetted** with the intent to kill, or if he aided and abetted with reckless indifference to human life and was a major participant in the crime. In other words, if three individuals kidnap a person who subsequently dies, all three defendants may be charged with Felony Murder with Special Circumstances and receive the death penalty. These rules vary considerably by state, and you should check your state's laws to learn whether it has a Felony Murder Rule and whether it imposes capital punishment under a Special

statutory rape the rape of a minor.

infraction a minor offense, such as a traffic violation, that is punishable by fine.

homicide the unlawful killing of another without justification.

Felony Murder Rule a doctrine that holds that if a death occurs during the commission of a serious felony, all defendants who were involved may be convicted of first-degree murder, regardless of which defendant actually caused the death.

Special Circumstances Rule a rule that holds that if a victim dies during the commission of a serious felony, as specified by statute, the defendant may receive the death penalty if he committed the felony, if he aided or abetted its commission with the intent to kill, or if he aided or abetted with reckless indifference to human life and was a major participant in the crime.

aided and abetted assisted someone in committing a crime; knowledge of unlawful purpose with intent to commit, encourage, or facilitate commission of the crime by act or advice.

Circumstances Rule. Record your findings in the State Specific Information box.

STATE SPECIFIC INFORMATION

The state of _____ has the following rules for murder.

Murder is defined in the statutes as follows:

_____

_____

_____

Felony Murder Rule:

_____

_____

_____

Special Circumstances:

_____

_____

_____

Capital Punishment:

_____

_____

_____

---

2. *Mayhem.* Most states define **mayhem** as the permanent disfigurement of another: it includes the loss of a limb, eye, or other part of the body. The act must be purposeful and not accidental.

3. *Rape.* In most states, a forcible sexual attack on a female by a male constitutes **rape**. Some states have expanded this definition to include unnatural sex acts on men as well as women. Rape can be further defined as sexual intercourse with a person without consent. Most state laws consider any sexual activity with a minor to be statutory rape, even if the minor consented to the act. Under earlier laws, a man could not be guilty of raping his wife, but modern law has overruled this holding in most states, so that today a man may be found guilty of raping his wife.

mayhem the purposeful and permanent disfigurement of another.

rape a forcible sexual attack; sexual intercourse without consent.

All states have instituted laws against child molestation. Sexual activity with children is forbidden, even if no rape is involved.

4. *Assault and Battery.* In the criminal sense, an **assault** is an attempted battery. Once the battery is successful, then the perpetrator may be charged with both. **Battery** is the harmful or offensive touching of another. Most states consider battery with a weapon to be a more serious crime than battery without a weapon. In addition, if an individual is deliberately attacked with a weapon by another but not killed, the crime may escalate to attempted murder. A defendant who attempts a battery but does not succeed may be charged with assault. in some states, once the battery is completed, the assault merges into the battery, and the defendant is charged only with battery.

5. *Kidnapping.* The transportation of an individual from one place to another against her will is **kidnapping**. In many states, transporting the victim only a few feet may be sufficient to constitute the crime. If an individual is taken across state lines, the kidnapping escalates to a federal crime.

Crimes against the Public. Crimes against the public can be divided into two groups: crimes against public morality and crimes against public order.

Crimes against Public Morality. Many crimes against the public are considered to be crimes against public morality. The following are examples of such crimes:

1. *Prostitution.* **Prostitution** is the providing of sexual favors in exchange for money. It is illegal in all states except Nevada, where each county may decide whether it is a crime in the county.

2. *Indecent Exposure.* **Indecent exposure** is the intentional exposure of private parts of the body in a public place. Nude dancing is an example of indecent exposure. The appellate courts in most states have upheld statutes prohibiting nude dancing and requiring dancers to have certain body parts covered.

3. *Obscenity.* Although purveyors of pornography use their First Amendment rights to free speech as a defense, the U.S. Supreme Court has consistently held that obscenity is not protected speech. In **Miller v. California**, 413 U.S. 15 (1973), the U.S. Supreme Court defined **obscenity** as any material that:

   a. appeals to the prurient interest,

   b. shows offensive sexual conduct as defined by applicable state law, and

   c. lacks serious literary, artistic, political, or scientific value.

The laws against child pornography are considerably more stringent, however. All exploitation of children is prohibited.

---

assault attempted battery.

battery harmful or offensive touching of another without consent.

kidnapping the transportation of an individual from one place to another against his will.

prostitution the provision of sexual favors in exchange for money.

indecent exposure the intentional exposure of private parts of the body in public.

Miller v. California the case in which the U.S. Supreme Court defined obscenity.

obscenity any material that appeals to the prurient interest, shows offensive sexual conduct as defined by applicable state law, and lacks serious literary, artistic, political, or scientific value.

Crimes against Public Order. Crimes against public order are offenses that disturb the orderly running of society. They include the following:

1. *Rioting.* When a group of individuals behave in a disorderly manner, their actions may constitute a riot. In most states a riot must involve a very large number of "rioters" who refuse to disperse even when told to do so by the police. Those individuals may be subject to arrest and may be charged with rioting. Generally, rioting will also involve the destruction of property or the harassment of others.

2. *Disorderly Conduct.* Disorderly conduct is a less serious crime and may include playing loud music late at night, being very loud in a public place, or committing any other act that disturbs the peaceful environment of others.

3. *Drug Sales.* The sale and use of illicit drugs is illegal in all states. Drug trafficking has become a very serious problem in today's society. The federal government has enacted drug trafficking statutes in an attempt to stop drug smuggling.

Crimes against Property. Most crimes against property involve unlawfully taking the property of another by stealing, force, fire, or deceit. The most serious crime against property is **arson**, which is the unlawful and intentional burning of another's property. In some states, the property must be a house or other building. In most states, arson has been extended to include the burning of one's own house or building if the purpose is to defraud an insurance company.

Burglary is the unlawful entry of another's building with the intention of committing a felony inside the building. In some states, unlawful entry with the intent to commit a misdemeanor is also a burglary. Only part of the body needs to enter the building; thus, reaching through a window in order to steal money is a burglary.

Robbery is the taking of another's property from his person by threat or force. An individual who threatens a storekeeper in order to get the money in the cash register may be guilty of robbery. If someone were to break into the store at night after the storekeeper has left, that individual may be guilty of burglary if he intended to commit a felony.

Many different kinds of theft are considered criminal acts. **Larceny** is the taking and carrying away of another's personal property with the intent to steal it. Taking property that is lawfully in your possession with the intent to steal is **embezzlement**. An example is an attorney who uses her client's settlement funds that have been deposited in a trust account for her own purposes.

The crimes described here are among the most common, but many other crimes also exist, and when committed, they can lead to imprisonment in a state or federal prison or county jail. Any student who is interested in learning more about this field of law is encouraged to take a course in Criminal Law.

arson the intentional burning of another's home or building.

burglary the unlawful entry of a building belonging to another with the intent to commit a felony inside the building

robbery taking another's property from her person by threat or force.

larceny taking and carrying away another's property with the intent to steal.

embezzlement taking property that is lawfully in one's possession with the intent to steal.

Defenses

Although the defendant may actually have committed the criminal act with which she is charged, various defenses that create an excuse can be presented at the trial. If the defendant's attorney can prove the defense, the accused will be found "not guilty." They most common defenses are listed in Exhibit 6-1; not all of these defenses may be valid in every state, however. Of course, instead of presenting one of these defenses, the defendant may contend that she did not commit the crime and plead "not guilty."

CRIMINAL PROCEDURES ✦

Once an individual commits a crime, certain procedures are followed from the time of arrest to the trial and sentencing. This section will present the steps in the criminal justice process, including a brief overview of what happens at trial.

Arrest

The ideal situation arises when a police officer actually sees a crime being committed and arrests the perpetrator at the scene. No **warrant**, or order authorizing an arrest, is required in this case because **probable cause** exists; that is, the police officer has cause to reasonably believe the perpetrator committed the criminal act because he personally saw it being committed.

Such situations are rare, however, and the police usually must investigate the evidence in the case before arresting a suspect. Often police detectives spend a considerable amount of time and effort conducting an investigation prior to making an arrest. Once an arrest warrant is issued for an individual, the police may seek her out and arrest her. After the police take the suspect into custody, she is transported to the police station, fingerprinted, photographed, and booked (charged) with a crime.

Interview and Investigation

Most individuals who have been charged with a crime call their lawyers at this time. As a paralegal employed by a criminal defense attorney, you may be asked to interview the client in jail. If you are working for the prosecuting attorney, you may be asked to begin investigating the defendant's background, prior crimes, and alibi. Among other things, you may have to search out any witnesses to the crime. If you visit the neighborhood where the crime was committed, you should go on the same day of the week at approximately the same time that the crime was committed.

Individuals who are arrested may not be interrogated unless they have been read their Miranda rights, which were first set out in the famous case ***Miranda v. Arizona***. Confessions obtained without reading the Miranda rights may not be admissible into evidence, but can be used for impeachment purposes in some states (that is, used to

warrant an order issued by a magistrate authorizing the police to make an arrest, conduct a search, or carry out other procedures as part of the criminal justice process.

probable cause a reasonable ground for believing that a person has committed a crime.

Miranda v. Arizona the case in which the U.S. Supreme Court set out the rights of the accused during interrogation by the police. The rights are known as the *Miranda* rights.

📖 **EXHIBIT 6-1 Valid Defenses to Crimes**

Self-defense	The defendant must prove he was defending himself. A person may not use more force to defend himself than is reasonable or more than was used by the other party. An individual may use deadly force only to defend his person, not his property. Deadly force is only allowed if it is also being used by the other party.
Defense of others	Similar to self-defense. The defendant must prove the individual being defended was not the aggressor. A person may not use more force than was being used by the other party and may not use deadly force unless deadly force was being used against the person being defended. Deadly force may not be used in defense of property.
Insanity	The defendant must prove that when the crime was committed, she was not capable of understanding the nature of the criminal act or that it was wrong. (The insanity defense varies by state.)
Temporary insanity	The defendant must prove that she was "insane" at the time the criminal act was committed even though she later regained her sanity.
Coercion	The defendant must prove that he committed the criminal act under compulsion from another, who used threats or force to make him commit the crime.
Entrapment	The defendant must prove that he was coerced into committing the criminal act by a police officer. For the defense to succeed, the crime must have been initiated by the officer, not the defendant. A person may also be entrapped by someone (i.e., a snitch) who was directed to entrap him by a police officer.

challenge the credibility of the defendant if she tells a different story at trial). If the accused wishes to speak to her attorney at any time, the interrogation must stop. If the accused knowingly discusses the crime with the police at this point, anything she says may be used against her in court. Often, the defendant's attorney will file a Motion to Suppress Evidence arguing that the confession should be suppressed because the accused did not knowingly give up her rights and that the interrogation consequently violated her Fifth Amendment right against self-incrimination. More commonly, Motions to Suppress Evidence argue that evidence should be suppressed because it was seized illegally in violation of the Fourth Amendment to the Constitution.

Arraignment

At the **arraignment**, the accused and his attorney appear before the judge to hear the charges and enter a plea. If the defendant cannot afford an attorney, the court will appoint one, usually a public defender. The judge may allow the accused to post bail to get out of jail, or if

arraignment the step in the criminal justice process when the defendant is brought before a judge to hear the charges and enter a plea.

the accused has ties to the community and is not likely to flee or commit another crime, the judge may release him on his "own recognizance" (known as an "OR" release). The judge will also ask the defendant whether he pleads guilty, not guilty, or **nolo contendere**. Literally translated from the Latin, nolo contendere means "I will not contest it." Although this plea is treated as an admission of guilt, the defendant is not actually admitting guilt or innocence. An accused may plead "nolo" (nolo contendere) to prevent a guilty plea from being used against him in a subsequent proceeding. For instance, if the accused is charged with battery in the criminal proceeding and his victim wishes to bring a civil suit against him for her personal injuries, a nolo contendere plea may not be used against the defendant at the civil trial. If he had pleaded guilty, however, the plaintiff could use that plea against him at the civil trial.

Preliminary Hearing or Pretrial Settlement

Some states have **preliminary hearings** to determine whether enough evidence exists against the defendant to hold a trial. Other states have settlement conferences where the defendant may plead to a lesser offense or plead guilty. Once the defendant pleads guilty, the judge renders the sentence and the case ends.

Plea Bargaining

Since many states' prisons are very crowded, a defendant may be given an opportunity to plead guilty to a lesser offense and have the charges reduced from a serious felony to a less serious one or from a felony to a misdemeanor. This process is known as **plea bargaining**. For example, after discussions between the prosecutor and the defense attorney, the defendant who is charged with rape (a felony) may agree to plead guilty to a related misdemeanor, such a sexual battery. The defendant then receives a less stringent sentence such as incarceration in the county jail for several months, instead of several years in the state prison. As another example, the defendant may be charged with a more serious felony (e.g., murder) and plead guilty to a lesser felony (e.g., manslaughter) to receive a shorter sentence in the state prison.

Plea bargaining has been the subject of considerable debate. Proponents say it saves money and helps alleviate the court's workload by reducing the number of cases that must go to trial. It also makes it possible for a defendant to be found guilty without the prosecution having to prove his guilt at trial. In addition, in some cases the defendant may implicate others in exchange for a plea bargain. Then the prosecution can bring charges against the other perpetrators.

Opponents of plea bargaining say that it allows repeat offenders to be freed quickly and, in some cases, to commit the same crimes again. Whatever its advantages and disadvantages, plea bargaining is used in most states, especially those with high crime rates and very crowded prisons.

To plea bargain effectively, both the prosecution and the defense must be well prepared for the discussions. The more evidence the

nolo contendere Latin for "I will not contest it." A plea by which the defendant does not admit guilt, but also does not contest the charges.

preliminary hearing a hearing in court to determine whether enough evidence exists to hold the defendant for trial.

plea bargaining pleading guilty to a lesser offense with less jail time than the offense that was originally charged.

prosecution has amassed, the better the prosecutor can argue that the defendant should plead guilty to a serious charge. Similarly, the more thoroughly the defense attorney has prepared his case, the better the plea bargain he can get for his client. In most cases, plea bargains are utilized with guilty defendants.

Grand Jury

In some states a grand jury hears testimony to determine if the prosecution has sufficient evidence to go to trial. The prosecutor presents evidence to the grand jury, but the defendant is not present and is not given an opportunity to present a defense. The prosecutor can call witnesses who usually must appear before the grand jury without an attorney. After hearing the evidence, the grand jury decides whether to hand down an indictment; if it does so, the defendant is held over for trial. As described earlier, some states use a preliminary hearing instead of a grand jury. Some states call a grand jury only in cases of major crimes that have been well publicized.

Trial and Sentencing

In most states, the defendant chooses whether or not to have the case heard by a judge or a jury. A few states, however, allow the prosecuting attorney to request a jury trial.

In order to find the defendant guilty, the judge or jury must find that the evidence shows guilt beyond a reasonable doubt, which is a very high standard. In most states all twelve jurors must agree on the defendant's guilt. However, Oregon allows a guilty verdict if ten out of twelve jurors agree, while Louisiana allows a guilty verdict if only nine of the twelve agree.

The prosecution presents its witnesses first, followed by the defense. To ensure that a witness will appear at the trail or other court proceeding, a subpoena may be used. Exhibit 6-2 shows a sample subpoena prepared by a prosecuting attorney.

After all of the evidence is presented, the verdict is rendered. If the jury reaches a guilty verdict, the judge imposes the sentence on the defendant. Some states, such as Virginia and Kentucky, allow the jury to impose the sentence. The *sentencing phase* is a separate proceeding in most states. The defendant may present character witnesses in an attempt to persuade the judge to impose a lighter sentence. A report indicating whether the defendant might successfully be released on probation may also be submitted as part of the sentencing recommendations.

Hung Jury.   If the jury is divided and cannot agree on a verdict (or, in states that allow nonunanimous verdicts, less than the required number agree), a "hung jury" results. In this case, the defendant is found neither guilty nor not guilty. States use various procedures when a hung jury results, but usually the district attorney has the option of retrying the defendant. In that case, a new trial is conducted with a new jury.

EXHIBIT 6-2   Subpoena (Criminal or Juvenile)

ATTORNEY OR PARTY WITHOUT ATTORNEY *(Name and Address):* TELEPHONE NO:	FOR COURT USE ONLY
ATTORNEY FOR *(Named):*	
Insert name of court, judicial district or branch court, if any, and post office and street address:	
Title of case:	

SUBPOENA (CRIMINAL OR JUVENILE) ☐ DUCES TECUM	CASE NUMBER:

THE PEOPLE OF THE STATE OF CALIFORNIA, TO (NAME):

1. **YOU ARE ORDERED TO APPEAR AS A WITNESS in this action at the date, time, and place shown in the box below UNLESS you make a special agreement with the person named in Item 3:**

a. Date: Time: ☐ Dept.:   ☐ Div.:   ☐ Room:
b. Address:

2. AND YOU ARE
   a. ☐ ordered to appear in person.
   b. ☐ not required to appear in person if you produce the records described in the accompanying affidavit and a completed declaration of custodian of records in compliance with Evidence Code sections 1560, 1561, 1562, and 1271. (1) Place a copy of the records in an envelope (or other wrapper). Enclose your original declaration with the records. Seal them. (2) Attach a copy of this subpoena to the envelope or write on the envelope the case name and number, our name and date, time, and place from item 1 (the box above). (3) Place this first envelope in an outer envelope, seal it, and mail it to the clerk of the court at the address in item 1. (4) Mail a copy of your declaration to the attorney or party shown at the top of this form.
   c. ☐ ordered to appear in person and to produce the record described in the accompanying affidavit. The personal attendance of the custodian or other qualified witness and the production of the original records is required by this subpoena. The procedure authorized by subdivision (b) of section 1560, and sections 1561 and 1562 of the Evidence Code, will not be deemed sufficient compliance with this subpoena.
   d. ☐ ordered to make the original business records described in the accompanying affidavit available for inspection at your normal business hours, conditions during normal business hours.
3. **IF YOU HAVE ANY QUESTION ABOUT THE TIME OR DATE FOR YOU TO APPEAR, OR IF YOU WANT TO BE CERTAIN THAT YOUR PRESENCE IS REQUIRED, CONTACT THE FOLLOWING PERSON BEFORE THE DATE ON WHICH YOU ARE TO APPEAR:**
   a. Name: b. Telephone number:
4. **WITNESS FEES:** You may be entitled to witness fees, mileage, or both, the discretion of the court. Contact the person named in item 3 **AFTER** your appearance.

DISOBEDIENCE OF THIS SUBPOENA MAY BE PUNISHED BY A FINE, IMPRISONMENT, OR BOTH. A WARRANT MAY ISSUE FOR YOUR ARREST IF YOU FAIL TO APPEAR.

FOR COURT USE ONLY	Date: ▶ _____
	(SIGNATURE OF PERSON ISSUING SUBPOENA)
	(TYPE OR PRINT NAME)
	(TITLE)

(See reverse for proof of service)

Form Adopted by Rule 982
Judicial Council of California
982(a)(16) [Rev. January 1, 1991]   **SUBPOENA (CRIMINAL OR JUVENILE)**   WEST GROUP Official Publisher   Penal Code, § 1326 et seq.
Welfare and Institutions Code, §§ 341, 664, 1727

continued

Exhibit 6-2 *continued*

SHORT TITLE:	CASE NUMBER:

PROOF OF SERVICE OF SUBPOENA

1. I served this ☐ Subpoena ☐ Subpoena Duces Tecum and supporting affidavit by personally delivering a copy to the person served as follows:

    a. Person served *(name)*:

    b. Address where served:

    c. Date of delivery:
    d. Time of delivery:

2. ☐ **NON-SERVICE RETURN OF SUBPOENA**
    a. ☐ After due search, careful inquiry, and diligent attempts at the dwelling, house, or usual place of abode or usual place of business, I have been unable to make personal delivery of this ☐ Subpoena ☐ Subpoena Duces Tecum in this county on the following persons *(specify)*:

    b. ☐ Reason:
        (1) ☐ Unknown at address.   (4) ☐ Out-of-county address.
        (2) ☐ Moved, forwarding address unknown. (5) ☐ Unable to serve by hearing date.
        (3) ☐ No such address.   (6) ☐ Other reasons *(explanation required)*:

4. Person serving:
    a. ☐ Not a registered California process server.   e. ☐ Exempt from registration under Bus. & Prof. Code section
    b. ☐ California sheriff, marshal, or constable.   22350(b).
    c. ☐ Registed California process server.   f. Name, address, and telephone number and, if applicable,
    d. ☐ Employee or independent contractor of a   county of registration and number.
        registered California process server.

I declare under penalty of perjury under the laws of the State of California that the foregoing is true and correct.

(For California sheriff, marshal, or constable use only.)
I certify that the foregoing is true and correct.

Date:

Date:

▶ _____
          (SIGNATURE)

▶ _____
          (SIGNATURE)

982(a)(16) [Rev. January 1, 1991]

PROOF OF SERVICE OF SUBPOENA
(CRIMINAL OR JUVENILE)

WEST GROUP
Official Publisher

Page two

Double Jeopardy. When an individual is tried for the same crime twice, he may claim **double jeopardy** as a defense at the second trial. Note that if the first trial results in a hung jury, a second trial does not constitute double jeopardy. For a second trial to constitute double jeopardy, the first trial must have been completed to the point where the judge or jury rendered a verdict. A defendant who has been found "not guilty," may not be retried for the same crime.

Appeals

Only death penalty cases are automatically appealable to the state's highest court, usually called the State Supreme Court. Other cases may be appealed if legal errors were made at the trial or if the defense attorney can prove that the judge or jurors were biased or prejudiced against the defendant.

Defendant's Right to Be Present

With the exception of a grand jury, the defendant has the right to be present at all stages of the proceedings described in this section, including oral arguments on any motions that the attorney may make before the court.

The defendant must always be present at felony proceedings, but may sign a waiver relinquishing the right to be present at hearings on motions in misdemeanor proceedings in Municipal Court. The waiver may apply to any or all of the following hearings:

1. When the case is set for trial
2. When a continuance is ordered
3. When a motion to set aside the indictment is heard
4. When a motion for bail is heard
5. When questions of law are presented to the court

Paralegals may be asked to draft these waivers and/or have them signed by the defendant during the initial interview. A sample Waiver of Personal Appearance is shown in Exhibit 6-3.

PRETRIAL PREPARATIONS BY THE PROSECUTION ✦

A paralegal who is employed by the prosecution will be very busy finding witnesses and additional evidence during the pretrial stage of the case. He may work with the investigating officer who initiated the case, check computer records to determine if the defendant has been found guilty of other crimes, and do research in the law library or on the computer. Other tasks include interviewing defense witnesses and preparing subpoenas for prosecution witnesses (see Exhibit 6-2).

Paralegals may also conduct discovery on the defense to determine what evidence they will present and what witnesses they will call to testify. A paralegal may be asked to read over any statements made by the

double jeopardy being tried for the same crime twice when a verdict was reached in the first trial.

EXHIBIT 6-3   Waiver of Personal Appearance

1   John P. Evans

2   Attorney at Law

3   1122 Main Street

4   Torrance, CA 90503

5

6   MUNICIPAL COURT OF THE STATE OF CALIFORNIA

7

8   COUNTY OF LOS ANGELES

9

10   PEOPLE OF THE STATE OF CALIFORNIA,   )   Case No.: C-1234-5999

11   )

12   Plaintiff,   )   DEFENDANT'S WAIVER OF PERSONAL

13   )   APPEARANCE

14   vs.   )

15   )

16   MICHAEL R. FELDSTEIN,   )

17   )

18   Defendant   )

19   _____)

20   I, MICHAEL R. FELDSTEIN, have been advised of my right to be present at all stages

21   of the proceedings, including but not limited to presentation of and arguments on

22   questions of law, and to be confronted by and to cross-examine all witnesses.

23   I hereby waive the right to be present at the hearing of any motion or order proceeding in this

24   cause, including when the case is set for trial, when a continuance is ordered, when a motion to set

25   aside the indictment or information under the provisions of Penal Code section 995 is heard, when

26   a motion for reduction of bail or for a personal recognizance release is heard, when a motion to

27   reduce sentence is heard, and when questions of law are presented to or considered by the court.

28

                                              1

continued

Exhibit 6-3 *continued*

1   I hereby ask the court to proceed when I am absent pursuant to this waiver with
2 the court's permission, and agree that my interest is deemed represented at all times by
3 the presence of my attorney, the same as if I myself were personally present in court.
4   I further agree that notice to my attorney that my presence in court on a particular
5 day at a particular time is required will be deemed notice to me.

6
7 Dated this 8th day of January, 2005.

8
9 _____
   MICHAEL R. FELDSTEIN
10

11 Dated this 8th day of January, 2005
12

13
14 _____
   JOHN P. EVANS
15 Attorney at Law
   1122 Main Street
16 Torrance, CA 90503

17
18
19
20
21
22
23
24
25
26
27
28

2

defendant to compare them to statements made at the preliminary hearing or statements made by other witnesses. Other assignments may include preparing exhibits for the trial and completing preliminary research on motions to be filed with the court.

Paralegals on the prosecution side should conduct as thorough an investigation as possible so that the district attorney can prove the defendant is guilty beyond a reasonable doubt.

PRETRIAL PREPARATIONS BY THE DEFENSE ✦

The prosecution's evidence and the circumstances under which it was obtained must be examined to determine its value and whether it was obtained legally. If not, a Motion to Suppress Evidence must be prepared. Most Motions to Suppress Evidence challenge the evidence as the product of an illegal search and seizure and/or a warrantless search. The motion may also challenge the admissibility of confessions or other statements made by the defendant. Any time a search of a building is conducted without a warrant, the search presents an opportunity for the defendant to challenge the admissibility of any evidence seized on the basis of an illegal search and seizure. Research must be conducted for the preparation of the motion and the Points and Authorities to accompany the motion. Evidence and witnesses obtained by the prosecution must be examined.

Any information that the prosecution will introduce into evidence at the trial may be obtained in advance by the defense attorney. A paralegal working for the defense must examine the evidence and witnesses' statements carefully to determine any discrepancies. The paralegal's investigation may involve examining the manner in which all the evidence was obtained against the client to determine whether any of her constitutional rights were violated. If violations occurred, the attorney may file a Motion to Suppress Evidence, and the judge will rule on whether the evidence will be disallowed.

USING THE INTERNET ✦

An excellent source for finding information about criminal law is the FindLaw site discussed and pictured above. The Institute for Law and Justice in Virginia provides links to criminal justice sites at:

http://www.ilj.org/#favorite

In addition to providing research and consulting services related to criminal justice, this site provides links to government agencies and various criminal sub-specialty areas such as substance abuse, corrections, sentencing, juvenile justice, courts, federal and state court decisions, and state and federal criminal codes.

A page that provides a number of links to other pages about criminal law is located at:

http://www.payles.com/law/criminal.html

Included are sites about criminal justice, criminal defense, defense litigation, constitutions, statutes, codes, Supreme Court decisions, noteworthy criminal decisions, prison law, uniform crime reports, search-and-seizure issues, and sentencing.

CHAPTER SUMMARY ✦

This chapter has presented an introduction to criminal law and the criminal justice system. Criminal law deals with wrongful acts against society. In contrast to civil law where suits are brought by an individual or an entity, in criminal law the plaintiff is the state or society, represented by the prosecuting attorney.

More serious crimes such as murder and rape are felonies, while less serious crimes such as petty theft and malicious mischief are misdemeanors. Minor offenses such as traffic violations are infractions; they are punishable by a fine and are not considered crimes. Most crimes have two elements: criminal intent and the commission of the criminal act. Crimes can be further classified into three categories: crimes against the person, crimes against the public, and crimes against property. The chapter presented representative examples in each category.

The criminal justice process begins with the arrest of a suspect. The chapter traced the process through all of its steps: arrest, interview, investigation, arraignment, preliminary hearing, grand jury, trial, sentencing, and the appeals process. Some possible defenses that a defendant might use were also presented. The chapter concluded by describing typical duties of a paralegal in both a criminal prosecution and a defense.

ETHICS and ETIQUETTE

Most states require criminal defendants to be represented in court by attorneys. A few states have exceptions for individuals who are incarcerated under limited circumstances. For instance, a few states allow nonlawyers to prepare a writ of habeas corpus petition for inmates in prison. This writ is a petition to bring the prisoner before the court to determine whether the imprisonment is valid. In some cases, prison inmates who study the law in prison are allowed to represent their fellow prisoners in disciplinary actions or to determine whether the other prisoner's time served was calculated correctly. However, for the most part, paralegals are not allowed to represent criminal defendants.

The issue of confidentiality is particularly critical in the prosecution and representation of individuals accused of crimes. Even if the accused admits to the commission of the crime to the attorney, paralegal, or legal assistant, they are bound by ethical considerations not to reveal the information. However, as was discussed in earlier chapters, one is obligated to reveal information about a crime that will be committed and will cause bodily harm or death. For example, the client may admit he killed the person he is accused of killing, and the rules of attorney/client privilege protect him from you revealing this fact. However, the client may tell you that he is about to kill someone else and, if you are reasonably certain that he will kill that person, you are obligated to reveal that fact. Always discuss this type of information with the attorney before proceeding.

Both prosecutors and criminal defense attorneys are often involved in cases that are the subject of publicity from the news media. If your office is involved in such a case, you are obligated not to reveal any facts to any member of the public, including the media. You must be especially careful when speaking on the telephone to be sure you are addressing the person actually identified. For instance, suppose someone calls the office and says she is your client. She proceeds to ask you questions about the case, which you answer because you think she is the client. However, there may be an occasion where it is someone pretending to be the client, and you have just revealed information protected by the attorney/client privilege. When in doubt, ask the person to make an appointment with you to come into the office to get the information.

✦ KEY TERMS

aided and abetted	*Miller v. California*
arraignment	*Miranda v. Arizona*
arson	misdemeanor
assault	nolo contendere
battery	obscenity
burglary	plea bargaining
double jeopardy	preliminary hearing
embezzlement	probable cause
felony	prostitution
Felony Murder Rule	rape
homicide	recidivism
indecent exposure	robbery
infraction	Special Circumstances Rule
kidnapping	statutory rape
larceny	warrant
mayhem	

✦ SELF TEST

Indicate whether the following statement are true (T) or False (F).

_____ 1. Felonies include murder and robbery.

_____ 2. Misdemeanors include kidnapping and arson.

_____ 3. Robbery involves entering a residence at night to steal.

____ 4. Burglary involves taking another's property from his person.

____ 5. The preliminary hearing is held to determine whether enough evidence exists to hold the defendant over for trail.

Circle the correct answer for the following questions:

1. The proceeding where the accused is brought before the judge to hear the charges against him is called
   a. a preliminary hearing.
   b. an arraignment.
   c. a trial.
   d. bail.

2. When the defendant's attorney wants evidence excluded from the trial because the police conducted an illegal search of the premises, she files a
   a. Motion to Exclude Evidence.
   b. Motion to Stop Evidence.
   c. Motion to Waiver.
   d. Motion to Suppress Evidence.

3. The elements of most crimes are
   a. intent and planning.
   b. act and planning.
   c. planning and motive.
   d. intent and act.
   e. motive and act.

4. Plea bargaining involves
   a. a not-guilty plea.
   b. pleading guilty to a lesser offense.
   c. having a trial.
   d. none of the above.

5. Crimes punishable by incarceration in the county jail are called
   a. felonies.
   b. infractions.
   c. misdemeanors.
   d. homicides.

Fill-in-the-blanks

1. To ensure the presence of a witness at the trial, a _____ is prepared and served.

2. The document signed by the defendant so that he does not have to be at a hearing to reduce sentence is called a _____.

3. In order to exclude evidence from the trial, a _____ must be filed.

4. The process whereby the defendant pleads guilty to a lesser charge and receives a shorter sentence is known as _____.

5. If an individual helps the defendant commit a murder, she is said to be _____ and _____.

✦ REVIEW QUESTIONS

1. Describe the procedures followed after the accused is arrested.

2. What are the paralegal's responsibilities when employed by the prosecutor?

3. What are the paralegal's responsibilities when employed by the defense?

4. What is the difference between assault and battery? May a defendant be charged with both? If so, under what circumstances?

5. Define the terms *felony* and *misdemeanor* and explain the differences between them.

✦ NOTEBOOK PROJECTS

1. You are employed by a criminal defense attorney. The client, Jonathan Reese, has been arrested for drunk driving. The attorney asks you to interview Mr. Reese at the county jail. What questions would you ask about the charge?

2. You are investigating the case in Project 1 above and have found a witness who Mr. Reese claims was with him at the time of his arrest. According to Mr. Reese, the witness, Jane Adams, will testify that he was not drinking alcohol on the evening in question. Make a list of questions to ask Ms. Adams.

3. Our client is Scott Marshall, whose address is 222 Gilltee Lane, your town, your state. He has been accused of killing Jose Ortiz with a .38 pistol. You have been asked by the attorney to research the following question and prepare a memo to the attorney on your findings.

   Our client and his wife, Ashley, were separated, but he had some items in her apartment that he had not yet picked up. The police went to Ashley's apartment and asked to search it. She said they could. In the closet among our client's belongings, the police found the .38 pistol used in the killing. We are seeking to suppress the evidence (the gun) because the wife did not have a right to give permission to search items belonging to her estranged husband. The question you must answer is: Did the police have the right to search the closet containing the husband's possessions if the husband and wife are separated and only the wife gave permission for the search? Cite appropriate cases because the next step will be to prepare a motion to suppress the gun.

4. Prepare a Motion to Suppress Evidence for the situation in Project 3. Use the format and headings appropriate for your state.

CIVIL LITIGATION

CHAPTER OUTCOMES

As a result of studying this chapter, the student will learn:

- How to conduct a client interview in a civil litigation case
- The requirements for filing a lawsuit
- To distinguish between the documents used in a civil case
- To know when to use various documents during a civil case

STATUTE OF LIMITATIONS

In most states, personal injury and tort actions must be filed with the court within a year of the time the injury occurred, a year from the time the plaintiff knew about the injury, or a year from the time the plaintiff should have known about the injury. Check your own state code for the **statute of limitations** in your state. The statute may be tolled (or lengthened) for reasons stated in the statute itself, such as those cases where the injured party was a minor at the time of injury. Record the time limitations in your state's statute below.

> STATE SPECIFIC INFORMATION
>
> In the state of _____ , the statute of limitations
> (Section _____) for personal injury actions is: _____
>
> _____ .
>
>
> The statutes of limitations (Section _____) for other civil litigation matters
> are: _____
>
> _____
>
> _____
>
> _____
>
> _____ .

statute of limitations a law that sets a maximum amount of time after something happens for it to be taken to court.

CLAIMS AGAINST THE GOVERNMENT ◆

In most states, claims against the government have a shorter statute of limitations, generally between three and six months. State governments require that certain information be included in civil litigation claims against them, including:

1. Name and address of claimant
2. Post office address to send notices to claimant
3. Date, place, and circumstances of the occurrence giving rise to the claim
4. General description of the injury, damages, or loss incurred
5. Names of public employees causing injury, damage, or loss, if known
6. Amount claimed if less than $10,000 as of the date of the claim, including estimate of future injury
7. Signature of the claimant or person acting on the claimant's behalf

In some cases, the public entity will provide forms for filing claims. However, in many states the claimant is not required to use these forms as long as all information required by their state's Government Code is provided to the government entity.

The government entity must grant or deny the claim within a certain time period after it is filed. This time varies by state. Both parties may agree, however, to extend this time period by written agreement. If the government entity rejects the claim, the plaintiff has a certain period of time, generally about six months from the date of notice of the rejection, to file a court action. Be sure to check with your own state for these time line and information requirements.

GUARDIAN AD LITEM ◆

Most states require a **guardian ad litem** to be appointed for a minor or incompetent who is a party to the action. This guardian acts for the minor or incompetent in this case only. The age of majority varies by state but is usually eighteen. The court where the action is pending will appoint the guardian upon petition by the attorney. The paralegal may be required to file the appropriate documentation with the court to appoint the guardian ad litem before commencing the lawsuit.

Generally, if the plaintiff is under the age of 14, the application for a guardian ad litem must be made by a relative, usually a parent. A minor plaintiff over 14 may be allowed to file his or her own application for a guardian.

In some states, defendant minors who are 14 or older must make application to the court within 10 days after service of the summons. If the application is not made within this period of time, a relative or friend may apply to the court on behalf of the minor, on their own motion. The form and content of the application varies by state, so

guardian ad litem a guardian appointed by a court to take care of the interests of a person who cannot legally take care of him- or herself in a lawsuit involving that person.

it is advisable to check the applicable rules in your state before filing the application. A sample application for appointment of a guardian ad litem for a minor plaintiff under the age of 14 is shown in Exhibit 7-1.

THE CLIENT INTERVIEW   ✦

The initial contact with the prospective client usually takes place in the attorney's office to determine whether the attorney will take the case and what action will be taken. Initial factual investigation begins with information obtained from the client at this interview. In addition to gathering facts, the initial contact is the opportunity for the client and attorney to establish a foundation for a business relationship. The client will determine whether he has a favorable impression of the attorney and the firm, and the attorney will make the same determination about his impression of the client. At this time, either the attorney or the client may decide they do not wish to proceed further. The attorney may choose not to take the case, or the prospective client may decide not to hire the law firm.

Therefore, prior to the interview, it is imperative that the attorney obtain some basic facts about the client's case. If the client has telephoned the law firm, the legal assistant or paralegal should be prepared to ask some preliminary questions preparatory to conducting an introductory investigation into the facts and legal issues of the case. Either the paralegal or attorney may conduct this preliminary investigation as well as the initial client interview. Typical questions to ask prior to the interview follow:

1. How did the prospective client hear about the firm?
2. Explain the general nature of the complaint/situation/action. In other words, what happened to the individual that precipitated his call to the law firm?

Other preliminary questions may be asked before the interview is scheduled. Based on this preliminary conversation, the paralegal or legal assistant may ask the client to bring certain items to the interview, such as a police report, accident report, insurance papers, or any other documentary evidence about the incident.

A typical form used for initial client interviews is shown in Exhibit 7-2 on page 133. Prior to asking the questions on the form, the individual conducting the interview should introduce herself to the client and attempt to put the client at ease. Remember that the majority of people who seek out lawyers have a major problem and may be highly agitated or stressed at the time of the interview. Therefore, the interviewer should make every attempt to calm down the client by asking preliminary unrelated questions. Once the interviewer feels that the client is no longer agitated or upset, then it is time to begin asking the questions on the interview form. It is usually advantageous to begin by asking the client to tell his story in chronological order, thereby

EXHIBIT 7-1   Petition and Order for Appointment of Guardian Ad Litem

1 John P. Evans

2 Attorney at Law

3 1122 Main Street

4 Torrance, CA 90503

5

6 LOS ANGELES COUNTY SUPERIOR COURT

7

8 NORTHEAST SUPERIOR COURT DISTRICT

9

10 KATHERINE AGNESS SPRINGER,   )   Case No.: PI-95-CC81

11   )

12 A Minor, By and Through   )   PETITION FOR APPOINTMENT OF GUARDIAN

13   )   AD LITEM, AND ORDER APPOINTING

14 MARGARET MARY SPRINGER, Her Guardian   )   GUARDIAN AD LITEM

15   )

16 ad Litem,   )

17   )

18   Plaintiff,   )

19   )

20   vs.   )

21   )

22 JOHN Q. MARTINEZ,   )

23   )

24   Defendant   )

25 _____   )

26   Petitioner, KATHERINE AGNES SPRINGER, alleges that she is a minor of the age of twelve (12) years, born April 15, 1991.

27   Petitioner has a cause of action arising out of an automobile accident on September 25, 2002, where she sus-

28 tained physical injuries.

1

continued

Exhibit 7-1 *continued*

1   Petitioner has no general Guardian, and no previous Petition for Appointment of a Guardian Ad Litem has

2   been filed in this matter.

3   MARY MARGARET SPRINGER is the mother of Petitioner and is competent to act as Guardian Ad Litem.

4   WHEREFORE, Petitioner prays that MARY MARGARET SPRINGER be appointed as Guardian Ad Litem for

5   Petitioner.

6   I declare under penalty of perjury under the laws of the State of California that the foregoing is true and correct.

7   DATED: July 9, 2003

8

9   _____

10   KATHERINE AGNES SPRINGER

11

12   CONSENT OF NOMINEE

13   I, MARY MARGARET SPRINGER, the nominee of Petitioner, consent to act as Guardian Ad Litem for the minor

14   Petitioner in the above action.

15   DATED: July 9, 2003

16

17   _____

18   MARGARET MARY SPRINGER

19

20   ORDER APPOINTING GUARDIAN AD LITEM

21   The court, having considered the petition of KATHERINE AGNES SPRINGER for the appointment of a Guardian

22   Ad Litem for petitioner, a minor, who is the plaintiff in the above action, and good cause appearing,

23   IT IS ORDERED that MARY MARGARET SPRINGER be appointed Guardian Ad Litem for KATHERINE AGNES

24   SPRINGER in the above action.

25   DATED: July 20, 2003

26

27   _____

28   JUDGE OF THE SUPERIOR COURT

2

EXHIBIT 7-2   Client Interview Form

CLIENT INTERVIEW FORM

Client's Name: _____

Address: _____

Telephone No.: (H) _____ (W) _____

Social Security No.: _____

Date of birth: _____ Birthplace: _____

Former address: _____

Spouse's Name: _____

Address: _____

Telephone No.: (H) _____ (W) _____

Social Security No.: _____

Date of birth: _____ Birthplace: _____

Date of marriage: _____ Place: _____

Was a divorce ever filed? If so, when? _____

Spouse's employer: _____

Employer's address: _____

Telephone No.: (H) _____ (W) _____

Former Spouse's Name: _____

Address: _____

Telephone No.: (H) _____ (W) _____

Social Security No.: _____

Date of termination of marriage: _____ Where: _____

Divorce or death? _____

List All Natural Children of Client:

1. Name: _____

   Address: _____

   Telephone No.: (H) _____ (W) _____

   Social Security No.: _____

   Date of birth: _____ Birthplace: _____

   Other parent's name, address, and telephone number: _____

   _____

2. Name: _____

   Address: _____

   Telephone No.: (H) _____ (W) _____

   Social Security No.: _____

   Date of birth: _____ Birthplace: _____

   Other parent's name, address, and telephone number: _____

   _____

3. Name: _____

   Address: _____

   Telephone No.: (H) _____ (W) _____

   Social Security No.: _____

continued

Exhibit 7-2 *continued*

Date of birth: _____ Birthplace: _____

Other parent's name, address, and telephone number: _____

_____

4. Name: _____

   Address: _____

   Telephone No.: (H) _____ (W) _____

   Social Security No.: _____

   Date of birth: _____ Birthplace: _____

   Other parent's name, address, and telephone number: _____

   _____

List Any Other Dependent Children of Client:

1. Name: _____

   Address: _____

   Telephone No.: (H) _____ (W) _____

   Social Security No.: _____

   Date of birth: _____ Birthplace: _____

   Other parent's name, address, and telephone number: _____

   _____

2. Name: _____

   Address: _____

   Telephone No.: (H) _____ (W) _____

   Social Security No.: _____

   Date of birth: _____ Birthplace: _____

   Other parent's name, address, and telephone number: _____

   _____

Did Client Support Any Others Not Listed Above?

1. Name: _____

   Address: _____

   Telephone No.: (H) _____ (W) _____

   Relationship to client: _____

   Percentage or amount of client's income provided to this person: _____

2. Name: _____

   Address: _____

   Telephone No.: (H) _____ (W) _____

   Relationship to client: _____

   Percentage or amount of client's income provided to this person: _____

Client's Father's Name: _____

Address: _____

Telephone No.: (H) _____ (W) _____

continued

Exhibit 7-2   *continued*

Date of birth: _____ Birthplace: _____

If deceased, state date of death: _____

Place of death: _____

Cause of death: _____

Client's Mother's Name: _____

Address: _____

Telephone No.: (H) _____ (W) _____

Date of birth: _____ Birthplace: _____

If deceased, state date of death: _____

Place of death: _____

Cause of death: _____

Client's Brothers and Sisters (including step-siblings):

1. Name: _____

   Address: _____

   Telephone No.: (H) _____ (W) _____

   Date of birth: _____ Birthplace: _____

   If deceased, state date of death: _____

   Place of death: _____

   Cause of death: _____

2. Name: _____

   Address: _____

   Telephone No.: (H) _____ (W) _____

   Date of birth: _____ Birthplace: _____

   If deceased, state date of death: _____

   Place of death: _____

   Cause of death: _____

3. Name: _____

   Address: _____

   Telephone No.: (H) _____ (W) _____

   Date of birth: _____ Birthplace: _____

   If deceased, state date of death: _____

   Place of death: _____

   Cause of death: _____

Economic Losses (client's annual income for five years before injury):

19_____ $_____

19_____ $_____

19_____ $_____

19_____ $_____

19_____ $_____

continued

Exhibit 7-2 *continued*

Client's Current Employer:

Name, address, and telephone number: _____

_____

Title and duties performed: _____

_____

Dates employed: _____

Employers for Last Five Years:

1. Name, address, and telephone number: _____

   _____

   Title and duties performed: _____

   _____

   Dates employed:_____

2. Name, address, and telephone number: _____

   _____

   Title and duties performed: _____

   _____

   Dates employed:_____

3. Name, address, and telephone number: _____

   _____

   Title and duties performed: _____

   _____

   Dates employed:_____

Educational Information of Client:

High School Graduate? _____ Year: _____
Name of college attended: _____
Years: _____ Degree achieved: _____
Name of college attended: _____
Years: _____ Degree achieved: _____

Other Technical/Trade Training:
Describe:

Occupation at Time of Injury:

enabling the interviewer to complete the form and understand events in the order in which they happened.

PRELIMINARY CONSIDERATIONS ✦

Before the attorney and client file suit, some preliminary considerations should be discussed.

Statute of Limitations

Some clients may come to the law office to file a lawsuit after the statute of limitations has run. If this occurs, then the attorney must notify the client of that fact. In most cases, the client will be barred from filing suit. In order to avoid a malpractice suit by the client, it is imperative that the attorney notify the client not only orally at the interview, but in writing as well.

Damages

Some clients may have unrealistic expectations regarding damages they will collect in a lawsuit. Individuals read about large settlements in the newspaper and think that they can also be compensated in these amounts. However, they often do not realize that those individuals who get the large amounts of money have been very seriously injured. In most cases, damages will amount to the following:

1. *General Damages.* These damages are those which are a direct result of the act of the defendant's wrongful act, such as pain and suffering.

2. *Special Damages.* Indirect losses or harm are known as special damages. For instance, the plaintiff may have lost salary because of not being able to work after being injured. She may have medical bills as a result of her injuries. She may have small children and had to hire someone to care for them while she was in the hospital or bedridden. All of these are examples of special damages.

3. *Punitive (or Exemplary) Damages.* Damages that punish the defendant for his grossly negligent or purposeful conduct are known as punitive damages. This is extra money given to the plaintiff to punish the defendant and to help keep a particularly bad act from happening again. These damages are awarded in addition to all other damages.

4. *Nominal Damages.* If the loss suffered by the plaintiff is a particularly small amount or if the actual amount lost is not proven, but the plaintiff proves that a wrong was committed, the court may award nominal damages, sometimes only $1. (Note that in cases where the attorney determines that a court is likely to award nominal damages, he will likely discuss with the client the option to settle the case with the defendant out of court.)

Equitable Remedies

If the damages suffered by the plaintiff are not monetary in nature, an equitable remedy may be sought. Equitable remedies seek to stop the defendant from doing something that he should not be doing or force him to perform an act that he should perform. Some examples of equitable remedies include:

1. *Injunction.* A court order to an individual or entity to do or refrain from doing a wrongful act. For instance, a company may be pouring its toxic waste in a lake near your house. You would seek an injunction to stop the company from continuing to do so.
2. *Temporary restraining order (TRO).* A temporary emergency order of the court that acts as an injunction until a certain time period has elapsed, which gives the court the opportunity to investigate the facts of the condition to determine whether to issue a permanent injunction in the situation. These TROs are often used in cases of domestic violence.

Other less commonly used equitable remedies include a declaratory judgment, where the individual asks the court to determine the rights of parties to a controversy where no money damages are being sought, and the writ of mandate (or mandamus), where a government official is ordered to perform a certain act.

THE LAWSUIT ✦

Once the attorney and client determine that a lawsuit will be commenced, the attorney will draft the Complaint and Summons to be served on the defendant and filed with the court. The complaint is filed with the court of appropriate jurisdiction depending on the remedies sought or the amount of money damages. The courts will vary by state. Typically, a Superior Court will hear major cases and the Municipal Court will hear minor ones.

Complaint

complaint the first main paper filed in a civil lawsuit; it includes, among other things, a statement of the wrong or harm done to the plaintiff by the defendant, a request for specific help from the court, and an explanation why the court has the power to do what the plaintiff wants.

The initial pleading filed by the plaintiff is called the **complaint**. It sets forth the causes of action against the defendant and informs the defendant that he is being sued. It notifies the defendant of the allegations against him. The allegations represent the factual statements of the plaintiff that must be proven. Each allegation set forth in the complaint must ultimately be proven before damages can be awarded. The complaint contains a demand for relief (prayer for damages), which includes general, special, and punitive damages. In California, the Judicial Council provides forms that may be used for the preparation of a complaint. A sample is included as Exhibit 7-3.

Other states that do not provide forms for the complaint require that it must be prepared on lined and numbered pleading paper with the caption shown above. Exhibit 7-4 on page 142 shows a sample heading for a complaint prepared on pleading paper.

EXHIBIT 7-3 Judicial Council Form Complaint

Courtesy: Reprinted from *West's California Judicial Council Forms 2003*, with permission of West, a Thomson business. For more information about this publication please visit **http://west.thomson.com**.

982.1(1)

ATTORNEY OR PARTY WITHOUT ATTORNEY *(Name, state bar number, and address)*	FOR COURT USE ONLY

TELEPHONE NO: FAX NO. *(Optional)*:
E-MAIL ADDRESS *(Optional)*:
ATTORNEY FOR *(Name)*:

NAME OF COURT:
STREET ADDRESS:
MAILING ADDRESS:
CITY AND ZIP CODE:
BRANCH NAME:

PLAINTIFF:

DEFENDANT:

☐ DOES 1 TO _____

COMPLAINT—Personal Injury, Property Damage, Wrongful Death
☐ **AMENDED** *(Number)*:
Type *(check all that apply)*:
☐ **MOTOR VEHICLE**   ☐ **OTHER** *(specify)*:
☐ **Property Damage**   ☐ **Wrongful Death**
☐ **Personal Injury**   ☐ **Other Damages** *(specify)*:

CASE NUMBER:

Jurisdiction *(check all that apply)*:
☐ **ACTION IS A LIMITED CIVIL CASE**
Amount demanded ☐ does not exceed $10,000
        ☐ exceeds $10,000, but does not exceed $25,000
☐ **ACTION IS AN UNLIMITED CIVIL CASE (exceeds $25,000)**
☐ **ACTION IS RECLASSIFIED** by this amended complaint
☐ from limited to unlimited
☐ from unlimited to limited

1. PLAINTIFF *(name)*:

   alleges causes of action against DEFENDANT *(name)*:
2. This pleading, including attachments and exhibits, consists of the following number of pages: _____
3. Each plaintiff named above is a competent adult
   a. ☐ **except** plaintiff *(name)*:
      (1) ☐ a corporation qualified to do business in California
      (2) ☐ an unincorporated entity *(describe)*:
      (3) ☐ a public entity *(describe)*:
      (4) ☐ a minor   ☐ an adult
         (a) ☐ for whom a guardian or conservator of the estate or a guardian ad litem has been appointed
         (b) ☐ other *(specify)*:
      (5) ☐ other *(specify)*:

   b. ☐ **except** plaintiff *(name)*:
      (1) ☐ a corporation qualified to do business in California
      (2) ☐ an unincorporated entity *(describe)*:
      (3) ☐ a public entity *(describe)*:
      (4) ☐ a minor   ☐ an adult
         (a) ☐ for whom a guardian or conservator of the estate or a guardian ad litem has been appointed
         (b) ☐ other *(specify)*:
      (5) ☐ other *(specify)*:

   ☐ Information about additional plaintiffs who are not competent adults as shown in complaint—Attachment 3.

Page 1 of 3

Form Approved for Optional Use
Judicial Council of California
982.1(1) [Rev. July 1, 2002]

**COMPLAINT—Personal Injury, Property
Damage, Wrongful Death**

Code of Civil Procedure, § 425.12

continued

Exhibit 7-3 *continued*

SHORT TITLE:	CASE NUMBER:

4. ☐ PLAINTIFF *(name)*:
   is doing business under the fictitious name *(specify)*:

   and has complied with the fictitious business name laws.

5. Each defendant named above is a natural person
   a. ☐ **except** defendant *(name)*:
      (1) ☐ a business organization, form unknown
      (2) ☐ a corporation
      (3) ☐ an unincorporated entity *(describe)*:

      (4) ☐ a public entity *(describe)*:

      (5) ☐ other *(specify)*:

   c. ☐ **except** defendant *(name)*:
      (1) ☐ a business organization, form unknown
      (2) ☐ a corporation
      (3) ☐ an unincorporated entity *(describe)*:

      (4) ☐ a public entity *(describe)*:

      (5) ☐ other *(specify)*:

   b. ☐ **except** defendant *(name)*:
      (1) ☐ a business organization, form unknown
      (2) ☐ a corporation
      (3) ☐ an unincorporated entity *(describe)*:

      (4) ☐ a public entity *(describe)*:

      (5) ☐ other *(specify)*:

   d. ☐ **except** defendant *(name)*:
      (1) ☐ a business organization, form unknown
      (2) ☐ a corporation
      (3) ☐ an unincorporated entity *(describe)*:

      (4) ☐ a public entity *(describe)*:

      (5) ☐ other *(specify)*:

   ☐ Information about additional defendants who are not natural persons is contained in Complaint—Attachment 5.

6. The true names and capacities of defendants sued as Does are unknown to plaintiff.

7. ☐ Defendants who are joined pursuant to Code of Civil Procedure section 382 are *(names)*.

8. This court is the proper court because
   a. ☐ at least one defendant now resides in its jurisdictional area.
   b. ☐ the principal place of business of a defendant corporation or unincorporated association is in its jurisdictional area.
   c. ☐ injury to person or damage to personal property occurred in its jurisdictional area.
   d. ☐ other *(specify)*:

9. ☐ Plaintiff is required to comply with a claims stature, **and**
   a. ☐ plaintiff has complied with applicable claims statutes, or
   b. ☐ plaintiff is excused from complying because *(specify)*:

continued

Exhibit 7-3 *continued*

SHORT TITLE:	CASE NUMBER:

10. The following causes of action are attached and the statements above apply to each *(each complaint must have one or more causes of action attached)*:
   a. ☐ Motor Vehicle
   b. ☐ General Negligence
   c. ☐ Intentional Tort
   d. ☐ Products Liability
   e. ☐ Premises Liability
   f. ☐ Other *(specify)*:

11. Plaintiff has suffered
   a. ☐ wage loss
   b. ☐ loss of use of property
   c. ☐ hospital and medical expenses
   d. ☐ general damage
   e. ☐ property damage
   f. ☐ loss of earning capacity
   g. ☐ other damage *(specify)*:

12. ☐ The damages claimed for wrongful death and the relationships of plaintiff to the deceased are
   a. ☐ listed in Complaint—Attachment 12.
   b. ☐ as follows:

13. The relief sought in this complaint is within the jurisdiction of this court.

14. PLAINTIFF PRAYS for judgment for costs of suit; for such relief as is fair, just, and equitable, and for
   a. (1) ☐ compensatory damages
       (2) ☐ punitive damages
   b. the amount of damages is *(you must check (1) in cases for personal injury or wrongful death)*:
       (1) ☐ according to proof
       (2) ☐ in the amount of: $

15. ☐ The paragraphs of this complaint alleged on information and belief are as follows *(specify paragraph numbers)*:

Date:

_____   ▶ _____
(TYPE OR PRINT NAME)   (SIGNATURE OF PLAINTIFF OR ATTORNEY)

982.1(1) [Rev. July 1, 2002]   **COMPLAINT—Personal Injury, Property**   Page 3 of 3
                                                Damage, Wrongful Death

EXHIBIT 7-4 Complaint Prepared on Pleading Paper

1	John P. Evans
2	Attorney at Law
3	1122 Division Street
4	Peekskill, NY 11022
5	
6	COUNTY OF WESTCHESTER
7	
8	STATE OF NEW YORK
9	
10	
11	KATHERINE SPRINGER,) Case No.: PI-95-CC81
12	)
13	Plaintiff,) COMPLAINT- PERSONAL INJURY
14	)
15	vs.)
16	)
17	JOHN Q. MARTINEZ,)
18	)
19	Defendant)
20	_____)
21	
22	{BODY OF COMPLAINT GOES HERE}
23	
24	
25	Dated this 19th day of January, 2003
26	_____
27	John P. Evans
28	Attorney at Law

SERVICE OF SUMMONS

The **summons** should be prepared and filed with the court along with the complaint. Most states have forms for this purpose, which may be found on their Web sites or at the clerk's office of the court in which the complaint is being filed. Enough copies for each defendant should be prepared as well as a copy for the office files. The complaint and summons are presented to the clerk of the appropriate court. A case number is assigned and stamped on the complaint and summons. The original will be signed and copies conformed for service on the defendant. In most cases, the attorney will sign all copies of the complaint that are being served.

Personal Service

The most common method of service is by personal service, which is accomplished by handing the complaint and summons to the defendant and telling him what they are. If the defendant refuses to accept the documents, they may be dropped at his feet. They must be given to the defendant personally, however, and not left in a mailbox, on a front porch, or on a desk. The time and date served must be noted by the server on the proof of service, usually located on the summons form itself. After service, the signed copy is filed with the court.

Service by Mail

Service by mail is accomplished by sending the documents to the defendant by certified mail with a return receipt requested. The date received must be noted, because the response will be due 30 days from the date the receipt is signed, plus an additional five days for mailing.

Substituted Service

If the defendant cannot be served personally or by mail, another individual may be served in place of the defendant. If at home, an adult member of the household may be served; if at a business, an adult who is in charge of the business may be served. A copy must then be sent to the defendant at the address served.

Service by Publication

As a last resort, the defendant may be served by publication in a newspaper of general circulation at the location where the defendant was last located. For instance, if the last known address of the defendant was in Topeka, Kansas, the publication would be made in the local paper for that city. The plaintiff must first prove that the defendant could not be served by any other means. The attorney must make a motion to the court with accompanying affidavits indicating how service was attempted on the defendant. The court will then issue a ruling on the motion, allowing or denying service by publication.

summons a notice delivered by a sheriff or other authorized person informing a person of a lawsuit against him; it tells the person to be in court at a certain time or risk losing the suit without being present.

Agents for Process

If a corporation is a defendant, the authorized agent for the organization must be served. Corporations are required to designate agents for process in each state where they operate. This information is available from the office of the secretary of state in the state in which the suit is being filed.

DATE OF SERVICE
✦

The date of service should be noted in the tickler file or calendar, along with the date responding documents are due. This date is 30 days from the day after the complaint and summons are personally served on the defendant, or 35 days if service is accomplished by mail.

RESPONSES BY DEFENDANT
✦

The defendant may respond to the complaint in the allotted time by one or more of the following methods:

1. Answer
2. Cross-complaint
3. Demurrer
4. Motion to Strike

REQUEST TO ENTER DEFAULT
✦

If the defendant fails to answer the complaint in the allotted time, the plaintiff may file a default judgment. This is accomplished by the preparation of a request to enter default along with accompanying documentation. The court will issue a judgment in favor of the plaintiff in most cases if the defendant fails to appear at the default hearing. The request to enter default must be filed with the appropriate court and will be served on the defendant.

ANSWER
✦

The **answer** contains factual issues in response to the complaint that must be proven by the plaintiff at the time of the trial. In many cases, the defendant will issue a general denial to all issues raised in the complaint, thereby compelling the plaintiff to prove all allegations. An Answer with General Denial is included as Exhibit 7-5.

By filing an answer, the defendant is submitting to the court's jurisdiction. Therefore, if the defendant wishes to object to this court's jurisdiction over her, she must file and serve a motion to quash service of summons before answering the complaint.

answer the first pleading by the defendant in a lawsuit responding to the charges and demands of the plaintiff's complaint.

EXHIBIT 7-5 Answer with General Denial

1	JEFFREY W. WILLIAMS
2	Attorney at Law
3	8166 Michigan Avenue
4	Chicago, IL 82233
5	
6	Attorneys for Defendant
7	COUNTY OF COOK
8	
9	STATE OF ILLINOIS
10	
11	PATRICIA MARRO,) Case No.: PI-95-CC81
12	)
13	Plaintiff,) ANSWER TO COMPLAINT OF PATRICIA MARRO
14	) – PERSONAL INJURY
15	vs.)
16	)
17	JOHN Q. BADD,)
18	)
19	Defendant)
20	_____)
21	COMES NOW THE DEFENDANT JOHN Q. BADD who generally denies each and every
22	allegation of the unverified complaint of the plaintiff PATRICIA MARRO, and prays that
23	the plaintiff take nothing from her suit and for costs of suit herein.
24	
25	Dated this 19th day of June, 2003
26	_____
27	JEFFREY W. WILLIAMS
28	Attorney at Law

In some cases, the defendant may wish to admit to some allegations in the complaint and to deny others. In those situations, she would submit specific denials to those numbered allegations in the complaint and admissions to others. For instance, the answer might state:

> Defendant denies allegations contained in Paragraphs 1, 2, and 3 of the Plaintiff's Complaint and admits allegations contained in Paragraph 4.

If the defendant wishes to bring up additional issues or facts constituting a defense in the action, she must do so in the answer. If additional facts constituting a defense are presented, each one must be explained separately and must be listed in numbered paragraphs. Some of examples of defenses include:

1. Statute of limitations has run and therefore the plaintiff is barred from filing a complaint regarding the matter.
2. Comparative negligence, if the plaintiff was partially at fault in the action.
3. Assumption of the risk of injury by the plaintiff. (For instance, if the plaintiff was engaging in an unusually dangerous activity, in many cases she assumes the risk of injury.)
4. The proper remedy is a Worker's Compensation action, because the plaintiff was acting within the scope of her employment at the time of the incident.
5. Immunity, such as a public officer may have if acting within the scope of his employment.

Several other defenses exist and may be asserted by the attorney for the defendant. Check your own state's codes to determine legitimate defenses to a civil complaint and record them below.

STATE SPECIFIC INFORMATION

The state of _____ allows the following additional defenses in a civil action:

1. _____

_____

_____.

2. _____

_____

_____.

FORM ANSWERS ─────────────────────────────◆

In some states, such as California, the Judicial Council provides forms for answers for personal injury, wrongful death, property damage, unlawful detainer, or contract actions. Be sure to check the rules for your own state on your state court's Web site and indicate the rules below.

STATE SPECIFIC INFORMATION

The state of _____ *allows* *does not allow* *requires* the use of forms for answers. Forms may be found at: _____
_____.

CROSS-COMPLAINT ────────────────────────◆

A **cross-complaint** may be filed with the answer when the defendant has a claim against the plaintiff or third parties arising from the same or a related transaction. The terminology used for these parties is as follows:

1. Party filing the cross-complaint—*cross-complainant*
2. Third party against whom the cross-complaint is filed— *third-party defendant*
3. Party against whom the cross-complaint is filed— *cross-defendant*
4. Defendant who files the cross-complaint against a third party— *third-party plaintiff*

In cases where many different parties are involved, it is possible to have a number of cross-complaints being filed against parties to the action as well as third parties. In those cases, the paralegal must pay particular attention, not only to whom is filing against whom, but also to the due dates of responsive pleadings. Each time a cross-complaint is filed, the responsive pleading is subject to the same 30-day answer requirements described earlier.

The heading in a cross-complaint should contain two separate captions:

1. The names of the parties in the initial action
2. The names of all cross-complinnts and cross-defendants

The second set of titles should be placed immediately below the initial title.

The body of the cross-complaint must include the facts constituting the cause of action and a precise demand for damages. Judicial Council forms are available for cross-complaints in actions for

cross-complaint a claim brought by one defendant against another or by a defendant against a plaintiff based on the same subject matter as the plaintiff's lawsuit.

personal injury, wrongful death, property damage, and contracts. Separate sections on the form may be marked for different causes of action and damages. If the defendant fails to file a cross-complaint against the plaintiff in a related or the same transaction, she may be barred from filing it at the later time. A sample form for a cross-complaint is contained in Exhibit 7-6.

DEMURRER

Sometimes, a plaintiff will file a complaint that has no legal grounds. Perhaps the defendant committed an act, but there is no statute forbidding the action. Or perhaps the plaintiff's attorney misstated the cause of action or made other legal errors. In those instances, the defendant's attorney will file a **demurrer**, a pleading which maintains that the plaintiff's complaint has no legal basis (see Exhibit 7-7 on page 152). Points and authorities (P&As) supporting the defendant's contentions must accompany the demurrer. These will include a statement of the issue or argument along with the citation of the case or statute from which it was obtained. For instance, if the defendant is objecting on the ground that the plaintiff does not have the legal capacity to sue, the points and authorities must include the number of the statute or code section that states what constitutes legal capacity to sue.

The court will hold a hearing on the demurrer. Both attorneys will present their oral arguments to the judge, who then issues a ruling. If the court rules that the demurrer is sustained without leave to amend, the defendant wins the lawsuit. In some cases, however, the court will allow the plaintiff to amend the complaint. If the court overrules the demurrer, the defendant must file an answer within the allotted time period.

RESPONSE TO DEMURRER

The party against whom a demurrer was filed may respond either by amending the complaint to alleviate the insufficiencies raised by the demurrer or by filing points and authorities in opposition to the demurrer. Papers opposing the demurrer must be served and filed at least five court days prior to the hearing.

Notice of hearing must be provided at least 15 days before the hearing if service is in person, or 20 to 40 days (depending on when the notice was received by the adverse party) if service is by mail. Responses to opposition to the demurrer must be served at least two court days prior to the hearing.

demurrer a legal pleading that states that the other side's argument does not give them a legal argument that can be upheld in court.

MOTION TO STRIKE

In some cases the complaint may be legally sufficient, but some of its allegations may be legally objectionable. In that event, the defendant

EXHIBIT 7-6   Sample Form for a Cross-Complaint

Courtesy: Reprinted from West's California Judicial Council Forms 2003, with permission of West, a Thomson business. For more information about this publication please visit **http://west.thomson.com**.

982.1(14)

ATTORNEY OR PARTY WITHOUT ATTORNEY *(Name, state bar number, and address)*:	FOR COURT USE ONLY
TELEPHONE NO: FAX NO. *(Optional)*: E-MAIL ADDRESS *(Optional)*: ATTORNEY FOR *(Name)*:	

NAME OF COURT:
STREET ADDRESS:
MAILING ADDRESS:
CITY AND ZIP CODE:
BRANCH NAME:

CROSS-COMPLAINANT:

CROSS-DEFENDANT:

☐ DOES 1 TO _____

CROSS-COMPLAINT—Personal Injury, Property Damage, Wrongful Death
☐ **AMENDED** *(Number)*:
Causes of Action *(check all that apply)*:
☐ **Apportionment of Fault**   ☐ **Declaratory Relief**
☐ **Indemnification**   ☐ **OTHER** *(specify)*:

Jurisdiction *(check all that apply)*:
☐ **ACTION IS A LIMITED CIVIL CASE ($25,000 or less)**
☐ **ACTION IS AN UNLIMITED CIVIL CASE (exceeds $25,000)**
It ☐ is ☐ is not   reclassified as unlimited by this cross-complaint

CASE NUMBER:

1. CROSS-COMPLAINANT *(name)*:

   alleges causes of action against CROSS-DEFENDANT *(name)*:

2. This pleading, including exhibits and attachments, consists of the following number of pages: _____

3. Each cross-complainant named above is a competent adult
   a. ☐ **except** cross-complainant *(name)*:
      (1) ☐ a corporation qualified to do business in California
      (2) ☐ an unincorporated entity *(describe)*:
      (3) ☐ a public entity *(describe)*:
      (4) ☐ a minor   ☐ an adult
         (a) ☐ for whom a guardian or conservator of the estate or a guardian ad litem has been appointed
         (b) ☐ other *(specify)*:
      (5) ☐ other *(specify)*:

   ☐ Information about additional cross-complainants who are not competent adults is contained in Cross-Complaint—Attachment 3.

(Continued on reverse)

Page 1 of 3

Form Approved for Optional Use Judicial Council of California 982.1(14) [Rev. January 1, 2001]	**CROSS-COMPLAINT—Personal Injury,** **Property Damage, Wrongful Death**	Code of Civil Procedure, § 425.12

continued

Exhibit 7-6 *continued*

SHORT TITLE:	CASE NUMBER:

4. Each cross-defendant named above is a natural person
   a. ☐ **except** cross-defendant *(name)*:
      (1) ☐ a business organization, form unknown
      (2) ☐ a corporation
      (3) ☐ an unincorporated entity *(describe)*:

      (4) ☐ a public entity *(describe)*:

      (5) ☐ other *(specify)*:

   b. ☐ **except** cross-defendant *(name)*:
      (1) ☐ a business organization, form unknown
      (2) ☐ a corporation
      (3) ☐ an unincorporated entity *(describe)*:

      (4) ☐ a public entity *(describe)*:

      (5) ☐ other *(specify)*:

   ☐ Information about additional cross-defendants who are not natural persons is contained in Cross-Complaint—Attachment 4.

5. The true names and capacities of cross-defendants sued as Does are unknown to cross-complainant.

6. ☐ Cross-complainant is required to comply with a claims stature, **and**
   a. ☐ has complied with applicable claims statutes, **or**
   b. ☐ is excused from complying because *(specify)*:

7. ☐ _____ **Cause of Action—Indemnification**
         (NUMBER)

   a. Cross-defendants were the agents, employees, co-venturers, partners, or in some manner agents or principals, or both, for each other and were acting within the course and scope of their agency or employment.
   b. The principal action alleged, among other things, conduct entitling plaintiff to compensatory damages against me. I contend that I am not liable for events and occurrences described in plaintiff's complaint.
   c. If I am found in some manner responsible to plaintiff or to anyone else as a result of the incidents and occurrences described in plaintiff's complaint, my liability would be based solely upon a derivative from of liability not resulting from my conduct, but only from an obligation imposed upon me by law; therefore, I would be entitled to complete indemnity from each cross-defendant.

8. ☐ _____ **Cause of Action—Apportionment of Fault**
         (NUMBER)

   a. Each cross-defendant was responsible, in whole or in part, for the injuries, if any, suffered by plaintiff.
   b. If I am judged liable to plaintiff, each cross-defendant should be required: (1) to pay a share of plaintiff's judgment which is in proportion to the comparative negligence of that cross-defendant in causing plaintiff's damages; and (2) to reimburse me for any payments I make to plaintiff in excess of my proportional share of all cross-defendants' negligence.

(Continued on page three)

982.1(14) [Rev. January 1, 2001]
**CROSS-COMPLAINT—Personal Injury,
Property Damage, Wrongful Death**
Page 2 of 3

continued

Exhibit 7-6 *continued*

SHORT TITLE:	CASE NUMBER:

9. ☐ _____ **Cause of Action—Declaratory Relief**
    (NUMBER)

    An actual controversy exists between the parties concerning their respective rights and duties because cross-complainant contends and cross-defendant disputes ☐ as specified in Cross-Complaint—Attachment 9
    ☐ as follows:

10. ☐ _____ **Cause of Action—***(specify)*:
    (NUMBER)

11. ☐ The following additional causes of action are attached and the statements below apply to each (*in each of the attachment, "plaintiff" means "cross-complainant" and "defendant" means "cross-defendant"*):
    a. ☐ Motor Vehicle
    b. ☐ General Negligence
    c. ☐ Intentional Tort
    d. ☐ Products Liability
    e. ☐ Premises Liability
    f. ☐ Other *(specify)*:

12. **CROSS-COMPLAINANT PRAYS** for judgment for costs of suit; for such relief as is fair, just, and equitable, and for
    a. ☐ total and complete indemnity for any judgments rendered against me.
    b. ☐ judgment in a proportionate share from each cross-defendant.
    c. ☐ a judicial determination that cross-defendants were the legal cause of any injuries and damages sustained by plaintiff and that cross-defendants indemnity me, either completely or partially, for any sums of money which may be recovered against me by plaintiff.
    d. ☐ compensatory damages
        (1) ☐ (unlimited civil cases) according to proof.
        (2) ☐ (limited civil cases) in the amount of: $
    e. ☐ other *(specify)*:

13. ☐ The paragraphs of this cross-complaint alleged on information and belief are as follows (*specify paragraph numbers*):

Date:

_____
(TYPE OR PRINT NAME)

▶ _____
(SIGNATURE OF CROSS-COMPLAINANT OR ATTORNEY)

982.1(14) [Rev. January 1, 2001]   **CROSS-COMPLAINT—Personal Injury,**   Page 3 of 3
Property Damage, Wrongful Death

EXHIBIT 7-7 Demurrer

```
 1  Attorney Name and Bar No.
 2  Office Address
 3  City, State and Zip Code
 4  Telephone Number
 5  Attorney for Defendant
 6
 7
 8              SUPERIOR COURT OF THE STATE OF NEW HAMPSHIRE
 9                          COUNTY OF CHESHIRE
10
11  STANLEY L. ROSEN,              )        Case No. OCV94999
12                                 )        DEFENDANT JOAN D. PALM'S
13              Plaintiff,         )        DEMURRER TO PLAINTIFF STANLEY L.
14      v.                         )        ROSEN'S COMPLAINT, NOTICE OF
15  JOAN D. PALM,                  )        HEARING; MEMORANDUM OF POINTS
16              Defendant.         )        AND AUTHORITIES [Code Civ. Proc. § 430.10]
17                                 )        Date:      July 13, 2005
18                                 )        Time:      10:00 A.M.
19                                 )        Location:  Department 5, Cheshire County
20                                                     Superior Court
21  _____
22        Defendant JOAN D. PALM demurs to the complaint filed by plaintiff STANLEY L. ROSEN
23  on the following grounds:
24        1.  The court has no jurisdiction of the subject matter of the causes of action alleged in
25  the complaint.
26        2.  The complaint does not state facts sufficient to constitute a cause of action against the
27  defendant.
28        WHEREFORE, defendant requests that:

                                          2
```

continued

may file a motion to strike, asking that the objectionable allegations be removed. The motion must set forth the objectionable wording along with points and authorities to support the defendant's contentions. The exact page and line number(s) of the objectionable words must be noted in the motion. The court will hold a hearing on the motion similar to the hearing held for demurrers.

The motion to strike may be filed along with a demurrer with the motion is requesting that the court disallow the complaint because its language conflicts with the Code of Civil Procedure, or a direct order of the court.

Exhibit *7-7* *continued*

1	1. The defendant's demurrer be sustained without leave to amend;
2	2. The court enter an order dismissing this action;
3	3. The defendant be awarded the costs of this action; and
4	4. The court grant such other and further relief that the court considers proper.

Dated: [date signed]   Respectfully submitted,
                                              JULIAN AND DI CECCO

_____

By: DONNA L. DI CECCO
Attorney for Defendant

2

MOTION FOR SUMMARY JUDGMENT ✦

Either party may file a motion for **summary judgment**. The plaintiff files such a motion to assert that there is not a defense that the defendant can claim in the action. The defendant files the motion to claim that the action has no merit. In either case, affidavits of witnesses or parties to the action must be filed along with the motion.

The judge will hold a hearing on the motion, where the attorneys present their oral arguments. The court will then issue an order setting forth its decision. If the judge grants the motion, the lawsuit is over and the party who made the motion prevails, but if the judge denies the motion, the lawsuit continues.

As a practical matter, these motions are filed in cases in which no factual issues are in question. The remaining issues are legal in nature and can be decided by the judge.

A motion for summary judgment may not be filed until at least 60 days after the first appearance by the defendant, usually the date the responding document (i.e., the answer) is filed. At this point either side may file this motion.

Service requirements are 28 days before the hearing if in person or 33 if by mail. All supporting papers must accompany the motion. Filing requirements are at least 15 days before the hearing.

A sample motion for summary judgment is shown in Exhibit 7-8. Supporting documentation must accompany this motion.

DISCOVERY ✦

Paralegals perform many important functions during the discovery phase of the lawsuit, during which time each side obtains information about the other side's case. It is considered to be the formal investigation phase of the lawsuit. Typically, paralegals working in discovery draft documents, keep track of all discovery papers, summarize and catalog documents, and maintain document control. The most common discovery devices are:

1. Depositions
2. Written interrogatories
3. Requests for admission
4. Demand for inspection
5. Demand for physical examination

Any requests by the adverse party for information or material that is covered by the attorney-client privilege or work product privilege is not discoverable. Additional privileges enumerated in the Evidence Code are:

1. Privilege against self-incrimination
2. Spousal privilege
3. Physician or psychotherapist privilege
4. Clergy-penitent privilege

These privileges may be waived by the holder only. A claim of privilege should be made upon being served with the discovery request, by an objection setting forth the nature of the privilege along with a refusal to respond.

DEPOSITION ✦

A deposition is a pretrial examination of a party or a witness to a lawsuit. The person whose testimony is taken is called the deponent.

EXHIBIT 7-8   Motion for Summary Judgment

```
 1 │ Attorney Name and Bar No.
 2 │ Office Address
 3 │ City, State and Zip Code
 4 │ Telephone Number
 5 │ Attorney for Plaintiff
 6 │
 7 │
 8 │              SUPERIOR COURT OF THE STATE OF PENNSYLVANIA
 9 │                         COUNTY OF YORK
10 │
11 │ SUSAN SIMON,                    )    Case No. SC94555
12 │                                 )    NOTICE OF MOTION FOR SUMMARY
13 │             Plaintiff,          )    JUDGMENT; POINTS AND AUTHORITIES;
14 │     v.                          )    AND DECLARATION UNDER CODE CIV.
15 │                                 )    PROC. § 437c(a)
16 │ LAURA ATKINS,                   )    Date:  December 1, 2005
17 │                                 )    Time:  2:00 P.M.
18 │             Defendant.          )    Location:  Department D
19 │                                      Trial Date:  September 1, 2005
20 │ ─────────────────────────────────────────────────────────
21 │ To all parties and their attorneys of record:
22 │     PLEASE TAKE NOTICE that on December 1, 2005, at 2:00 P.M., or as soon thereafter as
23 │ the matter can be heard in York County Superior Court, 400 Main Street, York, Pennsylvania,
24 │ the Plaintiff SUSAN SIMON, will and does move this Court for summary judgment in
25 │ favor of Plaintiff, and against Defendant, LAURA ATKINS. This motion is made pursuant to Code
26 │ of Civil Procedure section 437c, on the grounds that there is no defense to the action, there is no
27 │ triable issue as to any material fact, and that Plaintiff, SUSAN SIMON, is entitled to a judgment as a
28 │
```

1

continued

Paralegals may be asked to schedule depositions of either parties or witnesses to the action. A deposition may be taken of anyone in California and must be scheduled either within 75 miles of the deponent's residence or in the county where the case has been filed, provided that the latter is within 150 miles of the deponent's residence. Typically a deposition is scheduled at the law office of the attorney who is requesting it.

If the individual whose deposition is being taken may not be available at trial, the attorney may choose to have a video recording made of the deposition so that it may be used in place of testimony at trial. In that case, the paralegal must insert a notation of this intention in the notice of deposition, unless all parties agree to the recording.

Exhibit 7-8 *continued*

1	matter of law.
2	This motion will be based on the Memorandum of Points and Authorities accompanying this
3	motion, the Separate Statement of Undisputed Material Facts of Plaintiff, and the declarations of
4	DOUGLAS RICHARDS, RACHEL MARTINEZ, and MARIA MONTES, filed with this motion.
5	Dated: [date signed]
6	
7	
8	_____
	JAMES AARONSON
9	Attorney for Plaintiff
10	
11	
12	
13	
14	
15	
16	
17	
18	
19	
20	
21	
22	
23	
24	
25	
26	
27	
28	

2

In scheduling the deposition, the paralegal should also schedule a court reporter to take the transcript. The reporter may also administer the oath to the deponent, thus acting as the deposition officer, who must be a person who is not a party or attorney in the action.

Although a deponent is required to appear at a deposition if she is served with the notice, professional courtesy requires that a representative of the law firm contact the deponent or her attorney to schedule a mutually convenient time prior to service of the notice. A paralegal should follow these steps to schedule deposition:

1. Determine whether the site of the deposition meets the distance requirements for this deponent.
2. Select a date and time mutually convenient to the attorney, deponent, and other attorney. (This may be done more rapidly via email.)

3. Hire a certified reporter to take the deposition transcript on the date and time required.

4. Prepare a notice of deposition and serve it on all individuals who have filed an appearance in the case and file it with the court. (See Exhibit 7-9.) The plaintiff may serve a notice of deposition 20 days from the date the initial summons is served on the defendant or the defendant files an appearance. The defendant may serve a notice of deposition any time after she is served or appears.

5. If deposing a nonparty witness:
   a. Prepare a deposition subpoena, or
   b. Prepare a deposition subpoena indicating items that must be brought to the deposition if the individual is required to

---

EXHIBIT 7-9   Notice of Deposition

1	NAME OF ATTORNEY AND BAR NO.
2	Address
3	City, State and Zip Code
4	Telephone: (408) 555-1111
5	
6	Attorney for Plaintiff
7	
8	SUPERIOR COURT OF THE STATE OF CALIFORNIA
9	COUNTY OF SANTA CRUZ
10	
11	WILLIAM M. SANCHEZ,) CASE NO. XX-6Y99
12	) NOTICE OF ORAL DEPOSITION OF DANIEL
13	Plaintiff,) ROMERO AND PRODUCTION OF
14	) DOCUMENTS PURSUANT TO CODE CIV.
15	v.) PROC. § 2025(d)
16	)
17	DANIEL ROMERO,)
18	Defendant.)
19	_____)
20	
21	To the parties who have appeared in the above cause of action, and their attorneys of record:
22	YOU ARE NOTIFIED THAT ON January 5, 2006, at 11:00 A.M., the plaintiff will take the
23	oral deposition of the defendant DANIEL ROMERO, at the office of PLAINTIFF ATTORNEY
24	LAW FIRM, LOCATED AT 23344 Soquel Avenue, Suite 456, in the City of Capitola, County of Santa
25	Cruz, and State of California. The deposition will continue from day to day until completed.
26	Deponent is required to produce at deposition the materials described in Exhibit A attached to
27	this notice and incorporated by reference.
28	

1

continued

Exhibit 7-9 *continued*

1	Pursuant to section 2025(l)(1) of the Code of Civil Procedure, Plaintiff intends to record the
2	deposition of defendant stenographically and by video tape.
3	The attorney representing the defendant served with this notice is:
4	STEVEN P. STOFER
5	481 Oroville Road
6	Castroville, CA 92231
7	DATED: November 15, 2005
8	
9	
10	_____
	PLAINTIFF ATTORNEY NAME
11	Attorney for Plaintiff
12	
13	
14	
15	
16	
17	
18	
19	
20	
21	
22	
23	
24	
25	
26	
27	
28	

2

bring items or records with her. If the individual is not required to testify but merely produce business records, no notice of deposition is required. Service of a deposition subpoena with required items listed will suffice.

c. The individual must be served with the deposition subpoena in person.

d. Witness fees and mileage must be paid to the witness.

See Exhibit 7-10 for a sample deposition subpoena form requiring the deponent to appear and bring items with her.

Monetary sanctions may be imposed by the court if a deponent who has been subpoenaed fails to appear or the attorney scheduling the deposition cancels without notice to all interested parties.

EXHIBIT 7-10 Judicial Council Form Deposition Subpoena

Courtesy: Reprinted from *West's California Judicial Council Forms 2003*, with permission of West, a Thomson business. For more information about this publication please visit http://west.thomson.com.

ATTORNEY OR PARTY WITHOUT ATTORNEY (Name and Address):	TELEPHONE NO.:	FOR COURT USE ONLY

ATTORNEY FOR (Name):

NAME OF COURT:
STREET ADDRESS:
MAILING ADDRESS:
CITY AND ZIP CODE:
BRANCH NAME:

PLAINTIFF/PETITIONER:

DEFENDANT/RESPONDENT:

DEPOSITION SUBPENA
For Personal Appearance
☐ **and Production of Documents and Things**

CASE NUMBER:

THE PEOPLE OF THE STATE OF CALIFORNIA, TO *(name, address, and telephone number of deponent, if known):*

1. **YOU ARE ORDERED TO APPEAR IN PERSON TO TESTIFY AS A WITNESS** in this action at the following time and place:

Date: Time: Address:

a. ☐ As a deponent who is not a natural person, you are ordered to designate one or more persons to testify on your behalf as to the matters described in item 3. (Code of Civil Procedure section 2025(d)(6).)
b. ☐ You are ordered to produce the documents and things described in item 3.
c. ☐ This deposition will be recorded stenographically and by ☐ audiotape ☐ videotape.
d. ☐ This videotape deposition is intended for possible use at trial under Code of Civil Procedure section 2025(u)(4).

2. ☐ The **personal attendance** of the custodian of records or other qualified witness ☐ and the **production of the original documents** are required by this deposition subpena. The procedure authorized by Evidence Code sections 1560(b), 1561, and 1562 will not be deemed sufficient compliance with this subpena.

3. ☐ **The documents and things to be produced and any testing or sampling being sought are described as follows:**

☐ Continued on attachment 3.

4. *A deposition permits an attorney to ask questions of a witness who is sworn to tell the truth. An attorney for other parties may then ask questions also. Questions and answers are recorded stenographically at the deposition; later they are transcribed for possible use at trial. A witness may read the written record and change any incorrect answers before signing the deposition. The witness is entitled to receive witness fees and mileage actually traveled both ways. The money must be paid, at the option of the party giving notice of the deposition, either with service of this subpena or at the time of the deposition.*

DISOBEDIENCE OF THIS SUBPENA MAY BE PUNISHED AS CONTEMPT BY THIS COURT. YOU WILL ALSO BE LIABLE FOR THE SUM OF FIVE HUNDRED DOLLARS AND ALL DAMAGES RESULTING FROM YOUR FAILURE TO OBEY.

Date issued:

_____
(TYPE OR PRINT NAME)

▶ _____
(SIGNATURE OF PERSON ISSUING SUBPENA)

_____
(TITLE)

(See reverse for proof of service)

Form Adopted by Rule 982
Judicial Council of California
982(a)(15.1) [Rev. January 1, 1993]

DEPOSITION SUBPENA—PERSONAL APPEARANCE | WEST GROUP Official Publisher | Code of Civil Procedure, §§ 2020, 2025 Government Code § 68097.1

continued

Exhibit 7-10 *continued*

PLAINTIFF/PETITIONER:	CASE NUMBER:
DEFENDANT/RESPONDENT:	

PROOF OF SERVICE OF DEPOSITION SUBPENA—PERSONAL APPEARANCE

1. I served this Deposition Subpena—Personal Appearance by personally delivering a copy to the person served as follows:

   a. Person served *(name)*:

   b. Address where served:

   c. Date of delivery:

   d. Time of delivery:

   e. Witness fees and mileage both ways *(check one)*:
     (1) ☐ were paid. Amount: . . . .$ _____
     (2) ☐ were not paid.
     (3) ☐ were tendered to the witness's
         public entity employer as
         required by Government Code
         section 68097.2. The amount
         tendered was *(specify)*: . . . .$ _____

   f. Fee for service: . . . .$ _____

2. I received this subpena for service on *(date)*:

3. Person serving:
   a. ☐ Not a registered California process server.
   b. ☐ California sheriff, marshal, or constable.
   c. ☐ Registered California process server.
   d. ☐ Employee or independent contractor of a registered California process server.
   e. ☐ Exempt from registration under Bus. & Prof. Code section 22350(b).
   f. ☐ Registered professional photocopier.
   g. ☐ Exempt from registration under Bus. & Prof. Code section 22451.
   h. Name, address, and telephone number and, if applicable, county of registration and number:

I declare under penalty of perjury under the laws of the State of California that the foregoing is true and correct.

Date:

▶ _____
(SIGNATURE)

(For California sheriff, marshal, or constable use only)
I **certify** that the foregoing is true and correct.

Date:

▶ _____
(SIGNATURE)

982(a)(15.1) [Rev. January 1, 1993]   **PROOF OF SERVICE DEPOSITION SUBPENA—PERSONAL APPEARANCE**   WEST GROUP Official Publisher   Page two

Format of Notice of Deposition

The format for a notice of deposition is similar to that of other documents. A Judicial Council form is available for this notice. It should contain the following information:

1. Caption—names of the parties to the action and the case number.
2. Body—name and address of the deponent, status, and individual asking for deposition; location, date, and time of deposition.
3. Items to bring—items listed here that witness must bring to deposition.
4. Date of notice and attorney's name and address.

Deposition Summaries

Because depositions often elicit considerably more information than is required, the paralegal is often called upon to summarize the deposition testimony. The summary should point out any discrepancies in the witness's testimony. The most common types of summaries are a topical deposition summary, a page/line deposition summary, an issue deposition summary, and an index to a video deposition. Exhibits 7-11 and 7-12, and Exhibits 7-13 and 7-14 show samples of each type of summary; Exhibit 7-15 on page 164 shows instructions for their completion.

EXHIBIT 7-11   Topical Deposition Summary

①

FIELD V. RIVERS

Case No. 42196

Deponent Name: Lucelly Oso

Date of Deposition: May 1, 2005

Deposition Volume: No. 1

Topic/Subject	Transcript Page/Line	Summary Page
Personal	2/15	1
Employment history	3/5	1
Medical history	8/2	1
Psychiatric treatment	10/4	1
Psychiatric treatment	14/5	2
Educational history	17/19	2

② ③ ④

EXHIBIT 7-12 Page/Line Deposition Summary

Morgan v. Castillo

Case No. 33333

Deponent Name: Linda Stoner
Date of Deposition: March 6, 2005
Deposition Volume No. 1

①

② Page/Line	③ Subject	④ Summary
2/15	Personal	Resides at 222 Western Avenue, Akron, Ohio, phone: (999) 222-1111
3/5	Procedures	Explanation of deposition procedures
6/4	Employment	Currently employed by Ross Enterprises, 435 Irvine Boulevard, Akron, Ohio, as accountant for 6 months. Prior to that, accountant for Attorney Deanna Caudillo, 123 Broad Street, Akron, Ohio, 8 months
8/2	Medical	No present medication. Treated for back pain and psychiatric problems last three years.
10/4	Psychiatric	Saw Dr. Danielli for one year in Akron.
14/5	Psychiatric	Denies seeing psychiatrist for emotional or psychiatric problems.
16/9	Psychiatric	Dr. Danielli's office located on Madison Street but can't remember address. Deponent's attorney will provide.
17/19	Education	Completed Whittier School in Whittier, Ohio, 1992. Completed paralegal classes in 1994. CPA 1995.

EXHIBIT 7-13   Issue Deposition Summary

Morgan v. Guerrero

Case No. 55555

Deponent Name: Susan Dawson

Date: May 1, 2005

Deposition Volume No. 1

①

Subject/Issue	Page(s)
Personal/background	
Personal information	2
Employment history	6
Educational history	9
Medical history	
Current status	8
Psychiatric history	11, 16

②   ③

EXHIBIT 7-14   Index to a Video Deposition

Daniels v. Kenell—Case No. 11111

Deponent: William Minot

Date: December 26, 2005

Volume No. 1

①

Time/Date No.*	Page/Line	Summary
00:40:08	5/9	Identification of parties and attorneys
01:38:00	7/14	Witness William Minot sworn in
01:55:20	8/25	Attorney Melissa Chan begins direct examination
02:22:07	9/20	Exhibit 1 identified and authenticated by deponent (contract between Minot and Daniels dated 7/17/92)
02:50:03	10/25	Personal background of witness
03:30:02	12/5	Educational history of witness

* Times and dates are indicated as they appear on the video display.

②   ③   ④

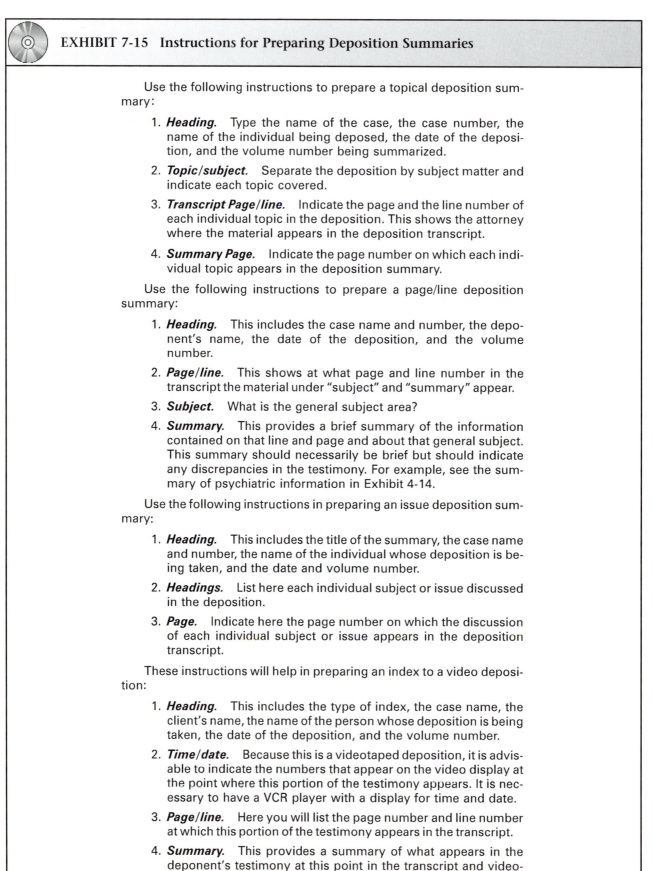

EXHIBIT 7-15 Instructions for Preparing Deposition Summaries

Use the following instructions to prepare a topical deposition summary:

1. *Heading.* Type the name of the case, the case number, the name of the individual being deposed, the date of the deposition, and the volume number being summarized.

2. *Topic/subject.* Separate the deposition by subject matter and indicate each topic covered.

3. *Transcript Page/line.* Indicate the page and the line number of each individual topic in the deposition. This shows the attorney where the material appears in the deposition transcript.

4. *Summary Page.* Indicate the page number on which each individual topic appears in the deposition summary.

Use the following instructions to prepare a page/line deposition summary:

1. *Heading.* This includes the case name and number, the deponent's name, the date of the deposition, and the volume number.

2. *Page/line.* This shows at what page and line number in the transcript the material under "subject" and "summary" appear.

3. *Subject.* What is the general subject area?

4. *Summary.* This provides a brief summary of the information contained on that line and page and about that general subject. This summary should necessarily be brief but should indicate any discrepancies in the testimony. For example, see the summary of psychiatric information in Exhibit 4-14.

Use the following instructions in preparing an issue deposition summary:

1. *Heading.* This includes the title of the summary, the case name and number, the name of the individual whose deposition is being taken, and the date and volume number.

2. *Headings.* List here each individual subject or issue discussed in the deposition.

3. *Page.* Indicate here the page number on which the discussion of each individual subject or issue appears in the deposition transcript.

These instructions will help in preparing an index to a video deposition:

1. *Heading.* This includes the type of index, the case name, the client's name, the name of the person whose deposition is being taken, the date of the deposition, and the volume number.

2. *Time/date.* Because this is a videotaped deposition, it is advisable to indicate the numbers that appear on the video display at the point where this portion of the testimony appears. It is necessary to have a VCR player with a display for time and date.

3. *Page/line.* Here you will list the page number and line number at which this portion of the testimony appears in the transcript.

4. *Summary.* This provides a summary of what appears in the deponent's testimony at this point in the transcript and videotape.

WRITTEN INTERROGATORIES ✦

Written questions asked by one party of another party are know as interrogatories. In addition to the questions on the form, each party may ask the other party an additional 35 questions specific to the case. Responses are written and signed under oath so they may be used as evidence against the party.

Generally, state courts require that interrogatories be served no earlier than 10 days after service of the summons and complaint. Additionally, discovery is not allowed after 30 days before trial.

Written interrogatories are the most used discovery tool, as well as the least expensive. They may be propounded relatively quickly merely by checking or "x"-ing the appropriate boxed on the form. All evidentiary information within the party's knowledge may be obtained.

A sample of a written interrogatory is shown in Exhibit 7-16.

The responding party has 30 days to issue answers to the interrogatories. Unless an objection is submitted, all questions must be answered within the 30-day time period. Proper grounds for objecting to questions follow. Individual objections must be stated for each question that is unacceptable. Acceptable grounds are:

1. If the question is irrelevant to the case or will not lead to the discovery of admissible evidence, then the question exceeds the scope of discovery and will not be allowed.

2. If the question seeks to obtain information covered by attorney-client privilege, it will be objectionable.

3. Questions about the contents of documents are not allowed; however, questions about the identity or location of documents may be obtained.

4. If the question would take an extraordinary amount of time and effort by the respondent, it is said to be burdensome and oppressive, and will not be allowed.

5. If the question has subparts, instructions, or compound requests within one question, none of the compound questions will be allowed.

Challenging Objections

If the answering party objects to answering questions propounded in the interrogatories, the propounding party (asking party) must first meet with opposing counsel to work out the dispute. If this is not possible, he may file a motion to compel further answers with the court, in which the court is asked to order the respondent to provide answers. The court will decide whether the answers previously provided are adequate and, if not, what additional information the answering party must provide.

Responses to Written interrogatories

Paralegals may be asked to assist the client in answering written interrogatories that have been propounded to them. The question asked

EXHIBIT 7-16 Written Interrogatories

STATE OF ILLINOIS)   IN THE FRANKLIN COUNTY
) SS.   CIRCUIT COURT
COUNTY OF FRANKLIN)
                                        CASE NO.

DAVID M. KASHEN,   )
)
            Plaintiff,   )
)
vs.   )
)
INSURANCE COMPANY,   )
CLAIMS, and J. A.   )
)
            Defendants.   )
)
_____   )

INTERROGATORIES

Comes now the Plaintiff, David M. Kashen, by Barbara Grasso, and pursuant to the Illinois Rules of Trial Procedure, propounds the following Interrogatories to be answered separately and fully, under oath, by each Defendant, on or before April _____, 2006. The Interrogatories which follow are to be deemed continuing, and you are requested to provide, by way of supplementary answers thereto, such additional information as you or any other person acting on your behalf may hereafter obtain which will augment or modify your answers now given to the Interrogatories below. Such supplementary responses are to be served upon the Plaintiff within thirty (30) days after receipt of such information.

All information is to be divulged which is in Defendants' possession or control, or within the possession and control of Defendants' attorneys, investigators, agents, employees or other representatives of Defendants.

INTERROGATORIES

1.   State the name, address, title, and duties of the person answering these interrogatories and the place where these interrogatories are answered.
     ANSWER:

2.   State the name, address, and job title of each person who was contacted in answering these interrogatories or who provided information relevant to the answering of the interrogatories and the proper designation of each book, document, or record which was searched in answering interrogatories.
     ANSWER:

3.   Are all Defendants' names correctly stated in the Complaint on file in this cause? If not, state the correct name of each party Defendant at the time of the conduct complained of in the Complaint and at the present time.
     ANSWER:

continued

Exhibit 7-16   *continued*

    4.   State the general corporate history of each corporate Defendant from the date of incorporation to the present, including the date and place of incorporation, date first qualified to do business in Illinois and Wisconsin, whether or not you continuously carried on business in Illinois and Wisconsin since that date, and the specific or primary business engaged in by Defendant corporations.
    ANSWER:

    5.   Please state whether each corporation Defendant is a subsidiary, parent corporation or sister corporation to another corporation. If so, give complete details as to the other corporation's state of incorporation, address of its principal place of business in state or registered office, date of incorporation, and the specific or primary business engaged in by that corporation. Additionally, state whether the corporation is qualified to do business in Illinois, and whether it has continuously carried on business in Illinois since the date of qualification.
    ANSWER:

    6.   State the name and address of each person who acted as a director of each corporate Defendant, from the dates of incorporation to the date of these interrogatories. Please specify what period of time each director served.
    ANSWER:

    7.   State the full legal name, address, and job title of the employee of each corporate Defendant who is best qualified to testify as to the type of information relating to each corporate Defendants' insurance and/or adjusting business in Illinois and Wisconsin which is stored in each Defendants' computers, as well as to how easily said information may be retrieved. If you state that no employee in Illinois or Wisconsin is qualified to testify as to said information, please state the full legal name, address, and job title of the person or persons, wherever located, who is or are best qualified to testify as to such information.
    ANSWER:

    8.   Please state the following:
        a. The date each claim referred to in the Complaint herein was filed with Defendants;
        b. The date said claims became due and payable under the terms of said policy;
        c. The date said claims were acknowledged as being due and payable by Defendants;
        d. The date said claim or claims were actually paid;
        e. The inception and expiration dates of said policy purchased by Joan Kashen as referred to in the Complaint.
    ANSWER:

    9.   State the name of each person who participated in the decision to pay or not pay the claims for benefits of Joan Kashen and Ann Kashen, arising out of the accident referred to in the Complaint.
    ANSWER:

continued

Exhibit 7-16 *continued*

10.   State the name, address, and job title at the time of issuance of the policy of the person who issued the policy to Joan Kashen. Also state the name, address, and job title of the person who authorized the insurance.
ANSWER:

11. Please state in detail on what grounds Plaintiff's claim for $25,000.00 was denied.
ANSWER:

12. If Defendants assert that Plaintiff's claim for compensation was not "denied," state in detail why Defendants did not pay Plaintiff's uninsured motorist claim commensurate with his injuries, and also state in detail why Defendants paid the uninsured claims of Joan Kashen and Ann Kashen rather than the Plaintiff's.
ANSWER:

13. If Defendant stated to Barbara Grasso, counsel for Joan Kashen, that D. would pay the Plaintiff $5,000.00 of uninsured motorist coverage and $25,000.00 of liability coverage of Joan Kashen's policy, which statements were untrue, please state in detail why such statements were made.
ANSWER:

14. State whether or not there have been, or are now, lawsuits pending against any and all Defendants herein or any agents of Defendants herein, claiming injury or damage due to breach of contract, breach of fiduciary duty, fraudulent, wanton or intentional misrepresentation, fraud in the inducement, unethical business practices, and any other negligent or wanton conduct involving the settlement of claims by Defendants. If so, for each such lawsuit state:
   a. The date of the filing of each lawsuit.
   b. The court in which such lawsuit was filed.
   c. The action or court number of each such lawsuit.
   d. The name and addresses of all parties, including plaintiff and defendant to each such lawsuit.
   e. The jurisdiction in which each such action was filed.
   f. The jurisdiction in which each such action came or will come to trial if different from answer in (e).
   g. The disposition of each such lawsuit.
   h. The name and address of each person or entity having possession, control, or custody of any and all records relating to such legal action against Defendants involving such a claim or similar claim.
ANSWER:

15. State whether Defendants or any agent of Defendants, employees, independent contractors or other representatives of Defendants had any knowledge whatsoever prior to the occasion made the basis of this suit, of any alleged, reckless, or intentional misrepresentation of the type or similar to the type made the basis of this lawsuit. If so, for each person or entity, state:
   a. The date on which such person or entity first had such knowledge.
   b. The substance and extent of such knowledge.
   c. The name and address of such person or entity.
   d. Whether any notes, correspondence, memorandum, or other documents created or helped to create such knowledge.
   e. Whether any notes, correspondence, memorandum, or other documents which were made by such person or entity reflect or depict such knowledge.
ANSWER:

continued

Exhibit 7-16   *continued*

16. Please attach a copy of each document referred to in the immediate preceding interrogatory.

17. State the name and address of each person or persons known by Defendants to have any knowledge whatsoever of matters pertinent to the occurrence made the basis of Plaintiff's Complaint.
ANSWER:

18. List each and every defense known to Defendants at this time which Defendants presently intend to assert.
ANSWER:

19. State whether or not any representative of Defendants has obtained a statement from any person or persons in connection with this matter which is the subject of Plaintiff's lawsuit, and the automobile accident which gave rise to Plaintiff's claim herein. If the answer is yes, state the following:
a. The name and address of each individual from whom such a statement was taken.
b. The date said statements were taken.
c. The identity of the person or entity who has present possession of said statements.
ANSWER:

20. State whether any communications, notes, correspondence, memorandum, or other documents were ever made by Defendant or any agent of Defendants regarding the alleged misrepresentations made by Defendant, as set forth in Plaintiff's Complaint. If so, please attach a copy of each document or the contents of any such communication referred to in the immediately preceding interrogatory.
ANSWER:

21. State whether any communications, notes, correspondence, memorandum, or other documents of any kind were made by Defendant regarding conversations between Defendant and Joan Kashen and conversations between Defendant and the Plaintiff. If so, please attach a copy of each document or the content of any such communication referred to in the immediately preceding interrogatory.
ANSWER:

22. Please state the substance of the facts and opinions to which each and every expert is expected to testify and set forth a summary of the grounds of each such opinion held by each and every said expert.
ANSWER:

23. Please state the conclusions or opinions of each and every expert witness you have retained, hired, or consulted in the preparation of the above-captioned case.
ANSWER:

continued

Exhibit 7-16 *continued*

24. Please state the names and addresses of each and every expert witness with whom Defendants have consulted in and about the handling and preparation of this case.
ANSWER:

25. Please set for the educational background of each and every expert witness that you expect to testify in the trial of this case with whom you have consulted in the preparation and handling of this case.
ANSWER:

_____

Barbara Grasso
Supreme Court #15624-79
1480 Penn Avenue
Chicago, Illinois
(500) 471-2601

CERTIFICATE OF SERVICE

I hereby certify that a copy of the foregoing has been served upon Defendants by United States mail, first class, postage prepaid, this _____ day of April, 2006.

_____

Barbara Grasso

Barbara Grasso
Grasso & Deitz
1480 Penn Avenue
Chicago, Illinois

ATTORNEY FOR PLAINTIFF

may be answered, or the individual may object to it. A format for preparing answers to written interrogatories is included as Exhibit 7-17. Some attorneys list the interrogatory question as well as the response on the response to written interrogatories.

Objections to Questions

If the individual objects to a question based on any of the allowed privileges, then the responding party must specifically claim each privilege separately. The responding party's attorney and the party must sign any answers in which objections occur. If no objections are raised in the answers, the party responding must sign under oath.

EXHIBIT 7-17   Response to Written Interrogatories

```
 1   Attorney Name and Bar No.
 2   Address
 3   City, State, and Zip Code
 4   Telephone Number
 5
 6   Attorney for Plaintiff
 7
 8                    SUPERIOR COURT OF THE STATE OF UTAH
 9                              COUNTY OF KING
10
11   JANET GOOD,                        )        Case No. CC44444
12                                      )        RESPONSE TO DEFENDANT'S
13              Plaintiff,              )        FIRST SET OF INTERROGATORIES
14        v.                            )        CODE CIV. PROC. § 2030(f)
15                                      )
16   SUSAN SMITH,                       )
17              Defendant.              )
18   _____
19
20   Responding Party:    Plaintiff JANET GOOD
21   Interrogatory Set No. 1
22   Propounding Party:   Defendant SUSAN SMITH
23        Responding party, JANET GOOD, the plaintiff in the above-entitled cause of action, makes
24   the following response to defendant's first set of interrogatories, served on plaintiff on October 1,
25   2006.
26        Response No. 1:   [set forth response here]
27        Response No. 2:   [set forth response here]
28

                                        1
```

continued

REQUESTS FOR ADMISSIONS ✦

A request for admissions is served on a party to the action only. The request asks the opposing party to admit any points that are not in dispute and do not have to be litigated (see Exhibit 7-18 on page 173). The plaintiff may choose to serve a set of requests asking the defendant to admit each and every allegation in the complaint.

For example, the party may be asked to admit that a document is genuine, that relevant facts or opinions are true, or that the law is applied to the facts truthfully.

Requests for admissions may be filed by the plaintiff at least 10 days after the summons has been served on the defendant or the defendant

Exhibit 7-17 *continued*

1	VERIFICATION
2	
3	I, JANET GOOD, am the plaintiff in the above-entitled cause of action. I have read the first
4	set of interrogatories propounded to me by the defendant, SUSAN SMITH, and my response to those
5	interrogatories. I am familiar with the contents of both. Based on my knowledge, the responses to
6	defendant's interrogatories are true.
7	I declare under penalty of perjury under the laws of the state of California that the foregoing
8	responses are true and correct.
9	Dated: [date signed]
10	
11	
12	JANET GOOD, Plaintiff
13	Responding Party

2

has appeared, whichever is first. Each party may submit up to 35 requests to the other party, except for those requests dealing with the genuineness of documents, which are not limited.

DEMAND FOR INSPECTION ✦

Demands for inspection allow parties to examine physical evidence that is within the other party's control. This may include documents or other items. There is no limit to the number of demands that may be served. Parties may examine and copy documents or inspect, photograph, and perform tests on other tangible evidence. Real property may be entered, measured, photographed, or otherwise tested pursuant to a

---

EXHIBIT 7-18   Request for Admissions

1	ATTORNEY NAME AND BAR NUMBER
2	Address of Attorney
3	City, State, and Zip Code
4	Telephone Number: (310) 222-3333
5	Attorney for Defendant
6	
7	
8	SUPERIOR COURT OF THE STATE OF UTAH
9	COUNTY OF KING
10	

```
11  NAME OF PLAINTIFF,              )      CASE NO. XXYYYY
12                                  )      PLAINTIFF'S FIRST
13              Plaintiff,          )      SET OF REQUESTS FOR ADMISSION
14       v.                         )      PURSUANT TO CODE CIV. PROC. § 2033(a–c)
15                                  )
16  NAME OF DEFENDANT,              )
17                                  )
18              Defendant.          )
19  _____
20  REQUESTING PARTY:   Plaintiff NAME OF PLAINTIFF
21  ADMISSION REQUESTS SET NO. 1
22  RESPONDING PARTY:   Defendant NAME OF DEFENDANT
23  TO DEFENDANT [name] AND [name of attorney] HIS ATTORNEY OF RECORD:
24       PLAINTIFF NAME, the plaintiff in the above cause of action, requests that [name], the
25  defendant in the above cause of action, admit the truth of the following matters.
26       1. [List here the first fact requesting defendant to admit. Some attorneys go through each and
27  every allegation in the complaint and list all of them as requests.]
28
```

1

continued

demand for inspection. Responses to a demand for inspection must be served within 20 days of the date of service of the demand. Inspection must be allowed within 30 days of service of the demand.

A sample demand for production/inspection is included as Exhibit 7-19 on page 175.

DEMAND FOR MEDICAL EXAMINATION   ✦

Demands for physical examination are typically made by defendants of personal injury plaintiffs. Only one examination is allowed, and it must be scheduled within 75 miles of the plaintiff's residence. The plaintiff has 30 days to comply with the defendant's demand.

Exhibit 7-18 *continued*

```
 1        2. Second cause of action, or other fact here.
 2        Plaintiff requests that defendant admit the genuineness of the following documents, copies of
 3   which are attached to this Request for Admission:
 4        [list documents here; describe each; attach copy to Requests]
 5        3. Medical report of Dr. Susan Shipman, dated November 1, 2007, indicating the extent of
 6   the personal injuries of Plaintiff, suffered in the incident on which this cause of action is based.
 7        Defendant is required to serve responses to this Request for Admission no later than
 8   _____[date]_____.
 9   Dated: Date Signed
10
11                                              [signature of attorney]
12                                              ATTORNEY FOR PLAINTIFF
13
14
15
16
17
18
19
20
21
22
23
24
25
26
27
28

                                         2
```

In some cases a motion must be filed with the court requesting an examination. This motion is required if either party demands a mental examination or if the plaintiff demands a physical examination of the defendant.

A sample demand by the defendant for physical examination of the plaintiff in a personal injury action is included as Exhibit 7-20 on page 177.

SUBPOENAS

To force a party or witness to appear at a deposition or other proceeding, you may issue a subpoena, which is signed by the judge and orders the person to appear at the designated time and place. Because a subpoena is a court-issued document, a person may be held in contempt of court for failure to appear and may also be required to

---

EXHIBIT 7-19   Demand for Production

1	GREGORY WALTERS, ESQ. State Bar #222333
2	500 West Robertson Boulevard
3	Los Angeles, CA 90000
4	(213) 555-5555
5	
6	Attorney for Plaintiff ROBERT GARRISON
7	
8	SUPERIOR COURT OF THE STATE OF CALIFORNIA
9	FOR THE COUNTY OF LOS ANGELES
10	CENTRAL DISTRICT
11	

12	ROBERT GARRISON,	)	CASE NO. XXXX
13		)	
14	Plaintiff,	)	DEMAND FOR PRODUCTION OF
15	v.	)	DOCUMENTS PROPOUNDED TO
16		)	DEFENDANT ALAN WEISS BY
17	ALAN WEISS,	)	PLAINTIFF ROBERT GARRISON
18	Defendant.	)	[CODE CIV. PROC. § 2031]
19			

20	PROPOUNDING PARTY:	PLAINTIFF ROBERT GARRISON
21	RESPONDING PARTY:	DEFENDANT ALAN WEISS
22	SET NUMBER:	ONE
23	PRODUCTION DATE:	Twenty (20) days from service
24	PRODUCTION TIME:	10:00 A.M.
25	PRODUCTION SITE:	Law Offices of Gregory Walters
26		500 West Robertson Boulevard
27		Los Angeles, CA 90000
28	Demand is hereby made by plaintiff that you produce, pursuant to Code of Civil Procedure,	

1

continued

pay damages. The witness will be paid witness fees and mileage. The subpoena must be served in person and proof of service must be filed with the court. If the individual is required to bring any items with her to the proceeding, the box for "subpoena duces tecum" must be checked on the form. Materials required, which must be listed on the form, may include letters, documents, payroll records, or any other tangible item that may be used as evidence.

Subpoenas are issued to force an individual's appearance at either a deposition or a court proceeding, such as a hearing or a trial. If the individual who is served with the subpoena does not appear at the date and time specified, then she may be held in contempt of court and incarcerated and/or fined.

Exhibit 7-19 *continued*

1	Section 2031, and Rule 1719, on the date and time indicated above, each, every, and all
2	items in your possession, custody, or control included in each of the following categories; you are
3	further requested to produce each of the items identified at the time and place herein specified, and to
4	permit the inspection and copy thereof by the requesting plaintiff and his attorneys.
5	As to the photographs requested, the plaintiff would accept exact duplicates of any and all
6	items referred to below. Pursuant to the California Code of Civil Procedure, plaintiff respectfully
7	requests that the defendant verify such responses.
8	Said items are to be produced on November 22, 2005, at the Law Offices of Gregory Walters,
9	at 500 West Robertson Boulevard, Los Angeles, California 90000.
10	The above-described items are not privileged and are relevant to the action or are reasonably
11	calculated to lead to the discovery of admissible evidence in this action.
12	1. Each employment contract between defendant and his employer relative to liability for
13	negligent acts of defendant during the scope of his employment.
14	2. A statement of repairs and refurbishing for the vehicle defendant was driving at the
15	time of the incident.
16	3. Ownership and registration materials of said vehicle stating the true owner of the
17	vehicle.
18	4. Pictures of the scene of the incident that is the subject of this lawsuit taken both at the
19	time of the incident and thereafter.
20	5. Pictures of the damages to the plaintiff's and defendant's automobiles at the time of
21	the incident.
22	DATED: November 2, 2005
23	
24	
25	
26	GREGORY WALTERS
27	Attorney for Plaintiff
28	

2

STIPULATIONS

Stipulations are agreements that are made between the attorneys but are binding on the parties to the action. A stipulation may be in the form of a written document or may be made in open court. The most common stipulations relate to extending time or amending pleadings.

SETTLEMENT

During the course of the investigation and discovery phase of the lawsuit, both attorneys will be discussing settlement. Most civil cases are settled before the trial date. The attorneys will meet with the judge during a mandatory settlement conference to try to settle the issues in the case shortly before the trial, and many cases do in fact settle at that time.

EXHIBIT 7-20 Demand for Physical Examination

```
1   NAME OF ATTORNEY AND BAR NUMBER
2   Address of Attorney
3   City, State, and Zip Code
4   Telephone Number: (408) 123-4555
5
6   Attorney for Defendant
7
8              SUPERIOR COURT OF THE STATE OF CALIFORNIA
9                      COUNTY OF CONTRA COSTA
10
11  NAME OF PLAINTIFF,              )    CASE NO. XXXXX
12                                  )    DEFENDANT'S DEMAND FOR PHYSICAL
13              Plaintiff,          )    EXAMINATION OF PLAINTIFF JOHN DOE
14                                  )
15      v.                          )    [Code Civ. Proc. § 2032(c)(2)]
16                                  )
17  NAME OF DEFENDANT,              )
18                                  )
19              Defendant.          )
20  _____
21  TO PLAINTIFF JOHN DOE and [name of attorney] his attorney:
22       Defendant  [name] , demands that plaintiff appear on [date at least thirty (30) days after service
23  of demand] at 10 A.M. at Suite 200, 123 Costa Boulevard, Contra Costa, Contra Costa County,
24  California, for a routine physical examination by Jacob Morley, who is a licensed orthopedic
25  specialist.
26       The physical examination of plaintiff, which does not involve any diagnostic test or
27  procedures that are painful, protracted, or intrusive, will be conducted in order to determine the
28
                                    1
```

continued

If the case reaches final settlement, it will be dismissed with prejudice, meaning that the plaintiff may not file a suit in the same action at a later date. If the case is dismissed without prejudice, the plaintiff may file the suit again later within the statute of limitations.

Arbitration

Another way of settling a dispute is to submit the case to arbitration where a disinterested third party (the arbitrator) hears the evidence and issues a decision based on the merits of the case. Both parties must agree to the choice of arbitrator. In some states, arbitrators are retired judges or attorneys. The arbitration proceeding itself is similar to a settlement conference.

Exhibit 7-20 *continued*

1	nature and extent of the injuries claimed by the plaintiff in his complaint. The examination will be
2	conducted as a routine physical examination along with X-rays of the spine, legs, and arms.
3	DATE: June 27, 2006
4	
5	
6	/s/_____
7	Attorney for Defendant
8	
9	
10	
11	
12	
13	
14	
15	
16	
17	
18	
19	
20	
21	
22	
23	
24	
25	
26	
27	
28	

2

If the case is submitted to binding arbitration, the arbitrator's decision is final. If the parties agree only to nonbinding arbitration, however, then either party may appeal the arbitrator's decision to the courts. Although the rules vary among the states, it is unusual to have binding arbitration because our system of government allows all individuals to have their "day in court." If the parties have agreed to mandatory arbitration prior to the institution of the lawsuit, they must try to resolve their dispute through the arbitration process before they will be granted a trial date. If no prior agreement on mandatory arbitration has been reached, the parties may agree to voluntary arbitration. Some states have both private arbitration, which is administered by a private organization, and court arbitration, which is governed by local court rules. Ascertain the rules for your own state and write them in the State Specific Information box.

STATE SPECIFIC INFORMATION

Arbitration procedures in the state of _____ are as follows:

_____

_____

_____

_____

_____

_____

ETHICS and ETIQUETTE

Civil litigation cases generally involve money damages. Attorneys are required to keep the client's money in a separate trust account. In cases involving insurance companies, the usual method of settlement is a check from the insurance company made out to the client and the attorney. The attorney will have the client sign the check, the attorney will deposit the check into her client trust account, and then write a check from the trust account to the client for the client's share of the settlement. Prior to this time, however, the amount of the attorney's fee must be clear to the client.

Some states require that attorneys have written and signed fee arrangements with the client. Be sure that the client and the attorney both sign the written agreement at the beginning of the case. The agreement should set forth the exact fee being charged as well as any additional charges. For instance, some attorneys charge for various administrative fees, such as copies and mailings. In addition to being sure the client signs the agreement, each item should be explained carefully to him. Many complaints against attorneys are made by clients who misunderstood or were not fully aware of the fee arrangement.

Conflict of interest situations most often arise in the civil litigation area. Attorneys may not represent clients on one side of an action and later represent clients on the other side. This representation also holds true for paralegals. In one case, a supervising paralegal in a large litigation case between two large corporations was employed by the attorney for the plaintiff. The defense attorney offered the paralegal a substantially higher salary to work on the defense side of this case. However, the courts did not allow the paralegal to work on that particular case after he had gone to work for the defense firm.

In order to avoid potential conflict of interest situations, many large law firms keep computer databases of their former clients and adverse parties. Imagine the firm with several hundred lawyers in a large city. Without the computer database, it would be virtually impossible to determine all former clients and adverse parties without the use of the computer database system.

If the legal professional changes jobs, it is important to reveal any potential conflict of interest situation to the attorney. If a situation arises after accepting the position, then the attorney should be informed immediately. For instance, suppose a client of your former firm was the plaintiff in a lawsuit against a client of your new firm. You would be precluded from working on this case because of the conflict of interest involved. You would have gained confidential information about the former client that could be valuable to the new client. Thus, a conflict of interest is created. See <u>In Re Complex Asbestos Litigation</u>, 232 Cal. App. 3d 572, 283 Cal. Rptr. 732 (1991), where the plaintiffs' attorney hired a paralegal who had worked for the defense attorney. After a complaint by the attorney for the defendant corporation, the paralegal and attorney were disqualified from working on the case.

CHAPTER SUMMARY ✦

Lawsuits are filed by individuals or entities against other individuals or entities. This chapter has taken the student though a civil lawsuit from the initial interview of the client to the pretrial stage. Most suits involve torts, or civil wrongs, committed by the defendant against the plaintiff. Negligence and products liability are important concepts in torts law.

Paralegals assist the attorney in conducting the preliminary investigation by interviewing the client and witnesses. After these interviews, the attorney determines whether or not a formal lawsuit should be filed. If a lawsuit is filed, a complaint and summons must be filed with the court and served on the defendant. Formal discovery is conducted by both sides, utilizing written interrogatories, depositions, requests for admission, and requests for production. Settlement negotiations with insurance companies are utilized to negotiate a fair settlement for the client without having to go to trial. In some cases, however, the two sides cannot reach an agreement, then the case goes to trial.

✦ KEY TERMS

answer	demurrer
complaint	statute of limitations
cross-complaint	summons

✦ SELF TEST

Match the following terms with their definitions:

____ 1. plaintiff

____ 2. defendant

____ 3. lawsuit

____ 4. complaint

a. first pleading filed in lawsuit

b. litigation

c. individual instituting a lawsuit

d. person or entity being sued

Indicate whether the following statements are true (T) or false (F).

____ 1. The defendant responds to the plaintiff's complaint with a deposition.

____ 2. The deposition may be used for parties and witnesses.

____ 3. During the client interview, legal advice may be given freely by the paralegal or legal administrative assistant.

Fill-in-the-blanks.

1. Written questions sent by one party to the other party in a lawsuit are called _____.

2. If the questions in (1) are sent to the defendant, answers must usually be provided to the plaintiff in _____ days.

3. The lawsuit is commenced by the filing of a _____.

4. The most common response by the defendant is called: _____.

5. If a party wishes the other party to provide documents during the discovery process, the proper document to prepare is the _____.

✦ REVIEW QUESTIONS

1. List the different parts of the complaint.

2. Describe each part of the complaint you listed in Question 1 and explain its purpose.

3. List the various discovery documents and tools available to each party in a lawsuit.

4. Describe each of the discovery documents you listed in Question 3.

5. Which discovery documents may be used for witnesses, and which documents are reserved for parties to the action?

✦ NOTEBOOK PROJECTS

1. Make a caption for a complaint in your state for a personal injury action by John Sanchez against Kevan Farmer for personal injuries of $50,000 arising from an automobile accident.

2. Using the format for your state, prepare a complaint in the following action:

Joseph Goode is suing Daniel Injurer for injuries sustained in an automobile accident on March 2, 2004, at the corner of Broad and Division Streets in your town. Plaintiff was stopped at a red light in his 2004 Lexus LX 400 (license MYLEXS) when defendant failed to stop and his 2003 Ferrari coupe (license HOTCAR) hit the rear of plaintiff's car. The plaintiff requests $25,000 for damages to his car and $32,000 for personal injuries.

3. Prepare Mr. Injurer's answer to the complaint in Project 2 in the form of a general denial.

4. Using the format or forms for your state, prepare a summons and proof of service to accompany the complaint in Project 2.

ESTATE PLANNING

CHAPTER OUTCOMES

As a result of studying this chapter, the student will learn:

- The different types of wills and the terminology used in them
- The methods of preparing a formal will
- The advantages of trusts, and how to prepare an inter vivos trust
- The laws relating to wills and inter vivos trusts

WHAT IS ESTATE PLANNING?

Estate planning involves the discussion and planning, with the client, of how he wishes to have his property distributed upon his death. With large estates, this can be a complicated process involving both estate planning attorneys and tax specialists in order to enable the client to gain the maximum legal benefit from that property. Generally, the more property is involved, the more expertise is required of different types of specialists to maximize the return to the heirs of the property concerned. In addition, an estate planning attorney will manage the probating of the estate when the client dies.

The paralegal or legal assistant working in an estate planning office will have to be knowledgeable about the laws related to wills, trusts, property, probate, insurance, and taxes. She may be required to draft wills and trusts, as well as prepare forms required for probating an estate.

WILLS

People write wills to indicate how they want their property to be distributed after they die. Often people say they do not need a will because they have very little property. However, having a **will** ensures that whatever you have will go to the person you want to have it. Furthermore, if an individual has minor children and wants to specify who will care for them after the parents' deaths, a will is essential. For these reasons, everyone needs a will.

will a document in which a person tells how his property is to be handed out after death.

Some terminology is unique to wills, as well as to the related fields of **probate** and estate planning. Therefore, the appropriate terms are defined as follows:

Administrator Individual appointed by the court to administer an estate when the decedent died without a will or did not name an executor in the will.

Bequest A gift of personal property by will; sometimes used to describe any property given in a will.

Decedent The deceased person.

Devise Gift of real property by will.

Executor An individual named in a will who is responsible for administering the will and distributing the property after the maker of the will dies.

Intestate Dying without a will.

Legacy Gift of personal property or money by will.

Probate The court procedure used to validate a will, appoint a personal representative, and distribute property.

Testate Dying with a will.

Testator The person who makes a will. (Formerly a female was called a testatrix; however, this term has become gender neutral in modern usage.)

TYPES OF WILLS   ✦

Most wills are formal, typed documents; but holographic, or handwritten, wills can also be valid. A few states still recognize nuncupative, or oral wills, in certain circumstances.

Formal Wills

To avoid potential disputes after the testator's death, a will should conform to certain formal standards. A formal will must be typed, and the **testator** must sign it in the presence of at least two witnesses, who also sign at the same time. It is advisable to choose witnesses younger than the testator so that they will be available to "prove up" the will upon the testator's death. In some states, the attorney and the legal secretary may witness the wills, but many states do not allow attorneys to witness the wills of their own clients.

Individuals who have large and/or complicated estates should seek the advice of an attorney in making a will, as should persons who wish to leave their property to nonrelatives. Some states require that all estates acquire the services of an attorney for probate purposes.

probate the court procedure used to validate a will, appoint a personal representative, and distribute property.

testator the person who makes a will.

Holographic Wills

A will created entirely in the handwriting of the testator is called a **holographic will**. It must be signed and dated in the testator's handwriting and does not require witnesses. Proving the validity of a holographic will may be difficult, however, unless someone can testify that the handwriting is indeed the testator's. Consequently, the will may be challenged in a will contest. For this reason, clients should be advised that formal wills are preferable to holographic wills.

Nuncupative Wills

A **nuncupative** will is an oral will. Such wills were originally used in wartime when soldiers dying on the battlefield would give instructions on the disposal of their property. Most states no longer recognize nuncupative wills, although a few still allow them in cases where an individual with very little property gives deathbed instructions on its disposition.

REQUIREMENTS FOR MAKING A WILL   ◆

To make a valid will, one must have testamentary capacity and testamentary intent.

Testamentary Capacity

To make a valid will, the maker must have testamentary capacity, or the mental capacity to understand the meaning of the material in the will. In other words, the testator must be capable of knowing that the document is a will and that it is disposing of his property. The testator must also meet the state's requirement for legal age, which is usually the age of majority. A will is void if the maker lacked testamentary capacity at the time the will was made.

Testamentary Intent

A testator must also have the intent to make a will disposing of her property at the time the will is made. There can be no mistake or undue influence on the testator when the will is made. *Mistake* is defined as an unintentional omission or error. For instance, if the testator does not sign the will in the presence of the witnesses, the will may be considered invalid. *Undue influence* is the taking advantage of the testator's weakness, age, or distress to affect the will. It includes any act that overpowers the intent of another. In cases of mistake and undue influence, testamentary intent is lacking because the will does not truly reflect the testator's intentions.

In some cases, when a testator leaves her property to nonrelatives, the relatives may challenge the validity of the will in a will contest, claiming that the beneficiaries (the persons who inherited the property) used undue influence. A court must then decide whether undue

holographic will handwritten will entirely in the writer's handwriting.

nuncupative will   oral will valid in few states.

influence was indeed exerted on the testator or whether she truly intended to leave her property to the beneficiaries—perhaps because they had been kind to her while her relatives ignored her. Since the testator cannot testify, will contests are difficult to prove and can become very emotional, particularly when large sums or property are involved. Witnesses must be obtained to prove or disprove the will.

The paralegal or legal assistant should attempt to find individuals who knew the testator at the time she was making her will and to whom she might have expressed her intentions. If there are no witnesses, then both parties will testify, and the court will decide the issue based on their credibility.

FORMAT FOR A FORMAL WILL ✦

The general format for the various parts of the will is described below. Formal wills are typed double-spaced. Each paragraph is numbered consecutively, either with words (e.g., FIRST, SECOND, THIRD) or numbers (e.g., 1, 2, 3). Each page must be numbered. Some law offices use numbered paper for wills, but most offices use bond paper. Some firms have special paper with "Last Will and Testament" printed at the top of the page. This paper would be used for the first page of the will, with bond paper used for subsequent pages.

The clauses of a simple formal will are outlined below. A Formal Will sample is included as Exhibit 8-1.

Statement of Intent/Introduction

This clause states the testator's intent to make this will and revokes earlier wills. A sample clause follows:

> I, KARA LOUISE KELSO, residing in the city of Seal Beach, County of Orange, State of California, being of lawful age and sound and disposing mind and memory, do hereby make, publish, and declare this to be my last will and testament. I hereby revoke all prior wills or codicils made by me.

Payment of Debts

All debts of the estate must be paid before the assets are distributed. The first bills paid are those of the testator's last illness, funeral expenses, and estate administration. After the debts are paid, the estate assets are distributed to the heirs. This paragraph is the first of the numbered paragraphs in the will:

> FIRST: I hereby direct that all of my just debts, estate expenses, expenses of last illness, and funeral expenses be paid as soon after my death as is practicable.

Statement of Family Relationships

This paragraph is a relatively simple clause that lists all of the testator's children and the spouse, if living. It should include the names and dates of birth of all children as in the following example:

EXHIBIT 8-1   A Simple Formal Will

LAST WILL AND TESTAMENT

of

JANE MARIE ROBERTSON

I, JANE MARIE ROBERTSON, of 559 Sunset Drive, Cordova, Texas, being of lawful age and of sound and disposing mind and memory and not acting under fraud, duress, menace of the undue influence of any person or thing, do hereby make, publish and declare this instrument to be my Last Will and Testament, and I do hereby revoke all other Wills and Codicils to Wills heretofore made by me as follows:

FIRST: I direct that all my just debts and expenses of last illness and funeral expenses be paid from my estate as soon after my demise as can lawfully and conveniently be done.

SECOND: I declare that at the time of the execution of this Will, I am married to JEFFREY WILLIAM ROBERTSON and have three children as follows:

JONATHAN MICHAEL ROBERTSON, date of birth: June 20, 1995

DANIELLE MARIE ROBERTSON, date of birth: December 19, 1998

JEFFREY MICHAEL ROBERTSON, date of birth: September 2, 2000

THIRD: I nominate and appoint as Executor Of my Last Will and Testament, my husband, JEFFREY WILLIAM ROBERTSON, of Cordova, Texas, to serve without bond. In the event JEFFREY WILLIAM ROBERTSON cannot or will not serve for any reason whatsoever, I then appoint MARC DAVID TIGER, of Memphis, Tennessee, to serve without bond.

FOURTH: I declare that all of my property is community property and from my share thereof, I bequeath all of my property to my husband JEFFREY WILLIAM ROBERTSON. In the event my said husband shall predecease me or shall not be alive at the time of the distribution of my estate, I then direct that my estate be divided equally among my children JONATHAN MICHAEL ROBERTSON, DANIELLE MARIE ROBERTSON, and JEFFREY MICHAEL ROBERTSON, in equal shares.

FIFTH: In the event any of my said children shall predecease me or shall not be alive at the time of the distribution of my estate, I then direct that his or her share shall lapse and shall be distributed in toto to the surviving child or children.

SIXTH: In the event my said husband shall predecease me or shall not be alive at the time of the distribution of my estate, and if any of my children, or all of them, are minors under the law at that time, I hereby appoint MARY ELIZABETH GALWAY, my sister, of Memphis, Tennessee, to serve as their guardian, with full authority to support them from the proceeds of my estate, until they reach the age of majority. If MARY ELIZABETH GALWAY shall be unable or

continued

Exhibit 8-1 *continued*

unwilling to serve, then I appoint my

brother, JAMES ALLEN ROBERTSON, to serve as their guardian, with full authority to support them from the proceeds of my estate, until they reach the age of majority.

SEVENTH: I have intentionally and with full knowledge failed to provide for any other persons living at the time of my demise except as otherwise provided herein. If any person, whether a beneficiary under this Will or not, shall contest this Will or object to any of the provisions hereof, I give to such person so contesting or objecting the sum of One Dollar ($1.00) and no more in lieu of the provisions which I have made herein or which I might have made herein to such person or persons so contesting or objecting.

EIGHTH: I give, devise, and bequeath the rest, residue, and remainder of my estate to my above-named spouse, JEFFREY WILLIAM ROBERTSON. If my said spouse shall predecease me, then I give, devise and bequeath the residue of my estate to my above-named children in equal shares.

IN WITNESS WHEREOF, I have hereunto set my hand this 9th day of June, 2003, at Cordova, Texas.

_____

The foregoing instrument, consisting of two (2) pages, was at this date hereof, by JANE MARIE ROBERTSON signed as and declared to be her Will, in the presence of us who, at her request and in her presence, and in the presence of each other, have subscribed our names as witnesses thereto. Each of us observed the signing of this Will by JANE MARIE ROBERTSON and by each other subscribing witness and knows that each signature is the true signature of the person whose name was signed. Each of us is more than twenty-one (21) years of age and a competent witness and resides at the address set forth after his or her name. We are acquainted with JANE MARIE ROBERTSON. At this time she is over the age of eighteen (18) years, and to the best of our knowledge, she is of sound mind and not acting under duress, menace, fraud, misrepresentation, or undue influence.

_____

_____

Name

_____

_____

Name

SECOND: I declare that I am married to DANIEL KELSO and have three children as follows:
  1. My daughter, MARIE ELIZABETH KELSO, date of birth: September 10, 1990;
  2. My son, MICHAEL WILLIAM KELSO, date of birth: March 1, 1991;
  3. My son, JASON DANIEL KELSO, date of birth: July 9, 1993.
All references to "my spouse" or "my children" shall refer to those individuals above named.

Pretermitted Heir Statute. Each state has a pretermitted heir statute that allows any child not included in this list to receive the amount of the estate that he would have received if there had been no will (this is called "taking against the will"). Pretermitted means "omitted," and these statutes presume that if a child's name is left out of the will, the omission was unintentional and occurred simply because the testator forgot to mention that child. Therefore, if a testator wished to disown a child and leave him no property, the attorney will advise her that the child must still be mentioned in this clause; otherwise the child may take against the will.

Divorce or Dissolution. The attorney should advise a client at the time of a divorce that her will should be changed to avoid leaving the estate to her ex-spouse. Other provisions of the will may also need to be changed.

Appointment of Guardian for Minor Children

This clause nominates the individual or individuals whom you wish to be guardian of your child upon your death. If an individual with children dies, the other parent will likely become their guardian. The will should also appoint an alternate guardian, however, in the event that both parents die at the same time. The testator should discuss the appointment with the prospective guardian before naming that person in the will. The testator may also wish to name a second guardian in case the first is unable or unwilling to serve. Great care should be taken in choosing the guardian, who should be someone with whom the children have a good relationship and who can be trusted to take care of the children with the proceeds from the estate. The following is an example of a clause appointing a guardian:

THIRD: In the event my spouse shall predecease me, or we should die together, then I nominate ALICIA SANCHEZ, of Los Angeles, California, to be guardian of the person and property of my minor children who survive me. If ALICIA SANCHEZ is unable or unwilling to serve, then I appoint MARIA GARCIA, of Whittier, California, as guardian.

Appointment of Executor

The **excutor** is the individual who handles the affairs of the estate, including payment of debts and distribution of assets. Some older wills use the term *executrix* to refer to a female executor. Many married individuals choose their spouse for this position. If the estate is large

executor an individual named in a will who is responsible for administering the provisions of the will and distributing the property after the maker of the will dies.

and/or complicated, however, some attorneys may advise that an accountant, an attorney, an expert in financial or property management, or an organization such as a bank be named as executor. In that case, the executor will charge the estate for services provided. State statutes establish fees for executors; however, an executor who is an heir will often waive the fee.

Clients should discuss their affairs and estate with the executor during their life time. If possible, an inventory of all assets should be made and given to the executor. If not, the executor should be told where all of the important documents are kept.

The executor is in charge of paying the bills of the estate from the estate assets, administering and supervising the probate of the estate (usually through an attorney), and distributing the estate assets. The executor may serve with bond or without bond. Generally, if the testator trusts the executor to handle all of the estate assets, the will would not require that a bond be posted. If a bond is required, its cost will be taken from the estate assets. The following is an example of a clause naming an executor:

FOURTH: I hereby nominate my spouse, DANIEL KELSO, to serve as Executor of my estate, without bond. If my said spouse should predecease me or be unable to serve, then I nominate my sister, KIMBELY FITZGARLD, to serve, without bond.

Distribution of Assets

The most important part of the will is the distribution of assets. This clause may be a general clause, leaving all property to a spouse and, if the spouse does not survive by a specified period (e.g., 180 days), then leaving it to the children in equal shares. It may also list various items, such as family heirlooms, that the testator wishes to go to certain individuals. Usually, attorneys will use several clauses for the distribution of assets, particularly if a number of items are to go to specified individuals. Each item must be listed and described in the will.

If an individual is married, both spouses should discuss the disposal of their property after death before the will is made. Generally, married couples leave the property to each other and to their children equally if one spouse predeceases (dies before) the other. In some states, a surviving spouse automatically inherits the other's property; in other states, the survivor gets a certain percentage of the property. In community property states, the distribution differs depending on whether the property is separate or community property. Separate property includes property obtained before marriage or by personal gift or inheritance after marriage. Community property, in states using this system, is property acquired during marriage that is not a personal gift or inheritance.

The testator will also have to decide whether the children will receive the assets by right of representation (per stirpes) or per capita (see Exhibit 8-2). Under the per stirpes method, if a child predeceases his parents but leaves children, those children will inherit the share of the estate their deceased parent would have received if he had not

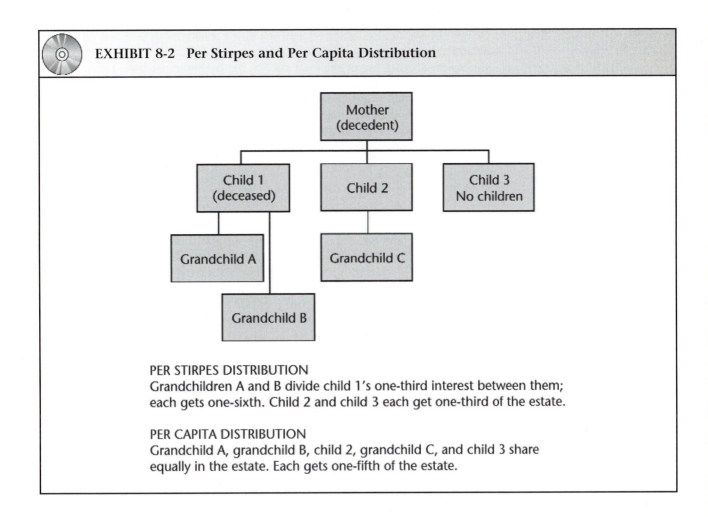

EXHIBIT 8-2   Per Stirpes and Per Capita Distribution

PER STIRPES DISTRIBUTION
Grandchildren A and B divide child 1's one-third interest between them; each gets one-sixth. Child 2 and child 3 each get one-third of the estate.

PER CAPITA DISTRIBUTION
Grandchild A, grandchild B, child 2, grandchild C, and child 3 share equally in the estate. Each gets one-fifth of the estate.

died. To illustrate, suppose the testator had three children (A, B, and C) who have two children each. Child A predeceases the testator. his children will each receive one-sixth of the estate because child A would have received one-third of the estate if he had lived ($\frac{1}{3} \div 2 = \frac{1}{6}$)

Under the per capita method of distribution, each surviving child and grandchild receives an equal percentage of the estate. For instance, if the decedent is survived by one child and three grandchildren, each heir receives one-fourth of the estate.

Sometimes individuals prefer a method that is neither per stirpes nor per capita. For example, a testator who is closer to her grandchildren than to her children might want to leave a larger portion of her estate to the grandchildren, as well as leaving a portion to her great-grandchildren in equal proportions for all. Or perhaps the grandchildren whose parents are deceased are in need of funds, while the testator's other children and grandchildren are well off. In that case, the testator might want to leave a disproportionate share to the poorer grandchildren. Whatever the case, all arrangements must be specified in the will.

Usually, though, the testator will agree to share the estate equally among the children and then among the grandchildren by right of representation, as in the following clause:

FIFTH: I give, **devise**, and bequeath all of my assets, both real and personal and wheresoever situated, to my spouse, DANIEL KELSO. If my spouse should predecease me or shall not survive me by 180 days, then I give all of my assets to my children in equal shares. If any of my children should predecease me, then I give their share of my assets to their children who survive me, by right of representation. If any predeceased child of mine shall have no surviving child or children, then I give, devise, and bequeath their share of my estate to my other children in equal shares.

If a testator has specific assets that she wishes to go to certain individuals, a clause such as the following may be used:

FIFTH: I give, **devise**, and bequeath my ruby and diamond ring and my diamond wedding band to my daughter, MARIE ELIZABETH KELSO. If my said daughter predeceases me or fails to survive me by 180 days, I give these rings to my eldest granddaughter. If no granddaughter survives me, then I give these rings to my son, MICHAEL WILLIAM KELSO.
   I give, devise, and bequeath all of my real property to my husband DANIEL KELSO. If my said husband should predecease me, then I give all of my real property to my children in equal shares.
   I give, devise, and bequeath all of my personal property in equal shares to my said husband and my children.

Joint Tenancy Property. Joint tenancy property is property that is owned by two or more persons, called the joint tenants. If one of the joint tenants dies, his interest in the property automatically passes to the other joint tenant(s). Therefore, any property owned in joint tenancy by the decedent and another person passes outside the will and is not affected by it. For instance, if an estate has more outstanding debts than its assets are worth (called a negative estate), joint tenancy property cannot be sold to pay the decedent's bills. Joint tenancy property passes to the other owner without having to go through the probate process. In some states, however, joint tenancy property must be included in the estate tax return for estate tax purposes.

Converting the joint tenancy property to the other owner is usually a simple matter. In the case of a bank account, most states require a copy of the death certificate and other formal probate papers naming the executor. Some states have forms that must be completed to "break the joint tenancy."

General and Specific Bequests.   General **bequests** are described only in general terms in the will. "All household furnishings" and "all of my property" are examples of general bequests.

In contrast, specific bequests describe specific property. "My 1987 Nissan Sentra" and "my property located at 211 Main Street in Prescott, Arizona," are examples. If the testator does not own that particular property at the time of her death, the gift lapses and the beneficiary gets nothing. For instance, if the testator sells the Nissan Sentra and buys a 1994 Honda Civic after making her will, the beneficiary does not receive the Honda. Specific bequests are the last to be disposed of in the case of a negative estate (an estate with more

devise gift of real property by will.

bequest a gift of personal property by will; sometimes used to describe any property given in a will.

liabilities than assets). Similarly, if estate assets must be sold to pay the decedent's debts, the property is sold in the following order: first, the residuary estate; then, general bequests; and last, specific bequests (the same order is used for a negative estate).

Testamentary Trust

If a trust is set up in the testator's will, it is known as a testamentary trust. The trust sets forth how the property will be distributed and nominates a trustee to manage the trust and distribute its proceeds. Although testamentary trusts were popular in the past, now more and more individuals are establishing formal trusts during their lifetime and putting all of their assets in them. This topic will be discussed more fully in the trusts section later in the chapter. Note that in some states if the deceased leaves minor children, the will must designate a trustee for the children's benefit.

A sample trust clause follows. However, this clause is used only when a separate trust instrument is prepared and made a part of the will.

> SIXTH: I nominate my attorney, LYNDA YAMASHITA, of Laguna Beach, California, as Trustee of the trusts established under this will and request that no bond be required.

The One Dollar Clause

This clause states that if any heirs should contest the will and lose, they will forfeit their inheritance under the will. Attorneys differ as to the importance of including a one-dollar clause in the will. Its purpose is to discourage will contests by disgruntled heirs who have not received as much of the testator's estate as they felt they deserved. Instead of a formal clause, some attorneys merely stipulate in the will that anyone who contests it shall receive nothing under the will. Some attorneys advise the testator to leave one dollar to any disinherited children. Others advise the client merely to mention that a child is being disinherited.

Residuary Clause

After all property has been distributed in the will, a clause must be added to distribute any items left out or acquired after the will is written. Such property is known as the residuary estate. In essence, then, the residuary clause distributes the remaining assets of the testator. In a negative estate, the residuary estate is used first to pay the bills of the estate. The residuary clause is generally included in the last paragraph of the will that disposes of property. The following is an example of a residuary clause:

> I give, devise, and bequeath the rest, residue, and remainder of my estate to my above-named children in equal shares.

Signature Clause

After all the assets have been distributed, the signatures of the testator and the witnesses are required. Some states require two witnesses, while others require three. You should always check the rules for your own state before preparing a will.

The signature clause should be on a page that contains at least two lines of the body of the will; the clause should not be on a separate page. The purpose of this requirement is to ensure that no one can substitute a new will later and merely attach the testator's signature page to it. Having the testator initial each page of the will at the bottom is another safeguard. Some attorneys also require that the last word on the page of the will be a hyphenated word. The following is an example of a signature clause:

IN WITNESS WHEREOF, I have hereunto subscribed my name this 1st day of July, 1994, at Seal Beach, California.

_____
KARA LOUISE KELSO

Witness Clause

Witnesses sign at the same time as the testator and state that they were present when the testator signed and that they knew the testator. Part of the witness (attestation) clause should be included on the same page as the testator's signature. It is advisable for the testator and the witnesses to sign the will on the same page. The witness clause may be single-spaced, although the rest of the will is double-spaced. Some states may require that the attestation clause include a statement by the testator that she is of legal age and is the maker of the will. The following is an example of a witness clause:

The foregoing document, consisting of four pages including this page, was on this date signed by KARA LOUISE KELSO and declared to be her will. We are familiar with the testator and know her to be the individual who signed in our presence and in the presence of each of us. We observed the signing of the will by KARA LOUISE KELSO and by each other witness. Each signature is the signature of the person whose name is signed.

Each of us is now more than eighteen (18) years old, is a competent witness, and resides at the address signed after her name. We are acquainted with the testator and know she is over the age of eighteen. To our knowledge, she is of sound mind and not acting uder duress, menace, fraud, or the undue influence of any person.

_____ Address: _____
_____

_____ Address: _____
_____

_____ Address: _____
_____

STORING THE WILL ✦

Once the will has been signed, the original must be kept in a safe place. Some lawyers choose to keep all clients' original wills in their offices. However, many years may pass between the preparation of the will and the death of the client. Therefore, some lawyers give the original will to their clients with instructions to keep it in a safe place. If the will is burned, torn, or changed or altered in any way, it may be considered void. Some lawyers advise their clients to keep their wills in a fireproof file cabinet. Someone whom the testator trusts should be made aware of the location of the will. It may not be appropriate to put the will in a safe deposit box because some states seal these boxes upon the individual's death.

CODICILS ✦

A codicil is a change made to a will after it has been signed. The codicil must be prepared with the same formality as the will itself. In many states, if the will is typed as a formal will, then the codicil must be typed formally as well. Therefore, be sure to prepare the codicil in the same manner as the will. If the will is holographic, the codicil should also be holographic.

Sometimes a testator may attempt to make several changes to the will by way of a codicil. In that event, the codicil may become so cumbersome and difficult to read that it may be advisable to rewrite the will itself. Whenever a codicil is prepared, be sure to read it over to be certain it is understandable. If you cannot understand the changes, then the probate court may not understand the changes at the time of death. In that case, a new will that reflects the changes should be prepared.

TRUSTS ✦

Most states have not enacted statutes related to trusts and use the common law for the primary source of law on trusts. Therefore, in most cases the laws related to trusts in your own states will be found in the court decisions. For this reason, the law of trusts may be complicated and may vary from state to state. Complete the form below for your own state.

STATE SPECIFIC INFORMATION

The state of _____ has/does not have a Trust Code. It is found at
_____.

As in the case of wills discussed earlier, special terminology is required when you are preparing trusts for a client. Some of the more common terms are defined below:

1. **Settlor or Trustor** The person who creates the trust instrument
2. **Beneficiary** The person who receives the benefit of trust property
3. **Trustee** The holder of legal title to the trust for the benefit of the beneficiary
4. **Trust corpus** All property held in the trust
5. **Legal title** Complete ownership
6. **Equitable title** The right of the beneficiary to have legal title of the trust corpus transferred to him

The trust instrument itself is a written document that creates the trust, whereby property is transferred from the settler of the trust to another (trustee) who holds the legal title to the trust property. The trustee must hold the property for the benefit of the beneficiary or beneficiaries, who hold equitable title as defined in the list above. For example, John may place all of his property in a trust instrument. He may also be the trustee of the trust and hold the property for the benefit of his children, who will obtain the property upon his death. The settlor may make up other conditions for the transfer of the property to the beneficiaries and may also appoint another person as the trustee. For instance, he may wish to have his friend and attorney, Michael, be the trustee who holds the property after John's death until his daughter reaches the age of 25 (or whatever age is specified in the trust instrument). In preparing the trust instrument, the settlor (also called a trustor) has options available to distribute the property at a time of his choosing.

Beneficiaries of the trust may receive income from the trust, the trust property, or both. For instance, one item of property in the trust may be an avocado ranch. The settlor may specify that the income from the ranch is to be received by his daughter and the ranch itself is to be transferred to his son upon the settlor's death.

Trustees owe a fiduciary duty to the beneficiaries of the trust to preserve the trust assets and to perform their duties in good faith. For example, if the terms of the trust require that the trustee must invest the income from the trust for the benefit of the beneficiaries, the trustee must use prudence and good judgment in investing in a stock portfolio that maximizes the income for the beneficiaries.

Trusts may be created for any legal purpose. In general, they are part of an estate plan whose function is to maximize the benefits of one's property for the beneficiaries upon his death. If the maker (grantor) of the trust wishes to have control of the trust assets during his lifetime, then an inter vivos trust is established. All of the grantor's property is put into the trust, and he may serve as trustee for the beneficiaries. This enables him to have the use of the property during his lifetime and have it pass to the beneficiaries at his death. If the trust is revocable, the grantor retains control and can revoke it; if it is irrevocable, he cannot. If the trust is irrevocable, the grantor relinquishes not only the control of the assets but also the right to receive income from them as well. If the trust is revocable, then the maker retains ownership and control of the assets during his lifetime.

In some cases, the grantor will be concerned about a beneficiary's ability to handle money. In this case, he may create a spendthrift trust, which provides the beneficiary with a regular income but prevents her from controlling the trust property. Various other provisions may be made, such as:

1. Providing funds for the support of family members
2. Tax savings
3. Providing specific funding for education, such as college for children or grandchildren
4. Avoidance of probate
5. Regular income for family members
6. Lump sum payments for specific purposes or on the occurrence of an event, such as a child getting married or reaching a certain age

Trust Fundamentals

Three different individuals or entities are required for the preparation of a trust instrument. The trust is created by the settlor or grantor, who initially has legal title to all of the trust property. The trustee is appointed by the grantor and holds the trust assets for the benefit of the beneficiaries, who receive equitable title. Thus, once the trust is created, legal title to the property passes from the grantor to the trustee, while equitable title remains with the beneficiaries. Although the grantor and the trustee may be the same person, the law requires that at least two different individuals hold the three positions of grantor, trustee, and beneficiary. A grantor may also be the trustee but may not also be the beneficiary. A grantor may be a beneficiary if another person is the trustee.

When the settlor initially creates the trust, he must specify in the trust instrument that the trustee is given certain active duties, such as managing the property. If the trust is created with the trustee's only duty being to hold the property, then it will not be declared a valid trust instrument. The trustee must have specific active duties for the trust to be valid.

Beneficiaries

Valid beneficiaries must be specifically named in the trust, either with their names, designations, or descriptions. For instance, a grantor may wish to establish a trust for the benefit of any of her children that are alive at the time of the settlor's death. Perhaps at the time the trust is created, the settlor has two children but two more children are born before the settlor's death. In that case, all four children would become beneficiaries if the trust was written to include "all children living at the time of X's death," X being the settlor. Most states require that if minors are beneficiaries under the trust, a guardian must be appointed to act for them.

Trust Property

Any ownership interest in property may be transferred by the settlor into the trust instrument. This includes real estate, personal property, money, business interests, shares of stock, or bank accounts.

Inter Vivos and Testamentary Trusts

Both of these trusts are expressly created for estate planning purposes. The difference is that the inter vivos trust is created during the settlor's lifetime, whereas the testamentary trust is created after the settlor's death. The testamentary trust is generally a part of the last will and testament of the settlor, or it is set up as a separate instrument to take effect upon the settlor's death.

Totten Trusts

Bank accounts may be set up by an individual, whereby the funds are held in trust for the benefit of the beneficiary upon the owner's death. The trust may be created by parents who hold the funds in trust for their children, or by any other person who wishes to hold funds in trust for another. Upon the owner's death, the beneficiaries may remove the funds from the account. Most banks require a certified copy of the death certificate for the funds to be transferred. In most states, the funds may be used by the owner until her death, and if there are no funds in the account at the time of death, then the trust is revoked.

Trust Clauses

Most trusts are very complicated and should be prepared by an attorney who specializes in this area. In some cases, an attorney may advise a client that a will would be sufficient for her estate plan and that a trust is not required. Various tax consequences must be considered before the drafting of a trust agreement.

A sample of a simple trust agreement is included as Exhibit 8-3.

CHAPTER SUMMARY   ✦

Individuals make wills to indicate how they want their property distributed upon their death. Generally, a formal will that adheres to all the requirements set by state statutes is preferable to a holographic (handwritten) will. Wills usually include a number of standard clauses

EXHIBIT 8-3 A Revocable Inter Vivos Trust

Courtesy: Reprinted from Hower, Wills, Trust, and Estate Administration for the Paralegal 5E, Thomson Delmar Learning

William T. Brown Trust Agreement

This trust agreement is made on _____, 20 _____, between William T. Brown of _____ County, State of _____, hereinafter called the "settlor," and William T. Brown of _____ County, State of _____, Charles T. Brown of _____ County, State of _____, and Sarah J. Brown of _____ County, State of _____, hereinafter collectively called the "trustees."

Recitals

I have transferred certain property to the trustees contemporaneously with signing this trust agreement, the receipt of which they acknowledge and which is described on Exhibit "A" attached hereto; and the parties to this agreement acknowledge that all property transferred or devised to the trust now or in the future is to be administered and distributed according to the terms of this trust agreement.

Article I

Reservation of Rights

During my life I reserve the following rights, to be exercised without the consent or participation of any other person:

1. To amend, in whole or in part, or to revoke this agreement by a written declaration.

2. To add any other real or personal property to the trust by transferring such property to the trustees, and to add any other property by my will. The trustees shall administer and distribute such property as though it had been a part of the original trust property.

3. To make payable to the trustees death benefits from insurance on my life, annuities, retirement plans, or other sources. If I do so, I reserve all incidents of ownership, and I shall have the duties of safekeeping all documents, of giving any necessary notices, of obtaining proper beneficiary designations, of paying premiums, contributions, assessments or other charges, and of maintaining any litigation.

4. To receive annual written accounts from all trustees (or the personal representative of any deceased trustee). My approval of these accounts by writings delivered to another trustee shall cover all transactions disclosed in these accounts and shall be binding and conclusive as to all persons.

5. To direct the trustees as to the retention, acquisition, or disposition of any trust assets by a writing delivered to the trustees. Any assets retained or acquired pursuant to such directions shall be retained as a part of the trust assets unless I otherwise direct in writing. The trustees shall not be liable to anyone for any loss resulting from any action taken in accordance with any such direction of mine.

6. To examine at all reasonable times the books and records of the trustees insofar as they relate to the trust.

continued

Exhibit 8-3   *continued*

Article II
Disposition of Trust Assets

Unless I am disabled, the trustees, after paying the proper charges and expenses of the trust, shall pay to me during my lifetime the entire net income from the trust property in monthly installments, and the trustees shall also pay to me and any other person who is a financial dependent of mine, in accordance with my written instructions, such portions of the principal of the trust property as I direct. If I become disabled by reason of illness, accident, or other emergency, or I am adjudicated incompetent, the trustees, other than myself, are authorized and directed to pay to me or for my benefit such portions of the trust income or principal as the trustees deem necessary to provide for my care, comfort, support, and maintenance.

On my death, the trustees, if requested by the personal representative of my estate shall, or in their own discretion may, directly or through the personal representative of my estate, pay the expenses of my last illness and funeral, my valid debts, the expenses of administering my estate, including nonprobate assets; and pay all estate, inheritance, generation-skipping, or other death taxes that become due because of my death, including any interest and penalties.

Also, on my death, I give all my tangible personal property to Charles T. Brown, my son, if he survives me, or if he does not survive me, to Sarah J. Brown, my daughter. (I request the recipient of any such tangible personal property to distribute the same as I may have indicated informally by memorandum or otherwise.) The trustees shall distribute all the trust property not effectively disposed of by the preceding provisions of this agreement in equal shares to the persons named below. If any person named below does not survive me, such person's share shall be distributed per stirpes to such person's descendants who survive me.

Charles T. Brown, my son
Sarah J. Brown, my daughter

Article III
Selection of Trustees

Trustees shall be appointed, removed, and replaced as follows: unless I am disabled, I reserve the right and power to remove any trustee and to appoint successor or additional trustees. If I become disabled, I shall cease to be a trustee. On my death or disability, my son, Charles T. Brown, may at any time appoint an individual or corporate trustee and may remove any individual or corporate trustee so appointed.

Article IV
Trustee Powers and Provisions

The powers granted to my trustees may be exercised during the term of this trust and after the termination of the trust as is reasonably necessary to distribute the trust assets. All of the

continued

Exhibit 8-3   *continued*

powers are to be discharged without the authorization or approval of any court. I hereby give to my trustees the following powers: (specific administrative powers are listed).

Among the administrative provisions of this trust, I request no bond or other indemnity shall be required of any trustee nominated or appointed in this trust. I expressly waive any requirement that this trust be submitted to the jurisdiction of any court, or that the trustees be appointed or confirmed, that their actions be authorized, or that their accounts be allowed, by any court. this waiver shall not prevent any trustee or beneficiary from requesting any of these procedures.

(General governing provisions may also be added).

The settlor and the trustees have signed this agreement in duplicate on or as of the date appearing at the beginning of this agreement and the trustees accept their appointments as trustees by signing this agreement

Note: Signatures and notary have been omitted.

ETHICS and ETIQUETTE

Estate planning practices generally involve clients who are making wills or trusts. The attorney prepares the will or trust based on the client's instructions. All information given to the attorney by the client is privileged.

Attorneys are not allowed to become beneficiaries under the client's will unless they are a relative of the client. This prevents the appearance of undue influence or coercion on the part of the attorney. If the client wishes to give the attorney (or other law office staff) a substantial gift under the will, the attorney must refer the client to another independent attorney who will counsel the client as to the proper procedure. In that case, the other attorney will discuss the gift with the client and draft the will.

Ethical rules allow attorneys and their staff to accept small gifts from clients, such as flowers or a box of candy at Christmas or for a birthday. However, substantial bequests in a will or large gifts outside the will are not allowed.

Separate accounts are particularly critical in the estate planning practice. Commingling of the funds of the attorney and the client is never allowed. If the attorney administers a trust account for the client, that trust account must be completely separate from the attorney's account. In some cases, an estate planning attorney may administer several different trust accounts for several different clients. Careful accounting practices must be utilized to assure that no questionable activities take place involving the trust.

such as the following: statement of intent, payment of debts, statement of family relationships, appointment of executor, distribution of assets, signature, and witnesses. Some property may pass outside the will, such as property held in joint tenancy or in trust.

Trusts may be established to avoid probate. Several different types of trusts are available, and one must discuss the situation carefully with the client to determine which trust is most beneficial in any given circumstances. Inter vivos (revocable living) trusts are among the most common trusts established today.

Wills must be probated upon the death of the maker. The executor administers the estate and sees to it that the testator's wishes are carried out. If the decedent died intestate (without a will), the court will appoint an administrator to administer the estate. After the formal process, the property is distributed to the heirs.

✦ KEY TERMS

bequest	nuncupative will
decedent	probate
devise	testator
executor	will
holographic will	

✦ SELF TEST

Indicate whether the following statements are true (T) or false (F).

_____ 1. A person who dies with a will dies intestate.

_____ 2. A devise is a gift of real property by will.

_____ 3. The executor is responsible for handling the decedent's affairs.

_____ 4. A gift of "all of my property" is a specific bequest.

_____ 5. A gift of "my house at 211 Main Street" is a specific bequest.

Circle the correct answer for the following questions:

1. Negative estates have
   a. no specific assets.
   b. no residuary estate.
   c. very few assets.
   d. more outstanding debts than property.

2. The residuary estate is
   a. what is left after all other property is disposed of.
   b. property purchased after the will was made and not mentioned in the will itself.
   c. both (a) and (b).
   d. none of the above.

3. To have testamentary capacity, an individual must
   a. be capable of knowing that the document is a will.
   b. know that property is being disposed of in the will.
   c. be of legal age to make a will.
   d. have the mental capacity to understand the meaning of a will.
   e. all of the above.

4. Holographic wills
   a. are typed but not witnessed.
   b. are written in the handwriting of the testator.
   c. are typed and witnessed.
   d. none of the above.

5. Nuncupative wills are
   a. formal wills.
   b. handwritten wills.
   c. witnessed wills.
   d. oral wills.

Fill-in-the-blanks.

1. The most common and the most advantageous will is a _____ will.

2. A child who is left out of the will may take against the will under the _____ _____ statute.

3. A change to a will made after the will has been signed is a _____.

4. When the terms of the grandparent's will specify that a child inherits his parent's share if the parent predeceases him, the _____ method of distribution is being used.

5. Formal wills require _____ witnesses.

✦ REVIEW QUESTIONS

1. Define the following terms: will, testate, intestate, executor, administrator, holographic will, inter vivos trust, beneficiary, codicil, and decedent.

2. How would you prepare for the signing of a will? Who should be there?

3. Discuss the advantages and disadvantages of each of the following:
   a. Formal will
   b. Holographic will
   c. Inter vivos trust

✦ NOTEBOOK PROJECTS

1. Using the sample clauses and will format in the chapter as models, prepare your own will or prepare a will for Maria Garcia using the following facts:

   Maria Garcia is unmarried and has three children: a daughter, Elsa Mary Garcia, born October 22, 2000; a daughter Joan Alicia Garcia, born May 5, 2002; and a son, Michael Alonzo Garcia, born June 27, 2003. Her property consists of a home in your town, your state; two diamond rings; and a 2000 Cadillac Eldorado. She wishes to have her property distributed evenly among the children, but she wants one diamond ring to go to each daughter. Her residuary estate goes to her son. Her executor is her brother, Philip Michael Garcia of your town, your state; alternate executor is her other brother, William Michael Garcia, of Phoenix, Arizona. The guardian of any minor children and their estate will be her sister, Anna Maria Garcia, who lives in your town, your state. Witnesses to the will are the paralegal and the legal assistant in your office.

2. How would you prepare for the signing of the will described above? Who should be there?

3. Assume Maria Garcia (see Project above) would like your office to prepare an inter vivos trust. Using the sample as a guide, prepare the document for her.

4. Research the law related to intestate succession in your state. In what order are the assets distributed if Maria Garcia were to die without a will?

PROBATE

CHAPTER OUTCOMES ◆

As a result of studying this chapter, the student will learn:

- The laws that relate to the probate of an estate
- How to prepare all documents required for a probate

INTRODUCTION ◆

The procedure for proving the validity of a will and distributing the assets of the estate is called **probate**. If an individual dies without a will (intestate), then the probate process determines the legal heirs of the decedent. The first step in the probate process is an interview with the executor of the estate; if there is no will, then the court will appoint an administrator to take care of the distribution.

Procedures vary considerably from state to state. Therefore, discussion here will center on the procedures for California. Be sure to review your own state's Probate Code or a state-specific text on this topic.

INITIAL INTERVIEW ◆

Many individuals appoint a close relative, such as a spouse, parent, brother, or sister, as **executor** of their estate. Therefore, the initial interview may be difficult for one who has just lost a loved one. The paralegal should be sympathetic and understanding but at the same time efficient and professional. A considerable amount of information must be elicited at this interview in order to begin the process of probating the estate. A probate checklist is included as Exhibit 9-1.

The paralegal must determine whether the decedent died with a will and if the executor can provide the original signed will to the law office. Several certified copies of the death certificate must also be obtained. A list of items that are not part of the probate estate must be acquired.

NONPROBATE PROPERTY—JOINT TENANCY ◆

Some property passes outside of the will and is not part of the probate estate. If the decedent owned property with another individual as a

probate the court procedure used to validate a will, appoint a personal representative, and distribute property.

executor an individual named in the will who is responsible for handling the decedent's affairs, including paying bills of the estate and distributing the property.

205

EXHIBIT 9-1 Probate Checklist

PROBATE PROCEDURES

NAME OF DECEDENT:

_____

EXECUTOR OR
ADMINISTRATOR:

_____

DATE OF DEATH: _____

List of Heirs:

1. Certified copy of death certificate   _____

2. List of assets and value at date of death   _____

3. List assets passing outside of will
   Community property _____
   Joint tenancy _____
   Insurance policies _____
   Trusts _____

4. Probate Petition   Prepared _____   Hearing: _____

5. Publication   Newspaper? _____   Date: _____

6. Appointment of executor or administrator? _____

7. Letters? _____

8. Creditors' notices? _____   Dates published? _____

9. Creditors' claims filed? _____
   Name of Creditor: *Claim Amount:*   *Accepted?*

10. Inventory and appraisal filed?
    Fee to appraiser: _____

11. Is federal estate tax due? ($600,000 value of estate?)

12. Does property have to be sold?
    a. Notice of proposed action to heirs?
    b. Hearing required?

13. Have all creditors' claims been satisfied and all property disposed of?

14. Final accounting and distribution _____   Hearing? _____

15. Final distribution of:
    a. Attorney fees
    b. Executor fees
    c. Property to heirs

16. Closed file on: _____

joint tenant, the joint tenancy property passes outright to the surviving joint tenant(s). However, various documents must be prepared depending on the type of property involved.

Joint Tenancy Bank Accounts

Banks and savings and loan institutions require a certified copy of the death certificate, along with the passbook for the bank account, in order to transfer a savings account to the surviving joint tenant. In the case of a checking account, the surviving joint tenant should write a check drawn against the balance in the account in addition to providing the death certificate.

Motor Vehicles Held in Joint Tenancy

Automobile or boat registrations to "John Adams or Sara Adams" or to "John Adams and Sara Adams as joint tenants" represent joint tenancy ownership. This wording should appear on the Ownership Certificate (pink slip). Transfer of ownership to the surviving joint tenant may be accomplished at the Department of Motor Vehicles or the local auto club. The following items are required:

1. Copy of the death certificate
2. Pink slip signed by surviving joint tenant
3. Vehicle's registration
4. A compliance certificate for smog is required if the surviving joint tenant is not the spouse or child.

Joint Tenancy Real Property

Real property includes land, buildings, and items permanently attached thereto. The first step in the transfer of title is preparation of an "Affidavit—Death of Joint Tenant" shown in Exhibit 9-2 on page 209.

A certified copy of the death certificate must be attached to the completed affidavit. A preliminary change of ownership report must accompany the recording of the affidavit.

Most of the information that must be included on the affidavit may be obtained from the original deed to the property. The surviving joint tenant should sign the deed in the presence of a notary public. Instructions for preparation of the affidavit are as follows:

TOP LEFT CORNER

Name and address of surviving joint tenant

    COUNTY OF: = insert name of county where signed

    _____, of legal age = insert name of person signing
                                       affidavit

continued

Affidavit *continued*

That _____	= insert name of decedent
"is the same person as ..."	= insert name of decedent as it appears on the joint tenancy deed
"in that certain"	= insert "deed"
"dated"	= insert date of deed
"executed by"	= insert names of persons who signed original joint tenancy deed
"to"	= insert names of persons owning property as joint tenants as shown on deed
Recording information	= obtain this from the joint tenancy deed
Large blank area	= insert legal description included as shown on deed

Be sure to have the joint tenant who is signing the affidavit sign it in front of a notary public.

Once the affidavit has been completed and signed, it must be recorded in the county recorder's office in the county in which the real property is located. The paralegal should prepare a letter to the county recorder requesting that the affidavit be recorded and returned to the address on the affidavit. A recording fee must accompany the letter. After the affidavit has been recorded, title to the property is in the name of the surviving joint tenant(s).

Arizona requires an affidavit to terminate a joint tenancy. The surviving joint tenant is required to sign this affidavit before a notary public. A sample form from Arizona is included herein as Exhibit 9-3.

Stocks and Bonds

Procedures for the transfer of stocks and bonds held in joint tenancy are relatively simple. If the decedent was the last surviving joint tenant, however, the stocks/bonds are a part of the estate that must be probated.

The first item required for the transfer is the original stock certificate. This may be in the decedent's safe deposit box, with his attorney or financial advisor, or in a place where he kept important papers. A certified copy of the death certificate is also required. (*Note:* Whenever a transfer of property occurs, a certified copy of the death certificate is needed.)

EXHIBIT 9-2 Affidavit—Death of Joint Tenant

RECORDING REQUESTED BY

AND WHEN RECORDED MAIL TO

Name

Street
Address

City &
State

——— SPACE ABOVE THIS LINE FOR RECORDER'S USE———

Affidavit — Death of Joint Tenant

A.P.N._____

STATE OF CALIFORNIA,   }
                                         } ss.
COUNTY OF_____   }

_____ , of legal age, being first duly sworn, deposes and says:

That_____ , the decedent mentioned in the attached certified copy of

Certificate of Death, is the same person as_____

named as one of the parties in that certain_____ dated_____ ,

executed by_____

to_____ ,

as joint tenants, recorded as Instrument No._____ , on_____ , in

Book/Reel_____ , Page/Image_____ , of Official Records of_____

County, California, covering the following described property situated in the_____

_____ , County of_____ , State of California:

That the value of all real and personal property owned by said decedent at date of death, including the full value of
the property above described, did not then exceed the sum of $_____ .

Dated_____   _____

SUBSCRIBED AND SWORN TO before me   _____

this_____ day of_____

Signature_____

(This area for official notarial seal)

Title Order No._____ Escrow or Loan No._____

EXHIBIT 9-3   Affidavit Evidencing Termination of Joint Tenancy

AFFIDAVIT EVIDENCING TERMINATION OF JOINT TENANCY

STATE OF ARIZONA   )
) ss
COUNTY OF _____)

The undersigned, being first duly sworn, says:

I am the surviving joint tenant of _____, who died on

_____.

At the time of death, decedent was the owner in joint tenancy with me of the following described real property:

The status of joint tenancy was created by Joint Tenancy Deed recorded on _____, in the Recorder's Office of _____ County, Arizona, at Book _____ at Pages_____.

This Affidavit is made from my own knowledge, and I will testify positively to the truth of the same in any court whenever called upon for that purpose.

A certified copy of the Certificate of Death of decedent, together with an Estate Tax Waiver from the Arizona Department of Revenue affecting said property, is attached hereto.

_____   _____

Date   Affiant's Signature

                                                  _____

                                                  Affiant's Printed Name

SUBSCRIBED AND SWORN TO before me on _____.
My Commission Expires: _____

_____

                                                  Notary Public

The surviving joint tenant must sign and complete a form transferring ownership. These forms may be obtained from a stationery store that sells legal forms, or, in some instances, from a bank or broker. The form is called an "Irrevocable Stock or Bond Power" or "Stock or Bond Assignment." Exhibit 9-4 is a sample form. The signature of the surviving joint tenant must be guaranteed by a bank officer or stockbroker handling the transaction.

Some transfer agents also require an affidavit of residence indicating that the decedent was a resident of the state. This form must be signed before a notary public by the surviving joint tenant.

Once all these materials have been prepared, they should be sent to the transfer agent with an accompanying letter. The name(s) of the new owner(s) of the stock must be indicated, along with their Social Security numbers and addresses.

LIVING TRUSTS

One method of avoiding probate is the preparation of a living trust. Typically, an individual prepares a trust with himself as trustee and a spouse as beneficiary. All items owned should be transferred into the name of the trust. If this is done, the paralegal must examine all documents of ownership to be certain each has been transferred into the name of the trust. Often a trustee forgets to transfer one or two items of property to the trust. These forgotten items must go through the probate process.

The transfer of most trust property to the beneficiaries is relatively simple. A copy of the trust instrument and certified copy of the death certificate are required. If real property is held in the trust, the successor trustee must execute a grant deed to the beneficiaries of the trust.

INSURANCE POLICIES

Life insurance policies pass to the beneficiary without having to go through the probate process. The insurance carrier will require a certified copy of the death certificate.

COMMUNITY PROPERTY

If your state is a community property state, any of the property held by a husband and wife as community property may pass to the surviving spouse without a formal probate. However, you should first determine whether your state is a community property state prior to following these procedures.

STATE SPECIFIC INFORMATION

The state of _____ *is/is not* a community property state.

EXHIBIT 9-4   Ex Parte Petition for Authority to Sell Securities and Order

Courtesy: Reprinted from *West's California Judicial Council Forms 2003*, with permission of West, a Thomson business. For more information about this publication please visit **http://west.thomson.com.**

DE-270, GC-070

ATTORNEY OR PARTY WITHOUT ATTORNEY *(Name, state bar number, and address):*	TELEPHONE AND FAX NOS:	FOR COURT USE ONLY

ATTORNEY FOR *(Named)*:

SUPERIOR COURT OF CALIFORNIA, COUNTY OF
STREET ADDRESS:
MAILING ADDRESS:
CITY AND ZIP CODE:
BRANCH NAME:

ESTATE OF (Name):

☐ DECEDENT ☐ CONSERVATEE ☐ MINOR

**EX PARTE PETITION FOR AUTHORITY TO SELL
SECURITIES AND ORDER**

CASE NUMBER:

1. **Petitioner** (name of each; see footnote[1] before completing):

   is the ☐ personal representative ☐ conservator ☐ guardian of the estate and requests a court order authorizing sale of estate securities.

2. a. The estate's securities described on the reverse should be sold for cash at the market price at the time of sale on an established stock or bond exchange, or, if unlisted, the sale will be made for not less than the minimum price stated on the reverse.
   b. ☐ Authority is given in decedent's will to sell property; or
   c. ☐ The sale is necessary to raise cash to pay
      (1) ☐ debts
      (2) ☐ legacies
      (3) ☐ family allowance
      (4) ☐ expenses
      (5) ☐ support of ward
      (6) ☐ other *(specify)*:

   d. ☐ The sale is for the advantage, benefit, and best interests of the estate, and those interested in the estate.
   e. Other facts pertinent to this petition are as follows:
      (1) ☐ Special notice has not been requested.
      (2) ☐ Waivers of all special notices are presented with this petition.
      (3) ☐ No security to be sold is specifically bequeathed.
      (4) ☐ Other *(specify)*:

Date:

*(Signature of all petitioners also required (Prob. Code. § 1020).)   ► _____
                                                                         (SIGNATURE OF ATTORNEY*)

I declare under penalty of perjury under the laws of the State of California that the foregoing is true and correct.

Date:

....   ► _____
(TYPE OR PRINT NAME)   (SIGNATURE OF PETITIONER)

....   ► _____
(TYPE OR PRINT NAME)   (SIGNATURE OF PETITIONER)

[1] Each personal representative, guardian, or conservator must sign the petition.

(Continued on reverse)

Form Approved by the Judicial Council of California	**EX PARTE PETITION FOR AUTHORITY TO SELL SECURITIES AND ORDER**	Probate Code, §§ 9630, 10000, 10200, 10201, 10252, 10261

continued

Exhibit 9-4 *continued*

ESTATE OF *(Name):*		CASE NUMBER:

LIST OF SECURITIES

Number of shares or face value of bonds	Name of security	Name of exchange (when required by local rule)	Recent bid asked (when required by local rule)	Minimum selling Price

ORDER AUTHORIZING SALE OF SECURITIES

THE COURT FINDS the sale is proper.
THE COURT ORDERS
The ☐ personal representative ☐ guardian ☐ conservator is authorized to sell the securities described above upon the terms and conditions specified. Notice of hearing on the petition is dispensed with.

Date: _____

_____
JUDGE OF THE SUPERIOR COURT

☐ SIGNATURE FOLLOWS LAST ATTACHMENT

DE-270, GC-070 [Rev. January 1, 1998]

**EX PARTE PETITION FOR AUTHORITY
TO SELL SECURITIES AND ORDER**

Page 2

The paralegal should read the will carefully to determine whether the property of the decedent is community property. In these cases, however, the surviving spouse must wait a short period of time before selling any property, to enable potential creditors to come forward. Each community-property state will vary somewhat as to the procedures to follow. However, in most cases, a form must be filed with the probate court by the surviving spouse, indicating that the decedent's property is community property.

In California, an affidavit of the surviving spouse is required to transfer title to real property. The deed to the property must show that the couple held title as "community property" or as "husband and wife" and not as "joint tenants."

Other Community Property Transfers

Other forms of community property may be transferred by filing a spousal property petition with the probate court. A sample form is shown in Exhibit 9-5.

Item 1-a must be completed only if there are assets in addition to community property that require a separate probate proceeding. In this case, the spousal property petition should have the same case number as the petition for probate of the estate. Local court rules determine whether a probate referee should be appointed (item 1-c). The paralegal should investigate local practices in the court in which the proceeding is being filed. The remainder of the form is self-explanatory.

These documents should be filed in the branch court in the county in which the decedent resided. Extra copies should be included for the court to conform and return to your office with the case number and hearing date, if one is required. If there is no other probate proceeding in this case, a filing fee must be included. However, if a petition for probate is filed, it should accompany this petition, along with one filing fee included for both. Some branches require a stamped, self-addressed envelope to return the documents to you if they are filed by mail.

After the court returns the documents, all individuals listed on the petition (items 9 and 10) must receive a notice of the hearing (Exhibit 9-6). In most counties, the probate clerk affixes the date and time of the hearing. A copy of the notice must be sent to the parties at least 15 days before the hearing date. After service is completed, the notice must be filed with the court prior to the hearing date.

To have all property declared community property that passes directly to the surviving spouse, a spousal property order must be prepared for the judge's signature at the hearing. The paralegal should complete this form and submit it to the court according to local court rules. Many counties require no appearance at the hearing if there is no opposition to the order. Check with the court to determine whether the order must be submitted prior to or after the hearing. Once the order is signed, a certified official copy is required for each item of property being transferred to the surviving spouse.

EXHIBIT 9-5   Spousal Property Petition with Order

Courtesy: Reprinted from *West's California Judicial Council Forms 2003*, with permission of West, a Thomson business. For more information about this publication please visit **http://west.thomson.com.**

DE-221

ATTORNEY OR PARTY WITHOUT ATTORNEY *(Name, state bar number, and Address):*	FOR COURT USE ONLY
TELEPHONE NO.: FAX NO.:	
ATTORNEY FOR *(Named)*:	

SUPERIOR COURT OF CALIFORNIA, COUNTY OF
STREET ADDRESS.
MAILING ADDRESS:
CITY AND ZIP CODE:
BRANCH NAME:

CASE NUMBER:

ESTATE OF *(Name)*:

DECEDENT

HEARING DATE:

SPOUSAL PROPERTY PETITION

DEPT.:   TIME:

1. **Petitioner** *(name):*   **requests**
   a. ☐ determination of property passing to the surviving spouse without administration (Prob. Code, § 13500).
   b. ☐ confirmation of property belonging to the surviving spouse (Prob. Code, §§ 100, 101).
   c. ☐ immediate appointment of a probate referee.

2. Petitioner is
   a. ☐ surviving spouse of the decedent.
   b. ☐ personal representative of *(name)*:   , surviving spouse.
   c. ☐ guardian of the estate or conservator of the estate of (name):   , surviving spouse.

3. Decedent died on *(date)*:

4. Decedent was
   a. ☐ a resident of the California county named above.
   b. ☐ a nonresident of California and left an estate in the county named above.
   c. ☐ intestate   ☐ testate and a copy of the will and any codicil is affixed as Attachment 4c or 7. *(Attach will.)*

5. a. (Complete in all cases) The decedent is survived by
      (1) ☐ child as follows: ☐ natural or adopted   ☐ natural, adopted by a third party   ☐ no child
      (2) ☐ issue of a predeceased child   ☐ no issue of a predeceased child.
   b. Decedent   ☐ is   ☐ is not   survived by a stepchild or foster child or children who would have been adopted by
      decedent but for a legal barrier. (See Prob. Code, § 6454.)

6. *(Complete only if no issue survived the decedent. Check **only the first** box that applies.)*
   a. ☐ The decedent is survived by a parent or parents who are listed in item 9.
   b. ☐ The decedent is survived by a brother, sister, or issue of a deceased brother or sister, all of whom are listed in item 9.

7. Administration of all or part of the estate is not necessary for the reason that all or a part of the estate is property passing to the
   surviving spouse. The facts upon which petitioner bases the allegation that the property described in Attachments 7a and 7b is
   property that should pass or be confirmed to the surviving spouse are stated in Attachment 7.
   a. ☐ Attachment 7a contains the legal description *(if real property add Assessor's Parcel Number)* of the deceased spouse's
      property that petitioner requests to be determined as having passed to the surviving spouse from the deceased spouse.
      This includes any interest in a trade or business name of any unincorporated business or an interest in any unincorporated
      business that the deceased spouse was operating or managing at the time of death, subject to any written agreement
      between the deceased spouse and the surviving spouse providing for a non pro rata division of the aggregate value of
      the community property assets or quasi-community property assets, or both.
   b. ☐ Attachment 7b contains the legal description *(if real property add Assessor's Parcel Number)* of the community or quasi-
      community property petitioner requests to be determined as having belonged under Probate Code sections 100 and 101
      to the surviving spouse upon the deceased spouse's death, subject to any written agreement between the deceased
      spouse and the surviving spouse providing for a non pro rata division of the aggregate value of the community property
      assets or quasi-community property assets, or both.

                                        (Continued on reverse, including footnotes)

Form Approved by the Judicial Council of California	**SPOUSAL PROPERTY PETITION** **(Probate)**	Probate Code, § 13650

continued

Exhibit 9-5 *continued*

ESTATE OF *(Name)*:	CASE NUMBER:
DECEDENT	

8. There ☐ exists ☐ does not exist   a written agreement between the deceased spouse and the surviving spouse providing for a non pro rata division of the aggregate value of the community property assets or quasi_community assets, or both. (If petitioner bases the description of the property of the deceased spouse passing to the surviving spouse or the property to be confirmed to the surviving spouse, or both, on a written agreement, a copy of the agreement must be attached to this petition as Attachment 8.)

9. The names, relationships, ages, and residence or mailing addresses so far as known to or reasonably ascertainable by petitioner of (1) all persons named in decedent's will and codicils, whether living or deceased, and (2) all persons checked in items 5 and 6 ☐ are listed below ☐ are listed in Attachment 9.

Name and relationship	Age	Residence or mailing address

10. The names and address of all persons named as executors in the decedent's will or appointed as personal representatives ☐ are listed below ☐ are listed in Attachment 9 ☐ none

11. ☐ The petitioner is the trustee of a trust that is a devisee under decedent's will. The names and addresses of all persons interested in the trust who are entitled to notice under Probate Code section 13655(b)(2) are listed in Attachment 11.

12. A petition for probate or for administration of the decedent's estate
    a. ☐ is being filed with this petition.
    b. ☐ was filed on (date):
    c. ☐ has not been filed and is not being filed with this petition.

13. Number of pages attached: _____

Date:

_____   ▶_____
(TYPE OR PRINT NAME)   (SIGNATURE OF PLAINTIFF OR ATTORNEY)

I declare under penalty of perjury under the laws of the State of California that the foregoing is true and correct.

Date:

_____   ▶_____
(TYPE OR PRINT NAME)   (SIGNATURE OF PLAINTIFF OR ATTORNEY)

1 See Prob. Code, § 13651(b) for the requirement that a copy of the will be attached in certain instances. If required, include in Attachment 4c or 7.

2 See Prob. Code, § 13658 for required filing of a list of known creditors of a business and other information in certain instances. If required, include in Attachment 7a.

DE-221 [Rev. July 1, 2000]   **SPOUSAL PROPERTY PETITION**   Page 2
                                                              (Probate)

EXHIBIT 9-6 Notice of Hearing (Probate)

Courtesy: Reprinted from *West's California Judicial Council Forms 2003,* with permission of West, a Thomson business. For more information about this publication please visit **http://west.thomson.com.**

DE-120

ATTORNEY OR PARTY WITHOUT ATTORNEY (Name, state bar number, and address) :	TELEPHONE AND FAX NOS.:	FOR COURT USE ONLY

ATTORNEY FOR (Name) :

SUPERIOR COURT OF CALIFORNIA, COUNTY OF

STREET ADDRESS:

MAILING ADDRESS:

CITY AND ZIP CODE:

BRANCH NAME:

ESTATE OF (Name):

DECEDENT

NOTICE OF HEARING **(Probate)**	CASE NUMBER:

> This notice is required by law. This notice does not require you to appear in court, but you may attend the hearing if you wish.

1. NOTICE is given that (name):

   (representative capacity, if any):

   has filed (specify):*

2. You may refer to the filed documents for further particulars. *(All of the case documents filed with the court are available for examination in the case file kept by the court clerk.)*

3. A HEARING on the matter will be held as follows:

   a. Date:　　　　　　Time:　　　　　　Dept.:　　　　　　Room:

   b. Address of court ☐ shown above ☐ is:

* Do not use this form to give notice of hearing of the petition for administration (see Probate Code, § 8100).

(Continued on reverse)

Form Approved by the Judicial Council of California DE-120 [Rev. January 1, 1998]	**NOTICE OF HEARING** **(Probate)**	WEST GROUP Official Publisher	Probate Code, §§ 1211, 1215, 1216, 1230

continued

Exhibit 9-6 *continued*

ESTATE OF *(Name):*	CASE NUMBER:
DECEDENT	

CLERK'S CERTIFICATE OF POSTING

1. I certify that I am not a party to this cause.
2. A copy of the foregoing *Notice of Hearing (Probate)*
   a. was posted at *(address):*

   b. was posted on *(date):*

Date: Clerk, by _____ , Deputy

PROOF OF SERVICE BY MAIL

1. I am over the age of 18 and not a party to this cause. I am a resident of or employed in the county where the mailing occurred.
2. My residence or business address is *(specify):*

3. I served the foregoing *Notice of Hearing (Probate)* on each person named below by enclosing a copy in an envelope addressed as shown below AND
   a. ☐ **depositing** the sealed envelope with the United States Postal Service with the postage fully prepaid.
   b. ☐ **placing** the envelope for collection and mailing on the date and at the place shown in item 4 following our ordinary business practices. I am readily familiar with this business' practice for collecting and processing correspondence for mailing. On the same day that correspondence is placed for collection and mailing, it is deposited in the ordinary course of business with the United States Postal Service in a sealed envelope with postage fully prepaid.

4. a. Date mailed: b. Place mailed *(city, state):*

5. ☐ I served with the *Notice of Hearing (Probate)* a copy of the petition or other document referred to in the notice.

I declare under penalty of perjury under the laws of the State of California that the foregoing is true and correct.

Date:

▶

....   _____
(TYPE OR PRINT NAME)   (SIGNATURE OF DECLARANT)

NAME AND ADDRESS OF EACH PERSON TO WHOM NOTICE WAS MAILED

☐ List of names and addresses continued in attachment.

DE-120 [Rev. January 1, 1998]	**NOTICE OF HEARING** (Probate)	WEST GROUP Official Publisher	**Page two** Probate Code, §§ 1261, 1263

PROBATE PROCEDURES ◆

If the decedent's property must go through a formal probate, the process occurs as described in this section. This procedure is required if there is property in addition to the following:

1. Property held in joint tenancy
2. Property held as community property
3. Insurance policies
4. Property held in a trust

None of the above-described property should be included in the formal probate process.

FORMAL PROBATE PROCEDURES ◆

In most cases, the client is the executor of the **estate** and is so named in the decedent's will. If there is no will, the court appoints an **administrator**. If the executor named in the will cannot or will not serve, or if no executor is appointed in the will, the court appoints an administrator CTA to administer the estate.

Prior to commencing the probate process, the paralegal should check with the individual court in which the case will be filed to ascertain if there are any special probate rules. Some courts provide a booklet that explains their special requirements.

Petition

Probate is commenced by the filing of the petition. The original will must be submitted attached to the petition. Usually filing is done in person. The petition is scrutinized carefully by the probate attorneys for errors and omissions. If any items are missing, discrepancies will be documented in the probate notes on file in the court clerk's office. All errors must be corrected prior to the hearing. If the probate notes indicate "RFA," no errors have been found and the petition is "recommended for approval." The hearing will be set approximately 30 days after the petition is filed. If no objections to the probate are raised, it is usually not necessary for the attorney to attend the hearing.

Preparing the Petition

A sample probate petition is included as Exhibit 9-7. The appropriate names and addresses for the attorney and the court should be indicated, as well as the name of the decedent. If the executor wishes to buy or sell property on behalf of the estate without prior court approval, then check the box indicating "authorization to administer under the Independent Administration of Estates Act" (item 2-c).

Item 1 requires the name of a local newspaper in the city in which the decedent lived immediately prior to his death. The paralegal should check with the probate clerk to determine the appropriate

administrator individual appointed to administer an estate when the decedent did not have a will or did not name an executor in the will.

estate the property a decedent owned at death.

EXHIBIT 9-7 Petition for Probate

Courtesy: Reprinted from *West's California Judicial Council Forms 2003*, with permission of West, a Thomson business. For more information about this publication please visit **http://west.thomson.com.**

DE-111

ATTORNEY OR PARTY WITHOUT ATTORNEY (Name, state bar number, and Address):	FOR COURT USE ONLY
TELEPHONE NO.: FAX NO (Optional): E-MAIL ADDRESS (Optional): ATTORNEY FOR (Named):	

SUPERIOR COURT OF CALIFORNIA, COUNTY OF
STREET ADDRESS.
MAILING ADDRESS:
CITY AND ZIP CODE:
BRANCH NAME:

ESTATE OF *(Name)*:

DECEDENT

PETITION FOR	☐ Probate of Will and for Letters Testamentary ☐ Probate of Will and for Letters of Administration with Will Annexed ☐ Letters of Administration ☐ Letters of Special Administration ☐ Authorization to Administer Under the Independent ☐ Administration of Estates Act ☐ with limited authority	CASE NUMBER: HEARING DATE: DEPT.: TIME:

1. Publication will be in (specify name of newspaper):
   a. ☐ Publication requested.   b. ☐ Publication to be arranged.

2. **Petitioner** (name of each): requests
   a. ☐ decedent's will and codicils, if any, be admitted to probate.
   b. ☐ *(name)*:
      be appointed   (1) ☐ executor   (3) ☐ administrator
                        (2) ☐ administrator with will annexed   (4) ☐ special administrator
      and Letters issue upon qualification.
   c. ☐ that ☐ full ☐ limited   authority be granted to administer under the Independent Administration of Estates Act.
   d. (1) ☐ bond not be required for the reasons stated in item 3d.
      (2) ☐ $ bond be fixed. It will be furnished by an admitted surety insurer or as otherwise provided by law.
            (Specify reasons in Attachment 2 if the amount is different from the maximum required by Probate Code section 8482.)
      (3) ☐ $ in deposits in a blocked account be allowed. Receipts will be filed. *(Specify institution and location):*

3. a. Decedent died on *(date)*: at *(place)*:
      (1) ☐ a resident of the county named above.
      (2) ☐ a nonresident of California and left an estate in the county named above located at *(specify location permitting publication in the newspaper named in item 1)*:
   b. Street address, city, and county of decedent's residence at time of death *(specify)*:

   c. Character and estimated value of the property of the estate:
      (1) Personal property: $
      (2) Annual gross income from
         (a) real property: $
         (b) personal property: $
                          Total: $
      (3) Real property: $ *(If full authority under the Independent Administration of Estates Act is requested, state the fair market value of the real property less encumbrances.)*
   d. (1) ☐ Will waives bond. ☐ Special administrator is the named executor and the will waives bond.
      (2) ☐ All beneficiaries are adults and have waived bond, and the will does not require a bond.
         (Affix waiver as Attachment 3d(2).)
      (3) ☐ All heirs at law are adults and have waived bond. *(Affix waiver as Attachment 3d(3).)*
      (4) ☐ Sole personal representative is a corporate fiduciary or an exempt government agency.
   e. (1) ☐ Decedent died intestate.
      (2) ☐ Copy of decedent's will dated: ☐ codicils dated: are affixed as Attachment 3e(2).
         ☐ The will and all codicils are self-proving (Prob. Code, § 8220).

(Continued on reverse)   Page 1 of 2

Form Approved by the   **PETITION FOR PROBATE**   Probate Code, §§ 13650, 10450
Judicial Council of California

continued

Exhibit 9-7   *continued*

ESTATE OF *(Name):* DECEDENT	CASE NUMBER:

3. f.   Appointment of personal representative (check all applicable boxes):

> | Include in Attachment 3e(2) a typed copy of a handwritten will and a translation of a foreign language will. |

(1)   Appointment of executor or administrator with will annexed:
- (a) ☐ Proposed executor is named as executor in the will and consents to act.
- (b) ☐ No executor is named in the will.
- (c) ☐ Proposed personal representative is a nominee of a person entitled to Letters. *(Affix nomination as Attachment 3f(1)(c).)*
- (d) ☐ Other named executors will not act because of ☐ death ☐ declination ☐ other reasons *(specify in Attachment 3f(1)(d)).*

(2)   Appointment of administrator:
- (a) ☐ Petitioner is a person entitled to Letters. *(If necessary, explain priority in Attachment 3f(2)(a).)*
- (b) ☐ Petitioner is a nominee of a person entitled to Letters. *(Affix nomination as Attachment 3f(2)(b).)*
- (c) ☐ Petitioner is related to the decedent as *(specify):*

(3) ☐ Appointment of special administrator requested. *(Specify grounds and requested powers in Attachment 3((3).)*

g.   Proposed personal representative is a ☐ resident of California ☐ nonresident of California *(affix statement of permanent address as Attachment 3g)* ☐ resident of the United States ☐ nonresident of the United States.

4. ☐ Decedent's will does not preclude administration of this estate under the Independent Administration of Estates Act.

5. a.   The decedent is survived by *(check at least one box in each of items (1)–(4)).*
- (1) ☐ spouse ☐ no spouse as follows: ☐ divorced or never married ☐ spouse deceased
- (2) ☐ domestic partner ☐ no domestic partner *(See Prob. Code, §§ 37(b), 6401(c), and 6402.)*
- (3) ☐ child as follows: ☐ natural or adopted ☐ natural adopted by a third party ☐ no child
- (4) ☐ issue of a predeceased child ☐ no issue of a predeceased child

b.   Decedent ☐ is ☐ is not survived by a stepchild or foster child or children who would have been adopted by decedent but for a legal barrier. *(See Prob. Code, § 6454.)*

6. *(Complete if decedent was survived by (1) a spouse or domestic partner but no issue (only a or b apply), or (2) no spouse, domestic partner, or issue. Check the first box that applies.):*
- a. ☐ Decedent is survived by a parent or parents who are listed in item 8.
- b. ☐ Decedent is survived by issue of deceased parents, all of whom are listed in item 8.
- c. ☐ Decedent is survived by a grandparent or grandparents who are listed in item 8.
- d. ☐ Decedent is survived by issue of grandparents, all of whom are listed in item 8.
- e. ☐ Decedent is survived by issue of a predeceased spouse, all of whom are listed in item 8.
- f. ☐ Decedent is survived by next of kin, all of whom are listed in item 8.
- g. ☐ Decedent is survived by parents of a predeceased spouse or issue of those parents, if both are predeceased, all of whom are listed in item 8.
- h. ☐ Decedent is survived by no known next of kin.

7. *(Complete only if no spouse or issue survived decedent)* Decedent ☐ had no predeceased spouse ☐ had a predeceased spouse who (1) ☐ died not more than 15 years before decedent owning an interest in **real property** that passed to decedent, (2) ☐ died not more than five years before decedent owning **personal property** valued at $10,000 or more that passed to decedent, (3) ☐ neither (1) nor (2) apply. *(If you checked (1) or (2), check only the first box that applies.):*
- a. ☐ Decedent is survived by issue of a predeceased spouse, all of whom are listed in item 8.
- b. ☐ Decedent is survived by a parent or parents of the predeceased spouse who are listed in item 8.
- c. ☐ Decedent is survived by issue of a parent of the predeceased spouse, all of whom are listed in item 8.
- d. ☐ Decedent is survived by next of kin of the decedent, all of whom are listed in item 8.
- e. ☐ Decedent is survived by next of kin of the predeceased spouse, all of whom are listed in item 8.

8.   Listed in Attachment 8 are the names, relationships, ages, and addresses, so far as known to or reasonably ascertainable by petitioner, of (1) all persons named in decedent's will and codicils, whether living or deceased; (2) all persons named or checked in items 2, 5, 6, and 7; and (3) all beneficiaries of a devisee trust in which the trustee and personal representative are the same person.

9.   Number of pages attached: _____

Date:

▶ _____

(Signature of all petitioners also required (Prob. Code, § 1020).)   (SIGNATURE OF ATTORNEY*)

I declare under penalty of perjury under the laws of the State of California that the foregoing is true and correct.

Date:

_____   ▶ _____
(TYPE OR PRINT NAME)   (SIGNATURE OF PLAINTIFF OR ATTORNEY)

_____   ▶ _____
(TYPE OR PRINT NAME)   (SIGNATURE OF PLAINTIFF OR ATTORNEY)

DE-111 [Rev. July 1, 2003]   **PETITION FOR PROBATE**   Page 2 of 2

newspaper to use. Arrangements must be made with the newspaper to post the notice of hearing (described later in this section).

Whether or not a bond must be posted (item 2-d) is determined by the will itself. The clause in the will appointing the executor indicates that he or she will serve with or without bond. The remainder of the petition is self-explanatory. However, the completed petition should be proofread carefully to avoid having to correct errors later, as this could delay the hearing on the probate. Be sure all applicable boxes are checked. The probate attorney at the court will examine the petition carefully and delay the hearing date until all errors have been corrected.

The original will (with decedent's and witnesses' signatures) and any later codicils must be filed with the petition. At least two additional copies of the petition should be submitted to the court for certification and conforming. One copy is kept in the files; the other is submitted to the newspaper with the notice. The petition should be signed by the executor prior to filing.

Certificate of Assignment

Some courts require a certificate of assignment, which is a request to the court to assign the probate action to a particular branch court. Check with the court clerk where the action will be filed to determine whether this form is required.

Notice of Petition to Administer Estate

The Notice of Petition to Administer Estate form must be published in a newspaper and mailed to all heirs and beneficiaries at least 15 days before the hearing. It gives notice to all concerned parties of the hearing date.

The notice must be published three times in a newspaper of general circulation in the city in which the decedent lived, commencing at least 15 days before the hearing; publication must be accomplished before the hearing. Proof of publication must be filed with the court before the hearing. Some newspapers will take care of filing the proof with the court; others will provide an affidavit for filing. All heirs and beneficiaries under the will must also obtain a copy of the notice.

Filing Fees

One filing fee is required for the whole probate action and must accompany the petition. This fee is paid from the estate's assets. If the executor or attorney advances the expense, they should be reimbursed after an estate checking account is established.

Proof of Subscribing Witness

If the will is not self-proving, one witness to the will must sign a proof of subscribing witness form attesting to the fact that the will was signed by the decedent in the witness's presence. However, most wills contain a **self-proving clause**, before the witness signatures, as follows:

> The foregoing document, consisting of three pages including this page, was on this date signed by MARY SMITH and declared to be her will. We are familiar with the testator and know her to be the individual who signed in our presence and in the presence of each of us. We observed the signing of the will by MARY SMITH and by each other witness. Each signature is the signature of the person whose name was signed.
>
> Each of us is now more than eighteen (18) years of age, is a competent witness, and resides at the address signed after her name. We are acquainted with the testator and know she is over the age of eighteen. To our knowledge, she is of sound mind and not acting under duress, menace, fraud, or the undue influence of any person.

_____   Address: _____

_____

_____   Address: _____

_____

_____   Address: _____

_____

If such a clause is included in the will, then the will is considered to be self-proving and no proof of subscribing witness form is required.

Notification to Director of Health Services and/or Retirement Funds

If the decedent had been receiving health care under Medical prior to death, a letter should be sent to the Director of Health Services along with a copy of the death certificate. In most cases, retirement funds obtained during the month of the decedent's death (such as Social Security, railroad retirement, etc.) must be returned to the organization or entity, along with a copy of the death certificate. No particular form is required; a short letter enclosing the death certificate should suffice.

Order for Probate

After the court approves the petition and prior to the hearing, an order for probate must be prepared and submitted to the court for the judge's signature. After the hearing, the judge will sign the order appointing the executor.

Letters Testamentary

The form for **letters testamentary** should be completed and submitted to the court with the order for probate. It should be accompanied by the "Duties and Responsibilities of Personal Representative" form.

self-proving clause clause in a will before the witness signatures that eliminates the need for the witnesses to sign a proof of subscribing witness form to attest to the fact that the will was signed by the decedent in the presence of the witness.

letters testamentary forms approved by the probate court that authorize an executor to administer the estate.

Additional copies should be submitted to the court with a request to return conformed copies of all documents, as well as two certified copies of the letters testamentary. Certification fees must accompany the request, which may be submitted by letter or in person.

Notice of Proposed Action

If the executor plans to sell real property prior to the closing of the estate, a notice of proposed action must be completed and filed with the court. All individuals who are beneficiaries of the property involved must receive a copy of the notice. For instance, if the executor must sell a house that was left to the decedent's two children, each child must receive a copy of the notice indicating the executor's intent.

Inventory and Appraisal Form

Within four months of the time the letters are issued, an inventory and appraisal form must be filed with the court. (This form was formerly known as "Inventory and Appraisement.") It must include attachments listing all of the assets of the estate as well as their value. Attachment 1 should include assets, the values of which are readily ascertainable, such as bank accounts, cash on hand, and salary or retirement fund proceeds issued after death. Attachment 2 lists all assets, the value of which must be determined by a probate referee who is appointed by the court and paid from estate funds. A sample inventory and appraisal form and attachments are shown in Exhibit 9-8.

Notice to Creditors

The executor is required to send a notice to all known creditors of the decedent. The notice is called a "Notice of Administration to Creditors" and tells the creditors where to file a claim against the estate, as well as the time requirements for filing. Creditors must file a claim against the estate before the later of:

1. Four months after the date letters were first issued to the executor
2. Sixty days after the date the notice was mailed or personally delivered to the creditor

The proof of service must be completed with the name and address of each entity to whom notice was mailed. If a creditor does not meet the deadline, it may be barred from making a late claim. Creditors must submit claims on a creditor's claim form.

Executors are under a fiduciary duty to the estate to preserve estate assets. Therefore, claims should not automatically be paid unless it can be ascertained that they are legitimate debts of the decedent. If the claim is rejected by the executor, the creditor may petition the court within three months by filing suit against the estate. For each claim received by the executor, an allowance or

EXHIBIT 9-8   Inventory and Appraisal Form and Attachments

Courtesy: Reprinted from *West's California Judicial Council Forms 2003*, with permission of West, a Thomson business. For more information about this publication please visit **http://west.thomson.com**.

DE-160/GC-040

ATTORNEY OR PARTY WITHOUT ATTORNEY *(Name, state bar number, and address)*:	FOR COURT USE ONLY

TELEPHONE NO.:   FAX NO. *(Optional)*:

E-MAIL ADDRESS *(Optional)*:

ATTORNEY FOR *(Named)*:

SUPERIOR COURT OF CALIFORNIA, COUNTY OF

STREET ADDRESS:
MAILING ADDRESS:
CITY AND ZIP CODE:
BRANCH NAME:

ESTATE OF *(Name)*:

☐ DECEDENT   ☐ CONSERVATEE   ☐ MINOR

INVENTORY AND APPRAISAL	CASE NUMBER:
☐ **Partial No.:** ☐ **Corrected**	
☐ **Final** ☐ **Reappraisal for Sale**	Date of Death of Decedent or of Appointment of Guardian or Conservator.
☐ **Supplemental** ☐ **Property Tax Certificate**	

APPRAISALS

1. Total appraisal by representative, guardian, or conservator (Attachment 1): $
2. Total appraisal by referee (Attachment 2): $
                                                                    TOTAL: $

DECLARATION OF REPRESENTATIVE, GUARDIAN, CONSERVATOR, OR SMALL ESTATE CLAIMANT

3. Attachments 1 and 2 together with all prior inventories filed contain a true statement of
    ☐ all   ☐ a portion of the estate that has come to my knowledge or possession, including particularly all money and all just claims the estate has against me. I have truly, honestly, and impartially appraised to the best of my ability each item set forth in Attachment 1.
4. ☐ No probate referee is required   ☐ by order of the court dated *(specify)*:
5. **Property tax certificate.** I certify that the requirements of Revenue and Taxation Code section 480
    a. ☐ are not applicable because the decedent owned no real property in California at the time of death.
    b. ☐ have been satisfied by the filing of a change of ownership statement with the county recorder or assessor of each county in California in which the decedent owned property at the time of death.

I declare under penalty of perjury under the laws of the State of California that the foregoing is true and correct.
Date:

_____   ► _____
(TYPE OR PRINT NAME; INCLUDE TITLE IF CORPORATE OFFICER)   (SIGNATURE)

STATEMENT ABOUT THE BOND
(Complete in all cases. Must be signed by attorney for fiduciary, or by fiduciary without an attorney.)

6. ☐ Bond is waived, or the sole fiduciary is a corporate fiduciary or an exempt government agency.
7. ☐ Bond filed in the amount of: $ ☐ Sufficient   ☐ Insufficient
8. ☐ Receipts for: $ have been filed with the court for deposits in a blocked account at
    (specify institution and location):
Date:

_____   ► _____
(TYPE OR PRINT NAME)   (SIGNATURE OF ATTORNEY OR PARTY WITHOUT ATTORNEY)

Page 1 of 2

Form Approved by the Judicial Council of California DE-160/GC-040 [Rev. January 1, 2003]	**INVENTORY AND APPRAISAL**	Probate Code, §§ 2610-2616, 8800-8980; Cal. Rules of Court, rule 7.501

continued

Exhibit 9-8 *continued*

ESTATE OF *(Name)*: ☐ DECEDENT ☐ CONSERVATEE ☐ MINOR	CASE NUMBER:

DECLARATION OF PROBATE REFEREE

9. I have truly, honestly, and impartially appraised to the best of my ability each item set forth in Attachment 2.
10. A true account of my commission and expenses actually and necessarily incurred pursuant to my appointment is:
   Statutory commission: $
   Expenses (specify): $
   TOTAL: $

I declare under penalty of perjury under the laws of the State of California that the foregoing is true and correct.
Date:

_____   ▶ _____
(TYPE OR PRINT NAME)   (SIGNATURE OF ATTORNEY OR PARTY WITHOUT ATTORNEY)

INSTRUCTIONS
(See Probate Code sections 2610–2616, 8801, 8804, 8852, 8905, 8960, 8961, and 8963 for additional instructions.)

1. See Probate Code section 8850 for items to be included in the inventory.

2. If the minor or conservatee is or has been during the guardianship or conservatorship confined in a state hospital under the jurisdiction of the State Department of Mental Health or the State Department of Developmental Services, mail a copy to the director of the appropriate department in Sacramento. (Prob. Code, § 2611.)

3. The representative, guardian, conservator, or small estate claimant shall list on Attachment 1 and appraise as of the date of death of the decedent or the date of appointment of the guardian or conservator, at fair market value, moneys, currency, cash items, bank accounts and amounts on deposit with each financial institution (as defined in Probate Code section 40), and the proceeds of life and accident insurance policies and retirement plans payable upon death in lump sum amounts to the estate, except items whose fair market value is, in the opinion of the representative, an amount different from the ostensible value or specified amount.

4. The representative, guardian, conservator, or small estate claimant shall list in Attachment 2 all other assets of the estate which shall be appraised by the referee.

5. If joint tenancy and other assets are listed for appraisal purposes only and not as part of the probate estate, they must be separately listed on additional attachments and their value excluded from the total valuation of Attachments 1 and 2.

6. Each attachment should conform to the format approved by the Judicial Council. (See *Inventory and Appraisal Attachment* (form DE-161/GC-041) and Cal. Rules of Court, rule 201.)

DE-160/GC-040 [Rev. January 1, 2003]   **INVENTORY AND APPRAISAL**   Page 2 of 2

continued

Exhibit 9-8   *continued*

DE-161, GC-041

ESTATE OF *(Name):*	CASE NUMBER:

**INVENTORY AND APPRAISAL
ATTACHMENT NO.:**

*(In decedents' estates, attachments must conform to Probate
Code section 8850(c) regarding community and separate property.)*

Page: _____ of: _____ total pages.
(Add pages as required.)

Item No.	Description	Appraised value
1.		$

Form Approved by the
Judicial Council of California
DE-161, GC-041 [Rev. January 1, 2003]

INVENTORY AND APPRAISAL ATTACHMENT

Probate Code, §§ 301,
2610-2613, 8800-8920,
10309

rejection form must be completed and filed with the court, along with a copy of the claim itself. This form (see Exhibit 9-9) must also be served on the creditor.

All bills paid on behalf of the decedent or the estate must be paid from a separate checking account. The executor must open this account in the name of the decedent's estate. To do so, a signed copy of the letters testamentary and death certificate are submitted to the bank with the request. In most cases, the bank will not have to keep the letters but will make a copy for its records. The account is then set up for "Estate of X" with the executor having signatory powers.

The executor is also required to pay all claims for funeral expenses, last illness expenses, and wage claims that have been approved, as well as any taxes due. An income tax return must be completed if the decedent had income in the year he or she died. Medical insurance payments should be checked against all bills received for last illness expenses, to avoid duplicate payment.

Petition for Final Distribution

Once the period for creditor's claims has passed and all estate matters have been concluded, the final petition may be filed. This may not be done until at least four months after the letters are issued. All taxes must also have been paid. This petition must be prepared on pleading paper by the attorney. Items to address include the following:

1. Name of decedent and date of death
2. Information about creditor claims and payments
3. Whether notice had to be given to the Director of Health Services
4. Indications that all debts have been paid
5. Actions taken by the executor in relation to the sale of estate property
6. Computation of payment to executor
7. List of creditors receiving notice
8. List of creditors' claims and when paid
9. List of property and its value
10. List of beneficiaries and the proposed distribution to them
11. Waiver forms signed by all beneficiaries waiving a final accounting
12. Verification signed by the executor

A cover letter should be prepared and all these items should be sent to the court for filing. An original and two extra copies of the petition should be sent, with instructions to return conformed copies. In some cases, a filing fee is required.

A notice of hearing form should be prepared and included in the mailing. When it is returned with the date and time of the hearing noted, a copy must be sent to all beneficiaries at least 15 days before the hearing.

EXHIBIT 9-9 Allowance or Rejection of Creditor's Claim

Courtesy: Reprinted from *West's California Judicial Council Forms 2003*, with permission of West, a Thomson business. For more information about this publication please visit **http://west.thomson.com.**

DE-174

ATTORNEY OR PARTY WITHOUT ATTORNEY *(Name, state bar number, and address):*

TELEPHONE NO.: FAX NO. *(Optional):*
E-MAIL ADDRESS *(Optional):*
ATTORNEY FOR *(Named):*

FOR COURT USE ONLY

SUPERIOR COURT OF CALIFORNIA, COUNTY OF
STREET ADDRESS:
MAILING ADDRESS:
CITY AND ZIP CODE:
BRANCH NAME:

ESTATE OF *(Name):* DECEDENT

ALLOWANCE OR REJECTION OF CREDITOR'S CLAIM CASE NUMBER:

NOTE: Attach a copy of the creditor's claim. If allowance or rejection by the court is not required, do not include any pages attached to the creditor claim form.

PERSONAL REPRESENTATIVE'S ALLOWANCE OR REJECTION

1. Name of creditor *(specify):*
2. The claim was filed on *(date):*
3. Date of first issuance of letters:
4. Date of Notice of Administration:
5. Date of decedent's death:
6. Estimated value of estate: $
7. Total amount of the claim: $
8. ☐ Claim is allowed for: $ *(The court must approve certain claims before they are paid.)*
9. ☐ Claim is rejected for: $ *(A creditor has three months to act on a rejected claim. See box below.)*
10. Notice of allowance or rejection given on *(date):*
11. ☐ The personal representative is authorized to administer the estate under the Independent Administration of Estates Act.

Date:

....
(TYPE OR PRINT NAME) ▶ _____
(SIGNATURE OF PERSONAL REPRESENTATIVE)

REJECTED CLAIMS: From the date notice of rejection is given, the creditor must act on the rejected claim (e.g., file a lawsuit) as follows:
a. **Claim due:** within three months after the notice of rejection.
b. **Claim not due:** within three months after the claim becomes due.

COURT'S APPROVAL OR REJECTION

12. ☐ Approved for: $
13. ☐ Rejected for: $
Date:

_____
SIGNATURE OF ☐ JUDGE ☐ COMMISSIONER

14. Number of pages attached: _____ ☐ SIGNATURE FOLLOWS LAST ATTACHMENT

(Proof of Service on reverse) Page 1 of 2

Form Approved by the
Judicial Council of California
DE-174 [Rev. January 1, 2000]

ALLOWANCE OR REJECTION OF CREDITOR'S CLAIM
(Probate)

Probate Code, §§ 9000 et seq.,

continued

Exhibit 9-9 *continued*

ESTATE OF *(Name)*:	CASE NUMBER:
DECEDENT	

PROOF OF ☐ MAILING ☐ PERSONAL DELIVERY TO CREDITOR

1. At the time of mailing or personal delivery I was at least 18 years of age and not a party to this proceeding.

2. My residence or business address is *(specify)*:

3. I mailed or personally delivered a copy of the *Allowance or Rejection of Creditor's Claim* as follows *(complete either a or b)*:

   a. ☐ Mail. I am a resident of or employed in the county where the mailing occurred.
      (1) I enclosed a copy in an envelope AND
         (a) ☐ deposited the sealed envelope with the United States Postal Service with the postage fully prepaid.
         (b) ☐ placed the envelope for collection and mailing on the date and at the place shown in items below following our ordinary business practices. I am readily familiar with this business's practice for collecting and processing correspondence for mailing. On the same day that correspondence is placed for collection and mailing, it is deposited in the ordinary course of business with the United States Postal Service in a sealed envelope with postage fully prepaid.
      (2) The envelope was addressed and mailed first-class as follows:
         (a) Name of creditor served:
         (b) Address on envelope:

         (c) Date of mailing:
         (d) Place of mailing *(city and state)*:

   b. ☐ Personal delivery. I personally delivered a copy to the creditor as follows:
      (1) Name of creditor served:
      (2) Address where delivered:
      (3) Date delivered:
      (4) Time delivered:

I declare under penalty of perjury under the laws of the State of California that the foregoing is true and correct.

Date:

....
(TYPE OR PRINT NAME OF DECLARANT)

► _____
(SIGNATURE OF DECLARANT)

DE-174 [Rev. January 1, 2000]   **ALLOWANCE OR REJECTION OF CREDITOR'S CLAIM**   Page 2
(Probate)

Order of Final Distribution

Some courts will prepare an order of final distribution; others require it to be prepared by the attorney's office. Check with the clerk's office to determine the proper procedure. Some courts require that the order be submitted to them a few days before the hearing. When the order is approved by the court, the assets may be distributed to the beneficiaries.

Receipts from Beneficiaries

Each individual receiving any property from the estate must sign a receipt indicating the exact property that was transferred. These receipts must be filed with the court to effectuate the final discharge.

Final Discharge

The executor must file an affidavit for final discharge with the court, with the accompanying receipts from the beneficiaries. If real property was distributed to beneficiaries in the order for final distribution, a notation should be made indicating that the order was recorded in the county recorder's office for the county where the property is located.

ESTATE CLOSE ✦

Once all of the preceding items have been taken care of, the estate is closed and the executor is relieved of all responsibilities regarding the estate.

ETHICS and ETIQUETTE

The client in a probate practice will generally be the executor of the estate of the decedent. During the administration of the estate, the assets of the estate must be divided among the beneficiaries. An estate account must be set up for all moneys belonging to the estate. For instance, the executor may have to sell a piece of property to pay probate expenses. The money received must be placed in the estate account. At the final accounting, the executor must list all moneys taken in and disbursed. Usually, the attorney will be responsible for carrying out these responsibilities. All moneys received and all moneys disbursed must come from the estate account.

CHAPTER SUMMARY ✦

Different states have various forms and procedures that must be followed that may be different from those described here. Probate procedures vary considerably from state to state. In some states, the probate process may take as little as six months. In others, particularly where all heirs are not known, the process may take several years. The forms book accompanying this text includes material from other states. The proper probate forms for your own state may be obtained at the office of the probate clerk of the probate court in your locality.

✦ KEY TERMS

administrator	letters testamentary
estate	probate
executor	self-proving clause

✦ SELF TEST

Indicate whether the following statements are true (T) or false (F).

____ 1. Probate procedures are the same from state to state.

____ 2. The executor is in charge of probating the estate.

____ 3. All joint tenancy property must be probated.

____ 4. The decedent's life insurance is part of the probate.

____ 5. The decedent's car passes to the spouse without probate.

Circle the correct answer for the following questions:

1. An individual may avoid probate with
   a. a will.
   b. a trust.
   c. only tangible assets.
   d. a living will.

2. The court appoints the executor with
   a. letters testamentary.
   b. a probate petition.
   c. a notice of hearing.
   d. a notice to creditors.

3. The probate petition
   a. is prepared on pleading paper.
   b. is a court form.
   c. is completed by the court.
   d. a and b are correct.
   e. all of the above.

4. When the court approves the executor, _____ is/are prepared.
   a. letters of administration
   b. a petition
   c. letters testamentary
   d. a notice to creditors

5. Who sets the hearing date for probate?
   a. the court clerk
   b. the executor
   c. the attorney
   d. the judge

Fill-in-the-blanks.

1. The most common method for the avoidance of probate is a _____.

2. In order to let creditors know the decedent has passed away, a _____ must be published.

3. The _____ must provide a written evaluation of certain assets of the estate.

4. The document that is prepared listing all assets of the estate and their estimated value is called the _____.

5. When the decedent's property must be sold to pay the estate's bills, the first property sold is the _____ portion of the estate.

✦ REVIEW QUESTIONS

1. Describe the probate process.

2. Research the probate process in your state and describe the differences from the California procedures.

3. List the types of property that are not probated.

4. Describe the difference in the probate procedures when the decedent dies with a will or without a will.

✦ NOTEBOOK PROJECTS

1. Obtain a packet of the forms used for probate in your state.

2. Using the information for Maria Garcia in the notebook projects in the previous chapter (Chapter 8), prepare the probate documents required in your state.

3. Find the probate procedures for your state in your state's statutes or a probate manual for your state. Make a copy of the pertinent parts.

FAMILY LAW

CHAPTER OUTCOMES

As a result of studying this chapter, the student will learn:

- To determine valid, void, voidable, and common law marriages
- The difference between divorce and dissolution, and the issues surrounding them
- How to draft required documents, such as prenuptial agreements, divorce papers, and required dissolution documents
- How to prepare necessary paperwork for an adoption

FAMILY LAW: AN OVERVIEW

Family lawyers specialize in domestic relations issues, such as divorce and adoption. Although family law is a broad area encompassing many aspects, most family law practices rely primarily on divorce (or dissolution) cases, which often raise issues of physical abuse, child custody, alimony and spousal support, child support, and visitation rights.

Family law is changing rapidly as a result of many new developments in recent years. For instance, in the past when a couple divorced, the mother regularly received custody of the children. Now, however, in many states the courts are making joint custody arrangements, where each parent had physical custody of the child for part of the time. Other courts award joint legal custody, where one parent has physical custody of the child and both parents make decisions together on legal issues arising in the child's life.

Family law is an area that requires a great deal of client contact. If you are a "people person" and can listen to other people's problems without becoming emotionally involved, then family law may be the field for you. Generally, divorce clients call the office frequently. Since the attorney may not always be available, the paralegal or legal assistant may have to speak to the client. Divorce and other domestic problems can be very traumatic, so the client may need considerable attention and reassurance.

MARRIAGE

marriage the legal union of a man and woman as husband and wife.

Marriage is the legal union of a man and woman as husband and wife in a marriage ceremony. The ceremony may be performed by a minister, priest, rabbi, judge, or justice of the peace. A marriage license is issued and becomes a binding agreement between the parties. Each state has different requirements for a valid marriage. For example, many states require the couple to be tested for various diseases and to wait for a certain period before applying for a marriage license.

Most states also have a waiting period between the application for the license and the marriage. Additionally, the parties must be residents of the state in which the marriage occurs for a specified period of time, as determined by the state statute. Therefore, you should check the rules of the state where you live. Fill in the State Specific Information box with the rules of your own state.

STATE SPECIFIC INFORMATION

The following rules for marriage apply in the state of _____:

Waiting Period for License: _____

_____

Blood Tests Required: _____

_____

Other Requirements: _____

_____

_____

_____

Common-Law Marriage

A **common-law marriage** exists when a man and woman agree to enter a marital relationship and subsequently live together, but never go through a formal marriage ceremony. Common-law marriage is recognized in the District of Columbia and in thirteen states, including Alabama, Colorado, Georgia, Idaho, Iowa, Kansas, Montana, Ohio, Oklahoma, Pennsylvania, Rhode Island, South Carolina, and Texas. Most states that do not allow common-law marriages will recognize one that was "celebrated" in another state. In the states where common-law marriage is recognized, its elements are as follows:

1. Both parties must be legally competent to marry.
2. Both parties must agree to enter into a marital relationship.
3. The parties must have an oral or written agreement, preferably written. (In some states the agreement may be implied by the parties' behavior.)
4. The parties must live together as husband and wife (cohabit) and represent themselves to the outside world as being married.

common-law marriage
when a man and woman agree to enter a marital relationship and live together as if married but never go through a formal marriage ceremony.

Void and Voidable Marriages

Some marriages are **void** at the outset and can never become valid; others are **voidable** by one of the parties. **Void marriages** include those between close relatives and those where one of the parties is already married to someone else and has not obtained a divorce. State statutes prohibit people from marrying any of the following close relatives:

1. Any ancestor or descendant (e.g., mother, father, grandmother, grandfather, son, daughter, grandchild)
2. A brother or sister
3. An aunt or uncle
4. A first cousin
5. A niece or nephew

Note that an adopted individual becomes a member of the adoptive family. Therefore, a marriage between an adopted child and any of the prohibited relatives would also be void.

A **voidable marriage** has certain defects that make it possible for one of the parties—generally, the innocent party—to have the marriage annulled. The marriage is not automatically void, however, and may become valid if certain events occur. Defects that can lead to a voidable marriage include the following:

1. One of the parties was not of legal age at the time of the marriage and did not have parental consent.
2. At the time of the marriage, one of the parties had a spouse from a former marriage who was still alive, although the party had believed the spouse was dead.
3. An incurable physical incapacity of one of the parties prevents the consummation of the marriage.
4. One of the parties was forced to consent to the marriage.
5. The consent of one of the parties was obtained by fraud.
6. Either party was of unsound mind at the time of the marriage.

With most of these defects, if the parties continue to live together as husband and wife for a specified period of time after the defect ceases to exist, the marriage will be considered valid and may not be voided at a later date. For example, if an individual who was under age at the time of the marriage lives with the spouse for a period of time after reaching legal age, their marriage will be valid. State statutes differ as to the time period involved.

Cohabitation

Cohabitation involves a man and woman living together as husband and wife without the benefit of a marriage contract and without the intent to enter into a common-law marriage. Recent cases have awarded **palimony** where couples part after living together for a long period. Usually, the party who is seeking support must show that there was an agreement, either oral or written, between the parties that one

void having no legal effect.

voidable capable of being adjudged void, but may also be made legal by taking certain steps.

void marriage a marriage that is not legal; includes marriages between close relatives and bigamous relationships.

voidable marriage a marriage that may be voided by one of the parties or may be made legal on the occurrence of certain events.

cohabitation living together without a marriage contract and without the intent to enter into a common law marriage.

palimony support paid to one party after a relationship ends based on an implied contract between the couple while they lived together.

person would keep house, cook, entertain, and run the household while the other person pursued a career outside the home. In such cases, the working party may have to pay support to the person who stayed home as compensation for services rendered. The courts may not award compensation for sexual services, however, because this would represent an illegal contract based on prostitution.

Disputes about the distribution of property may be avoided if the individuals decide early in their relationship to prepare a **cohabitation agreement** that states clearly which items belong to each person. In this document, the couple sets out how the property is to be distributed if they separate. It may also provide for support or a lump-sum payment for one party.

Prenuptial Agreements

Many couples who are planning to marry prepare a **prenuptial agreement** that states how their property will be divided if the couple obtains a divorce. The agreement lists the property each party owned before the marriage and sets out the manner in which property acquired during the marriage will be divided. The agreement also stipulates the manner in which debts will be paid and provides for child and/or spousal support. Some clients may feel that a prenuptial agreement is unnecessary because they do not plan to get a divorce. Nevertheless, as divorce becomes more common, more couples are deciding to draw up prenuptial agreements. Such agreements are also popular with divorced individuals who are planning a second marriage and have already experienced the problems that property divisions, support, custody, and other issues can present. Exhibit 10-1 shows an example of a prenuptial agreement.

ENDING A MARRIAGE ◆

A marriage may be ended by an annulment (also known as nullity), legal separation, divorce, or dissolution. In this section, annulment and legal separation will be discussed. Separate sections will be devoted to divorce and dissolution, which vary depending on the state in which the parties reside.

Annulment/Nullity

Individuals who are involved in a voidable marriage may seek an annulment or nullity. In most states, the grounds for **annulment** are the same as those for voidable marriages. Usually these marriages must be of relatively short duration. The length of the marriage is set by state statute. Many states also allow marriages to be annulled that have not been consummated.

Legal Separation

A legal separation is treated in the same manner as a divorce or dissolution. Most states require the same documents to be prepared and

cohabitation agreement an agreement made between a couple who live together that sets out how their property is to be divided if the relationship ends.

prenuptial agreement an agreement made in contemplation of marriage that delineates the separate property of each party and sets out how property acquired during marriage will be divided if the couple separates.

annulment the act of making a marriage void; also called nullity.

EXHIBIT 10-1 A Sample Prenuptial Agreement

This Prenuptial Agreement is entered into this 20th day of June, 2003, by and between JEFFREY WILLIAM ALTERIO, of Peekskill, New York, and DONNA MARIE GALLO, of Seal Beach, California, in contemplation of the marriage of the parties.

This agreement is being made on the basis of the parties' contemplated marriage on December 26, 2003. Neither party has been previously married. Both parties wish to define their rights and responsibilities regarding property and finances.

In consideration of the contemplated marriage between the parties and other consideration enumerated below, the parties agree.

1. REVOCATION

    If the parties wish to revoke this Agreement, they must prepare a writing signed by both parties.

2. RELATED INSTRUMENTS

    Additional instruments required to accomplish the intent of this Agreement shall be promptly delivered, executed, and acknowledged, at the request of the other party on a timely basis.

3. DISCLOSURES

    Each of the parties to this agreement is of lawful age and competent to enter into a contract. Neither party knows of any reasons why he/she may not enter into the contemplated marriage. Both parties enter into this agreement voluntarily and without duress or coercion.

    Both parties are fully aware of all terms and provisions of this agreement. Each party has disclosed to the other prior to signing this agreement the extent and value of their individual property holdings and the respective value of each holding described herein. All properties described herein represent a full and complete enumeration of their respective property interests as of this date.

4. TAX LIABILITY

    No clause in this agreement shall waive the right of either party to report income for federal or state tax purposes in the manner permissible for any other spouses. No rights are hereby waived under the Federal Gift Tax laws or the Federal Estate Tax laws regarding any transfers of property.

5. BINDING CLAUSES

    This agreement shall be binding upon and benefit both parties and their heirs, assigns, administrators, executors, and personal representatives.

6. COMPLETE AGREEMENT

    This agreement is complete in its entirety with respect to the rights of the individuals herein. All prior agreements and representations regarding the subject matter of this agreement are waived or merged into this agreement.

continued

Exhibit 10-1   *continued*

7. VALIDITY

If any of the clauses of this agreement shall be invalid or unenforceable, then the remaining provisions shall continue to be effective.

8. ASSETS

A. All assets of JEFFREY WILLIAM ALTERIO that shall remain his separate property after the contemplated marriage to DONNA MARIE GALLO are enumerated below:

1999 Rolls Royce, NY License No. BIGJEFF

2-carat diamond men's ring with the initial "J" in rubies

One-acre parcel of land located in Peekskill, New York

B. All assets of DONNA MARIE GALLO that shall remain her separate property after the contemplated marriage to JEFFREY WILLIAM ALTERIO are enumerated below:

2002 Lexus ES 2000 automobile, California License No. DNNA

One-carat emerald-cut amethyst ring

9. LIABILITIES

All liabilities listed below are considered to be the separate property responsibility of each of the parties and are not to be paid from community funds:

A. JEFFREY WILLIAM ALTERIO is responsible for the following:

1. VISA card no. VISA0000 for $2,500

2. Discover card no DISCCC for $1,500

B. DONNA MARIE GALLO is responsible for the following:

1. VISA card no. VISSSS for $3,500

2. MAXX card no. MXXX for $2,322

Signed this 20th day of June, 2003, in the City of Seal Beach, State of California.

_____

JEFFREY WILLIAM ALTERIO

_____

DONNA MARIE GALLO

filed. The couple's property is divided as if they had been divorced. The primary difference between a divorce or dissolution and a legal separation is that the couple may not remarry until they obtain a divorce or dissolution. In most states, the waiting period for finalization of the legal separation is shorter than that for a divorce or dissolution.

DIVORCE ACTIONS ◆

The primary differences between divorce and dissolution are:

1. The divorce is an adversary proceeding and the dissolution is not. The parties to a divorce are the plaintiff and defendant. In dissolution, the parties are the petitioner and respondent.

2. In order to obtain a divorce, one must have grounds for the divorce. Neither party is held responsible for a dissolution, which is also known as a no-fault divorce.

Grounds for Divorce

Although each state utilizing the **divorce** process has different grounds, the most common ones are listed here.

1. **Physical or mental cruelty.** Extreme physical or mental cruelty by one spouse on the other is **grounds for divorce** in most states. The injured spouse must prove the abuse by testimony of witnesses, police reports, pictures, or other forms of physical evidence. For example, in New York, the treatment of the plaintiff by the defendant must rise to the level that the physical or mental well being of the plaintiff is endangered, and conditions must be unsafe for the plaintiff to continue living with the defendant.

2. **Incurable insanity.** In states that allow these grounds, the other party must be able to prove that the spouse is incurably insane. Proof may take the form of medical reports, expert testimony, or other physical evidence.

3. **Abandonment.** One spouse must depart the family home for a period of time, such as one year, without any intention of returning. Other forms of abandonment allowable in some states are constructive abandonment, where one spouse refuses to engage in sexual relations with the other spouse continuously for a period of time such as one year, or lock out, where one spouse refuses to allow the other spouse into the home continuously for a period of time.

4. **Imprisonment.** If the defendant is imprisoned for three consecutive years after the marriage, a divorce action may be commenced in some states if the defendant is still in prison. Other states require that the defendant must have been imprisoned for a felony conviction.

5. **Adultery.** If the defendant voluntarily performs sexual intercourse with a person other than the spouse during the marriage,

divorce adversary proceeding to end a marriage.

grounds for divorce reasons the state allows a couple to obtain a divorce.

a divorce action may be filed on the grounds of adultery. Proof must be obtained in the form of testimony of witnesses or physical evidence. However, admission by the guilty spouse is generally sufficient to prove adultery.

6. **Separation agreement.** In a few states, the parties may choose to live apart for more than one year based on the terms of assigned separation agreement. The agreement must generally be signed by both parties before a notary public and filed in the county where one party resides.

If your state allows the plaintiff to file for divorce only with grounds, complete the State Specific Information box below.

STATE SPECIFIC INFORMATION FOR THE STATE OF _____.

The grounds for divorce are the following:

1. _____

2. _____

3. _____

4. _____

5. _____

Residency Requirements

All states require that the plaintiff, defendant, or both must have lived in that state long enough to establish residency before filing for a divorce. Some state statutes require that the defendant be a resident of the state for a specified period as well. Research your own state statutes to determine the residency requirements and complete the State Specific Information box.

STATE SPECIFIC INFORMATION FOR THE STATE OF _____.

In the state of _____, the plaintiff must be a resident of the state for _____ years/months and the county for _____ years/months before filing a divorce action in that state. The defendant must be a resident of the state for _____ years/months and the county for _____ years/months.

STARTING THE DIVORCE ACTION ──────────────── ✦

In most states, the divorce action is commenced by the completion of a Summons and Complaint. Exhibits 10-2 and 10-3 are sample complaints from Tennessee and New York. Exhibit 10-4 is the format for a Verified Complaint in a divorce action in New York.

As in other civil actions, the summons and complaint are filed with the county clerk and served on the defendant. A fee is paid to the county clerk's office. Most states require that the defendant be personally served by a resident of the state who is not a party to the action and who is not a minor.

If the defendant agrees to the divorce, then the action is considered uncontested and the procedure is considerably easier than if the defendant contests the divorce. The defendant in an uncontested divorce must sign a document to that effect. In New York the document is called an Affidavit of Defendant. The affidavit is filed with the court. However, if the defendant does not agree to the divorce, then it may be contested in most states by the filing of an answer that states the reasons why the divorce should not be granted. It may also include an affirmative defense such as one of the following:

1. **Condoning misconduct.** If the plaintiff is asking for the divorce based on the defendant's misconduct, the defendant must prove that the plaintiff accepted this misconduct. For example, if Wanda wishes to divorce Harry because he has committed adultery, Harry can contest the divorce by saying that Wanda had been aware of the adultery for some time and accepted it.

2. **Mental impairment.** The defendant must prove that the behavior that provided grounds for the divorce was caused by a mental defect.

3. **Connivance.** The defendant must prove that the plaintiff lured her into the misconduct that provided the grounds for divorce.

4. **Recrimination.** If the defendant can prove that the plaintiff was also guilty of the misconduct that established grounds for the divorce, the court may deny the divorce. This defense is based on the English common-law theory of "clean hands;" that is, an individual who seeks relief from the court cannot also be at fault in the situation. Both parties must come into the court with "clean hands."

In most cases, the defendant agrees to the divorce but contests the support, property division, custody, or visitation rights offered by the other party. If the parties cannot agree on those issues, the court will decide the most equitable settlement.

A complete packet of instructions for the preparation of a divorce in New York is included in the forms resource book accompanying this textbook.

condoning misconduct when one spouse is aware of the other's misconduct and accepts it.

mental impairment mental defect.

connivance when one spouse lures the other into misconduct.

recrimination when both parties to a divorce have committed the same misconduct.

EXHIBIT 10-2 Divorce Complaint from Tennessee

1	IN THE CIRCUIT COURT FOR THE COUNTY OF SHELBY, TENNESSEE

IN THE CIRCUIT COURT FOR THE COUNTY OF SHELBY, TENNESSEE

MELANIE L. CONLIN,   )

)

          Plaintiff   )

vs.   )

)   No. D-42222

JEREMY W. CONLIN,   )

)

          Defendant.   )

COMPLAINT FOR DIVORCE

TO THE HONORABLE CHANCELLORS AND CIRCUIT COURT JUDGES OF SHELBY COUNTY, TENNESSEE:

The Plaintiff would respectfully show the Court the following:

I.

JURISDICTION

Plaintiff or Defendant has resided in Shelby County, Tennessee more than six months preceding the filing of this complaint.

Plaintiff is a bona fide resident of Tennessee and the acts complained of were committed while the Plaintiff was a bona fide resident of Shelby County, Tennessee.

II.

STATISTICAL DATA

	WIFE:	HUSBAND:
NAME:	Melanie L. Conlin	Jeremy W. Conlin
PRESENT	247 Carrollwood Lane	299 Germantown Road
ADDRESS:	Cordova, Tennessee	Germantown, Tennessee
BIRTHPLACE:	Memphis, Tennessee	Biloxi, Mississippi
BIRTHDATE:	October 29, 1970	April 1, 1965
NUMBER OF PREVIOUS MARRIAGES:	0	0
MARRIAGE:	June 6, 1995	

1

continued

Exhibit 10-2 *continued*

1	SEPARATION: February 1, 2006
2	MINOR CHILDREN OF THE MARRIAGE
3	AND BIRTHDATES:
4	Jeremy William Conlin, Jr. March 21, 1998
5	Rebecca Jane Conlin December 9, 1999
6	Bradley Willis Conlin September 20, 2003
7	III.
8	GROUNDS
9	Irreconcilable differences have arisen between the parties that will prevent them from living
10	together as husband and wife.
11	IV.
12	AVERMENTS
13	The parties' children live and have lived in Shelby County, Tennessee, for the last six months and
14	specifically at the following places within the last five years:
15	999 Mt. Moriah Road, Memphis, Tennessee 3/21/98–4/1/04
16	247 Carrollwood Lane, Cordova, Tennessee 4/2/04–present
17	Plaintiff has not participated in any other litigation relating to the custody of the subject of this
18	custody litigation. Plaintiff does not have information of any other custody proceeding concern-
19	ing the subject of this custody litigation in any Court of this or any other state. Plaintiff does not
20	know of any person not a party to this proceeding, who has physical custody of the subject of
21	the custody litigation, or claims to have custody, or visitation rights with respect to the subject
22	of this custody litigation.
23	
24	V.
25	PRAYERS
26	WHEREFORE, PREMISES CONSIDERED, Plaintiff prays that:
27	1. Proper process issue and be served upon the Defendant requiring the Defendant to
28	answer this complaint.

2

continued

Exhibit 10-2   *continued*

1	2. Upon the hearing of this cause the Plaintiff be awarded a Final
2	Decree of Absolute Divorce from the Defendant.
3	3. The Court adjust and adjudicate the respective rights and interests
4	of the parties in all jointly owned property.
5	4. The Court approve a Marital Dissolution Agreement if entered into
6	between the parties.
7	5. Plaintiff be awarded exclusive custody of the parties' minor children, child support both

pendente lite and permanent and attorney's fees and suit expenses for defending the interest of said children; that a hearing be held to determine said pendente lite relief and that said child support shall be assigned from the Defendant's income.

6.   Plaintiff be awarded such other further and general relief to which Plaintiff may prove
entitled.

RICHARD DREY, Attorney for Plaintiff
4953 Front Street, Suite 555
Memphis, Tennessee 38018
(901) 555-5555
Supreme Court No.: 99995

EXHIBIT 10-3 Divorce Verified Complaint from New York

SUPREME COURT OF THE STATE OF NEW YORK
COUNTY OF WESTCHESTER

— —

MARY ANN GUERRERO: Index No.:

:

Plaintiff:

:

-against-:   VERIFIED COMPLAINT
                                                                      ACTION FOR DIVORCE
:

:

JONATHAN GUERRERO:

:

Defendant.

— —

The plaintiff, complaining of the defendant, by her attorneys, BURNS & DAILY, alleges:

1. That on or about the 27th day of June, 1989, plaintiff and defendant were married in Peekskill, New York.

2. That for a continuous period of at least two years immediately preceding the commencement of this action, the plaintiff and defendant were and still are residents of the County of Westchester, State of New York.

3. That there are two infant issue of this marriage, to wit: JUDY ANN, born the 25th day of October, 1992; and PHILIP MICHAEL, born the 15th day of September, 1994.

4. After their marriage, as aforesaid and until the 20th day of May, 1995, the plaintiff lived with defendant as man and wife, in various places in the State of New York, and during all that period of time, plaintiff was a true and dutiful wife to the defendant and duly performed all of her duties and obligations as such.

5. That during the course of their marriage, plaintiff and defendant encountered irreconcilable differences which led to their separation and subsequent agreement, entered into the 20th day of June, 1995, and that the parties have lived separate and apart pursuant to this written agreement for a period of more than one year.

WHEREFORE, plaintiff asks judgment against the defendant dissolving the bonds of matrimony existing between the plaintiff and defendant herein, for custody of the minor children of this marriage, and child support; and for such other and further relief as this Court may deem just and proper.

DATED: Peekskill, New York

June 30, 2006

Yours, etc.

BURNS & DAILY
Attorneys for Plaintiff
11223 Main Street
Peekskill, New York 19007
(914) 555-2222
By: _____

EXHIBIT 10-4 Verified Complaint Action for Divorce from New York

1 **SUPREME COURT OF THE STATE OF NEW YORK**
COUNTY OF _____
--X

2 3
                        Plaintiff,
  -against-

4
                      Defendant.
--X

Index No.:

VERIFIED COMPLAINT

ACTION FOR DIVORCE

5 **FIRST:**
Plaintiff *herein / by* _____, complaining of the Defendant, alleges that the parties are over the age of 18 years and;

6 **SECOND:**
- The Plaintiff has resided in New York State for a continuous period in excess of two years immediately preceding the commencement of this action.

OR

- The Defendant has resided in New York State for a continuous period in excess of two years immediately preceding the commencement of this action.

OR

- The Plaintiff has resided in New York State for a continuous period in excess of one year immediately preceding the commencement of this action, and:
  a. • the parties were married in New York State.
  b. • the Plaintiff has lived as husband or wife in New York State with the Defendant.
  c. • the cause of action occurred in New York State.

OR

- The Defendant has resided in New York State for a continuous period in excess of one year immediately preceding the commencement of this action, and:
  a. • the parties were married in New York State.
  b. • the Defendant has lived as husband or wife in New York State with the Plaintiff.
  c. • the cause of action occurred in New York State.

OR

- The cause of action occurred in New York State and both parties were residents thereof at the time of the commencement of this action.

7 **THIRD:** The Plaintiff and the Defendant were married on_____ in (city, town or village; and state or country)_____.

8 The marriage was not performed by a clergyman, minister or by a leader of the Society for Ethical Culture. (If the word "not" is deleted above check the appropriate box below).
- *To the best of my knowledge I have taken all steps solely within my power to remove any barrier to the Defendant's remarriage.*   **OR**
- *I will take prior to the entry of final judgment all steps solely within my power to the best of my knowledge to remove any barrier to the Defendant's remarriage.*   **OR**
- *The Defendant has waived in writing the requirements of DRL §253 (Barriers to Remarriage).*

9 **FOURTH:** • There are no children of the marriage.   **OR**
                • There is (are) _____ child(ren) of the marriage, namely:

Name	Date of Birth	Address
_____	_____	_____
_____	_____	_____
_____	_____	_____
_____	_____	_____
_____	_____	_____

10 The Plaintiff resides at _____
The Defendant resides at _____

continued

Exhibit 10-4 *continued*

11   The parties are covered by the following group health plans:

Plaintiff   **Defendant**
Group Health Plan:_____   Group Health Plan:_____
Address:_____   Address:_____
Identification Number:_____   Identification Number:_____
Plan Administrator:_____   Plan Administrator:_____
Type of Coverage:_____   Type of Coverage:_____

12   **FIFTH:** The grounds for divorce that are alleged as follows:

Cruel and Inhuman Treatment (DRL 6170(1)):
• At the following times, none of which are earlier than (5) years prior to commencement of this action. the Defendant engaged in conduct that so endangered the mental and physical well-being of the Plaintiff, so as to render it unsafe and improper for the parties to cohabit (live together) as husband and wife.

   (State the facts that demonstrate cruel and inhuman conduct giving dates, places and specific acts. Conduct may include physical, verbal, sexual or emotional behavior.)
   _____
   _____
   _____

   (Attach an additional sheet, if necessary).

Abandonment (DRL 176(2):
• That commencing on or about _____, and continuing for a period of more than one (1) year immediately prior to commencement of this action, the Defendant left the marital residence of the parties located at _____. and did not return. Such absence was without cause or justification, and was without Plaintiff's consent.
• That commencing on or about _____, and continuing for a period of more than one (1) year immediately prior to commencement of this action, the Defendant refused to have sexual relations with the Plaintiff despite Plaintiff's repeated requests to resume such relations. Defendant does not suffer from any disability which would prevent *her / him* from engaging in such sexual relations with Plaintiff. The refusal to engage in sexual relations was without good cause or justification and occurred at the marital residence located at
   _____.

• That commencing on or about _____, and continuing for a period of more than one (1) year immediately prior to commencement of this action, the Defendant willfully and without cause or justification abandoned the Plaintiff, who had been a faithful and dutiful *husband / wife*, by depriving Plaintiff of access to the marital residence located at _____. This deprivation of access was without the consent of the Plaintiff and continued for a period of greater than one year.

Confinement to Prison (DRL §170(3)):
• (a) That after the marriage of Plaintiff and Defendant, Defendant was confined in prison for a period of three or more consecutive years, to wit: that Defendant was confined in _____ prison on _____, and has remained confined to this date; and
   (b) not more that five (5) years has elapsed between the end of the third year of imprisonment and the date of commencement of this action.

Adultery (DRL §170(4)):
• (a) That on _____, at the premises located at _____ the Defendant engaged in sexual intercourse with _____, without the procurement nor the connivance of the Plaintiff, and the Plaintiff ceased to cohabit (live) with the Defendant upon the discovery of the adultery; and
   (b) not more than five (5) years elapsed between the date of said adultery and the date of commencement of this action.

   (Attach a corroborating affidavit of a third party witness or other additional proof).

continued

Exhibit 10-4   *continued*

<u>**Living Separate and Apart Pursuant to a Separation Decree or Judgment of Separation**</u>
<u>**(DRL §170(5))**</u>
- (a)   That the _____ Court, _____ County, _____ (Country or State) rendered a decree or judgment of separation on _____, under Index Number _____;and
- (b)   that the parties have lived separate and apart for a period of one year or longer after the granting of such decree; and
- (c)   that the Plaintiff has substantially complied with all the terms and conditions of such decree or judgment.

<u>**Living Separate and Apart Pursuant to a Separation Agreement (DRL §170(6))**</u>
- (a)   That the Plaintiff and Defendant entered into a written agreement of separation, which they subscribed and acknowledged on _____, in the form required to entitle a deed to be recorded; and
- (b)   that the *agreement / memorandum* of said agreement was filed on _____ in the Office of the Clerk of the County of _____, wherein *Plaintiff / Defendant* resided; and
- (c)   that the parties have lived separate and apart for a period of one year or longer after the execution of said agreement; and
- (d)   that the Plaintiff has substantially complied with all terms and conditions of such agreement.

13   **SIXTH:** There is no judgment in any court for a divorce and no other matrimonial action between the parties pending in this court or in any other court of competent jurisdiction.

14   **WHEREFORE,** Plaintiff demands judgment against the Defendant as follows: A judgment dissolving the marriage between the parties and
- _____
  _____
  _____
  _____

AND

- equitable distribution of marital property;

OR

- marital property to be distributed pursuant to the annexed separation agreement / stipulation;

OR

- I waive equitable distribution of marital property;

  and any other relief the court deems fitting and proper.

15   Dated:

16   • *Plaintiff*
                                                                     • *Attorney(s) for Plaintiff*
                                                                       Address:
                                                                       Phone No.:

17   STATE OF NEW YORK, COUNTY OF _____ ss:

I _____ (Print Name), am the Plaintiff in the within action for a divorce. I have read the foregoing complaint and know the contents thereof The contents are true to my own knowledge except as to matters therein stated to be alleged upon information and belief, and as to those matters I believe them to be true.

Subscribed and Sworn to
before me on   _____
_____   Plaintiff's Signature

_____
        NOTARY PUBLIC

TABLE 10-1 Terminology for Divorce and Dissolution	
Divorce	**No-Fault Divorce (Dissolution)**
Divorce	Dissolution
Complaint	Petition
Answer	Response
Plaintiff	Petitioner
Defendant	Respondent
Alimony	Spousal support
Smith v. Smith	*In RE Marriage of Smith*

No-Fault Divorce (Dissolution)

An important trend in recent years is the emergence of "**no-fault divorce**." Rather than having to prove grounds for the divorce, one spouse may merely file a document (usually a **petition**) and serve it on the other spouse to commence the action. About half the states allow some form of no-fault divorce, especially where the couple have lived apart under a separation agreement for a specified period. In most of these states, the other party may not contest the divorce, and no grounds are required. No-fault divorce is known as **dissolution** in many states. Table 10-1 lists the terms used in divorce and the corresponding terms in dissolutions.

Initiating the Dissolution.   Exhibit 10-5 on page 252 shows the petition that is used in California to initiate an action in dissolution. The petition is accompanied by statements of income, expenses, and property. All pleadings filed in California use forms that may be obtained from the county clerk's office. Most other states, however, require office-prepared pleadings.

It is important to learn your own state's rules for filing divorce actions. You should check the files in your office to determine how these actions were filed in the past. Do not hesitate to ask another paralegal or legal assistant if you are unsure.

Residency Requirements

All states require that the petitioner or plaintiff must have lived in that state long enough to establish residency before filing for a divorce. Some state statutes require that the defendant or respondent be a resident of the state for a specified period as well. In California, for instance, the petitioner must have been a resident of the state for six months and of the county for three months to initiate a dissolution proceeding. In contrast, Florida allows immediate residency by the filing of a Declaration of Domicile with the clerk of the court.

Research your own state statutes to find out the residency requirement, and fill in the State Specific Information box.

---

no-fault divorce a divorce available in many states that requires neither party to prove grounds. Either party desiring a divorce files a petition to commence the action; also called a dissolution.

petition the form filed to initiate a no-fault divorce or dissolution; also the form filed to initiate an adoption.

dissolution the term used for no-fault divorce in many states.

STATE SPECIFIC INFORMATION

RESIDENCY REQUIREMENTS

In the state of _____, the plaintiff/petitioner must be a resident of the state for _____ years/months and the county for _____ years/months before filing for a divorce/dissolution. The defendant/respondent must be a resident of the state for _____ years/months and the county for _____ years/months.

Marital Property (or Community Property)

Many states divide property from the marriage based on whether it was acquired during the marriage, before the marriage, or after the separation. In **community property** states, all property acquired during the marriage, except individual gifts or inheritances, is considered community property and is divided equally upon dissolution of the marriage. **Separate property** includes property acquired before the marriage, property acquired after the separation, and individual gifts and inheritances acquired during the marriage. A gift to the couple, however, would be considered community property and would be divided upon dissolution.

In one case, the wife's parents purchased a house for the couple for a wedding present. When the couple later divorced, the wife sought to keep the house as her separate property. The court held, however, that since the house was given to the couple and not to the wife individually, it was community property and must be divided between the parties.

Other states may make an unequal division of the property acquired during the marriage. However, more states have recognized that since both parties contribute equally to the finances of the marriage, the property acquired should be divided equally as well.

Quasi-community property includes property located in another state that would have been considered community property in the state of the couple's residence. For purposes of the divorce, this property is treated as if it were community property. However, for practical purposes, if the laws related to property ownership are different in the state in which the property is located, the courts will offset that property with other marital property in the settlement agreement. Sometimes, the state where the property is located is not a community property state. In that case, the court would award the property to one party, but would offset that property with other property in the settlement agreement. For instance, Mary and Bob live in a community property state, but also own a piece of land worth $20,000 in a non-community property state. Assume that Mary and Bob divorce, and the court awards the real estate to Bob. In that case, Mary would receive other property worth $10,000 (her half of the interest in the lad) to offset the award to Bob.

Pensions and retirement benefits are usually subject to division based on the period of time the individual has been paying into those

community property
property acquired during the marriage that is not a gift or inheritance. The concept applies only in community property states.

separate property
property acquired before marriage or during marriage through gift or inheritance. The concept applies only in community property states.

quasi-community property
property in another state that would be community property if located in the state where the couple reside.

EXHIBIT 10-5 Petition for Dissolution of Marriage, Legal Separation, or Nullity of Marriage

Courtesy: Reprinted from *West's California Judicial Council Forms 2003*, with permission of West, a Thomson business. For more information about this publication please visit **http://west.thomson.com**.

FL-100

ATTORNEY OR PARTY WITHOUT ATTORNEY *(Name, state bar number, and address)*:	FOR COURT USE ONLY

TELEPHONE NO. *(Optional)*:   FAX NO. *(Optional)*:

E-MAIL ADDRESS *(Optional)*:

ATTORNEY FOR *(Named)*:

SUPERIOR COURT OF CALIFORNIA, COUNTY OF

STREET ADDRESS:

MAILING ADDRESS:

CITY AND ZIP CODE:

BRANCH NAME:

MARRIAGE OF

PETITIONER:

RESPONDENT:

PETITION FOR	CASE NUMBER:
☐ **Dissolution of Marriage**	
☐ **Legal Separation**	
☐ **Nullity of Marriage** ☐ **AMENDED**	

1. RESIDENCE (Dissolution only) ☐ Petitioner ☐ Respondent has been a resident of this state for at least six months and of this county for at least three months immediately preceding the filing of this Petition for Dissolution of Marriage.

2. STATISTICAL FACTS
   a. Date of marriage: c. Period between marriage and separation
   b. Date of separation: Years: Months:

3. DECLARATION REGARDING MINOR CHILDREN *(include children of this relationship born prior to or during the marriage or adopted during the marriage)*:
   a. ☐ There are no minor children.
   b. ☐ The minor children are:

Child's name	Birth date	Age	Sex

   ☐ Continued on Attachment 3b.
   c. If there are minor children of the Petitioner and Respondent, a completed *Declaration Under Uniform Child Custody Jurisdiction and Enforcement Act (UCCJEA) (form FL-105)* must be attached.
   d. ☐ A completed voluntary declaration of paternity regarding minor children born to the Petitioner and Respondent prior to the marriage is attached.

4. ☐ Petitioner requests confirmation as separate property assets and debts for the items listed
   ☐ in Attachment 4 ☐ below:

Item	Confirm to

NOTICE: Any party required to pay child support must pay interest on overdue amounts at the "legal" rate, which is currently 10 percent.

Page 1 of 2

Form Approved by the Judicial Council of California FL-100 [Rev. January 1, 2003]	**PETITION** **(Family Law)**	Probate Code, §§ 2330, 3409; Cal. Rules of court, rule 1215 www.cortinfor.ca.gov

continued

Exhibit 10-5   *continued*

MARRIAGE OF *(last name, first name of parties):*	CASE NUMBER:

5. DECLARATION REGARDING COMMUNITY AND QUASI-COMMUNITY ASSETS AND DEBTS AS CURRENTLY KNOWN
   a. ☐ There are no such assets or debts subject to disposition by the court in this proceeding.
   b. ☐ All such assets and debts have been disposed of by written agreement.
   c. ☐ All such assets and debts are listed ☐ in Attachment 5c ☐ below *(specify):*

6. **Petitioner requests**
   a. ☐ Dissolution of the marriage based on
      (1) ☐ irreconcilable differences. Fam. Code, § 2310(a)
      (2) ☐ incurable insanity. Fam. Code, § 2310(b)
   b. ☐ Legal separation of the parties based on
      (1) ☐ irreconcilable differences. Fam. Code, § 2310(a)
      (2) ☐ incurable insanity. Fam. Code, § 2310(b)
   c. ☐ Nullity of void marriage based on
      (1) ☐ incestuous marriage. Fam. Code, § 2200
      (2) ☐ bigamous marriage. Fam. Code §2201

   d. ☐ Nullity of voidable marriage based on
      (1) ☐ Petitioner's age at time of marriage. Fam. Code, § 2210(a)
      (2) ☐ prior existing marriage. Fam. Code, § 2210(b)
      (3) ☐ unsound mind. Fam. Code, § 2210(c)
      (4) ☐ fraud. Fam. Code, § 2210(d)
      (5) ☐ force. Fam. Code, § 2210(e)
      (6) ☐ physical incapacity. Fam. Code, § 2210(f)

7. **Petitioner requests** that the court grant the above relief and make injunctive (including restraining) and other orders as follows:

	Petitioner	Respondent	Joint	Other
a. Legal custody of children to	☐	☐	☐	☐
b. Physical custody of children to	☐	☐	☐	☐
c. Child visitation be granted to	☐	☐	☐	☐
(1) ☐ Supervised for	☐	☐	☐	☐
(2) ☐ No visitation for	☐	☐	☐	☐
(3) ☐ Continued on Attachment 7c(3).	☐	☐	☐	☐

   d. ☐ Determination of parentage of any children born to the Petitioner and Respondent prior to the marriage.
   e. Spousal support payable to (earnings assignment will be issued).   ☐ Petitioner ☐ Respondent
   f. Attorney fees and costs payable by . . . .   ☐ Petitioner ☐ Respondent
   g. ☐ Terminate the court's jurisdiction (ability) to award spousal support to Respondent.
   h. ☐ Property rights be determined.
   i. ☐ Petitioner's former name be restored *(specify):*
   j. ☐ Other *(specify):*
   k. ☐ Continued on Attachment 7j.

8. If there are minor children born to or adopted by the Petitioner and Respondent before or during this marriage, the court will make orders for the support of the children. An earnings assignment will be issued without further notice.

9. **I HAVE READ THE RESTRAINING ORDERS ON THE BACK OF THE SUMMONS, AND I UNDERSTAND THAT THEY APPLY TO ME WHEN THIS PETITION IS FILED.**

I declare under penalty of perjury under the laws of the State of California that the foregoing is true and correct.

Date:

_____
(TYPE OR PRINT NAME)

▶ _____
(SIGNATURE OF PETITIONER)

Date:

_____
(TYPE OR PRINT NAME)

▶ _____
(SIGNATURE OF ATTORNEY FOR PETITIONER)

> NOTICE: Dissolution or legal separation may automatically cancel the rights of a spouse under the other spouse's will, trust, retirement benefit plan, power of attorney, pay on death bank account, transfer on death vehicle registration, survivorship rights to any property owned in joint tenancy, and any other similar thing. It does not automatically cancel the right of a spouse as beneficiary of the other spouse's life insurance policy. You should review these matters, as well as any credit cards, other credit accounts, insurance polices, retirement benefit plans, and credit reports to determine whether they should be changed or whether you should take any other actions. However, some changes may require the agreement of your spouse or a court order (see Family Code sections 231-235).

FL-100 [Rev. January 1, 2003]   **PETITION**   Page 2 of 2
                                            (Family Law)

benefits during the marriage. Therefore, the longer the marriage, often the greater the share of pension benefits the other spouse (the spouse who did not contribute to the benefits) receives.

Preliminary Hearing or Order to Show Cause

Since the whole divorce process often takes considerable time, the courts allow preliminary proceedings where one of the spouses may request a temporary order. Most attorneys advise their clients not to agree to a temporary order, however, if they would not agree to that same order on a permanent basis. Many courts use the temporary order when deciding the issues in the case on a permanent basis.

If one party needs financial support to provide for her needs, then it may be sought in the preliminary or **Order to Show Cause** hearing. Other items that might be requested at this time include attorneys' fees, temporary custody, child support, spousal support, and permission to live in the family home. If there is a problem with physical abuse, then a Temporary Restraining Order (or Stay-Away Order) may be request against the abusing spouse to keep that spouse away from the abused spouse and the home.

Child Custody Determination

Under modern statutes, both parents have an equal right to custody of their children. The primary principle used by the court in determining custody is the "best interests of the child." Some questions the court must answer are the following:

1. Which parent wants custody of the child?
2. Which parent does the child want to live with? (This question is more critical with older children. For instance, a judge may be more likely to ask a twelve-year-old which parent he wants to live with than a five-year-old.)
3. How well does the child get along with each parent and with other siblings?
4. How well established is the child in the community in which he lives? Has the family home been in this location for a considerable period of time? Does the child go to school in the neighborhood?
5. What is the mental and physical health of the child and the parents? If the child has physical or mental problems, which parent would be better able to take care of him?
6. What would a change in environment do to the child's stability at this time?
7. Which parent appears to the court to be better able to care for the child's needs.
8. Will changing the custodial arrangement removes the child from this court's jurisdiction?

Order to Show Cause (OSC) a preliminary hearing in a dissolution action where the court issues temporary orders on such matters as support and child custody.

In most cases, where both parents are stable and positive influences on the child, the noncustodial parent will be awarded liberal visitation rights. If there has been a history of abuse by one of the parents, however, the court may order supervised visitation or, in extreme cases, no visitation at all.

From a practical standpoint, custody issues are the most difficult problems in which the family lawyer will be involved. As a paralegal or legal assistant in a family law practice, one must often listen to extremely difficult problems. Being able to leave one's job "at the office" is particularly beneficial in this type of environment.

Child Support

Both spouses are legally required to support their children. Generally, the noncustodial parent pays support for the child to the custodial parent. The amount of support awarded is determined by the best interests of the child. The court looks at the age of the child, the salaries of both parents, the manner in which the child has been living, and the number of children. Child support payments may not be discharged in bankruptcy proceedings. Therefore, a parent who files for bankruptcy must still pay child support.

In addition to food, clothing, and shelter, the parent may be required to provide the following items:

1. Medical, vision, and/or dental insurance
2. Education expenses
3. Medical and hospital expenses

The requirements for child support end when the child reaches the age of majority, usually eighteen.

Some states have instituted criminal penalties against absent parents who do not support their children. For instance, in California, the District Attorney's office has a special Child Support Division that investigates nonpaying parents and obtains support for the custodial parent through salary garnishment, wage assignments, and tax liens. Sometimes criminal penalties such as incarceration are imposed on a nonpaying parent.

Alimony or Spousal Support

Some spouses are required to pay alimony or support to the other spouse when a divorce is obtained. In deciding whether to award support, the court will consider whether the spouses are both capable of earning a living for themselves or whether one has not worked before and lacks job skills. In the latter case, the court may order a vocational rehabilitation counselor to interview the nonworking spouse to determine the amount of time and training required to make that person a contributing member of the workforce. In such cases, the court may order temporary support for months or years to allow the person to obtain job training.

Other factors that the court may look at in determining alimony include the ages of the parties, the length of the marriage, the couple's standard of living, the ages of the children and the salary of the paying spouse. Generally, an individual is more likely to get spousal support after a long-term marriage. Some states have defined long-term marriages as those lasting five years or more. Spousal support often lasts until the spouse who is receiving the support dies or remarries.

Marital Settlement Agreement

To expedite the divorce settlement, the attorneys may negotiate an agreement between the parties to divide their assets. If the parties can agree to the division of property, support, visitation rights, custody, and all other issues, then the court will not intervene in the settlement process. The **Marital Settlement Agreement** sets out all of the terms of the settlement and is signed by both parties. If the parties can arrive at an agreement, the court proceedings are less complicated, and the process becomes more tolerable. A sample Marital Settlement Agreement is shown in Exhibit 10-6.

Final Decree of Divorce or Dissolution

After a certain period of time has elapsed, usually about six months or a year after the initial complaint or petition was filed with the court, the final decree may be filed. In most states, this is a separate document that is prepared by the attorney. As the paralegal or legal assistant, you should put a note in your "tickler file" to file this document at the appropriate time. There are many horror stories about individuals who thought their divorces were final and remarried, only to find that the final papers were never filed.

California has attempted to address this problem by allowing the parties to file a **Final Decree Nunc Pro Tunc**, which is a final dissolution that is retroactive; that is, it becomes effective as of the time the dissolution would have taken place if the final decree had been filed at the appropriate time. This procedure solves the problem of a person who has inadvertently remarried without being divorced.

ADOPTION

The legal procedure whereby an individual or a couple become parents to a child who has not been born to them is known as **adoption**. The child relinquishes all rights and responsibilities that previously existed with the biological parents. The new parents then assume these responsibilities as though the child had been born to them. Clients should be made fully aware of the consequences of the adoption process. The birth parents are no longer considered the legal parents of the child, and their parental rights are terminated, while the adoptive parents assume all rights and responsibilities for that child. The child loses all right to inherit from the birth parents and receives the right to inherit from the adoptive parents. In addition, the child acquires a new set of relatives, including siblings, grandparents, aunts, uncles, and cousins, just as if he had been born into the family.

Marital Settlement Agreement an agreement made by a married couple contemplating divorce that sets forth the manner in which property is to be divided.

Final Decree Nunc Pro Tunc a final dissolution of a marriage that is filed after the appropriate time for filing a final decree, but is effective as of the time the dissolution would have taken place if the final decree had been filed in a timely manner.

adoption a legal proceeding where adoptive parents become the legal parents of an adopted child. The birth parents give up all legal rights and responsibilities for the child.

EXHIBIT 10-6   Marital Settlement Agreement

1   MARITAL SETTLEMENT AGREEMENT

2   BETWEEN

3   JAMES R. MARTIN AND

4   BARBARA S. MARTIN

5

6   The parties above named are husband and wife and hereby agree that irreconcilable differences have

7   caused the irremediable breakdown of their marriage. It is their mutual desire to bring about a final division

8   of their property and a complete settlement of their respective property rights to all of their property. To

9   this end, the parties agree to the following:

10

11   FIRST: The parties agree that the following items are community property and should be divided equal-

12   ly between them:

13   1. House located at 333 Sycamore Lane. Austin, Texas

14   2. Lot 264 in the Subdivision Map of Carrollwood Estates, known as 64 Treetop Road, Cordova, Tennessee

15   These properties shall be sold and the proceeds equally divided between the parties.

16

17   SECOND: The parties agree that the following items are separate property and shall remain with the owner.

18   The separate property of JAMES R. MARTIN consists of the following:

19   1. 2005 Lexus GS300 sedan, License No. JIMBOW

20   2. All of his jewelry as previously agreed upon

21   The separate property of BARBARA S. MARTIN consists of the following:

22   1. 2002 Ferrari, License No. FASTTT

23   2. All of her jewelry as previously agreed upon.

24

25   THIRD: The parties agree that neither party shall receive either support or maintenance and that each

26   party will maintain his/her own medical insurance, life insurance, and retirement plans.

27

28

1

continued

Exhibit 10-6 *continued*

1   FOURTH: Both parties have read this agreement and accept and understand its terms. No further

2   promises have been made by the parties outside of this Marital Settlement Agreement.

3

4   FIFTH: Both parties agree to execute all documents required to effectuate the sale and/or transfers of

5   property required by this agreement.

6

7   SIXTH: Subject to the approval of the Texas Family Law Court, this document shall be made a part of

8   the decree of divorce of the parties.

9

10   Executed on the _____ day of _____ , 2006 by:

11

12   _____

13   JAMES R. MARTIN

14

15   _____

16   BARBARA S. MARTIN

17

18

19

20

21

22

23

24

25

26

27

28

2

Independent adoptions have become a new specialty area for some attorneys. Pregnant women contact the attorney, who provides them with resumes of prospective parents for their child. The birth mother can review the resumes of the prospective adoptive parents and interview those that she feels would be appropriate. She thus has the option of actually choosing her child's new parents. In most states, both parents must consent to the adoption in writing.

Agency adoptions are becoming less common because very few babies are given up to agencies for adoption. One or both birth parents must sign a document that relinquishes the child to the agency. The birth parent does not have the opportunity of knowing where the child is placed.

In **stepparent adoptions**, a new spouse adopts the other spouse's child from a previous marriage. The child's other parent must give permission for this adoption to occur. For instance, during Sue and Bob's marriage, they have a son, Michael. Sue and Bob are divorced, and Sue marries Stan. Stan would like to adopt Michael. Bob must sign a form giving permission for the adoption to occur. Stan then becomes Michael's father, and Bob has no rights or responsibilities for Michael.

If one adult adopts another adult, the adopting parent must be at least ten years older than the adopted adult. Although this type of adoption is rare, it offers the advantage of giving the adopted adult the right to inherit from the other adult. The majority of states require the permission of the spouse of the adopting adult before such an adoption may occur.

Procedures for Adoptions

Most states have basic forms or documents that must be filed to accomplish the adoption. These involve a petition, a **Consent and Agreement**, and a **decree**. When the client comes into the office to initiate the adoption, the paralegal or legal secretary must complete the petition, which includes the names of the new parents, the name of the child at birth, the date of birth, and the signatures of the adopting parents. A sample Adoption Petition is shown in Exhibit 10-7 on page 261.

In many states, a Consent and Agreement form must be completed by the adopting parents and by the child if she is over twelve years of age. Permissions must be obtained from the birth parents.

After the hearing is held before the court, the judge will issue a Decree of Adoption, stating that the child may be adopted and the new name for the child. At this time, a copy of the decree may be sent to the state agency where birth records are kept so that a new birth certificate may be issued to the child with her new name and the names of her new parents. Note that single individuals may also adopt children in most states.

independent adoption
an adoption that is not carried out through an agency; usually carried out though an attorney who acts as a middleperson between the biological mother and the adoptive parents.

agency adoption
the adoption of a child through a public or private agency.

stepparent adoption
the adoption by one spouse of the other spouse's child or children from a former marriage.

Consent and Agreement
in adoption proceedings, the forms by which the adopting parents obtain the approval of the biological parents.

decree in adoption proceedings, a form issued by the court that states that the child may be adopted and indicates the child's new name.

ETHICS and ETIQUETTE

One of the major conflicts that arise in the Family Law practice is that of attempting to represent both parties in a divorce action. Oftentimes, those divorces that start out amicably do not end up that way. Attorneys should avoid representing both parties. Conflict of interest situations occur in those cases for many reasons. Suppose both parties want custody of the children. One attorney cannot be an advocate for both parties in that situation. Or suppose there is a question whether a piece of property is one spouse's separate property or whether the property is marital or community property. Since the attorney is required to zealously represent her client, it would be difficult to choose which client should prevail.

Some paralegals open offices to prepare legal documents for clients who are getting a divorce. However, the paralegal must be sure that he is only typing the information supplied by the client and not giving legal advice. The paralegal may not explain the rights of the parties, nor may he advise the client as to her options. Most states require that these paralegals call on an attorney or refer the client to an attorney when the client needs legal advice. Likewise, those paralegals or legal assistants employed in law offices must refer all such issues to the attorney. The paralegal or legal assistant may prepare forms based on information obtained from the client. However, they may not tell the client how to prepare the form or the ramifications of including various information.

CHAPTER SUMMARY ✦

Family law centers on questions related to marriage, divorce, and adoption. States have various requirements for marriage, including such things as blood tests and residency requirements. Thirteen states and the District of Columbia also recognize common-law marriages. Marriages between closely related individuals are never valid and are void from the onset. A voidable marriage has a defect that makes it possible for one of the parties to have the marriage voided; the marriage is not automatically void, however, and may become valid under certain circumstances. A growing trend in family law is the preparation of prenuptial agreements that set out how the couple's property will be divided if they divorce.

Divorce law varies by state. Some states require grounds for divorce, while others have no-fault divorce or dissolution. In some states, a petition is used to initiate the dissolution proceeding, while divorces generally require a complaint. Property division, spousal support or alimony, child custody, and child support are all issues that may arise in a divorce. Marital Settlement Agreements are prepared to set out how the property is to be divided upon divorce or dissolution.

Adoptions may be undertaken privately or through an agency. In some cases, stepparents adopt their stepchildren. A petition, consent, and decree are usually required for an adoption.

EXHIBIT 10-7 Adoption Petition

1   Michelle M. Tanaka

2   Attorney at Law

3   1122 Main Street

4   Roanoke, VA 99999

5   (315) 999-5555

6   IN THE CIRCUIT COURT FOR THE CITY OF ROANOKE

7   STATE OF VIRGINIA

8   In the Matter of the Adoption Petition of:

9

10 JENNIFER LEE and   )

11   )

12 ROBERT LEE,   )

13   )   ADOPTION PETITION

14 Adoptive Parents and Petitioners.   )   NO. A-48999

15 _____

16

17 Petitioners herein allege as follows:

18   1. That at the time of the birth of the minor who is the subject of this petition, her name was MARY MARTINE.

19   2. That the petitioners herein are husband and wife and presently reside in the City of Roanoke, State of

20 Virginia, and wish to adopt the minor child, MARY MARTINE, who was born in Marysville County, Virginia, on

21 October 26, 2005. The petitioners are adults and are both more than ten years older than the minor child.

22   3. The parents of the minor child will consent to the adoption by said petitioners. The minor child

23 presently resides with the Adoptive Parents.

24   4. Both parties agree to the adoption of this child by the other party.

25   5. This child is a proper subject for adoption. The home of the Adoptive Parents is a proper home for

26 this child, and they are able to provide suitable care.

27   6. All background information required by the Virginia Department of Adoptions will be promptly sub-

28 mitted thereto by the undersigned petitioners.

1

continued

Exhibit 10-7 *continued*

1	WHEREFORE, petitioners pray that the Court grant this adoption request to enable the parties to maintain a
2	relationship of parent and child. The new name for the child shall be MARY ELIZABETH LEE.
3	
4	
5	ROBERT LEE
6	
7	
8	JENNIFER LEE
9	
10	
11	
12	
13	
14	
15	
16	
17	
18	
19	
20	
21	
22	
23	
24	
25	
26	
27	
28	

2

◆ KEY TERMS

adoption	marriage
agency adoption	mental impairment
annulment	no-fault divorce
cohabitation	Order to Show Cause (OSC)
cohabitation agreement	palimony
common-law marriage	petition
community property	prenuptial agreement
condoning misconduct	quasi-community property
connivance	recrimination
decree	separate property
dissolution	stepparent adoption
divorce	void
Final Decree Nunc Pro Tunc	voidable
grounds for divorce	voidable marriage
independent adoption	void marriage
Marital Settlement Agreement	

◆ SELF TEST

Indicate whether the following statements are true (T) or false (F).

_____ 1. All states recognize common-law marriage.

_____ 2. Recent cases have awarded "palimony" when couples who have lived together for a long time part company.

_____ 3. A cohabitation agreement is prepared by a couple in contemplation of marriage and provides for a subsequent division of property.

_____ 4. Void marriages include those between a person and his ancestor and between a person and her descendant.

_____ 5. A marriage may be voidable if either party was of unsound mind at the time of the marriage.

Circle the correct answer for the following questions:

1. Annulment means
   a. the marriage is treated as if it had never existed.
   b. the same thing as divorce.
   c. a legal separation.
   d. a no-fault divorce.

2. Property acquired during a marriage that is not a gift or an inheritance is known as
   a. separate property.
   b. community property.
   c. communal property.
   d. quasi-community property.

3. A divorce action is initiated by filing a
   a. complaint.
   b. answer.
   c. default.
   d. financial statement.

4. A dissolution action is initiated by filing a
   a. complaint.
   b. petition.
   c. default.
   d. financial statement.

5. The requirement that a person filing for divorce must have lived in that state for a sufficient period of time is called a(n)
   a. domiciled requirement.
   b. residency requirement.
   c. live-in requirement.
   d. address requirement.

Fill-in-the-blanks

1. Preliminary support may be obtained at the _____.

2. Which spouse is legally required to support the children? _____

3. The court determines the amount of child support based on the _____.

4. The first document filed in a divorce or dissolution action is called the _____ in a no-fault divorce state and the _____ in a state that has grounds for divorce.

5. Marriages that are void include _____.

✦ REVIEW QUESTIONS

1. Explain the difference between void and voidable marriages.

2. List the procedures followed for private adoptions.

3. Explain what the court considers in setting the amount of child support a parent must pay.

4. List the issues that are decided at the Order to Show Cause hearing.

✦ NOTEBOOK PROJECTS

1. Depending on the law in your state, prepare either a petition for dissolution or a complaint for divorce using the case information provided. If you live in a state that requires grounds for divorce, your instructor will tell you the proper grounds. Prepare the form for your state. If your state forms are not available, use Exhibit 10-2, 10-3, or 10-4. *Note:* 10-4 is not provided on disk.

CASE INFORMATION

- Client's name: Mary E. Gallo
- Address: 245 Sunset Drive, Your Town, Your State
- Court: Use the closest appropriate court in your state.
- Spouse: Michael P. Gallo
- Spouse's address: 459 Academy Street, Your Town, Your State
- Married: June 15, 1995
- Separated: July 4, current year
- Minor children: Anna Gallo, born 9/9/1997
                            Paul Gallo, born 4/29/2000

The children are currently living with their mother.

The client requests that the following items be designated as her separate property: a three-carat marquise-cut diamond ring, 1995 Chevrolet station wagon, service for 12 Lennox china, service for 12 International sterling silver, and International sterling silver six-piece tea service.

Community (or marital) assets include the following and should be divided between the parties:

- Residence located at 245 Sunset Drive, Your Town, Your State; valued at $250,000 with equity of $200,000.

- Vacation home located at 999 Brentwood Drive, Lake Arrowhead, California; valued at $150,000, which was paid in cash; therefore, total equity is $150,000.

- Furniture and furnishings located at residence: $50,000.

- Furniture and furnishings located at California home: $25,000.

- Bank account at National Savings Bank, Your Town: $20,000.

The client requests dissolution or divorce, full custody of the children, spousal support of $3,000 per month, and child support of $1,000 per month. She also requests that her spouse pay her attorney's fees.

  2. Our clients, John and Norma Ray, wish to adopt a child, Virginia Steadman, whose parents are Steven and Roberta Steadman. Virginia was born May 30, 2004, in your state. The Steadmans will consent to the adoption, and Virginia's new name will be Virginia Ray. Using the format for your state, prepare a Petition for Adoption. If you do not know the format for your state, use Exhibit 10-6 as a guide.

3. List the grounds for divorce recognized in your state. If your state is a no-fault state, describe the procedures for filing for divorce or dissolution in your state.

4. Research and determine the divorce laws in your state as they relate to the following. Prepare a written report on your findings.
   a. Grounds
   b. Filing procedures and fees
   c. Child support
   d. Child custody
   e. Spousal support

5. Our client, Nancy Hallam, put her baby up for adoption on June 1, 1997. She is interested in obtaining the records of the child's adoptive parents and learning where they are located. The child was adopted through the county agency in your state. Research the laws in your state to determine whether the records may be obtained by the client. Prepare a memorandum to Mr. Williams indicating your findings.

BUSINESS ORGANIZATIONS

CHAPTER OUTCOMES

As a result of studying this chapter, the student will learn:

- To distinguish the characteristics of the different types of business organizations, including sole proprietorships, partnerships, and corporations
- The role the legal professional plays in the formation of each type of business organization
- To prepare partnership agreements, corporate formation, and corporate dissolution documents

TYPES OF BUSINESS ORGANIZATIONS

The most common types of business organizations are the sole proprietorship, partnership, and corporation. Although most businesses are operated as sole proprietorships, one of the other forms of organization may be more advantageous, depending on the client's preferences.

SOLE PROPRIETORSHIPS

The mainstay of the United States economy is the **sole proprietorship**, an unincorporated business that is usually owned by one person. You probably deal with sole proprietorships every day. The dry cleaner's where you take your clothes, the service station where you buy gas, and the local convenience store may be organized in this manner.

Sole proprietorships offer both advantages and disadvantages. One advantage is that sole proprietorships are relatively easy to establish and are not costly to organize. Because they usually are owned by only one individual, the owner does not have to be concerned about disagreements with other owners.

The owner of a sole proprietorship is subject to unlimited personal liability, however, which can be a major disadvantage in today's litigious society. For instance, if someone sues the business and is awarded damages of $200,000 when the assets of the business are worth only $50,000, he would be able to take the owner's personal assets as well as those of the business in settlement of the claim. Most small business

sole proprietorship
unincorporated business, usually owned by one person.

owners will have liability insurance to protect them against these eventualities, however.

The sole proprietor is responsible for the management operations of the business. If a manager for the business is hired by the sole proprietor, the owner may be responsible for any actions of the manager which are done in the scope of her employment. This concept is known as "vicarious liability." The owner of the business may purchase inventory, equipment, and any other items needed to run the operation. She may incur loans and debts. As in the case of the liability for injuries to customers discussed above, she also has unlimited liability for the debts of the sole proprietorship. The owner is liable to all creditors of the business for unpaid bills.

In most cases, the individual wishing to set up a small business will seek a loan from a financial institution. When the bank reviews the business assets and collateral, the owner's personal assets will be evaluated as well.

One major disadvantage of the sole proprietorship is that the owner has less access to capital to undertake new projects than a partnership or corporation. If the owner wishes to expand the business, she is limited to obtaining personal loans using the business assets or her personal assets as security.

Having a single owner can also lead to problems. If the owner dies or becomes disabled, there may be no one else who can run the business. The only recourse might be to sell the business, which could result in a loss of profit and revenues.

In many cases, other forms of organization will provide certain tax benefits. The owner should consult an accountant or tax attorney for advice before changing the form of ownership to save taxes. Sometimes little or no tax savings results.

If the business sells items to the public and the state imposes a sales tax, then a sales tax permit must be obtained. If the proprietorship operates under a name other than the owner's name, a Fictitious Business Name Certificate must be filed in the county where the business is located. A business license must be obtained in the city where the business is located. A sample Fictitious Business Name Certificate is shown in Exhibit 11-1.

PARTNERSHIPS
✦

A **partnership** is an association of two or more individuals who have joined together to operate a business for profit. The major reasons for forming a partnership are to share expenses and to increase capital. Although a partnership is a business, the partnership itself is not taxed; instead, partners must declare their share of the partnership profits on their personal income tax return.

partnership
an association of two or more individuals who have joined together to operate a business for profit.

The partnership demonstrates the feature of straightforward joint ownership. Partnerships are generally larger than sole proprietorships, which can explain the need for more capital and increased sharing of expenses. Where the most favorable business size is small, a partnership is often advantageous. Where the business size is large, most

EXHIBIT 11-1   Fictitious Business Name Statement

FICTITIOUS BUSINESS NAME STATEMENT

File No. 425222

The following persons are doing business as:

GOLFF FOR LESS, 166 East Airport Road, Scottsdale, AZ 85013

Danielle M. Gallo, 5111 Sunset Drive, Scottsdale, AZ 85011

Jeffrey W. Longman, 4315 East Desert Drive, Scottsdale, AZ 85011

This business is conducted by two individuals.

DANIELLE M. GALLO	JEFFREY W. LONGMAN

This statement was filed with the County Clerk of Maricopa County on May 19, 2003.

The registrants commenced to transact business under the fictitious name listed above on May 11, 2003.

NOTICE: This Fictitious Business Name Statement expires five years from the date it was filed with the office of the County Clerk. A new Fictitious Business Name Statement must be filed before that time.

The filing of this statement does not of itself authorize the use in this state of a Fictitious Business Name in violation of the rights of another under Federal, State, or common law (See Section 9222 et seq., Business Code.)

individuals would prefer some form of corporate ownership arrangement. More than any other type of business arrangement, the partnership must be based on trust among the partners. All partners are equally responsible for the acts of the others. Each partner may bind the partnership to contracts or other business arrangements. Each partner is responsible for the liability and debts of the other partners when that debt or liability involves the partnership. For example, if Partner A decides to purchase a yacht in the partnership's name, each of the partners is also liable for payment of the purchase price of the yacht. If one partner enters into a contract for the partnership, then all partners will be liable for the terms of the contract. Although one partner may deal honestly and fairly and without fraudulent intent, another partner may engage in illegal activities or dishonest practices for which the honest partner could be held liable.

With all of the disadvantages described above, one wonders why individuals would form a partnership when they could gain extra business capital by taking loans and acquiring assistance in the operation of the business by hiring employees. The organization of the partnership is basically the same as that of a sole proprietorship, except that the partners take on the responsibilities of the sole proprietor.

Clients should be advised to choose their partners carefully and to select partners whose management practices and beliefs are similar to their own. Knowing an individual's business ethics is only the first step in determining whether to choose an individual for a partner. Partnership agreements should be scrutinized to determine the exact terms of the agreement as well as who is responsible for the actions of the partnership and whose decisions are final. In many cases, when the client is apprised of all of the disadvantages of the partnership arrangement, he will choose either a sole proprietorship or a corporate arrangement.

General and Limited Partners

Although a partnership may have only two partners, many partnerships have numerous partners and include both general and limited partners. **General partners** are involved in the day-to-day operations of the business. They not only invest money in the partnership but are also responsible for its management. In many partnerships, all partners are general partners.

Sometimes individuals have capital to invest but do not wish to be responsible for the management of the partnership. These partners are **limited partners**. Unlike general partners, limited partners are not personally liable for the other partners' actions. A limited partner may only be held liable for the amount of money he contributed to the business. However, a limited partner has no power to make business decisions related to the partnership. If a general partner makes a decision that is displeasing to a limited partner, he has no recourse but to leave the partnership if the partnership agreement allows him to do so.

A partnership must have at least one general partner who is responsible for the partnership liability; thus, a partnership cannot have only limited partners. Some states have more stringent regulations on limited partners. You should research the statutes in your own state to learn the rules for limited partnerships. List the main requirements in the State Specific Information box.

general partners individuals who invest money in the business and are involved in its day-to-day operations.

limited partners individuals who invest capital in the business without management responsibility or personal liability.

STATE SPECIFIC INFORMATION

Requirements for limited partnerships in the state of _____ include the following:

_____

_____

_____

The General Partnership Agreement

When the partnership involves only general partners, they must negotiate an agreement for the operation of the business. Because of the complexity of a general partnership and the responsibilities and liabilities involved in this type business arrangement, it is advisable to have a written partnership agreement that enumerates the following elements:

1. Title—name and address of partners
2. Name—name, purpose, and location of the partnership
3. Duration of the partnership
4. Each partner's contribution in money and time
5. How profits will be divided and allocation of expenses and losses
6. How a partner may transfer her interests
7. How a partner's interest may be "bought out" or purchased by the other partners. (This issue will be particularly critical if your client is the partner whose interest is purchased.)
8. The procedure for voting on issues
9. Duties and responsibilities of each partner
10. Procedures for dissolving the partnership
11. Procedures for removing a partner or obtaining new partners
12. How policy disagreements will be settled
13. Accounting procedures used in the business
14. Each partner's liability to the other partners
15. How partners will be compensated
16. What effect the death or resignation of a partner will have
17. Signatures of the partners

A sample general partnership agreement is included as Exhibit 11-2.

Format for General Partnership Agreement

Title.   The title of the partnership agreement should identify the parties and the nature of the agreement. For instance, in Exhibit 11-2, Adams and Harmon are identified as the parties to the agreement. The nature of the agreement is that it is a General Partnership Agreement.

Name, Nature, and Location.   Exhibit 11-2 shows that the partnership is being formed to manufacture candles and that the partnership name is Adams and Harmon. Its principal place of business is given under No. 4.

Capital Contribution.   Under the title "Initial Capital," the agreement indicates the initial capital that each partner must contribute as well as how the partners share in profits and losses. It indicates the accounting procedures, management rights, compensation, and profits allocation.

The partnership agreement also indicates the procedures for dissolution of the partnership on the death of one of the partners, as well

EXHIBIT 11-2 Partnership Agreement

ADAMS AND HARMON
GENERAL PARTNERSHIP AGREEMENT

This Agreement is made on May 6, 2006 by Gregory Adams and Lisa Harmon, referred to as "Partners" under the following provisions.

1. The Partners shall associate to form a General Partnership for the purpose of manufacturing candles and any other businesses agreed upon by the Partners.

2. The Partnership name shall be Adams & Harmon.

3. The Partnership shall commence on the execution of this Agreement and shall continue until dissolved by agreement of the Partners or terminated under the Agreement.

4. The Partnership's principal place of business shall be 24 Colonial Road, Salem, Massachusetts.

Initial Capital

5. The Partnership's initial capital shall be $100,000. Each Partner shall contribute toward the initial capital by depositing the following amounts in the Partnership checking account at the Main Office of the Community Bank in Salem, Massachusetts, May 20, 2006:
Each party shall contribute $50,000.

6. No Partner shall withdraw any portion of the Partnership capital without the other Partner's express written consent.

7. The Partners shall share equally in Partnership net profits and shall bear Partnership losses equally.

8. Partnership books of account shall be accurately kept and shall include records of all Partnership income, expenses, assets, and liabilities. The Partnership books of account shall be maintained on a cash basis. Each Partner shall have the right to inspect the Partnership books at any time.

9. The Partnership's fiscal year shall end on December 31 each year.

10. Complete accountings of the Partnership affairs at the close of business on the last days of March, September, and December of each year shall be rendered to each Partner within 10 days after the close of each such month. At the time of such accounting, the net profits of the Partnership shall be distributed to the Partners as provided in this Agreement. Except as to errors brought to the Partners' attention within 10 days after it is rendered, each accounting shall be final and conclusive.

11. Each Partner shall devote undivided time to and use utmost skill in the Partnership business.

12. Each Partner shall have an equal right in the management of the Partnership. Each Partner shall have authority to bind the Partnership in making contracts and incurring obligations in the Partnership name or on its credit. No Partner, however, shall incur obligations in the Partnership name or on its credit exceeding $10,000 without the other Partner's express written consent. Any obligation incurred in violation of this provision shall be charged to and collected from the Partner who incurred the obligation.

13. In compensation for services in the Partnership business, each Partner shall be entitled to a salary of $3,000 per month. The Partnership shall deduct the Partners' salaries as ordinary business expenses prior to computing net profits. A Partner's salary may be increased or reduced at any time by mutual agreement of the Partners.

14. The term "net profits," as used in this Agreement, shall mean the Partnership net profits as determined by generally accepted accounting principles for each accounting period specified in this Agreement.

15. Upon 30-days written notice of intent to the other Partner, either Partner may withdraw from the Partnership at the end of any accounting period specified in this Agreement.

continued

Exhibit 11-2 *continued*

16. On dissolution of the Partnership by the death, withdrawal, or other act of either Partner, the remaining Partner may continue the Partnership business by purchasing the outgoing Partner's interest in the Partnership assets and goodwill. The remaining Partner shall have the option to purchase the outgoing Partner's interest by paying to the outgoing Partner or the appropriate personal representative the value of the outgoing Partner's interest as determined under Paragraph 17 of this Agreement.

17. On exercise of the option described in Paragraph 16 of this Agreement, the remaining Partner shall pay to the outgoing Partner or appropriate personal representative the value of the outgoing Partner's Partnership interest as determined by the last regular accounting preceding dissolution plus the full unwithdrawn portion of the outgoing Partner's share in net profits earned between the date of that accounting and the date of dissolution.

18. If the Partnership is dissolved by the death of either Partner, the remaining Partner shall have 30 days from the date of death in which to purchase the deceased Partner's Partnership interest. The purchase price for the deceased Partner's interest shall be determined under Paragraph 17 of this Agreement. During the 30-day period following either Partner's death, the remaining Partner may continue the Partnership business. The liability of the deceased Partner's estate for Partnership obligations incurred during the period of continuation shall be limited to the amount that the deceased Partner had invested or involved with the Partnership at the time of death and that is includable in the deceased Partner's estate. The deceased Partner's estate shall be entitled, at the election of the personal representative, to either one-half of the Partnership profits earned during the period of continuation or to interest at 10 percent (10%) per annum for the Partnership's use of the deceased Partner's interest as determined under Paragraph 17 of this Agreement during the period of continuation.

19. On any purchase and sale made pursuant to Paragraphs 16, 17, or 18 of this Agreement, the remaining Partner shall assume all Partnership obligations. The remaining Partner shall hold the withdrawing Partner or the deceased Partner's estate and personal representative, as well as any property belonging to either a withdrawing or deceased Partner, free and harmless from all liability for Partnership obligations. Immediately upon purchase of a withdrawing or deceased Partner's interest, the remaining Partner shall prepare, file, serve, and publish all notices required by law to protect the withdrawing Partner or the deceased Partner's estate and personal representative from liability for future Partnership obligations. All costs incident to the requirements of this Paragraph shall be borne by the remaining Partner.

20. On dissolution of the Partnership, except as provided in Paragraphs 16, 17, and 18 of this Agreement, the Partnership affairs shall be wound up, the Partnership assets liquidated, its debts paid, and the surplus divided among the Partners according to their then net worths in the Partnership business.

21. All notices between the Partners shall be in writing and shall be deemed served when personally delivered to a Partner, or when deposited in the United States mail, certified, first-class postage prepaid, addressed to a Partner at the Partnership's principal place of business or to such other place as may be specified in a notice given pursuant to this Paragraph as the address for service of notice on such Partner.

22. All consents and agreements provided for or permitted by this Agreement shall be in writing. Signed copies of all consents and agreements pertaining to the Partnership shall be kept with the Partnership books.

23. On all accountings provided for in this Agreement, the goodwill of the Partnership business shall be valued at one dollar ($1) and no more.

24. This instrument contains the Partner's sole agreement pertaining to their Partnership. It correctly sets out the Partners' rights and obligations. Any prior agreements, promises, negotiations, or representations not expressly set forth in this instrument have no force or effect.

Executed at Salem, Massachusetts, This _____ day of May, 2006.

_____

GREGORY ADAMS

_____

LISA HARMON

as procedures for purchase and sale by the partners. It is signed by both partners.

Should the Client Form a Partnership?

The decision of whether to form a partnership or continue as a sole proprietorship can become very complex. When the client comes to the office to discuss the type of organization that is appropriate for her business, the following questions should be asked:

1. Why do you want to change your form of business ownership?

2. Do you need more capital for expansion or another purpose? If so, would a loan be preferable to forming a partnership? Are other methods of raising capital available?

3. How well do you know your partner(s)? Have you had prior business dealings or are you personal friends?

4. Do you have any information about the prospective partner's business ethics? Has he been convicted of a crime? Has he been involved in unethical practices?

5. Do you know the partner's management practices? Are they similar to your own?

6. Have you considered forming a corporation instead of a partnership? (At this point, the difference between a corporation and a partnership should be explained to the client, who may not be aware of the advantages of a corporation. The ultimate decision, however, rests with the client.)

If the paralegal conducts the discussion with the client, no legal advice may be given. Any questions that require the paralegal to "advise" the client should be referred to the attorney. However, the paralegal may explain the various types of business structures to the client and the advantages and disadvantages of each. If the client asks, "What type of business do you think I should form, a sole proprietorship, partnership, or corporation?" the client should be referred to the attorney. This is a typical example of a question that should not be answered by the paralegal because it constitutes legal advice.

CORPORATIONS ✦

corporation business entity existing separate and apart from its owners.

shareholders owners of a corporation.

A **corporation** is a business entity that exists separately and apart from its owners, who are called **shareholders**. Some corporations have just a few shareholders, while others have thousands. A corporation is said to have "perpetual life" because it is not dissolved upon the death of any of the shareholders. A shareholder's ownership interest is represented by shares of stock. The interest can easily be transferred to another by selling the stock.

The primary advantages of the corporate structure are the ability to raise considerably larger sums of capital, the limited liability of the owners of shares, and the corporation's perpetual life. Because many individuals pool their capital to form a corporation, potentially, large sums of money can be raised. Unlike sole proprietors and general partners, owners of shares of a corporation's stock will not be liable for damages if a lawsuit is brought against the corporation. If the corporation must pay damages, only the corporate assets may be used to satisfy the claim. Having perpetual life means that when a shareholder dies, his shares of stock pass to his heirs; but the corporation itself continues. As we have seen in other forms of business organizations, the death of an owner may mean the dissolution of the business.

In some cases, a corporation enjoys lower tax rates than other forms of business organization. In a small, closely held corporation, the business income may be divided between the owner and the corporation. By dividing the income, the owner will be in a lower tax bracket and will be assessed lower taxes than if he were a sole proprietor and reported all the business income on his personal tax return. For instance, if the owner works in the business and collects a salary, he must report the salary on his personal income tax return; but his salary is deducted from the income of the corporation, which pays no tax on it. If the corporation's income amounts to $150,000 to $200,000 a year or less after deducting all expenses including salaries, this method of dividing the corporate income between the owner and the business will probably result in lower taxes than if the business were run as a partnership or a sole proprietorship. Obviously, this system will only be advantageous in a small corporation with a few owners who collect a salary from the corporation.

One disadvantage of corporations is that they are regulated more stringently than other types of organizations. Creating and maintaining the corporate structure can involve a considerable amount of paperwork. The government may require various documents including Articles of Incorporation, Bylaws, Minutes of Meetings, and Proxy statements. The next sections will discuss preincorporation concerns to discuss with the client as well as the mechanics of how the corporation is formed.

Preliminary Considerations

The attorney and client must discuss some preliminary matters before the corporate documents are prepared. The following items must be addressed:

1. The type of corporate structure
2. The form of stock ownership
3. The corporation's purpose
4. The financial foundation
5. The state of incorporation (usually the state where the attorney and client are located).

State of Incorporation. Although most corporations are incorporated in the state where the attorney and client are located, some clients may prefer to choose a state where the statutes and taxes are more favorable to the corporate structure. The paralegal may be called upon to research the laws of different states to determine the feasibility of incorporating in the client's state or another state, thereby providing greater advantages for the client. In an office specializing in corporate law, the statutes of different states for corporations will be readily available for the paralegal's research. The state that is chosen for the incorporation is known as the domicile state of the corporation.

Exhibit 11-3 on page 278 shows a checklist for the formation of a corporation.

Preincorporation Agreement. If more than one individual is establishing the corporation, it is advisable to prepare a preincorporation agreement, which lists the preliminary agreements of the parties, known as the promoters of the corporation. These individuals are responsible for the organization of the corporation, including obtaining funds for the corporation and complying with all necessary statutes of the state of incorporation.

The preincorporation agreement should contain all preliminary agreements of the promoters and should be signed by all parties. Included therein should be the name and address of the corporation, its purpose, information about stock subscriptions and corporate capital, and the choice of corporate officers. A sample preincorporation agreement is found at Exhibit 11-4 on page 279.

Agent for Process. Once the client decides on a state of domicile and the type of corporation, an agent for process must be chosen. The agent is authorized to act for the corporation and receives service of process and other communications from the office of the state's secretary of state for the benefit of the corporation. An agent must be chosen for each state in which the corporation operates.

The agent should be a trusted employee of the corporation and should be chosen with the utmost care. The paralegal should keep a record of the agent's name and address; the address will generally be the office of the corporation.

Choosing a Name. Before choosing a name for the corporation, permission must be obtained from the state's secretary of state. Various methods are used in different states. Some states have forms on their Web sites for this purpose. Other states allow an inquiry to be made by telephone if a prepaid account has been established with the secretary of state's office. Most states require that the name contain the word "corporation," "company," "incorporated," or some other name that indicates the corporate structure.

In addition, other laws should be checked to determine the rights to the reservation of a name, including:

1. Federal Trademark Act (15 U.S.C. Sec. 1051)
2. Your own state's Trademark Act
3. Your state's Fictitious Business Name Act
4. Common-law rights, including rights to a trade name.

Complete the rules for your state in the State Specific Information box below.

STATE SPECIFIC INFORMATION FOR THE STATE OF _____
FOR CORPORATE NAME RESERVATION:

A name for a corporation may be reserved by the following procedure:
_____
_____
_____
_____.

STATE LAWS RELATED TO NAME RESERVATION:

1. Fictitious Business Name Statement—Section _____ of the
   _____ Code.

2. State Trademark Act, found at: _____
   _____.

3. Other pertinent state statutes: _____
   _____.

Articles of Incorporation

The first document prepared for corporate formation is the **Articles of Incorporation**, which include the following:

1. The name of the corporation
2. The purpose of the corporation
3. The name and address of the agent for process
4. The stock structure of the corporation (the number of shares issued and their value)
5. The duration of the corporation and the names of its initial incorporators and Board of Directors (not required in all states)

Exhibit 11-5 on page 281 shows an example of Articles of Incorporation. The articles must be filed with the secretary of state's office in the state where the corporation is being formed. A name for the corporation must be reserved with that same office.

A corporation may not use the same name as another corporation, nor may it use a name that is so similar to another corporate name that the two organizations could be confused. In the past, a considerable amount of time was spent writing letters back and forth to the secretary of state's office to determine the available names for the corporation. Now, however, the paralegal can use software packages to determine if a particular name is available so that the articles may

Articles of Incorporation
first document in corporate formation. Lists the name, purpose, agent for process, stock structure, and duration of the corporation.

EXHIBIT 11-3 Checklist for Corporate Formation

Courtesy: Reprinted from Cummins, Basics of Legal Document Preparation, Thomson Delmar Learning

TICKLER/CHECKLIST FOR INCORPORATION OF

1. Name:
   Call secretary of state re: name availability _____
   Reserve corporate name _____

2. Draft incorporation documents:
   Articles _____
   Designation of registered agent _____
   Bylaws _____
   Minutes and waiver or consent _____
   Subscriptions _____
   Stock certificates _____

3. Prepare miscellaneous forms:
   Application for federal employer identification number _____
   Application for sales tax _____
   Application for business license _____

4. Prepare miscellaneous letters:
   Secretary of state/articles _____
   City/business licenses _____
   IRS filing, subchapter S, election and power of attorney. _____

5. Prepare minute books _____

6. Send articles to secretary of state _____
   Rec'd _____

7. Send city/business licenses _____
   Rec'd _____

8. Send application for federal employer identification number _____
   Rec'd _____

9. Send application for sales tax _____
   Rec'd _____

10. Order corporate seal/corporate kit _____
    Rec'd _____

11. Schedule organizational meeting of board of directors _____

12. Hold organizational meeting of board _____

13. Prepare corporate bank account resolution _____

14. Prepare the waiver of notice of the annual shareholders'
    and directors' meeting _____

15. Prepare the annual shareholders' and directors' resolution _____

EXHIBIT 11-4   Preincorporation Agreement

AGREEMENT TO INCORPORATE

Agreement made this 30th day of February, 2005, between WALTER GATES, of City of Boulder, County of Citrus, State of Fremont, and HUGH PACK, City of Boulder, County of Citrus, State of Fremont, hereinafter sometimes called the "incorporators."

In consideration of the mutual promises herein contained, the incorporators agree to form a corporation under the laws of the State of Fremont, and particularly the General Corporation Law of the state, for the purpose of undertaking and carrying on a business or businesses, as follows:

SECTION ONE
NAME OF CORPORATION

Subject to availability, the name of the corporation shall be CYBERSPACE, INCORPORATED.

SECTION TWO
PURPOSE AND POWERS

The corporation shall be formed for the purpose of engaging in and maintaining a computer software business and such other lawful businesses as may from time to time be determined by the board of directors. The authorized corporate purposes shall include any lawful business purpose or purposes which a corporation organized under the General Corporation Law may be permitted to undertake.

SECTION THREE
PRINCIPAL OFFICE

The principal office for the transaction of the business of the corporation shall be located in the County of Citrus, State of Fremont.

SECTION FOUR
CAPITALIZATION

The authorized capital of the corporation shall be Ten Thousand Dollars ($10,000.00). The authorized capital stock of the corporation shall be all common stock with a par value of One Dollar ($1.00) per share.

SECTION FIVE
STOCK SUBSCRIPTION

Each of the incorporators subscribes as capital of the corporation the sum set out opposite his name below and agrees to accept in exchange for the amounts so specified the shares of stock following his name:

Name of Subscriber	Subscription	Stock
WALTER GATES	$5000.00	5000 shares
HUGH PACK	$5000.00	5000 shares

SECTION SIX
INCORPORATION; PERMIT TO ISSUE SHARES;
PAYMENT OF SUBSCRIPTION

The incorporators shall cause the corporation to be formed under the provisions of section 1010 of the Fremont Business Corporation Act, formed within ninety (90) days from the date of this agreement, and thereupon with all reasonable diligence shall cause the corporation to apply for and secure a permit authorizing issuance of stock as hereinabove subscribed.

continued

Exhibit 11-4 *continued*

SECTION SEVEN
SIGNING ARTICLES; FIRST DIRECTORS

The parties to this agreement, or so many of them as may be necessary for the purpose, shall sign the articles of incorporation as incorporators. The persons named below shall be designated in the articles of incorporation as the first directors of the corporation and shall serve as such until their respective successors are duly elected and qualified:

Office	Name of officer
President	WALTER GATES
Vice president	HUGH PACK
Secretary-treasurer	I. B. HEMMINGWAY

IN WITNESS WHEREOF the undersigned incorporators have executed this agreement at Boulder, Fremont, the day and year first above written.

_____
WALTER GATES

_____
HUGH PACK

---

be prepared simultaneously. A name may usually be reserved via computer modem or fax.

After the name has been obtained, the Articles of Incorporation are prepared for mailing to the secretary of state's office. If the articles have been prepared properly, a Certificate of Incorporation will be returned to the law office. At that time, the paralegal will usually be asked to order the corporate seal and minute book from a legal stationery store.

Organizational Meeting

At this point, the new corporation usually holds an initial organizational meeting to elect officers and to draft the **Bylaws**, which are the rules that govern the day-to-day operations of the corporation. Bylaws include such information as the following:

1. The location of the corporation's office
2. The date and place of the annual shareholders' meeting
3. The powers of the Board of Directors, the date and place of their meetings, and the method by which shareholders may remove individual directors
4. The types of corporate officers and their terms, duties, and responsibilities
5. Information about the corporation's stock

Bylaws rules that govern the day-to-day operations of the corporation.

EXHIBIT 11-5   Sample Articles of Incorporation

ARTICLES OF INCORPORATION
OF
ABC CORPORATION

I.

The name of this corporation is: ABC CORPORATION.

II.

The purpose of this corporation is to engage in any lawful act or activity for which a corporation may be organized under the General Corporation Law of California other than the banking business, the trust company business, or the practice of a profession permitted to be incorporated by the California Corporations Code.

III.

The name and address in the State of California of this corporation's initial agent for service of process is:

Dana M. Morrison
45 Sunset Boulevard
Memphis, CA 90555

IV.

This corporation is authorized to issue only one class of shares of common stock; and the total number of shares which this corporation is authorized to issue is two hundred (200).

V.

The liability of the directors of the corporation for monetary damages shall be eliminated to the fullest extent permissible under California law.

VI.

The corporation is authorized to provide indemnification of agents, as that term is defined in Section 317 of the California Corporations Code, for breach of duty to the corporation and its shareholders in excess of that expressly permitted by said Section 317 under any bylaw, agreement, vote of shareholders or disinterested directors or otherwise, to the fullest extent such indemnification may be authorized hereby, subject to the limits on such excess indemnification set forth in Section 204 of the California Corporations Code. The corporation is further authorized to provide insurance for agents as set forth in Section 317 of the California Corporations Code, provided that, in cases where the corporation owns all or a portion of the shares of the company issuing the insurance policy, one of the two sets of conditions set forth in Section 317, as amended, is met.

VII.

Any repeal or modification of the foregoing provisions of Articles V and VI, by the shareholders of this corporation, shall not adversely affect any right or protection of a director or agent of this corporation existing at the time of such repeal or modification.

DATED: June 27, 2006

_____
WILLIAM M. LANGLEY
Sole Incorporator

6. Methods of changing the Bylaws

7. Other general operational information

Exhibit 11-6 shows an example of corporate Bylaws.

Once all these formalities have been accomplished, the corporation may operate. The corporate paralegal will generally be responsible for keeping track of the time line of the corporate organization to be sure that all matters are handled in a timely fashion.

Annual Report

Once each year the corporation is required to file an **Annual Report**, which is sent to the shareholders and the secretary of state of the state where the corporation is incorporated. This report describes the actions and business in which the corporation was engaged during the previous year. It also lists the corporation's income and expenses for the year, along with its assets and liabilities. The paralegal and/or assistant should record the date the Annual Report is due in the tickler file and also note an earlier date when preparations should begin to allow the report to be completed by the due date. The Annual Report may be prepared by the attorney or by the corporation itself.

Special Types of Corporations

Close Corporations.   A **close corporation** is a corporation formed by a few individuals who also run the corporation. Unlike other corporations, in a close corporation, shareholders actually manage and control the business operations of the corporation. A close corporation may not offer its stock to the public, and the number of shareholders is restricted.

Professional Corporations.   In recent years, states have enacted statutes to allow professionals to incorporate. **Professional corporations** are most commonly formed by doctors and lawyers, but may also be formed by many other professionals including accountants, dentists, optometrists, and psychologists. "P.C." after a professional's name shows that the practice is incorporated in this manner. Most states have much more stringent rules and regulations for professional corporations than for ordinary corporations. In addition, many professions have their own rules for incorporation.

Professionals who incorporate may still be held personally liable for their own malpractice, as well as for malpractice committed by persons whom they supervise. A professional cannot be held personally liable, however, for malpractice committed by other professionals in the corporation whom she does not supervise. For example, Doctors Roth and Wilmot decide to form a professional corporation. Neither supervises the other. If Doctor Roth is sued for malpractice, Doctor Wilmot's personal assets cannot be used to settle the suit; only the assets of the professional corporation and Doctor Roth's personal assets may be sued. It should be noted that all professionals are required to carry malpractice insurance.

Annual Report a yearly report issued by a corporation describing the past year's activities.

close corporation a corporation formed by a small number of people who manage and control the business.

professional corporation a corporation formed by professionals, such as doctors or lawyers.

EXHIBIT 11-6   Example of Corporate Bylaws

Bylaws
of
ABC Corporation
Article One: Shareholders

Section 1. MEETINGS.

(A) TIME. An annual meeting of the shareholders shall be held each year on the first day of April at 2:00 p.m., unless such day should fall on a legal holiday. In such event, the meeting shall be held at the same hour on the next succeeding business day that is not a legal holiday.

(B) PLACE. Annual meetings shall be held at the principal executive office of the corporation or at such other place within the state of California as may be determined by the board of directors and designated in the notice of such meeting.

(C) CALL. Annual meetings may be called by the directors, by the Chairman of the Board, if any, Vice-Chairman of the Board, if any, the President, if any, the Secretary, or by any other officer instructed by the Directors to call the meeting.

(D) SPECIAL MEETINGS. If in any year, the election of directors is not held at the annual meeting of the shareholders or an adjournment of the meeting, the board of directors shall call a special meeting of the shareholders as soon as possible thereafter as is reasonably possible for the purpose of holding the election and transacting such other business as may properly be brought before the meeting.

In the event the board of directors fails to call a special meeting within three months after the date set for the annual meeting, any shareholders may call such a meeting; at such a meeting, the shareholders may elect directors and transact all other business as may be properly brought before the meeting.

(E) NOTICE. Written notice stating the place, day, and hour of each meeting, and, in the case of a special meeting, the general nature of the business to be transacted or, in the case of an Annual Meeting, those matters which the Board of Directors, at the time of mailing of the notice, intends to present for action by the shareholders, shall be given not less than ten (10) days (or not less than any such other minimum period of days as may be prescribed by the General Corporation Law) or more than sixty (60) days (or more than any maximum period of days as may be prescribed by the General Corporation Law).

(F) ACTION BY WRITTEN CONSENT. Any action required by law to be taken at a meeting of the shareholders, except for the election of the directors, and any other action that may be taken at a meeting of shareholders may be taken without a meeting if written consent, setting forth the action so taken, is signed by the holders of outstanding shares having not less than the minimum number of votes that would be necessary to authorize or take such an action at a meeting at which all shares entitled to vote thereon were present and voted, if the consents of all shareholders entitled to vote were solicited in writing. Directors may not be elected by written consent except by unanimous written consent of all shares entitled to vote for the election of directors.

continued

Exhibit 11-6   *continued*

(G) WAIVER OF NOTICE. A shareholder may waive notice of any annual or special meeting by signing a petition notice of waiver either before or after the date of such meeting.

(H) RECORD DATE. For the purpose of determining those shareholders entitled to notice of or to vote at any meeting of shareholders, or to receive payment of any dividend, or in order to make a determination of shareholders for any other proper purpose, the board of directors may fix, in advance, a date as the record date for the determination of shareholders. Such date shall not be more than sixty (60) days, and for a meeting of shareholders, not less than ten (10) days, or in the case of a meeting where a merger or consolidation will be considered, not less than twenty (20) days, immediately preceding such meeting.

If a record date is not fixed for the determination of shareholders entitled to notice of or to vote at a meeting of shareholders, the record date shall be at the close of business on the business day next preceding the day on which notice is given, or, if notice is waived, at the close of business on the business day next preceding the day on which the meeting is held.

If no record date is fixed, the record date for determining shareholders entitled to give consent to corporate action in writing without a meeting shall be the day on which the first written consent is given, when no prior action by the board of directors is necessary.

If no record date is fixed, the record date for determining shareholders for any other purpose shall be at the close of business on the day on which the board of directors adopts the resolution relating thereto or the 60th day prior to the date of such other action, whichever is later.

When a determination of shareholders entitled to vote at any meeting of shareholders has been made as provided in this section, such determination shall apply to adjournment of such meeting, unless the board of directors fixes a new record date for the adjourned meeting.

(I) QUORUM. The presence, at the shareholders' meeting, in person or by proxy, of persons entitled to vote a majority of the shares of the corporation then outstanding shall constitute a quorum for the transaction of business. In determining whether quorum requirements for a meeting have been met, any share that has been enjoined from voting or that cannot be lawfully voted for any reason shall not be counted.

(J) PROXIES. Every person entitled to vote at a shareholders' meeting of the corporation, or entitled to execute written consent authorizing action in lieu of a meeting, may do so either in person or by proxy executed in writing by the shareholder or by his duly authorized attorney in fact. No proxy shall be valid after 11 months from the date of its execution unless otherwise provided in the proxy.

(K) VOTING. Except in elections of directors, in which each shareholder shall have the right to cumulate his votes, each outstanding share, regardless of class, shall be entitled to one vote on each matter submitted to a vote at a meeting of shareholders. The affirmative vote of the majority of shares represented at a meeting at which a quorum is present shall be the act of the shareholders unless the vote of a greater number or a vote by classes is required by the articles, these bylaws, or the laws of the State of California.

(L) ORDER OF BUSINESS. The order of business at the annual meeting of the shareholders and, insofar as possible, at all other meetings of shareholders, shall be as follows:

continued

Exhibit 11-6 *continued*

1. Call to order.
2. Proof of notice of meeting.
3. Reading and disposing of any unapproved minutes.
4. Reports of officers.
5. Reports of committees.
6. Election of directors.
7. Disposition of unfinished business.
8. Disposition of new business.
9. Adjournment.

Article Two: Board of Directors

Section 1. GENERAL POWERS.

(A) AUTHORITY. Subject to the limitations of the articles of incorporation, these bylaws, and the Corporations Code of the State of California, and the provisions of the Corporations Code concerning corporate action that must be authorized or approved by the shareholders of the corporation, all corporate power shall be exercised by or under the authority of the board of directors, and the business and affairs of the corporation shall be controlled by the board.

(B) NUMBER, TENURE, QUALIFICATIONS, AND ELECTION. The board of directors shall consist of ten persons who shall be shareholders of the corporation. The number of directors may be increased or decreased by approval of the outstanding shares. Directors of the corporation shall be elected at the annual meeting of the shareholders, or at a meeting held in lieu thereof as provided in Article One above, and shall serve until the next succeeding annual meeting and until their successors have been elected and qualified.

Section 2. MEETINGS.

(A) ORGANIZATIONAL MEETING. The board of directors shall hold an organizational meeting immediately following each annual meeting of the shareholders. Additionally, regular meetings of the board of directors shall be held at such times as shall be fixed by resolution of the board. Special meetings of the board may be called at any time by the president or, if the president is absent or refuses to act, any vice-president or any two members of the board.

(B) NOTICE. Notice need not be given of regular meetings of the board of directors, nor is it necessary to give notice of adjourned meetings. Notice of special meetings shall be in writing by mail at least four days prior to the date of the meeting or 48 hours' notice delivered personally or by telephone or telegraph. Neither the business to be transacted at nor the purpose of any such meeting need be specified in the notice. Attendance of a director at a meeting shall constitute a waiver of notice of that meeting except when the director attends for the express purpose of objecting to the transaction of any business in that the meeting is not lawfully called or convened.

(C) QUORUM AND VOTING. A majority of the authorized number of directors shall constitute a quorum for the transaction of business, and the acts of a majority of directors present at a meeting at which a quorum is present shall constitute the acts of the board of directors. At any meeting of the board of directors, if less than a quorum is present, a majority of those present may adjourn the meeting until a

continued

Exhibit 11-6 *continued*

quorum is present. If the meeting is adjourned for more than 24 hours, notice of any adjournment to another time or place shall be given prior to the time of the adjourned meeting to the directors who were not present at the time of adjournment.

(D) COMPENSATION. Directors who are not employed as officers of the corporation shall be entitled to receive from the corporation as compensation for their services as directors such reasonable compensation as the board may determine, and shall also be entitled to reimbursement for any reasonable expenses incurred in attending meetings of directors.

(E) INDEMNIFICATION. The corporation shall indemnify all persons who have served or may serve at any time as officers or directors of the corporation, and their heirs, executors, administrators, successors, and assigns, from and against any and all loss and expense, including amounts paid in settlement before or after suit is commenced, and reasonable attorneys' fees, actually and necessarily sustained as a result of any claim, demand, action, proceeding, or judgment that may be asserted against any such persons, or in which any such persons are made parties by reason of their being or having been officers or directors of the corporation. However, this right of indemnification shall not exist in relation to matters where it is adjudged in any action, suit, or proceeding that any such persons are liable for negligence or misconduct in the performance of duty.

(F) COMMITTEES. The board of directors may, by resolution adopted by a majority of the whole board, designate two or more directors to constitute an executive committee. The executive committee, to the extent provided in the resolution, shall have and may exercise all of the authority of the board of directors in the management of the corporation, except that the committee shall have no authority in reference to amending the articles of incorporation, adopting a plan of merger or consolidation, suggesting to shareholders the sale, lease, exchange, mortgage, or other disposition of all or substantially all the property and assets of the corporation other than in the usual course of business, recommending to the shareholders a voluntary dissolution or a revocation thereof, amending, altering, or repealing any provision of these bylaws, electing or removing directors or officers of the corporation, or members of the executive committee, fixing the compensation of any member of the executive committee, declaring dividends, or amending, altering, or repealing any resolution of the board of directors which, by its terms, provides that it not be amended, altered, or repealed by the executive committee. The board of directors shall have power at any time to fill vacancies in, to change the size or membership of, and to discharge any such committee.

Any such executive committee shall keep a written record of its proceedings and shall submit such record to the whole board at each regular meeting, and at such other times as may be requested by the board. However, failure to submit such record, or failure of the board to approve any action indicated therein shall not invalidate such action to the extent it has been carried out by the corporation prior to the time the record thereof was or should have been submitted to the board as provided herein.

Article Three: Officers

(A) ENUMERATION OF OFFICERS. The corporation shall have as officers a president, vice-president, secretary, and chief financial officer. The board of directors, at its discretion, may appoint such officers as the business of the corporation may require.

(B) ELECTION AND TERM OF OFFICE. The principal officers of the corporation shall be elected by the board of directors at its organizational meeting immediately following the annual meeting of

continued

Exhibit 11-6 *continued*

shareholders or as soon thereafter as is reasonably possible. Subordinate officers may be elected as the board may see fit. Each officer shall hold office until his successor is elected and qualified, or until his resignation, death, or removal.

(C) REMOVAL. Any officer may be removed from office at any time, with or without cause, on the affirmative vote of a majority of the board of directors. Removal shall be without prejudice to any contract rights of the officer removed.

(D) VACANCIES. Vacancies in office, however caused, may be filled by election of the board of directors at any time for unexpired terms of such offices.

(E) OFFICERS—POWERS AND DUTIES. The president, vice-president, secretary, chief financial officer, and other officers appointed by the board of directors shall have such powers and duties as prescribed by the board of directors.

(F) ABSENCE OR DISABILITY OF OFFICERS. In the case of the absence or disability of any officer of the corporation and of any person hereby authorized to act in his place during his absence or disability, the board of directors may, by resolution, delegate the powers and duties of such officer, or to any director, or to any other person whom it may select.

(G) SALARIES. The salaries of all officers of the corporation shall be fixed by the board of directors.

Article Four: Stock Certificates

(A) FORM. The shares of the corporation shall be represented by certificates signed by the chairman or a vice-chairman of the board of directors, if any, or the president or a vice-president, and by the chief financial officer or an assistant financial officer, or the secretary or an assistant secretary. Any or all of such signatures may be facsimile. Each such certificate shall also state:

1. The name of the record holder of the shares represented by such certificate;

2. The number of shares represented thereby;

3. A designation of any class or series of which such shares are a part;

4. That the shares are without par value;

5. Any rights of redemption and the redemption price;

6. Any rights of conversion, and the essential terms and periods for conversion;

7. Any liens or restrictions on transfer or on the voting power of such shares;

8. That the shares are assessable, if that is the fact;

9. That assessments to which the shares are subject are collectible by personal action, if that is the fact;

10. When the shares of the corporation are classified or any class has two or more series, the rights, preferences, privileges, and restrictions granted to or imposed on the respective classes or series of

continued

Exhibit 11-6 *continued*

shares and the holders thereof, as established by the articles or by any certificate of determination of preferences, as well as the number of shares constituting each series and the designation thereof; or a summary of such preferences, privileges and restrictions with reference to the provisions of the articles or certificate or certificates of determination of preferences establishing same; or the office or agency of the corporation from which stockholders may obtain a copy of a statement of such right, preferences, privileges, and restrictions or of such summary.

11. Any right of the board of directors to fix the dividend rights, dividend rate, conversion rights, voting rights, rights in terms of redemption, including sinking fund provisions, the redemption price or prices, or the liquidation preferences of any wholly unissued class or of any wholly unissued series of any class of shares, or the number of shares constituting any unissued series of any class of shares, or designation of such series, or all or any of them; and

12. For any certificates issued for shares prior to the full payment therefor, the amount remaining unpaid, the terms of payment to become due, and any restrictions on the transfer of such partly paid shares on the books of the corporation.

13. All certificates for shares of the corporation shall bear the following legend: "These securities have not been registered under the Securities Act of 1933, and may not be offered, offered for sale, or sold in the absence of an effective registration statement under that Act or an opinion of counsel satisfactory to the corporation that registration is not required."

(B) LOST, DESTROYED, AND STOLEN CERTIFICATES. No certificate for shares of stock in the corporation shall be issued in place of any certificate alleged to have been lost, destroyed, stolen, or mutilated except on production of such evidence and provision of such indemnity to the corporation as the board of directors may prescribe.

Article Five: Corporate Actions

(A) CONTRACTS. The board of directors may authorize any officer or officers, and any agent or agents of the corporation, to enter into any contract or to execute and deliver any instrument in the name of and on behalf of the corporation, and such authority may be general or confined to specific instances.

(B) LOANS. No loans shall be made by the corporation to its officers or directors, and no loans shall be made by the corporation secured by its shares. No loans shall be made or contracted on behalf of the corporation and no evidence of indebtedness shall be issued in its name unless authorized by resolution of the board of directors. Such authority may be general or confined to specific instances.

(C) CHECKS, DRAFTS, OR ORDERS. All checks, drafts, or other orders for the payment of money by or to the corporation and all notes and other evidence of indebtedness issued in the name of the corporation shall be signed by such officer or officers, agent or agents of the corporation, and in such manner as shall be determined by resolution by the board of directors.

(D) BANK DEPOSITS. All funds of the corporation not otherwise employed shall be deposited to the credit of the corporation in such banks, trust companies, or other depositories as the board of directors may select.

continued

Exhibit 11-6 *continued*

Article Six: Miscellaneous

(A) INSPECTION OF CORPORATE RECORDS. The corporation shall keep correct and complete books and records of account and shall also keep minutes of all meetings of shareholders and directors. Additionally, a record shall be kept at the principal executive office of the corporation, giving the names and addresses of all shareholders, and the number and class or classes of shares held by each. Any person who is the holder of a voting trust certificate or who is the holder of record of at least ten percent of the outstanding voting shares of the corporation shall have the right to examine and copy, in person or by agent or attorney, at any reasonable time or times, for any proper purpose, the books and records of account of the corporation, the minutes, and the record of shareholders.

(B) INSPECTION OF ARTICLES OF INCORPORATION AND BYLAWS. The original or a copy of the articles of incorporation and bylaws of the corporation, as amended or otherwise altered to date, and certified by the secretary of the corporation, shall at all times be kept at the principal executive office of the corporation. Such articles and bylaws shall be open to inspection to all shareholders of record or holders of voting trust certificates at all reasonable times during the business hours of the corporation.

(C) FISCAL YEAR. The fiscal year of the corporation shall begin on the first day of April of each year and end at 11:59 p.m. on the 31st day of March of the following year.

(D) CORPORATE SEAL. The board of directors shall adopt an official seal for the corporation, which shall be inscribed with the name of the corporation, the state of incorporation, and the words "Corporate Seal."

(E) CONSTRUCTION AND DEFINITION. Unless the context requires otherwise, the general provisions, rules of construction, and definitions in the Corporations Code of the State of California shall govern the construction of these bylaws.

Without limiting the foregoing, the masculine gender includes the feminine and neuter; the singular number includes the plural, and the plural number includes the singular; "shall" is mandatory and "may" is permissive, and "person" includes a corporation as well as a natural person.

Article Seven: Amendments

These bylaws may be altered, amended, or repealed by approval of the outstanding voting shares or by a majority vote of the board of directors of the corporation.

If a client in a profession wishes to incorporate, you must check your state's rules and regulations for that profession. Contact the licensing board or state agency that oversees that particular profession for the specific regulations. In general all individuals owning shares in the corporation must be licensed in that particular profession. In addition, they must carry minimum amounts of liability (malpractice) insurance.

Fill in the rules for your own state in the State Specific Information box.

STATE SPECIFIC INFORMATION

Rules for professional corporation in the state of _____ are as follows:

_____

_____

_____

_____.

Subchapter S corporation
a corporation that is limited to twenty-five shareholders and to domestic operations; may offer significant tax advantages because the income and losses are reported on the owner's personal income tax returns. In size and structure, it is similar to a close corporation.

franchise the right to market a company's goods or services in a particular territory. After purchasing the franchise from a franchise organization, an individual owns the business and leases the equipment and facilities from the parent organization.

Subchapter S Corporations. A **Subchapter S corporation** is similar in size and structure to a close corporation. A Subchapter S corporation may have no more than twenty-five shareholders, and it is limited to domestic operations. Such a corporation may offer significant tax advantages in the early years of a business when profits are small or nonexistent because the corporate income and losses are reported on the owner's personal tax returns. If a corporation's taxable income is more than $175,000 a year, the owners will pay lower taxes if they organize as a Subchapter S corporation and report the profits on their personal income tax returns than if they organize as a regular corporation and file a corporate tax return. Owners may only deduct losses from their individual tax returns up to the amount of their investment in the corporation.

Franchises. In recent years, the franchise market has expanded considerably. A **franchise** is a business that obtains the right to market a company's goods or services in a particular territory; the term also refers to the right itself. Many fast-food restaurants, automobile repair shops, and other businesses are operated as franchises. In this type of operation, the individual owner owns the business itself but leases the facilities from the franchise organization (the parent company that grants the franchise and allows the business to use its name). Usually, the business owner is required to purchase supplies from the franchise organization. Some fast-food establishments are also required to buy their ingredients from certain suppliers to maintain uniform quality.

Franchise organizations employ paralegals and legal secretaries to assist in preparing franchise agreements, property leases, equipment leases, and purchase contracts. Individuals interested in purchasing a franchise often ask an attorney to review the franchise agreement that has been prepared by the franchise organization to be sure that their own rights are protected.

Although large franchise organizations are usually corporations, an individual who purchases a franchise may organize it as a sole proprietorship, a partnership, or a corporation.

Nonprofit Corporations. If a corporation is operated entirely for charitable, religious, scientific, educational, and/or literary purposes, it may qualify as a nonprofit corporation for tax purposes under the Internal Revenue Code. The corporation may not engage in other unrelated activities or benefit the owners economically, although the owners may collect a reasonable salary if they work in the business. All corporate profits must be used to benefit the purpose for which the corporation was formed, such as the individual charity. The corporation may not engage in any political activities, such as supporting political candidates or lobbying for new legislation. Some states may impose additional restrictions on nonprofit corporations: therefore, you should check your own state's statutes for other rules. Add them to the State Specific Information box.

STATE SPECIFIC INFORMATION

Rules for nonprofit corporations in the state of _____
are as follows:

_____

_____

_____

_____.

Corporate Board of Directors

The **Board of Directors** is a group of individuals who oversee the running of the corporation. The directors have a fiduciary duty to use ethical and sound judgment in managing the corporation's affairs. As fiduciaries of the corporation, the directors owe a duty of loyalty that includes placing the organization's needs before their own personal business interests. A director may not be involved in a conflict of interest such as working as a consultant for a competing company or taking a fee from a competing company. Nor may directors commit any acts that are beyond the scope of their enumerated duties and responsibilities. Directors may not be held personally liable for their mistakes, however, unless it can be proved that they engaged in fraudulent, illegal, or unethical practices, such as entering into agreements for their own personal profit or acting disloyally.

Board of Directors the individuals who oversee the running of a corporation.

Minute Book of the Corporation

The Corporate Minute Book is generally kept by the paralegal or attorney for the corporation. It contains a complete record of the business of the corporation, including the Articles of Incorporation, Bylaws, Minutes of all meetings, and the ledger of stock transfers.

A minute book may be obtained from a legal stationery store. Law offices that specialize in corporate law will have already established suppliers for this purpose. Web sites of legal stationery suppliers are also available. The book will contain the name of the corporation printed or embossed on the spine, sample corporate documents, blank stock certificates, and an index. The same supplier that provides the minute book will also have corporate seals available for purchase. These seals are similar to stamps that use a stamp pad. Embossed seals that make imprints on the paper are also sold, depending on the client's preference. In most cases, both types of seals are purchased for different purposes.

Annual Report

Each state requires that the corporation prepare a report at the end of its fiscal year for shareholders and the state secretary of state's office. It should contain a detailed account of the corporation's operations during the year. It also includes the name, date, and state of incorporation, the corporation's address and federal identification number, and the name of the corporation's agent for process in each state in which it does business. The corporation's financial operations for the last year should be explained in great detail.

Ultra Vires Acts

Any actions that are outside the scope of the powers or activities permitted by the Articles of Incorporation are considered **ultra vires acts**. An officer or director who commits an ultra vires act may be held personally liable for the endeavor through a process known as "piercing the corporate veil." If an officer or director commits an ultra vires act, an individual who is injured by it can pierce the corporate veil and sue the officer or director personally. If the action injures the shareholders, they may sue in the same manner.

Shareholder Suits against the Corporation

ultra vires acts acts outside the scope of the corporation's powers as set out in the Articles of Incorporation.

derivative suit a suit by shareholders against a corporation.

If a director or officer commits an ultra vires act that injures the shareholders, they may institute a direct action against that director or officer. If the ultra vires act has injured the corporation, the shareholders may file a **derivative suit**. To do so, the shareholders must have held their stock at the time the act occurred ("contemporaneous ownership") and must first have made a demand on the board of directors to take action to protect the corporation's rights in this instance. If the board fails to act, then the shareholders may file a derivative suit. To win the suit, the shareholders must show that the director or officer deliberately mismanaged or committed fraud against the corporation.

Dissolving the Corporation

A corporation may elect to voluntarily dissolve for any reason, by a vote of at least 50 percent of the voting power of the shareholders, without court intervention. The board of directors may also dissolve the corporation without shareholder approval under the following circumstances:

1. No shares have been issued by the corporation.
2. The corporation has filed a Chapter 7 bankruptcy.
3. All corporate assets have been disposed of.
4. No business has been conducted for the past five years.

All creditors and shareholders must be notified, and a notice must be filed with the state's secretary of state, indicating that the corporation is being dissolved. After the creditors are notified and paid and the assets are liquidated, the corporation is dissolved. Any monies left after the creditors are paid are distributed to the shareholders. A document is filed with the secretary of state reporting the **dissolution**.

Only the state may institute an **involuntary dissolution**. In some cases, however, the shareholders may petition the courts for involuntary dissolution if they can prove that the directors are not managing the corporation prudently or that management problems are affecting the operation of the corporation. Some states allow creditors to apply for an involuntary dissolution of the corporation if they are owed substantial sums and are not being paid.

Procedures for Voluntary Dissolution

The forms and documents required for corporate dissolution vary by state. It would be advisable to research the laws of your state and obtain the appropriate forms for this purpose.

The state of California has made the **voluntary dissolution** process relatively simple by requiring just a few forms to be completed and filed with the secretary of state's office, including:

1. Certificate of election to wind up and dissolve
2. Certificate of dissolution
3. Tax clearance certificate (filed with the Franchise Tax Board)

Samples of the first and second items are included as Exhibits 11-7 and 11-8. In addition to the filing of forms, all creditors must have been notified and paid in full. All shareholders must be notified of the dissolution. If assets remain after paying all creditors, then the shareholders should be paid a proportionate amount of the proceeds that are left.

dissolution terminating the existence of a corporation; can be voluntary or involuntary.

involuntary dissolution the termination of a corporation against the will of the directors; must be initiated by the state, but shareholders or creditors may petition to begin dissolution proceedings.

voluntary dissolution the termination of a corporation by the shareholders or the directors who act willingly and are not being forced to terminate by the state or creditors.

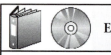

EXHIBIT 11-7 Certificate of Election to Wind Up and Dissolve

The undersigned certify that:

1. They are the president and the secretary, respectively, of ABC Enterprises, Inc., a New York corporation.

2. The corporation has elected to wind up and dissolve.

3. The election was made by the vote of 200 shares of the corporation, and representing at least 50 percent (50%) of the voting power of the corporation.

We further declare under penalty of perjury under the laws of the State of New York that the matters set forth in this certificate are true and correct of our own knowledge.
Date: March 2, 2003

_____
JANE A. RICHARDS, President

_____
STEVEN P. RICHARDS, Secretary

Consolidations and Mergers

When two or more corporations dissolve and then join together to form a new organization, a **consolidation** has occurred. The shareholders of both original corporations must approve the dissolution of their own corporation and the formation of the new one. In this case, the following occurs:

$$A + B = C$$

In a **merger**, one corporation takes over another corporation. One of the corporations survives and the other disappears, becoming part of the survivor. In this case, the following occurs:

$$A \text{ absorbs } B = A$$

consolidation the process in which two corporations dissolve and then join together to form a third corporation.

merger the process in which one corporation takes over another corporation.

The merger must be approved by the shareholders of the corporation that will no longer exist. Shareholders who do not want to have stock in the new corporation can sell their shares back to the corporation. Articles must be filed with the secretary of state providing notification of the merger.

Paralegals and legal assistants may be involved in preparing the documentation for dissolution, mergers, and consolidations. Form books and software packages are available to assist in this endeavor. You should always consult the files to determine if the same task has been performed in another case; if so, you can use the format as a guide.

EXHIBIT 11-8 Certificate of Dissolution

The undersigned certify that:

1. They constitute a majority of the directors now in office at ABC ENTERPRISES, INC.

2. The corporation has been completely wound up.

3. The corporation's known debts and liabilities have been actually paid.

4. The corporation never acquired any known assets.

5. A person or corporation assumes the tax liability, if any, of the dissolving corporation as security for the issuance of a tax clearance certificate from the State Tax Board and is responsible for additional corporate taxes, if any, that are assessed and that become due after the date of the assumption of the tax liability.

6. The corporation is dissolved.

We further declare under penalty of perjury under the laws of the State of New York that the matters set forth in this certificate are true and correct of our own knowledge.

Dated: March 25, 2003

_____

JANE A. RICHARDS, President

_____

STEVEN P. RICHARDS, Secretary

ETHICS and ETIQUETTE

Attorneys are precluded from entering into business arrangements with their clients when it relates to the legal profession. Additionally, great care must be undertaken if the client approaches the attorney with a business proposition in another type of business for which the attorney will represent the business. A conflict of interest situation must be avoided. Clients should be advised by the attorney to seek the advice of an independent counsel.

Attorneys may not enter into business arrangements involving the law with the paralegal or legal assistant. This includes allowing the paralegal or legal assistant to invest money in the law firm based on a partnership arrangement. Moreover, lay personnel may not share in the business profits of the law firm.

The paralegal or legal assistant employed in a corporation must also adhere to the principles of confidentiality with matters involving the corporation. As in a private law office, all confidential communications with employees of the corporation may not be divulged.

CHAPTER SUMMARY ✦

The different types of business organizations include the sole proprietorship, the partnership, and the corporation. A sole proprietorship is an unincorporated business that is usually owned by a single individual. Sole proprietorships are easy to establish, but they have several disadvantages: the owner is subject to unlimited personal liability; raising capital can be difficult; and the business may have to be dissolved on the death or disability of the owner.

A partnership has access to more capital than a sole proprietorship, and limited partners are liable only for the amount they have invested. General partners, however, are liable not only for their own actions but also for the actions of their partners.

A corporation has access to more capital than a sole proprietorship or a partnership and also offers the advantage of limited liability for shareholders. In addition, a corporation has perpetual life and may offer tax benefits. In addition to the standard stock corporation, several special types of corporations exist, including the professional corporation, Subchapter S corporation, and close corporation.

To form a corporation, the incorporators organize the corporation and file Articles of Incorporation with the secretary of state of the state where the corporation is located. Once the articles are accepted, an organizational meeting is held to elect a Board of Directors, develop an organization plan for the corporation and adopt Bylaws. Minutes of the meeting are taken.

The members of the Board of Directors owe a fiduciary duty to the corporation. If they commit ultra vires acts, they may be sued personally by shareholders or others. Shareholders may file a derivative suit.

A corporation may be dissolved voluntarily by the shareholders and Board or Directors or involuntarily by the state of incorporation. The corporation may also merge with another corporation or be consolidated. In a merger, one corporation absorbs the other; in a consolidation, a third corporation is formed from the combination of the original two.

✦ KEY TERMS

annual report

articles of incorporation

board of directors

bylaws

close corporation

consolidation

corporation

derivative suit

dissolution

franchise

general partner

involuntary dissolution

limited partner

merger

partnership

professional corporation

shareholder

sole proprietorship

Subchapter S corporation

ultra vires acts

voluntary dissolution

✦ SELF TEST

Indicate whether the following statements are true (T) or false (F).

_____ 1. Partnerships are preferable to corporations because a partner's personal assets are protected from suit in a partnership.

_____ 2. Articles of Incorporation are prepared to authorize a corporation to operate.

_____ 3. Ownership in a corporation is represented by shares of stock.

_____ 4. A corporation and its shareholders share responsibility when suits are brought against the corporation.

_____ 5. For legal purposes, a corporation exists separate and apart from its shareholders.

Circle the correct answer for the following questions:

1. The document that is validated by the state and authorizes the corporation to exist and operate is called
   a. Articles of Incorporation.
   b. common stock.
   c. preferred stock.
   d. Bylaws.

2. The rules of a corporation that govern its operations are called
   a. Articles of Incorporation.
   b. common stock.
   c. preferred stock.
   d. Bylaws.

3. The officers who are elected by the shareholders to control the operation of the corporation are called the
   a. Board of Trustees.
   b. Board of Directors.
   c. shareholder officers.
   d. corporate officers.

4. Ownership in a corporation may be proved by
   a. a certificate of stock.
   b. a certificate of ownership.
   c. the Bylaws.
   d. the Articles.

5. Partnerships are
   a. limited corporations.
   b. the same as sole proprietorships.
   c. associations of two or more individuals.
   d. formed to operate a business for profit.
   e. (c) and (d) are correct.

Fill-in-the-blanks.

1. The two types of partners are _____ and _____ partners.

2. The type of partner who is involved in the day-to-day operations of the business is a
   _____.

3. Define a sole proprietorship: _____.

4. Corporate formation begins with the preparation of the _____.

5. The individuals who own a corporation are called _____.

✦ REVIEW QUESTIONS

1. Explain how a name is reserved for a corporation.

2. Explain the difference between a sole proprietorship, a partnership, and a corporation.

3. What are the major advantages and disadvantages of a sloe proprietorship? A partnership?
   A corporation?

4. What information is included in a corporation's Articles of Incorporation?

5. What is a Subchapter S corporation?

✦ NOTEBOOK PROJECTS

1. Proofread the Certificate of Incorporation in Exhibit 11-9 and retype it using
   the format for your own state. Change the address of the corporation to your
   city and your state.

2. Our office has a new client, Scott Lipinski, who would like to form a corporation called SCOTTZ PLANEZ to sell airplanes in your state. Prepare the Articles
   of Incorporation for this endeavor. Use the format for your state, or use Exhibit
   11-5 as a guide.

3. Draft a letter that you would send to the secretary of state's office in your
   state to determine whether the name "SCOTTZ PLANEZ" may be used by the
   corporation formed in Project 2.

4. Using Exhibit 11-6 as a model, prepare the Bylaws for the corporation formed
   in Projects 2 and 3 with the following officers' signatures:

   Scott Lipinski, president; George Crock, vice-president; Jane Fitzgerald, secretary and treasurer; Jeffrey Langton, chairman of the board. These individuals
   comprise the Board of Directors of this corporation. *Note:* When revising the
   articles in Exhibit 11-6, Article Three (A) should be changed to indicate the
   names and titles of the officers. Article Three (E) may also require some
   changes.

5. Prepare the Articles of Incorporation for your own freelance legal professional
   corporation.

6. Research the statutes in your state to determine the rules for limited partnerships. Prepare a memorandum to your instructor listing these rules.

EXHIBIT 11-9 Certificate of Incorporation

CERTIFICATE OF INCORPORATION
OF
JANE'S BEAUTY SUPPLY, INC.

Under Section 402 of the Business Corporation Law
of the State of New York

The undersigned, for the purpose of forming a corporation pursuant to Section 402 of the Business Corporation Law of the State of New York, certifies:

1. The name of the corporation shall be Jane's Beauty Supply, Inc.
2. The purpose of the Corporation is to engage in any lawful act or activity for which corporations may be organized under the NY business corporation law; provided, however, that the Corporation is not formed to engage in any act or activity requiring the consent or approval of any State official, department, board, agency, or other body without such consent or approval first being obtained.
3. The office of the corporation is to be located at 1001 Kelly Avenue, Utica, NY.
4. The aggragate number of shares which the corporation shall have authority to issue is Two Hundred (200) shares all of which are to be of one class of common stock without par value.
5. The Secretary of State is designated as agent of the coproration upon whom process against it may be served. The post office address to which the Secretary of State shall mail a copy of any process against the corporation served upon him is 1001 Kelly Avenue, Utica, New York 13501.
6. No shareholder of the corporation shall have any preemptive or preferential right of subscription to any shares of any class of the corporation whether now or here after authorized, or to any obligations convertible into shares of any class of the corporation, issued or sold, nor any right of subscription to any thereof other than such right, if any, and at such price as the Board of Directors may in its discretion determine, and the Board of Directors may issue shares of the Corporation or obligations convertible into shares without offering such issue either in whole or in part to the shareholders of the corporation.

IN WITNESS WHEREOF; the undersigned have signed this certificate of incorporation on 2006 and affirms the statements contained herein as true under the penalties of perjury.

_____
Jane S. Smith
1001 Kelly Avenue
Utica, New York 13502

STATE OF New York   )
                          ss.:
County OF Oneida   )

On this _____ day of _____, 2006, before me personally came JANE S. SMITH, to me known and known to me to be the person described in and who executed the foregoing certificate of incorporation and she duly acknowledged to me that she executed the same.

_____
Notary

BANKRUPTCY LAW

CHAPTER OUTCOMES

As a result of studying this chapter, the student will learn:

- Different types of bankruptcy
- To explain the procedures to be followed for Chapter 7 and Chapter 11 bankruptcy
- To prepare the forms required for filing a bankruptcy

INTRODUCTION

Bankruptcy is a federal court proceeding. Businesses and individuals may file a Chapter 7 or Chapter 11 bankruptcy. Attorneys who handle these cases must file a statement of compensation with the bankruptcy court to report the fee the attorney is to be paid for handling the bankruptcy as well as all fees paid to the attorney by the bankruptcy client during the previous year. The attorney must be a disinterested party in the case except in a Chapter 7 filing, in which a party with an interest in the case may represent the debtor. Therefore, attorneys employed by the corporation may represent it in a Chapter 7 bankruptcy proceeding. The chapter numbers refer to the Bankruptcy Code wherein the information and laws are found. The applicable chapters of the Bankruptcy Code are:

1. General Provisions and Introduction
2. Case Administration
3. Creditors and their Claims, Debtor, Estate

bankruptcy a procedure by which a person is relieved of his debts once he has placed all property and money under the court's supervision.

Chapter 13 bankruptcy a bankruptcy for individuals with standard incomes who wish to adjust debts.

These sections of the code will likely be used more often by the attorney than by the paralegal or legal assistant, as they deal with substantive and procedural issues and definitions related to information that should be given to the paralegal prior to preparation of the bankruptcy documents.

Exhibit 12-1 indicates the types of bankruptcy proceedings available and the circumstances under which each is used. Those utilized by corporations are Chapter 7 and Chapter 11. **Chapter 13 bankruptcy** may be used by an individual with a standard income who wishes to adjust his debts.

EXHIBIT 12-1	Types of Bankruptcy

Chapter 7	Liquidation of debts
Chapter 9	Adjustment of the debts of a municipality (Only used by a city of local government entity)
Chapter 11	Reorganization
Chapter 12	Emergency debt relief for farmers
Chapter 13	Wage earner reorganization

CHAPTER 7 PROCEDURES

Filing Statement of Compensation

Attorneys and other professionals rendering services to the estate must file a statement of compensation with the court to have their employment and fees approved. Notes of this application must be given to all creditors.

Filing of Petition

The next step to a **Chapter 7 bankruptcy** is the filing of a petition, by the debtor corporation, with the bankruptcy court in the appropriate district. (See Exhibit 12-2.) The petition must be accompanied by a cover sheet indicating the various schedules that are attached thereto. (See Exhibit 12-3.)

Schedules must be prepared indicating all creditors holding secured and unsecured claims against the corporation. (See Exhibits 12-4 and 12-5.)

If the corporation has outstanding **executory contracts** and/or unexpired leases, then Schedule G—Executory Contracts and Unexpired Leases Form (see Exhibit 12-6) must also be prepared and submitted.

In addition to these general bankruptcy forms, each individual court may have its own local forms and local rules that must be followed. The paralegal should contact the court that has jurisdiction over the matter to determine whether any additional materials are required.

Other schedules may also be required, as noted in the following list.

A. Form 6, consisting of some of the forms outlined previously as well as:

1. A—Real Property
2. B—Personal Property
3. C—Exempt Property
4. D—Creditors Holding Secured Priority Claims
5. E—Creditors Holding Unsecured Priority Claims

Chapter 7 bankruptcy a type of bankruptcy handled under Chapter 7 of the Federal Bankruptcy Act; the bankrupt's property is distributed among creditors who file and prove their claims and the individual may keep some personal property.

executory contracts contracts in which the terms have not yet been carried out and may depend on a future event.

EXHIBIT 12-2   Voluntary Petition—Bankruptcy

(Official Form 1) (9/97)

FORM B1	United States Bankruptcy Court _____District of_____	Voluntary Petition

Name of Debtor (if individual, enter Last, First, Middle):	Name of Joint Debtor (Spouse) (Last, First, Middle):
All Other Names used by the Debtor in the last 6 years (include married, maiden, and trade names):	All Other Names used by the Joint Debtor in the last 6 years (include married, maiden, and trade names):
Soc. Sec./Tax I.D. No. (if more than one, state all):	Soc. Sec./Tax I.D. No. (if more than one, state all):
Street Address of Debtor (No. & Street, City, State & Zip Code):	Street Address of Joint Debtor (No. & Street, City, State & Zip Code):
County of Residence or of the Principal Place of Business:	County of Residence or of the Principal Place of Business:
Mailing Address of Debtor (if different from street address):	Mailing Address of Joint Debtor (if different from street address):

Location of Principal Assets of Business Debtor
(if different from street address above):

Information Regarding the Debtor (Check the Applicable Boxes)

Venue (Check any applicable box)
☐ Debtor has been domiciled or has had a residence, principal place of business, or principal assets in this District for 180 days immediately preceding the date of this petition or for a longer part of such 180 days than in any other District.
☐ There is a bankruptcy case concerning debtor's affiliate, general partner, or partnership pending in this District.

Type of Debtor (Check all boxes that apply)
☐ Individual(s)   ☐ Railroad
☐ Corporation   ☐ Stockbroker
☐ Partnership   ☐ Commodity Broker
☐ Other_____

Nature of Debts (Check one box)
☐ Consumer/Non-Business   ☐ Business

Chapter 11 Small Business (Check all boxes that apply)
☐ Debtor is a small business as defined in 11 U.S.C. § 101
☐ Debtor is and elects to be considered a small business under 11 U.S.C. § 1121(e) (Optional)

Chapter or Section of Bankruptcy Code Under Which the Petition is Filed (Check one box)
☐ Chapter 7   ☐ Chapter 11   ☐ Chapter 13
☐ Chapter 9   ☐ Chapter 12
☐ Sec. 304 - Case ancillary to foreign proceeding

Filing Fee (Check one box)
☐ Full Filing Fee attached
☐ Filing Fee to be paid in installments (Applicable to individuals only) Must attach signed application for the court's consideration certifying that the debtor is unable to pay fee except in installments. Rule 1006(b). See Official Form No. 3.

Statistical/Administrative Information (Estimates only)
☐ Debtor estimates that funds will be available for distribution to unsecured creditors.
☐ Debtor estimates that, after any exempt property is excluded and administrative expenses paid, there will be no funds available for distribution to unsecured creditors.

THIS SPACE IS FOR COURT USE ONLY

Estimated Number of Creditors	1-15	16-49	50-99	100-199	200-999	1000-over
	☐	☐	☐	☐	☐	☐

Estimated Assets							
$0 to $50,000	$50,001 to $100,000	$100,001 to $500,000	$500,001 to $1 million	$1,000,001 to $10 million	$10,000,001 to $50 million	$50,000,001 to $100 million	More than $100 million
☐	☐	☐	☐	☐	☐	☐	☐

Estimated Debts							
$0 to $50,000	$50,001 to $100,000	$100,001 to $500,000	$500,001 to $1 million	$1,000,001 to $10 million	$10,000,001 to $50 million	$50,000,001 to $100 million	More than $100 million
☐	☐	☐	☐	☐	☐	☐	☐

continued

Exhibit 12-2   *continued*

Name of Debtor _____

Case No. _____
(Court use only)

FILING OF PLAN

For Chapter 9, 11, 12 and 13 cases only. Check appropriate box.

☐ A copy of debtor's proposed plan dated _____ is attached.

☐ Debtor intends to file a plan within the time allowed by statute, rule, or order of the court.

PRIOR BANKRUPTCY CASE FILED WITHIN LAST 6 YEARS (If more than one, attach additional sheet)

Location Where Filed	Case Number	Dated Filed

PENDING BANKRUPTCY CASE FILED BY ANY SPOUSE, PARTNER, OR AFFILIATE OF THIS DEBTOR (If more than one, attach additional sheet)

Name of Debtor	Case Number	Date
Relationship	District	Judge

REQUEST FOR RELIEF

Debtor requests relief in accordance with the chapter of title 11, United States Code, specified in this petition.

SIGNATURES

ATTORNEY

X _____

Signature   Date

Attorney I.D. Number _____

INDIVIDUAL/JOINT DEBTOR(S)	CORPORATE OR PARTNERSHIP DEBTOR
I declare under penalty of perjury that the information provided in this petition is true and correct.	I declare under penalty of perjury that the information provided in this petition is true and correct, and that the filing of this petition on behalf of the debtor has been authorized.
X _____ Signature of Debtor	X _____ Signature of Authorized Individual
Date _____	Print or Type Name of Authorized Individual _____
X _____ Signature of Joint Debtor	Title of Individual Authorized by Debtor to File This Petition _____
Date _____	Date _____

EXHIBIT "A" (To be completed if debtor is a corporation requesting relief under Chapter 11.)

☐ Exhibit "A" is attached and made a part of this petition.

TO BE COMPLETED BY INDIVIDUAL CHAPTER 7 DEBTOR WITH PRIMARILY CONSUMER DEBTS (See P.L. 96-353 § 322)

I am aware that I may proceed under Chapter 7, 11, or 12, or 13 of title 11, United States Code, understand the relief available under each such chapter, and choose to proceed under Chapter 7 of such title.

If I am represented by an attorney, Exhibit "B" has been completed.

X _____
Signature of Debtor   Date

X _____
Signature of Joint Debtor   Date

EXHIBIT "B" (To be completed by attorney for individual Chapter 7 debtor(s) with primarily consumer debts.)

I, the attorney for the debtor(s) named in the foregoing petition, declare that I have informed the debtor(s) that (he, she, or they) may proceed under Chapter 7, 11, 12, or 13 of title 11, United States Code, and have explained the relief available under each such chapter.

X _____
Signature of Attorney   Date

EXHIBIT 12-3 Summary of Schedules

FORM B6-Cont.
(6/90)

UNITED STATES BANKRUPTCY COURT
_____ District of _____

In re _____,   Case No. _____
            Debtor   **(If known)**

SUMMARY OF SCHEDULES

Indicate as to each schedule whether that schedule is attached and state the number of pages in each. Report the totals from Schedules A, B, D, E, F, I, and J in the boxes provided. Add the amounts from Schedules A and B to determine the total amount of the debtor's assets. Add the amounts from Schedules D, E, and F to determine the total amount of the debtor's liabilities.

			AMOUNTS SCHEDULED		
NAME OF SCHEDULE	**ATTACHED (YES/NO)**	**NO. OF SHEETS**	**ASSETS**	**LIABILITIES**	**OTHER**
A - Real Property			$		
B - Personal Property			$		
C - Property Claimed as Exempt					
D - Creditors Holding Secured Claims				$	
E - Creditors Holding Unsecured Priority Claims				$	
F - Creditors Holding Unsecured Nonpriority Claims				$	
G - Executory Contracts and Unexpired Leases					
H - Codebtors					
I - Current Income of Individual Debtor(s)					$
J - Current Expenditures of Individual Debtor(s)					$

Total Number of Sheets of ALL Schedules ➤ [   ]

Total Assets ➤ $ [   ]

Total Liabilities ➤ $ [   ]

EXHIBIT 12-4 Schedule D—Creditors Holding Secured Claims

In re _____,   Case No._____
                Debtor   (If known)

SCHEDULE D—CREDITORS HOLDING SECURED CLAIMS

State the name, mailing address, including zip code, and account number, if any, of all entities holding claims secured by property of the debtor as of the date of filing of the petition. List creditors holding all types of secured interest such as judgment liens, garnishments, statutory liens, mortgages, deeds of trust, and other security interests. List creditors in alphabetical order to the extent practicable. If all secured creditors will not fit on this page, use the continuation sheet provided.

If any entity other than a spouse in a joint case may be jointly liable on a claim, place an "X" in the column labeled "Codebtor," include the entity on the appropriate schedule of creditors, and complete Schedule H—Codebtors. If a joint petition is filed, state whether husband, wife, both of them, or the marital community may be liable on each claim by placing an "H," "W," "J," or "C" in the column labeled "Husband, Wife, Joint, or Community."

If the claim is contingent, place an "X" in the column labeled "Contingent." If the claim is unliquidated, place an "X" in the column labeled "Unliquidated." If the claim is disputed, place an "X" in the column labeled "Disputed." (You may need to place an "X" in more than one of these three columns.)

Report the total of all claims listed on this schedule in the box labeled "Total" on the last sheet of the completed schedule. Report this total also on the Summary of Schedules.

☐ Check this box if debtor has no creditors holding secured claims to report on this Schedule D.

CREDITOR'S NAME AND MAILING ADDRESS INCLUDING ZIP CODE	CODEBTOR	HUSBAND, WIFE, JOINT, OR COMMUNITY	DATE CLAIM WAS INCURRED, NATURE OF LIEN, AND DESCRIPTION AND MARKET VALUE OF PROPERTY SUBJECT TO LIEN	CONTINGENT	UNLIQUIDATED	DISPUTED	AMOUNT OF CLAIM WITHOUT DEDUCTING VALUE OF COLLATERAL	UNSECURED PORTION, IF ANY
ACCOUNT NO.								
			VALUE $					
ACCOUNT NO.								
			VALUE $					
ACCOUNT NO.								
			VALUE $					
ACCOUNT NO.								
			VALUE $					

_____ continuation sheets attached

Subtotal ➡ $ _____
(Total of this page)

Total ➡ $ _____
(Use only on last page)

(Report total also on Summary of Schedules)

continued

Exhibit 12-4 *continued*

In re _____ ,   Case No. _____
                    Debtor   (If known)

SCHEDULE D—CREDITORS HOLDING SECURED CLAIMS
(Continuation Sheet)

CREDITOR'S NAME AND MAILING ADDRESS INCLUDING ZIP CODE	CODEBTOR	HUSBAND, WIFE, JOINT, OR COMMUNITY	DATE CLAIM WAS INCURRED, NATURE OF LIEN, AND DESCRIPTION AND MARKET VALUE OF PROPERTY SUBJECT TO LIEN	CONTINGENT	UNLIQUIDATED	DISPUTED	AMOUNT OF CLAIM WITHOUT DEDUCTING VALUE OF COLLATERAL	UNSECURED PORTION, IF ANY
ACCOUNT NO.			VALUE $					
ACCOUNT NO.			VALUE $					
ACCOUNT NO.			VALUE $					
ACCOUNT NO.			VALUE $					
ACCOUNT NO.			VALUE $					
ACCOUNT NO.			VALUE $					

Subtotal ➡ $ _____
(Total of this page)

Total ➡ $ _____
(Use only on last page)

Sheet no. _____ of _____ continuation sheets attached to
Schedule of Creditors Holding Secured Claims

(Report total also on Summary of Schedules)

EXHIBIT 12-5   Schedules E and F—Creditors Holding Unsecured Priority Claims and Nonpriority Claims

In re _____,   Case No._____
　　　　　　　　Debtor　　　　　　　　　　　　　　　　　　　　　　(If known)

SCHEDULE E—CREDITORS HOLDING UNSECURED PRIORITY CLAIMS

A complete list of claims entitled to priority, listed separately by type of priority, is to be set forth on the sheets provided. Only holders of unsecured claims entitled to priority should be listed in this schedule. In the boxes provided on the attached sheets, state the name and mailing address, including zip code, and account number, if any, of all entities holding priority claims against the debtor or the property of the debtor, as of the date of the filing of the petition.

If any entity other than a spouse in a joint case may be jointly liable on a claim, place an "X" in the column labeled "Codebtor," include the entity on the appropriate schedule of creditors, and complete Schedule H—Codebtors. If a joint petition is filed, state whether husband, wife, both of them, or the marital community may be liable on each claim by placing an "H," "W," "J," or "C" in the column labeled "Husband, Wife, Joint, or Community."

If the claim is contingent, place an "X" in the column labeled "Contingent." If the claim is unliquidated, place an "X" in the column labeled "Unliquidated." If the claim is disputed, place an "X" in the column labeled "Disputed." (You may need to place an "X" in more than one of these three columns.)

Report the total of all claims listed on each sheet in the box labeled "Subtotal" on each sheet. Report the total of all claims listed on this Schedule E in the box labeled "Total" on the last sheet of the completed schedule. Repeat this total also on the Summary of Schedules.

☐ Check this box if debtor has no creditors holding unsecured priority claims to report on this Schedule E.

TYPES OF PRIORITY CLAIMS (Check the appropriate box(es) below if claims in that category are listed on the attached sheets)

☐ **Extensions of credit in an involuntary case**

Claims arising in the ordinary course of the debtor's business or financial affairs after the commencement of the case but before the earlier of the appointment of a trustee or the order for relief. 11 U.S.C. § 507(a)(2).

☐ **Wages, salaries, and commissions**

Wages, salaries, and commissions, including vacation, severance, and sick leave pay owing to employees, up to a maximum of $2000 per employee, earned within 90 days immediately preceding the filing of the original petition, or the cessation of business, whichever occurred first, to the extent provided in 11 U.S.C. § 507(a)(3).

☐ **Contributions to employee benefit plans**

Money owed to employee benefit plans for services rendered within 180 days immediately preceding the filing of the original petition, or the cessation of business, whichever occurred first, to the extent provided in 11 U.S.C. § 507(a)(4).

☐ **Certain farmers and fishermen**

Claims of certain farmers and fishermen, up to a maximum of $2000 per farmer or fisherman, against the debtor, as provided in 11 U.S.C. § 507(a)(5).

☐ **Deposits by individuals**

Claims of individuals up to a maximum of $900 for deposits for the purchase, lease, or rental of property or services for personal, family, or household use, that were not delivered or provided. 11 U.S.C. § 507(a)(6).

☐ **Taxes and Certain Other Debts Owed to Governmental Units**

Taxes, customs, duties, and penalties owing to federal, state, and local governmental units as set forth in 11 U.S.C. § 507(a)(7).

_____ continuation sheets attached

continued

Exhibit 12-5 *continued*

In re _____, Case No._____
          Debtor   (If known)

SCHEDULE E—CREDITORS HOLDING UNSECURED PRIORITY CLAIMS
(Continuation Sheet)

TYPE OF PRIORITY

CREDITOR'S NAME AND MAILING ADDRESS INCLUDING ZIP CODE	CODEBTOR	HUSBAND, WIFE, JOINT, OR COMMUNITY	DATE CLAIM WAS INCURRED AND CONSIDERATION FOR CLAIM	CONTINGENT	UNLIQUIDATED	DISPUTED	TOTAL AMOUNT OF CLAIM	AMOUNT ENTITLED TO PRIORITY
ACCOUNT NO.								
ACCOUNT NO.								
ACCOUNT NO.								
ACCOUNT NO.								
ACCOUNT NO.								

Subtotal ➡ $ _____
(Total of this page)

Total ➡ $ _____
(Use only on last page)
(Report total also on Summary of Schedules)

Sheet no. _____ of _____ sheets attached to
Schedule of Creditors Holding Unsecured Priority Claims

continued

Exhibit 12-5 *continued*

FORM B6F (Official Form 6F) (9/97)

In re _____,   Case No. _____
　　　　　　　Debtor　　　　　　　　　　　　　　　　　　　　　**(If known)**

SCHEDULE F- CREDITORS HOLDING UNSECURED NONPRIORITY CLAIMS

State the name, mailing address, including zip code, and account number, if any, of all entities holding unsecured claims without priority against the debtor or the property of the debtor, as of the date of filing of the petition. Do not include claims listed in Schedules D and E. If all creditors will not fit on this page, use the continuation sheet provided.

If any entity other than a spouse in a joint case may be jointly liable on a claim, place an "X" in the column labeled "Codebtor," include the entity on the appropriate schedule of creditors, and complete Schedule H - Codebtors. If a joint petition is filed, state whether husband, wife, both of them, or the marital community maybe liable on each claim by placing an "H," "W," "J," or "C" in the column labeled "Husband, Wife, Joint, or Community."

If the claim is contingent, place an "X" in the column labeled "Contingent." If the claim is unliquidated, place an "X" in the column labeled "Unliquidated." If the claim is disputed, place an "X" in the column labeled "Disputed." (You may need to place an "X" in more than one of these three columns.)

Report total of all claims listed on this schedule in the box labeled "Total" on the last sheet of the completed schedule. Report this total also on the Summary of Schedules.

☐ Check this box if debtor has no creditors holding unsecured claims to report on this Schedule F.

CREDITOR'S NAME AND MAILING ADDRESS INCLUDING ZIP CODE	CODEBTOR	HUSBAND, WIFE, JOINT, OR COMMUNITY	DATE CLAIM WAS INCURRED AND CONSIDERATION FOR CLAIM. IF CLAIM IS SUBJECT TO SETOFF, SO STATE.	CONTINGENT	UNLIQUIDATED	DISPUTED	AMOUNT OF CLAIM
ACCOUNT NO.							
ACCOUNT NO.							
ACCOUNT NO.							
ACCOUNT NO.							

_____ continuation sheets attached　　　　　　Subtotal▶ | $

Total ▶ | $

(Report also on Summary of Schedules)

EXHIBIT 12-6 Schedule G—Executory Contracts and Unexpired Leases

In re _____ ,   Case No._____
                          Debtor   (If known)

SCHEDULE G—EXECUTORY CONTRACTS AND UNEXPIRED LEASES

Describe all executory contracts of any nature and all unexpired leases of real personal property. Include any timeshare interests.

State nature of debtor's interest in contract, i.e., "Purchaser," "Agent," etc. State whether debtor is the lessor or lessee of a lease.

Provide the names and complete mailing addresses of all other parties to each lease or contract described.

NOTE: A party listed on this schedule will not receive notice of the filing of this case unless the party is also scheduled in the appropriate schedule of creditors.

☐ Check this box if debtor has no executory contracts or unexpired leases.

NAME AND MAILING ADDRESS, INCLUDING ZIP CODE, OF OTHER PARTIES TO LEASE OR CONTRACT	DESCRIPTION OF CONTRACT OR LEASE AND NATURE OF DEBTOR'S INTEREST. STATE WHETHER LEASE IS FOR NONRESIDENTIAL REAL PROPERTY. STATE CONTRACT NUMBER OF ANY GOVERNMENT CONTRACT

6. F—Creditors Holding Unsecured Nonpriority Claims

7. G—Executory Contracts and Unexpired Leases

8. H—Codebtors [usually used for individuals]

9. I—Current Income

10. J—Current Expenditures

11. Summary Schedules

B. Statement of Financial Affairs—Form 7 (see Exhibit 12-7 located at the end of this chapter)

One may obtain all required forms from the local bankruptcy court or from the Federal Court's Web page (listed previously). Information to include in the forms is self-explanatory. Be sure to have the forms signed by an appropriate officer of the corporation prior to filing.

Trustee Appointment

The United States Trustee has the power to make an interim appointment of a trustee to serve in this capacity until the meeting of creditors. This individual will be chosen from a panel of individuals who assume such responsibility on a regular basis.

OVERVIEW OF CHAPTER 7 BANKRUPTCY ◆

The most common type of bankruptcy is the Chapter 7 liquidation. The individual, corporation, or business has its debts discharged in exchange for giving up property, which is sold to pay creditors. Some assets are exempt.

The bankruptcy must be filed in the district bankruptcy court where the principal place of the business was located or the principal corporate assets were situated during the previous 180 days.

The business or individual must enumerate assets and liabilities, as well as income and expenses, and must list any exempt property. The bankruptcy court appoints a trustee to administer the case. Once the case is completed, the debts that have been discharged in the bankruptcy need not be paid. However, the business must cease operation.

OVERVIEW OF CHAPTER 11 BANKRUPTCY ◆

Corporations that file under Chapter 11 intend to reorganize the company rather than liquidate it. In recent years, this method has been used by many large corporations. The major advantages is that the corporation may continue to operate even though it has serious financial problems. During this period, the business reorganizes to a more economically sound structure. The company must file stringent rules and its affairs become public knowledge, in that the creditors and the trustee may scrutinize its activities. In general, corporations that file for Chapter 11 bankruptcy have enough income to pay off a portion of their debts over a period of time.

Although the Chapter 11 is more expensive and time-consuming than a Chapter 7 bankruptcy, it is the best alternative for a business that wishes to remain in operation during the reorganization process. Strict deadlines exist for the filing of documents with the bankruptcy court.

DEFINITIONS

Unlike civil litigation, where the parties are the plaintiff and the defendant, the bankruptcy proceeding involves a **debtor**, and **creditors**, and the **trustee**. The debtor usually institutes the bankruptcy proceeding and is the individual or corporation who is bankrupt and owes the debts. The debts are owed to the creditors. The trustee is an independent party who is appointed by the court to liquidate the assets and distribute funds to the creditors.

Notice to Creditors

Approximately five to seven days after the petition is filed, notice will be sent to the debtor and creditors advising them of the filing of an order for relief and the appointment of the interim trustee, who will also receive the notice.

Notice of Creditors' Meeting

Notice will be given by the United States Trustee to all creditors, advising them of the creditors' meeting, including time, date, and place. This meeting must occur not less than 20 nor more than 40 days after the order for relief has been entered. The debtor and a representative of the United States Trustee's office must also appear at the meeting. Questions may be posed to the debtor by both the representative and the creditors, primarily to verify whether the previously submitted statements and schedules accurately reflect the assets owned by the debtor. The creditors will appoint a permanent trustee.

Discharge

If no objections are filed relating to the bankruptcy proceedings, a discharge will automatically be issued by the bankruptcy court. Most debts will be discharged at this point. Secured debts, however, are not dischargeable.

CHAPTER 11 PROCEEEDING

If the corporation wishes to remain in business, it may file a Chapter 11 reorganization proceeding and must follow these procedures:

creditor individual or entity to whom the debtor owes money.

debtor individual or entity that owes money and initiates a bankruptcy proceeding.

trustee independent party appointed by the court in a bankruptcy proceeding for the purpose of liquidating the assets and distributing funds to creditors.

1. *Initial filing.* Items to include at the initial filing are the petition, the $800 filing fee, a corporate resolution authorizing the bankruptcy, all creditors' names and addresses, and the 20 largest creditors' claims.

2. *Up to 15 days after initial filing.* Additional items that must be filed include a statement of financial affairs, a list of all equity security holders, schedules of assets and liabilities, and a statement of executory contracts.

3. *Within 30 days of initial filing.* The debtor must file an inventory of assets if the United States Trustee so orders. All operating reports must be filed. Applications to hire attorneys or other professionals must be filed. (Alternatively, an application may be filed within 30 days of retaining the professional.)

4. *Within 60 days of filing.* A debtor in possession of property must assume any lease, or it is considered rejected. The debtor must also deposit all funds in an approved bank. Old bank accounts must be canceled and new ones established, called general, tax, and payroll accounts. The corporation's checkbook must state that it is a "Debtor-in-Possession." These accounts operate like an attorney's trust account. That is, all funds received are deposited into the general account; disbursements are made into the payroll account as payroll must be paid. Regular reports must be filed with the court on income and disbursements.

5. *Filing of a plan of reorganization and disclosure statement.* The debtor must file its own reorganization plan, along with disclosures about the plan, telling the creditors information that might affect their vote for or against the plan.

6. *Notice to creditors 25 days before hearing.* A hearing will be held in the bankruptcy court to approve the disclosure statement; notice must be sent to creditors at least 25 days before this hearing.

   Accompanying the notice to creditors are the following:

   a. Copy of the reorganization plan

   b. Copy of the disclosure statement

   c. Copy of the approval of the disclosure statement

   d. A ballot to vote on the plan

   These documents are known as the confirmation packet.

7. *Confirmation hearing.* The court will either confirm or deny confirmation of the corporation's plan for reorganization. Typically the confirmation process takes approximately four or five months.

The only method for a corporation to use to discharge its debts, if it wishes to stay in business, is the **Chapter 11 bankruptcy** process. Confirmation of the Chapter 11 plan will result in a discharge of obligations pursuant to § 1141 of the Bankruptcy Code. See 11 U.S.C. § 1129 *et seq.*

Chapter 11 bankruptcy a bankruptcy for business reorganizations short of full bankruptcy.

Only a brief overview of the corporate bankruptcy process has been given here. The paralegal should consult a text on bankruptcy or the Bankruptcy Code to obtain further information. Forms used in the bankruptcy process may be downloaded from the Federal Courts Web site:

http://www.uscourts.gov/

ETHICS and ETIQUETTE

Freelance legal assistants may operate services for the preparation of the forms required in a bankruptcy action. The courts have found that these paralegals may type bankruptcy forms for the clients but may not offer any advice. The client must provide the information to include on the forms, and the paralegal may type the form using the supplied information. If the client makes a mistake, the paralegal may not advise the client as to the proper way to complete the form, as this could constitute legal advice. If the client asks the paralegal for legal advice, the paralegal must ask the client to seek the advice of an attorney.

CHAPTER SUMMARY ✦

Bankruptcy is a federal proceeding handled in federal courts; therefore, most bankruptcy rules are the same in all states. In Chapter 7 bankruptcy, business or individual debtors may have their debts discharged in exchange for giving up certain property that is sold to pay creditors. Chapter 11 bankruptcy was designed to help business debtors reorganize, while continuing to operate their business. Individuals may also file a Chapter 11 bankruptcy.

✦ KEY TERMS

bankruptcy	creditor
Chapter 7 bankruptcy	debtor
Chapter 11 bankruptcy	executory contracts
Chapter 13 bankruptcy	trustee

✦ SELF TEST

Indicate whether the following statements are true (T) or false (F).

_____ 1. Chapter 11 is the bankruptcy of choice for individuals.

_____ 2. Bankruptcies are done in state court.

_____ 3. Businesses may file a Chapter 7 or Chapter 13 bankruptcy.

_____ 4. Each state has its own bankruptcy court on the state level.

_____ 5. Attorneys file a statement of compensation with the client.

Circle the correct answer for the following questions:

1. Chapter 7 bankruptcy proceedings involve
   a. adjustment of debts.
   b. liquidation of debts.
   c. reorganization.
   d. family farmers.

2. The type of bankruptcy where individuals or businesses have their debts discharged in exchange for giving up property is
   a. Chapter 7.
   b. Chapter 9.
   c. Chapter 11.
   d. Chapter 12.
   e. Chapter 13.

3. Corporations file under Chapter _____ to reorganize the company:
   a. Chapter 7
   b. Chapter 9
   c. Chapter 11
   d. Chapter 13
   e. none of the above

4. The parties to a bankruptcy are the
   a. plaintiff and defendant.
   b. creditor and defendant.
   c. debtor, creditors, and trustee.
   d. debtor and trustee.

5. Chapter _____ proceedings commence with the filing of a Petition.
   a. 7
   b. 9
   c. 11
   d. 12
   e. 13

Fill-in-the-blanks.

1. The parties to a bankruptcy are _____.

2. In a Chapter 7 bankruptcy, _____ are prepared indicating all creditors holding secured and unsecured claims against the corporation.

3. The _____ has the power to make an interim appointment of a trustee to serve in this capacity until the meeting of creditors.

4. If a corporation wishes to remain in business, it may file a Chapter _____ bankruptcy.

5. Forms used in the bankruptcy process may be found at the _____ courts Web site.

✦ REVIEW QUESTIONS

1. Explain the procedures followed in the Chapter 7 bankruptcy.

2. Under what circumstances would a Chapter 7 bankruptcy be filed?

3. What is the intent of corporations filing a Chapter 11 bankruptcy?

4. Explain the procedure for filing a Chapter 11 bankruptcy.

5. What forms are found on the Federal Courts Web site? List the Web address.

✦ NOTEBOOK PROJECTS

1. Obtain all forms required for a Chapter 7 filing from the Web site.

2. Prepare the Petition for your own corporation's Chapter 7 bankruptcy using the name and address of your school as the name of the business. Do not include your social security number. You may use XXX-XX-XXXX or leave that section blank. The nature of the debts are business. You are attaching the full filing fee. You are estimating that funds will be available to distribute to unsecured creditors. You have 20 creditors, assets of $200,000, and debts of $150,000.

3. Where is the court in which you would file the petition in No. 2? Find any local rules or forms for this court and include them with this answer.

4. Write a memo to the attorney following these instructions:

   ABC Corporation is our client and they want to file a bankruptcy case. However, they wish to discharge their debts and remain in business. Prepare a memorandum describing their options in filing for bankruptcy. Describe the procedure for filing this type of bankruptcy. Cite appropriate code sections.

5. Prepare instructions for your notebook on how to prepare a Chapter 7 and a Chapter 11 bankruptcy case.

6. Research the bankruptcy court Web site within your federal circuit court and summarize the services and information available therein. Write a memo to your instructor with your findings.

EXHIBIT 12-7   Statement of Financial Affairs

FORM 7. STATEMENT OF FINANCIAL AFFAIRS

UNITED STATES BANKRUPTCY COURT

_____ DISTRICT OF _____

In re: _____,   Case No. _____
                   (Name)   (If known)
                      Debtor

STATEMENT OF FINANCIAL AFFAIRS

This statement is to be completed by every debtor. Spouses filing a joint petition may file a single statement on which the information for both spouses is combined. If the case is filed under Chapter 12 or Chapter 13, a married debtor must furnish information for both spouses whether or not a joint petition is filed, unless the spouses are separated and a joint petition is not filed. An individual debtor engaged in business as a sole proprietor, partner, family farmer, or self-employed professional, should provide the information requested on this statement concerning all such activities as well as the individual's personal affairs.

Questions 1-15 are to be completed by all debtors. Debtors that are or have been in business, as defined below, also must complete Questions 16-21. **Each question must be answered. If the answer to any question is "None," or the question is not applicable, mark the box labeled "None."** If additional space is needed for the answer to any question, use and attach a separate sheet properly identified with the case name, case number (if known), and the number of the question.

DEFINITIONS

"_In business._" A debtor is "in business" for the purpose of this form if the debtor is a corporation or partnership. An individual debtor is "in business" for the purpose of this form if the debtor is or has been, within the two years immediately preceding the filing of this bankruptcy case, any of the following: an officer, director, managing executive, or person in control of a corporation; a partner, other than a limited partner, of a partnership; a sole proprietor or self-employed.

"_Insider._" The term "insider" includes but is not limited to: relatives of the debtor; general partners of the debtor and their relatives; corporations of which the debtor is an officer, director, or person in control; officers, directors, and any person in control of a corporate debtor and their relatives; affiliates of the debtor and insiders of such affiliates; any managing agent of the debtor. 11 U.S.C. § 101(30).

    1.   **Income from employment or operation of business**

None
☐
    State the gross amount of income the debtor has received from employment, trade, or profession, or from operation of the debtor's business from the beginning of this calendar year to the date this case was commenced. State also the gross amounts received during the **two years** immediately preceding this calendar year. (A debtor that maintains, or has maintained, financial records on the basis of a fiscal rather than a calendar year may report fiscal year income. Identify the beginning and ending dates of the debtor's fiscal year.) If a joint petition is filed, state income for each spouse separately. (Married debtors filing under Chapter 12 or Chapter 13 must state income of both spouses whether or not a joint petition is filed, unless the spouses are separated and a joint petition is not filed.)

AMOUNT   SOURCE (If more than one)

continued

Exhibit 12-7 *continued*

2. Income other than from employment or operation of business

None   State the amount of income received by the debtor other than from employment, trade, profession, or operation of the debtor's business
☐   during the two **years** immediately preceding the commencement of this case. Give particulars. If a joint petition is filed, state income for each spouse separately. (Married debtors filing under Chapter 12 or Chapter 13 must state income for each spouse whether or not a joint petition is filed, unless the spouses are separated and a joint petition is not filed.)

AMOUNT   SOURCE

3. Payments to creditors

None   a.   List all payments on loans, installment purchases of goods or services, and other debts, aggregating more than $600 to any creditor,
☐   made within **90 days** immediately preceding the commencement of this case. (Married debtors filing under Chapter 12 or Chapter 13 must include payments by either or both spouses whether not a joint petition is filed, unless the spouses are separated and a joint petition is not filed.)

NAME AND ADDRESS OF CREDITOR	DATES OF PAYMENTS	AMOUNT PAID	AMOUNT STILL OWING

None   b.   List all payments made within **one year** immediately preceding the commencement of this case, to or for the benefit of, creditors who
☐   are or were insiders. (Married debtors filing under Chapter 12 or Chapter 13 must include payments by either or both spouses whether or not a joint petition is filed, unless the spouses are separated and a joint petition is not filed.)

NAME AND ADDRESS OF CREDITOR; RELATIONSHIP TO DEBTOR	DATES OF PAYMENTS	AMOUNT PAID	AMOUNT STILL OWING

4. Suits, executions, garnishments and attachments

None   a.   List all suits to which the debtor is or was a party within **one year** immediately preceding the filing of this bankruptcy case. (Married
☐   debtors filing under Chapter 12 or Chapter 13 must include information concerning either or both spouses whether or not a joint petition is filed, unless the spouses are separated and a joint petition is not filed.)

CAPTION OF SUIT AND CASE NUMBER	NATURE OF PROCEEDING	COURT AND LOCATION	STATUS OR DISPOSITION

continued

Exhibit 12-7   *continued*

None   b.   Describe all property that has been attached, garnished or seized under any legal or equitable process within **one year** immediately preceding the commencement of this case. (Married debtors filing under Chapter 12 or Chapter 13 must include information concerning property of either or both spouses whether or not a joint petition is filed, unless the spouses are separated and a joint petition is not filed.)

NAME AND ADDRESS OF PERSON FOR WHOSE BENEFIT PROPERTY WAS SEIZED	DATE OF SEIZURE	DESCRIPTION AND VALUE OF PROPERTY

5. Repossessions, foreclosures and returns

None   List all property that has been repossessed by a creditor, sold at a foreclosure sale, transferred through a deed in lieu of foreclosure or returned to the seller, within **one year** immediately preceding the commencement of this case. (Married debtors filing under Chapter 12 or Chapter 13 must include information concerning property of either or both spouses whether or not a joint petition is filed, unless the spouses are separated and a joint petition is not filed.)

NAME AND ADDRESS OF CREDITOR OR SELLER	DATE OF REPOSSESSION, FORECLOSURE SALE, TRANSFER OR RETURN	DESCRIPTION AND VALUE OF PROPERTY

6.   Assignments and receiverships

None   a.   Describe any assignment of property for the benefit of creditors made within **120 days** immediately preceding the commencement of this case. (Married debtors filing under Chapter 12 or Chapter 13 must include any assignment by either or both spouses whether or not a joint petition is filed, unless the spouses are separated and a joint petition is not filed.)

NAME AND ADDRESS OF ASSIGNEE	DATE OF ASSIGNMENT	TERMS OF ASSIGNMENT OR SETTLEMENT

continued

Exhibit 12-7 *continued*

None   b.   List all property which has been in the hands of a custodian, receiver, or court-appointed official within **one year** immediately preceding
☐   the commencement of this case. (Married debtors filing under Chapter 12 or Chapter 13 must include information concerning property
        of either or both spouses whether or not a joint petition is filed, unless the spouses are separated and a joint petition is not filed.)

NAME AND ADDRESS OF CUSTODIAN	NAME AND LOCATION OF COURT; CASE TITLE & NUMBER	DATE OF ORDER	DESCRIPTION AND VALUE OF PROPERTY

7.   Gifts

None   List all gifts or charitable contributions made within **one year** immediately preceding the commencement of this case except ordinary
☐   and usual gifts to family members aggregating less than $200 in value per individual family member and charitable contributions aggregating
      less than $100 per recipient. (Married debtors filing under Chapter 12 or Chapter 13 must include gifts or contributions by either or both
      spouses whether or not a joint petition is filed, unless the spouses are separated and a joint petition is not filed.)

NAME AND ADDRESS OF PERSON OR ORGANIZATION	RELATIONSHIP TO DEBTOR, IF ANY	DATE OF GIFT	DESCRIPTION AND VALUE OF GIFT

8.   Losses

None   List all losses from fire, theft, other casualty or gambling within **one year** immediately preceding the commencement of this case or since
☐   the commencement of this case. (Married debtors filing under Chapter 12 or Chapter 13 must include losses by either or both spouses
      whether or not a joint petition is filed, unless the spouses are separated and a joint petition is not filed.)

DESCRIPTION AND VALUE OF PROPERTY	DESCRIPTION OF CIRCUMSTANCES AND, IF LOSS WAS COVERED IN WHOLE OR IN PART BY INSURANCE, GIVE PARTICULARS	DATE OF LOSS

continued

Exhibit 12-7   *continued*

9.   Payments related to debt counseling or bankruptcy

None
☐

List all payments made or property transferred by or on behalf of the debtor to any person, including attorneys, for consultation concerning debt consolidation, relief under the bankruptcy law or preparation of a petition in bankruptcy within **one year** immediately preceding the commencement of this case.

NAME AND ADDRESS OF PAYEE	DATE OF PAYMENT; NAME OF PAYOR IF OTHER THAN DEBTOR	AMOUNT OF MONEY OR DESCRIPTION AND VALUE OF PROPERTY

10.   Other transfers

None   a.
☐

List all other property, other than property transferred in the ordinary course of the business or financial affairs of the debtor, transferred either absolutely or as security within **one year** immediately preceding the commencement of this case. (Married debtors filing under Chapter 12 or Chapter 13 must include transfers by either or both spouses whether or not a joint petition is filed, unless the spouses are separated and a joint petition is not filed.)

NAME AND ADDRESS OF TRANSFEREE; RELATIONSHIP TO DEBTOR	DATE	DESCRIBE PROPERTY TRANSFERRED AND VALUE RECEIVED

11.   Closed financial accounts

None
☐

List all financial accounts and instruments held in the name of the debtor or for the benefit of the debtor which were closed, sold, or otherwise transferred within **one year** immediately preceding the commencement of this case. Include checking, savings, or other financial accounts, certificates of deposit, or other instruments; shares and share accounts held in banks, credit unions, pension funds, cooperatives, associations, brokerage houses and other financial institutions. (Married debtors filing under Chapter 12 or Chapter 13 must include information concerning accounts or instruments held by or for either or both spouses whether or not a joint petition is filed, unless the spouses are separated and a joint petition is not filed.)

NAME AND ADDRESS OF INSTITUTION	TYPE AND NUMBER OF ACCOUNT AND AMOUNT OF FINAL BALANCE	AMOUNT AND DATE OF SALE OR CLOSING

continued

Exhibit 12-7 *continued*

12. Safe deposit boxes

None ☐   List each safe deposit or other box or depository in which the debtor has or had securities, cash, or other valuables within one year immediately preceding the commencement of this case. (Married debtors filing under Chapter 12 or Chapter 13 must include boxes or depositories of either or both spouses whether or not a joint petition is filed, unless the spouses are separated and a joint petition is not filed.)

NAME AND ADDRESS OF BANK OR OTHER DEPOSITORY	NAMES AND ADDRESSES OF THOSE WITH ACCESS TO BOX OR DEPOSITORY	DESCRIPTION OF CONTENTS	DATE OF TRANSFER OR SURRENDER, IF ANY

13. Setoffs

None ☐   List all setoffs made by any creditor, including a bank, against a debt or deposit of the debtor within 90 days preceding the commencement of this case. (Married debtors filing under Chapter 12 or Chapter 13 must include information concerning either or both spouses whether or not a joint petition is filed, unless the spouses are separated and a joint petition is not filed.)

NAME AND ADDRESS OF CREDITOR	DATE OF SETOFF	AMOUNT OF SETOFF

14. Property held for another person

None ☐   List all property owned by another person that the debtor holds or controls.

NAME AND ADDRESS OF OWNER	DESCRIPTION AND VALUE OF PROPERTY	LOCATION OF PROPERTY

15. Prior address of debtor

None ☐   If the debtor has moved within the two years immediately preceding the commencement of this case, list all premises which the debtor occupied during that period and vacated prior to the commencement of this case. If a joint petition is filed, report also any separate address of either spouse.

ADDRESS	NAME USED	DATES OF OCCUPANCY

continued

Exhibit 12-7   *continued*

The following questions are to be completed by every debtor that is a corporation or partnership and by any individual debtor who is or has been, with the two years immediately preceding the commencement of this case, any of the following: an officer, director, managing executive, or owner of more than 5 percent of the voting securities of a corporation; a partner, other than a limited partner, of a partnership; a sole proprietor or otherwise self-employed.

(An individual or joint debtor should complete this portion of the statement only if the debtor is or has been in business, as defined above, within the two years immediately preceding the commencement of this case.)

16. Nature, location and name of business

None a. If the debtor is an individual, list the names and addresses of all businesses in which the debtor was an officer, director, partner, or
☐   managing executive of a corporation, partnership, sole proprietorship, or was a self-employed professional within the **two years** immediately preceding the commencement of this case, or in which the debtor owned 5 percent or more of the voting or equity securities, within the **two years** immediately preceding the commencement of this case.

b. If the debtor is a partnership, list the names and addresses of all businesses in which the debtor was a partner or owned 5 percent or more of the voting securities, within the **two years** immediately preceding the commencement of this case.

c. If the debtor is a corporation, list the names and addresses of all businesses in which the debtor was a partner or owned 5 percent or more of the voting securities, within the **two years** immediately preceding the commencement of this case.

| | | | BEGINNING AND ENDING |
NAME	ADDRESS	NATURE OF BUSINESS	DATES OF OPERATION

17. Books, records and financial statements

None a. List all bookkeepers and accountants who within the **six years** immediately preceding the filing of this bankruptcy case kept or
☐   supervised the keeping of books of account and records of the debtor.

NAME AND ADDRESS	DATES SERVICES RENDERED

None b. List all firms or individuals who within the **two years** immediately preceding the filing of this bankruptcy case have audited the books of
☐   account and records, or prepared a financial statement of the debtor.

NAME AND ADDRESS	DATES SERVICES RENDERED

continued

Exhibit 12-7 *continued*

None c. List all firms or individuals who at the time of the commencement of this case were in possession of the books of account and records of
□ the debtor. If any of the books of account and records are not available, explain.

NAME ADDRESS
_____

None d. List all financial institutions, creditors and other parties, including mercantile and trade agencies, to whom a financial statement was
□ issued within the **two years** immediately preceding the commencement of this case by the debtor.

NAME AND ADDRESS DATE ISSUED
_____

18. **Inventories**

None a. List the dates of the last two inventories taken of your property, the name of the person who supervised the taking of each inventory,
□ and the dollar amount and basis of each inventor.

| | | DOLLAR AMOUNT OF INVENTORY |
DATE OF INVENTORY	INVENTORY SUPERVISOR	(Specify cost, market or other basis)

None b. List the name and address of the person having possession of the records of each of the two inventories reported in a., above.
□

| | NAME AND ADDRESSES OF |
DATE OF INVENTORY	CUSTODIAN OF INVENTORY RECORDS

19. **Current partners, officers, directors and shareholders**

None a. If the debtor is a partnership, list the nature and percentage of partnership interest of each member of the partnership.
□

NAME AND ADDRESS	NATURE OF INTEREST	PERCENTAGE OF INTEREST

continued

Exhibit 12-7   *continued*

None   b.   If the debtor is a corporation, list all officers and directors of the corporation, and each stockholder who directly or indirectly owns,
☐   controls, or holds 5 percent or more of the voting securities of the corporation.

NAME AND ADDRESS	TITLE	NATURE AND PERCENTAGE OF STOCK OWNERSHIP

20.   **Former partners, officers, directors and shareholders**

None   a.   If the debtor is a partnership, list each member who withdrew from the partnership within one year immediately preceding the
☐   commencement of this case.

NAME	ADDRESS	DATE OF WITHDRAWAL

None   b.   If the debtor is a corporation, list all officers or directors whose relationship with the corporation terminated within one year
☐   immediately preceding the commencement of this case.

NAME AND ADDRESS	TITLE	DATE OF TERMINATION

21.   **Withdrawals from a partnership or distributions by a corporation**

None   If the debtor is a partnership or corporation, list all withdrawals or distributions credited or given to an insider, including compensation
☐   in any form, bonuses, loans, stock redemptions, options exercised and any other perquisite during one year immediately preceding the
         commencement of this case

NAME AND ADDRESS OF RECIPIENT; RELATIONSHIP TO DEBTOR	DATE AND PURPOSE OF WITHDRAWAL	AMOUNT OF MONEY OR DESCRIPTION AND VALUE OF PROPERTY

continued

Exhibit 12-7 *continued*

[If completed by an individual or individual and spouse]

I declare under penalty of perjury that I have read the answers contained in the foregoing statement of financial affairs and any attachments thereto and that they are true and correct.

Date _____   Signature _____
                                  of Debtor

Date _____   Signature _____
                                  of Joint Debtor
                                  (if any)

CERTIFICATION AND SIGNATURE OF NON-ATTORNEY BANKRUPTCY PETITION PREPARER (See 11 U.S.C. § 110)

I certify that I am a bankruptcy petition preparer as defined in 11 U.S.C. § 110, that I prepared this document for compensation, and that I have provided the debtor with a copy of this document.

_____   _____
Printed or Typed Name of Bankruptcy Petition Preparer   Social Security No.

_____
Address

Names and Social Security numbers of all other individuals who prepared or assisted in preparing this document:

If more than one person prepared this document, attach additional signed sheets conforming to the appropriate Official Form for each person.

X_____   _____
Signature of Bankruptcy Petition Preparer   Date

A bankruptcy petition preparer's failure to comply with the provisions of title 11 and the Federal Rules of Bankruptcy Procedure may result in fines or imprisonment or both. 11 U.S.C. § 156.

[If completed on behalf of a partnership or corporation]

I, declare under penalty of perjury that I have read the answers contained in the foregoing statement of financial affairs and any attachments thereto and that they are true and correct to the best of my knowledge, information and belief.

Date _____   Signature _____

                                  _____
                                  Print Name and Title

[An individual signing on behalf of a partnership or corporation must indicate position or relationship to debtor.]

_____ continuation sheets attached

Penalty for making a false statement: Fine of up to $500,000 or imprisonment for up to 5 years, or both. 18 U.S.C. § 152 and 3571

REAL PROPERTY

CHAPTER OUTCOMES

As a result of studying this chapter, the student will learn:

- The role of the paralegal and legal assistant in real property law
- The various types of property ownerships
- The steps involved in transferring property
- The rights of landlords and tenants

REAL AND PERSONAL PROPERTY

Real property includes land and things permanently attached to the land. Homes, garages and other buildings, in-ground swimming pools, minerals in the ground, trees, and fixtures are examples of real property.

Personal property includes items that are not attached to the land or buildings and are movable or easily transportable from one location to another. For example, a camper and an automobile would be classified as personal property.

A **fixture** is an item of personal property that is affixed to land or to a building in such a way that it becomes a part of the real property. For example, a light fixture purchased at a store is personal property. Once the light fixture is permanently attached to the ceiling of your home, however, it becomes real property. Other examples of fixtures include furnaces, built-in bookcases, and wall-to-wall carpeting.

Fixtures can also become personal property. For example, a growing tree is considered to be real property because it is attached to the land. Once the tree is cut down, it becomes personal property. A chandelier attached to the ceiling is a fixture but can become personal property if it is removed from the ceiling.

THE ROLE OF THE LEGAL ASSISTANT

Many opportunities are available for paralegals trained in real estate law. Possible employers include private law offices specializing in real estate law, real estate offices, escrow offices, title companies, mortgage companies, and banks. Government offices, such as the Tax Assessor's

real property
includes land and things permanently attached to the land.

personal property items that are not attached to land or buildings and are movable or easily transportable from one location to another.

fixture an item of personal property that is permanently attached to land or to a building in such a way that it becomes part of the real property.

CHAPTER 12

Office and the Office of the County Recorder, may also be sources of employment.

In a private law firm, paralegals may prepare documents required for a real estate transaction, as well as do research into the ownership of property. They may also prepare the documents necessary for closings. If the attorney practices landlord/tenant law, then the paralegal may draft documents for evictions and discuss the rights and responsibilities of landlords and tenants with clients. Attention to detail is imperative for a paralegal employed in real estate law.

Property descriptions must be proofread carefully to make sure numbers are not transposed or typed incorrectly. Research is often conducted into property ownership. Tickler files are maintained for the sequence of events in a real estate transaction to ensure that each step is completed in a timely fashion.

TYPES OF OWNERSHIP ✦

Ownership in **fee simple** is the absolute ownership of that property with no ownership limitations. It may be conveyed by gift, sale, or inheritance. Most modern-day property is held in this manner. Several individuals may share an interest in the same piece of property in fee simple, as will be discussed later in this chapter.

Joint Tenancy

One of the most common forms of real estate ownership is **joint tenancy**. Any number of persons may own a piece of property in this manner with all ownership interests being equal. The title to the property is held in joint ownership in undivided equal shares. Each of the owners has an undivided ownership interest in the property with right of survivorship. Although joint tenancy ownership is not reserved for spouses, many married couples hold their real property in this fashion.

Any of the owners may sell or encumber the property without the other's permission. The new owner will become a tenant in common with the other owners of the property. The primary advantage of this type of ownership is the right of survivorship whereby the property passes automatically to the surviving joint tenant(s) upon the death of a joint tenant without having to be administered in a probate proceeding. In most states, a simple document is required to transfer full title to the survivor upon the death of the joint tenant.

This type of ownership must be specifically stated in the deed to the property. For example, the following wording would constitute a joint tenancy ownership:

DANIEL MICHAEL ROBERTSON and JULIANNE HENDRICKS in joint tenancy with right of survivorship.

Tenancy in Common

When two or more individuals own a piece of property together, with each having a certain proportion of the property, the property is

fee simple absolute ownership of property.

joint tenancy ownership of an undivided interest in property by two or more owners with a right of survivorship.

owned as a **tenancy in common**. Any number of people can divide a piece of property as tenants in common. For instance, if ten individuals owned Blacklake as tenants in common, then each would own one-tenth of the property. Property can be divided into any number of interests, and they can be equal or unequal. In the case of Blacklake, each tenant in common owned an equal interest in the property, but the title could be worded such that the interests were not the same.

Any co-owner of property may sell his share to another party, who will then own that percentage of interest in the property. Unlike joint tenancy, there is no right of survivorship except in the percentage owned. For instance if John Doe died with a one-quarter interest in Blacklake, his heirs at law would receive his one-quarter interest.

Community Property

In community property states, married couples may hold property acquired during the marriage as **community property**. Each spouse has equal control of the property and may not dispose of the property without the consent of the other spouse. This property will be liable for any debts of either of the spouses that were incurred during the marriage unless the other spouse can prove it should be treated as a separate debt. For instance, the spouse may have incurred the debt before the marriage; in this case, it would be a separate debt and not a debt of the community.

Some states have variations of this ownership rule. For instance, in California, if the parties own their property as "community property with right of survivorship," the property passes automatically to the surviving spouse in the event of the other spouse's death. Title passes by operation of law and excludes heirs and separate property creditors of the deceased spouse. The surviving spouse will then hold title to the property as her separate property.

PARTNERSHIP PROPERTY ✦

Partners in a business may hold property in the name of the partnership. The amount of ownership interest is the same percentage as the interest in the partnership. The property belongs to the business and not to the individual partners. A partner's personal creditor may take his share of the profits but not the partnership property.

TENANCY BY THE ENTIRETY ✦

A few states allow a married couple to acquire property in tenancy by the entirety. Neither party may sell or encumber the property without the express permission of the other party. Upon the death of one spouse, the property passes automatically to the survivor.

tenancy in common joint ownership of property with no right of survivorship.

community property property acquired by either spouse during marriage, except property acquired by gift or inheritance, and owned by both spouses equally.

```
┌────────────────────────────────────────────────────────────┐
│                                                              │
│   STATE SPECIFIC INFORMATION                                 │
│                                                              │
│   In the state of _____, property may be     │
│   held in the                                                │
│   following ways:                                            │
│                                                              │
│   1. _____ │
│                                                              │
│   2. _____ │
│                                                              │
│   3. _____ │
│                                                              │
│   4. _____ │
│                                                              │
│   5. _____ │
│                                                              │
└────────────────────────────────────────────────────────────┘
```

CONDOMINIUMS ◆

In the **condominium** form of ownership, different people own individual units within a multiple-unit complex. Each unit is owned in fee simple and may be owned by a single individual or by two or more individuals in any of the forms of ownership discussed above, such as joint tenancy or tenancy in common. The interior of the unit within the building is the bounds of what each owner owns. The owner of a unit may also have the use of a portion of the property not within the bounds of the individual unit, such as a garage, a storage cupboard, or a patio. Any other areas of the complex are known as common areas and are owned by all owners of condominiums within the complex as tenants in common. The individual owners may not transfer their ownership of the common areas unless they transfer ownership of their individual units.

The everyday management of the affairs of the complex is usually handled by a property management company that takes care of the building's maintenance and financial affairs. Each owner may obtain a loan on the individual unit he owns. A master loan is generally obtained for the complex itself.

Most states require that a master deed for the whole complex be recorded in the county recorder's office. (This process is similar to the manner in which tract maps are recorded, as will be described later in this chapter.) In addition, each owner of an individual unit will have his own deed that should also be recorded.

The individual owners elect a board of directors from among themselves to establish rules and regulations for the condominium complex. The board may also handle the maintenance and financial affairs of the condominium if a professional management company is not employed for this purpose.

condominium ownership of a unit within a multiple-unit building complex.

cooperative similar to a condominium except that the unit is represented by a share of stock.

COOPERATIVES ◆

A **cooperative** apartment is similar to a condominium except that, whereas a condominium owner actually owns an individual unit within a large complex, a cooperative owner owns a share of stock represented by a unit. Thus, ownership of a cooperative is necessarily more restrictive than ownership of a condominium.

The cooperative complex is governed by a board of directors, who are elected by the individual share owners. A cooperative owner may not sell his share without obtaining permission from the board. The board must also approve any prospective purchaser. An owner who wishes to rent his unit must also obtain permission from the board.

One of the major disadvantages of cooperative ownership is the difficulty of obtaining a loan on an individual unit (or share). Therefore, when an owner wishes to sell his apartment, he must either provide a personal loan for the buyer, or as happens more frequently, the buyer must pay cash. Some banks have begun to loan money for cooperative sales, however.

Although cooperative apartments may be less expensive than condominiums, they are also more difficult to sell. A client who is considering purchasing a cooperative unit should be advised of these disadvantages. Financing arrangements should be investigated to determine whether a loan may be obtained on the cooperative unit prior to making an offer on it.

TRANSFER OF REAL PROPERTY

Selling real property can be a complex transaction. The following steps represent the process in the sale of real estate:

1. **Finding a real estate agent.** Most real estate sales are negotiated through a real estate agent. The seller should talk to recent sellers in the geographical area where the property is located to determine the best agent. An agent can do a computerized analysis of recent sales to recommend the appropriate selling price for the property. A good agent will also offer advice to the seller on how to enhance the salability of the home. Agents are paid a commission that represents a percentage of the selling price, but the actual percentage number is usually negotiable, especially in a competitive market. In a complicated sale of real property, hiring an attorney to negotiate the agreement with the real estate agency may be appropriate.

2. **Listing agreement.** The **listing agreement** sets out the terms of the agreement with the real estate agent, including the agent's commission, the length of the agreement, and the rights and responsibilities of the seller and the agent. As with any other contract, the seller should read the agreement carefully before signing and should also have her attorney examine it. A good real estate agent will take the client through the agreement step by step, and explain all of the terms. One important item in the listing agreement is the period of time the agent will have the listing. Three to six months are typical terms, but if the seller has any doubts about the agent's ability to sell the property, a shorter term may be appropriate. Paralegals may be asked to

listing agreement
an agreement made with a real estate agent when property is put up for sale; sets out the agent's commission, the length of the agreement, and the rights and responsibilities of the parties.

prepare and/or review listing agreements for the client. They may draft recommendations for changes for the attorney's review.

3. **Offer.** At some point the real estate agent will receive an **offer** from a prospective buyer. At the time the offer is made, the prospective buyer will also give the agent a deposit, sometimes called a binder or earnest money deposit. Basically, this **deposit** is an indication to the seller that the buyer is genuinely interested in purchasing the property.

4. **Counteroffer.** In some cases, the seller will respond to the buyer's offer with a **counteroffer**, which will generally be higher than the price the buyer offered but may not be more than the original listing price.

5. **Acceptance.** At some point during the negotiations, the buyer and seller will agree on a mutually acceptable price for the property. Usually, the sale will be conditioned upon the buyer's obtaining appropriate financing. If the prospective buyer did not make a deposit at the time of the original offer, one must be made at this time.

6. **Real Estate Sales/Purchase Contract.** When the buyer and seller have agreed on a price, the agent or the attorney will draw up a real estate sales contract setting out the rights and responsibilities of both parties. In some states, standardized contracts prepared by the Realtors' associations are available. The agreement will include general property information, such as the location of the property and the purchase price, as well as the following:

   a. How the property will be paid for

   b. Total purchase price

   c. Closing information

   d. Date of possession (if different from closing date)

   e. Proration of taxes and any additional assessments

   f. Whether buyer is entitled to an inspection of the property prior to closing (walk through)

   g. The general condition of the property

   h. Listing of all personal property included in the sale

   i. If the property is covered by any home warranty plans

   j. Pest control information (some states require a termite inspection and report)

Once the contract is signed by both the buyer and seller, the buyer is said to have an **equitable interest** in the property; that is, the buyer has an ownership interest but not one that entitles him to possession of the property. That comes when the deed is transferred and the buyer obtains a legal interest in the property. Legal interest is also called **legal title**.

7. **Title insurance.** Before a deed may be issued, a title insurance company will check the title to the property to make sure that it is free of any liens, encumbrances, easements, or other items

---

offer proposal or bid to purchase property at a particular price.

deposit money given by a buyer to a seller as a pledge or down payment when an offer to purchase property is made; also called a binder or earnest money deposit.

counteroffer a higher price named by a seller after a would-be buyer has made an offer.

equitable interest an ownership interest that does not entitle one to possession of the property, which occurs at the transfer of the deed when the owner obtains a legal interest in the property.

legal title right to possession of property; transferred through a deed.

that might affect it. (A lien is a claim or charge against the property for payment of a debt, and an easement is the right of one property owner to use another's property, as when one owner must cross another's land to have access to his own.) The buyer and seller must agree on how these encumbrances will be removed before a clear title insurance policy will be issued.

Title insurance companies often employ paralegals and legal assistants to check the title to property. Some firms conduct their own title searches; in that case, the paralegal may be asked to examine the records in the office of the county recorder. Find out how and where these records are checked in your own state and include it here.

STATE SPECIFIC INFORMATION

In the state of _____, property records are located at the office of _____.

Titles are checked through the following procedure:

_____

_____

_____.

The buyer receives an abstract of title (or history of the property's ownership) that lists the results of the title search. Any liens against the property are indicated in the abstract. If a title insurance company has been hired and its search determines that the title is free of encumbrances, the company issues a **title insurance policy**, which ensures that the buyer has received a clear title.

8. **Closing or Escrow.**   Once the buyer has obtained all the loans needed to purchase the property, title has been cleared, and a title insurance policy has been issued, the deed may be prepared and ownership of the property transferred. This procedure is known as a **closing** in some states and an **escrow** in others.

DEEDS

A deed transfers legal title (the right to possession) from the seller to the buyer. All deeds must comply with certain requirements, including the following:

1. A deed must be a writing and signed by the seller.
2. The property being transferred must be described by metes and bounds, property address, plat map, or the legal name of the property.

title insurance policy policy issued by a title insurance company that insures that the buyer of property is receiving a clear title.

closing a formal proceeding held in a lawyer's office where property documents and property are transferred from the seller to the buyer.

escrow the time period during which a title search is conducted on property; extends up to the time the property is transferred from the seller to the buyer; used in some states instead of a closing.

3. Words indicating the intent to transfer the described property must be included.
4. The buyer's name must be included.

Some states have additional requirements, which may include any or all of the following:

1. The seller's signature must be witnessed.
2. The seller must sign the deed before a notary public.
3. The signature of the seller's spouse must be included.

Types of Deeds

Several different types of deeds are used. You will need to become familiar with warranty deeds, grant deeds, and quitclaim deeds.

Warranty Deed. Most states require a **warranty deed**, wherein the seller warrants to the buyer that the property is free of encumbrances and that she holds full and complete ownership in the property except for any which are specifically noted in the deed itself, such as mortgages or easements. The seller guarantees title to the property. In some states, the seller may guarantee the buyer's quiet enjoyment of the property. If the buyer learns after the transfer of the deed that the seller breached any of the warranties, the seller would be held liable for any damages. Exhibit 13-1 shows a warranty deed from North Carolina.

Grant Deed. Some states use a **grant deed**, which is similar to a warranty deed. In this case, the seller warrants that the property is free of any encumbrances except those that have been previously disclosed to the buyer. In addition, the seller guarantees that he has title to the property and the right to convey it to the buyer.

Quitclaim Deed. From a buyer's perspective, the least advantageous type of deed is a **quitclaim deed**. In this case, the seller merely conveys to the buyer any interest he may have in the property, which may be all, a part, or none. No guarantees or warranties accompany a quitclaim deed. The seller in essence states to the buyer, "you may have any interest in the property that I might have." If the seller has no interest in the property, the buyer will have no recourse against the seller.

Sometimes a quitclaim deed is used to clear title to the property. For example, if the seller is divorced, his ex-spouse may be asked to sign a quitclaim deed giving up any claim she might have to the property.

Property Descriptions

A deed must include a detailed description of the property so that all parties, along with the governing body, understand which piece of property is being transferred. Most states use a combination of metes and bounds and tract maps to describe property.

warranty deed deed in which the seller guarantees that he holds full and complete ownership in the property and that the property is free of encumbrances unless specifically noted in the deed.

grant deed deed in which the seller guarantees that she has title to the property and the right to convey it and that the property is free of encumbrances except any that have previously been disclosed to the buyer.

quitclaim deed deed in which the seller conveys any interest that he may have in the property; least advantageous type of deed; often used to clear title to property.

EXHIBIT 13-1 General Warranty Deed for North Carolina

Excise Tax | Recording Time, Book and Page

Tax Lot No. _____ Parcel Identifier No. _____

Verified by _____ County on the _____ day of _____, 20___

by _____

_____

Mail after recording to _____

_____

This instrument was prepared by _____

Brief description for the Index _____

NORTH CAROLINA GENERAL WARRANTY DEED

THIS DEED made this _____ day of _____, 20___ by and between _____

GRANTOR   GRANTEE

Enter in appropriate block for each party: name, address, and if appropriate, character or entity, e.g., corporation or partnership.

The designation Grantor and Grantee as used herein shall include said parties, their heirs, successors, and assigns, and shall include singular, plural, masculine, feminine, or neuter as required by context.

WITNESSETH, that the Grantor, for a valuable consideration paid by the Grantee, the receipt of which is hereby acknowledged, has and by these presents does grant, bargain, sell and convey unto the Grantee in fee simple, all that certain lot or parcel of land situated in the City of _____, _____ Township, _____ County, North Carolina and more particularly described as follows:

continued

Exhibit 13-1 *continued*

The property hereinabove described was acquired by Grantor by instrument recorded in _____
_____.

A map showing the above described property is recorded in Plat Book _____ page _____.

TO HAVE AND TO HOLD the aforesaid lot or parcel of land and all privileges and appurtenances thereto belonging to the Grantee in fee simple.

And the Grantor convenants with the Grantee, that Grantor is seized of the premises in fee simple, has the right to convey the same in fee simple, that title is marketable and free and clear of all encumbrances, and that Grantor will warrant and defend the title against the lawful claims of all persons whosoever except for the exceptions hereinafter stated.

Title to the property hereinabove described is subject to the following exceptions:

IN WITNESS WHEREOF, the Grantor has hereunto set his hand and seal, or if corporate, has caused this instrument to be signed in its corporate name by its duly authorized officers and its seal to be hereunto affixed by authority of its Board of Directors, the day and year first above written.

_____   _____(SEAL)
        (Corporate Name)

By: _____   _____(SEAL)
_____ President

ATTEST: _____(SEAL)

_____
_____Secretary (Corporate Seal)   _____(SEAL)

SEAL-STAMP   NORTH CAROLINA, _____ County.

Use Black Ink

I, a Notary Public of the County and State aforesaid, certify that _____Grantor, personally appeared before me this day and acknowledged execution of the foregoing instrument. Witness my hand and official stamp or seal, this _____ day of _____, 20___.

My commission expires: _____ Notary Public

SEAL-STAMP   NORTH CAROLINA, _____ County.

Use Black Ink

I, a Notary Public of the County and State aforesaid that _____ personally came before me this day and acknowledged that _____ he is _____ Secretary of _____ a North Carolina corporation, and that by authority duly given and as the act of the corporation, the foregoing instrument was signed in its name by its _____ President, sealed with its corporate seal and attested by _____ as its _____ Secretary. Witness my hand and official stamp or seal, this _____ day of _____, 20___.

My commission expires: _____ Notary Public

The foregoing certificate(s) _____
_____
_____

of is/are certified to be correct. This instrument and this certificate are duly registered at the date and time and in the Book and Page shown on the first page hereof _____ REGISTER OF DEEDS FOR _____ COUNTY.

By: _____ Deputy/Assistant-Register of Deeds

SOURCE: This form is used with the permission of the North Carolina Bar Association who publishes this form and others on behalf of the Real Property Section of the NCBA.

Metes and Bounds. Metes and bounds measure the size of a piece of property from a permanent marker on the property itself. The distance from the marker is generally measured in feet. The direction from the marker is measured in degrees, minutes, and seconds. For example, 33°20'35" would be read as 33 degrees, 20 minutes, and 35 seconds. Changes in the direction of the measurement are indicated by a semicolon: for example, 33°20'35"; 25°18'30".

Tract Maps. In most suburban areas, developers purchase a large plot of land and subdivide it into lots for houses. In those cases, the subdivider (developer) must file a tract map with the city in which the property is located. The map shows the size and shape of each lot. The city council (or other government agency) reviews the map. If the map is approved, the map is then filed with the county. The property description of an individual lot might be as follows:

> Lot 264 of Tract 33 of the Cordova Country Subdivision in the City of Cordova, County of Shelby, State of Tennessee, as recorded in Tract map 22, page 102.

Consider how easy it would be to transpose a number when typing the description. Studies have found that a considerable percentage property descriptions are incorrect. Therefore, the legal assistant and/or paralegal should proofread the descriptions carefully and plot them out on a piece of paper (if possible) to determine whether the lines actually intersect. In most cases, it is advantageous to have a private survey of the land taken by a surveyor to be sure the description is correct.

Recording Deeds

Most states require that all deeds be recorded in the county or state where they were issued. Recording gives notice to the world that the individual named in the deed is the true owner of the property. Any other documents concerning the property should also be recorded.

MORTGAGES OR DEEDS OF TRUST ◆

In most states, a purchaser who obtains a loan against the property has a mortgage on that property. The borrower (or mortgagor) borrows the money from the lender (or mortgagee), usually a bank or other lending institution. The borrower signs a promissory note that makes her liable for payment of the debt. Title to the property remains with the borrower, and the lender has a lien against the property. If the borrower defaults on the loan, the property may be sold for the benefit of the lender, with any additional funds from the sale being returned to the borrower. An example of the mortgage from used in Florida is shown in Exhibit 13-2.

Some states use a deed of trust instead of a mortgage. The only difference between a mortgage and a deed of trust is that with a deed of trust the lender retains title to the property until the mortgage is paid. (Exhibit 13-3 on page 342 shows an example of a deed of trust.)

EXHIBIT 13-2 Florida Mortgage

THIS INDENTURE, made this _____ day of _____ in the year of our Lord two thousand and _____, by and between _____ of the _____ County of _____ and State of Florida, hereinafter called the Mortgagor; and _____; hereinafter called the Mortgagee:

Whereas the said Mortgagor is justly indebted to the said Mortgagee in the principal sum of _____ _____ Dollars, as evidenced by a certain promissory note of even date herewith, executed by _____ and payable to the order of the Mortgagee, with interest and upon terms as provided therein.

Said note provides that all installments of principal and interest are payable in lawful money of the United States of America, which shall be legal tender for public and private debts at the time of payment, at the office of _____, or at such other place as the holder thereof may from time to time designate in writing. Said note also provides that the final installment of principal and interest shall be due and payable on the _____ day of _____, 20_____.

Said note provides that each maker and endorser, jointly and severally, shall pay all costs of collection, including a reasonable attorney's fee, on failure to pay any principal and interest when due thereon, and that all principal due thereunder shall bear interest at the maximum permissible rate per annum from due date until paid.

Said note further provides that if any installment of principal and/or interest shall not be paid when due, then the entire principal sum and accrued interest shall become due and payable at once, at the option of the holder thereof.

NOW THIS INDENTURE WITNESSETH, that the said Mortgagor, to secure said indebtedness and interest thereon, and also for and in consideration of the sum of One Dollar paid by Mortgagee, at or before the ensealing and delivery of these presents, the receipt whereof is hereby acknowledged, has granted, bargained, sold, and conveyed and by these presents does grant, bargain, sell and convey unto the Mortgagee all that certain lot, parcel or piece of land lying and being in the County of _____ and State of Florida, more particularly described as _____ _____.

ALSO TOGETHER WITH all buildings and improvements thereon situate or which may hereafter be erected or placed thereon and all and singular the tenements, hereditaments, appurtenances, and easements thereunto belonging or in anywise appertaining, and the rents, issues, and profits thereof, and together with all heating, ventilating and air conditioning equipment, all plumbing apparatus, fixtures, hot water heaters, water and sprinkler systems and pumps, all lighting fixtures and all screens, awnings, venetian blinds, built-in equipment, and built-in furniture (whether or not affixed to land or building) now or hereafter located in or on said premises, including all renewals, replacements and additions thereto.

TO HAVE AND TO HOLD the above granted and described premises unto the said Mortgagee; its successors or assigns, forever.

continued

Exhibit 13-2   *continued*

And the said Mortgagor hereby covenants with the Mortgagee that the said Mortgagor is indefeasibly seized of said land in fee simple; that the said Mortgagor has full power and lawful right to convey the same in fee simple as aforesaid; that it shall be lawful for the Mortgagee at all times peaceably and quietly to enter upon, hold, occupy and enjoy said land and every part thereof; that the land is free from all encumbrances, except as aforesaid; that said Mortgagor will make such further assurances to prove the fee simple title to said land in said Mortgagee as may be reasonably required, and that said Mortgagor does hereby fully warrant the title to said land and every part thereof and will defend the same against the lawful claims of all persons whomsoever.

PROVIDED ALWAYS, and these presents are on this express condition, that if said Mortgagor shall well and truly pay said indebtedness unto the said Mortgagee, and any renewals or extensions thereof, and the interest thereon, together with all costs, charges and expenses, including a reasonable attorney's fee, which the said Mortgagee may incur or be put to in collecting the same by foreclosure, or otherwise, and shall perform and comply with all other terms, conditions and covenants contained in said promissory note and this mortgage, then these presents and the estate hereby granted shall cease, determine and be null and void.

And the said Mortgagor hereby jointly and severally covenants and agrees to and with the said Mortgagee as follows:

1. To pay all and singular the principal and interest and the various and sundry sums of money payable by virtue of said promissory note and this mortgage, each and every, promptly on the days respectively the same severally become due.

2. To pay all and singular the taxes, assessments, levies, liabilities, obligations, and encumbrances of every nature and kind now on said described property, and/or that hereafter may be imposed, suffered, placed, levied, or assessed thereupon and/or that hereafter may be levied or assessed upon this mortgage and/or the indebtedness secured hereby, each and every, before they become delinquent, and in so far as any thereof is of record the same shall be promptly satisfied and discharged of record and the original official document (such as, for instance, the tax receipt or the satisfaction paper officially endorsed or certified) shall be placed in the hands of said Mortgagee within ten (10) days after next payment.

3. To keep the buildings now or hereafter situate on said land and all personal property used in the operation thereof continuously insured against loss by fire and such other hazards as may from time to time be requested by Mortgagee, in companies and in amounts in each company as may be approved by and acceptable to Mortgagee; and all insurance policies shall contain the usual standard Mortgagee clause making the loss under said policies payable, without contribution, to said Mortgagee as its interest may appear, and each and every such policy shall be promptly delivered to and held by said Mortgagee; and, not less than ten (10) days in advance of the expiration of each policy, to deliver to said Mortgagee a renewal thereof, together with a receipt for the premium of such renewal. Any insurance proceeds, or any part thereof, may be applied by Mortgagee, at its option, either to the indebtedness hereby secured or to the restoration or repair of the property damaged.

4. To keep said land and the buildings and improvements now or hereafter situate thereon in good order and repair, and to permit, commit or suffer no waste, impairment or deterioration of said property or any part thereof.

continued

Exhibit 13-2　*continued*

5. To comply, as far as they affect the mortgaged property, with all statutes, laws, ordinances, decrees and orders of the United States, the State of Florida and of any political subdivision thereof.

6. In case Mortgagor shall fail to promptly discharge any obligation or covenant as provided herein, the Mortgagee shall have the option, but no obligation, to perform on behalf of the Mortgagor any act to be performed by Mortgagor in discharging such obligation or covenant, and any amount which Mortgagee may expend in performing such act, or in connection therewith, with interest thereon at the rate of ten (10) percent per annum and together with all expenses, including reasonable attorney's fees, incurred by Mortgagee shall be immediately payable by Mortgagor and shall be secured by this mortgage; and Mortgagee shall be subrogated to any rights, equities, and liens so discharged.

7. That if the principal or interest on the note herein described, or any part of the indebtedness secured by this mortgage or interest thereon, be not paid within ten (10) days after they are due, or if default be made in the full and prompt performance of any covenant or agreement herein contained, or if any proceeding be instituted to abate any nuisance on the mortgaged property, or if any proceeding be instituted which might result to the detriment of the use and enjoyment of the said property or upon the rendering by any court of last resort of a decision that an undertaking by the Mortgagor as herein provided to pay any tax, assessment, levy, liability, obligation, or encumbrance is legally inoperative or cannot be enforced, or in the event of the passage of any law changing in any way or respect the laws now in force for the taxation of mortgages or debts secured thereby for any purpose, or the manner of collection of any such tax, so as to affect this mortgage or the debt secured hereby; or if the Mortgagor shall make an assignment for the benefit of creditors, or if a receiver be appointed for the Mortgagor or any part of the mortgaged property, or if Mortgagor files a petition in bankruptcy, or is adjudicated a bankrupt or files any petition or institutes any proceedings under the National Bankruptcy Act, then on the happening of any one or more of these events, this conveyance shall become absolute and the whole indebtedness secured hereby shall immediately become due and payable, at the option of the Mortgagee, and this mortgage may thereupon be foreclosed for the whole of said money, interest, and costs; or Mortgagee may foreclose only as to the sum past due, without injury to this mortgage or the displacement or impairment of the remainder of the lien thereof, and at such foreclosure sale the property shall be sold subject to all remaining items of indebtedness; and Mortgagee may again foreclose, in the same manner, as often as there may be any sum past due.

8. Except during such period or periods as the Mortgagee may from time to time designate in writing, the Mortgagor will pay to the Mortgagee on the first day of each month throughout the existence of this mortgage a sum equal to the Mortgagee's estimate of the taxes and assessments next due on the mortgaged property and premiums next payable on or for policies of fire and other hazard insurance thereon, less any sums already paid the Mortgagee with respect thereto, divided by the number of months to elapse before one (1) month prior to the date when such taxes, assessments, and premiums become due and payable, such sums to be held by the Mortgagee, without interest, to pay such items. If at any time the estimated sum is insufficient to pay an item when due, the Mortgagor shall forthwith upon demand pay the

continued

Exhibit 13-2 *continued*

deficiency to the Mortgagee. The arrangement provided for in this paragraph is solely for the added protection of the Mortgagee and entails no responsibility on the Mortgagee's part beyond the allowing of due credit, without interest, for sums actually received by it. Upon the occurrence of a default under this mortgage, the Mortgagee may apply all or any part of the accumulated funds then held, upon any obligation secured hereby. Upon assignment of this mortgage, any funds on hand shall be turned over to the assignee and any responsibility of the assignor with respect thereto shall terminate. Each transfer of the mortgaged property shall automatically transfer to the grantee all right of the grantor with respect to any funds accumulated hereunder.

9. That in case of default or the happening of any event which would enable the Mortgagee to declare the whole indebtedness secured hereby immediately due and payable, the Mortgagee shall be entitled to the appointment of a receiver of all the rents, issues, and profits, regardless of the value of the mortgaged property and the solvency or insolvency of the Mortgagor and other persons liable to pay said indebtedness.

10. That the Mortgagee may collect a "late charge" not to exceed four cents (4¢) for each dollar of each payment due hereunder made more than fifteen (15) days in arrears to cover the extra expense involved in handling delinquent payments.

11. That the words "Mortgagor" and "Mortgagee" when used herein shall be taken to include singular and plural number and masculine, feminine or neuter gender, as may fit the case, and shall also include the heirs, administrators, executors, successors and assigns of the parties hereto. Each and all of the terms and provisions hereof shall extend to and be a part of any renewal or extension of this mortgage.

12. That this mortgage and the note secured hereby constitute a Florida contract and shall be construed according to the laws of that state.

IN WITNESS WHEREOF, the said Mortgagor has hereunto set his hand and seal the day and year first above written.

[Parties' Signatures]

_____   _____

_____   _____

EXHIBIT 13-3 North Carolina Deed of Trust

Courtesy: Used with permission of the North Carolina Bar Association, who published this form and others on behalf of the Real Property Section of the NCBA.

SATISFACTION: the debt secured by the within Deed of Trust together with the note(s) secured thereby has been satisfied in full.
This the _____ day of _____ , 20_____ .
Signed: _____

Mail after recording to:

This instrument prepared by:

Recording: Time, Book, and Page

NORTH CAROLINA DEED OF TRUST

THIS DEED of TRUST made this _____ day of _____ , 20_____ , by and between:

GRANTOR	TRUSTEE	BENEFICIARY
		SOUTHERN NATIONAL BANK OF NORTH CAROLINA, a national banking association

Enter in appropriate block for each party: name, address, and, if appropriate, character of entity, e.g., corporation or partnership.

The designation Grantor, Trustee, and Beneficiary as used herein shall include said parties, their heirs, successors, and assigns, and shall include singular, plural, masculine, feminine, or neuter as required by context.

   WITNESSETH: The Grantor is indebted to the Beneficiary in the sum of _____
_____DOLLARS ($_____) (the "Debt") for money loaned, as evidenced by promissory Notes(s) of even date herewith, the terms of which are incorporated herein by reference.
   NOW, THEREFORE, as security for the Debt, together with interest thereon, and as security for all renewals, extensions, deferments, amortizations, and reamortizations thereof, in whole or in part, together with interest thereon whether at the same or different rates, and for a valuable consideration, receipt of which is hereby acknowledged, the Grantor has bargained, sold, granted, and conveyed and does by these presents bargain, sell, grant, and convey to the Trustee, his heirs, or successors, and assigns, the real property situated in the City of _____ , _____ Township, _____ County, State of North Carolina, particularly described as follows:

   DESCRIPTION SET FORTH HEREINBELOW AND ON SCHEDULE "A," IF ANY, ATTACHED HERETO AND MADE A PART HEREOF

continued

Exhibit 13-3   *continued*

TO HAVE AND TO HOLD said real property, including all buildings, improvements, and fixtures now or hereafter located thereon, with all the rights, privileges and appurtenances thereunto belonging to the Trustee, his heirs, or successors, and assigns forever, upon the trusts, terms and conditions, and for the uses hereinafter set forth.

If the Grantor shall pay the Dept secured hereby in accordance with the terms of the Note(s) evidencing the same, and all renewals, extensions, deferments, amortizations and reamortizations thereof, in whole or in part, together with interest thereon, and shall comply with all the convenants, terms and conditions of the deed to trust, then this conveyance shall be null and void and may be cancelled of record at the request of the Grantor. If, however, there shall be any default in any of the convenants, terms, or conditions of the Note(s) secured hereby, or any failure or neglect to comply with the convenants, terms, or conditions contained this deed of trust, then and in any of such events, if the default is not made good within (15) days, the Note(s) shall, at the option of the Beneficiary, at once become due and payable without notice, and it shall be lawful for and the duty of the Trustee, upon request of the Beneficiary, to sell the land herein conveyed at public auction for cash, after having first given such notice of hearing as to commencement of foreclosure proceedings and obtaining such findings or leave of court as may be then required by law and giving such notice and advertising the time and place of such sale in such manner as may be then provided by law, and upon such and any resales and upon compliance with the then law relating to foreclosure proceedings to convey title to the purchaser in fee simple.

The proceeds of the Sale shall, after the Trustee retains his commission, be applied to the costs of sale, the amount due on the Note(s) hereby secured and otherwise as required by the then existing law relating to foreclosures. The Trustee's commission shall be five (5%) percent of the gross proceeds of the sale.

And the said Grantor does hereby convenant and agree with the Trustee and with the Beneficiary as follows:

1. INSURANCE. Grantor shall keep all improvements on said land, now or hereafter erected constantly insured for the benefit of the Beneficiary against loss by fire, windstorm and such other casualties and contingencies, in such manner and in such companies and for such amounts as may be satisfactory to or required by the Beneficiary. Grantor shall purchase such insurance, pay all premiums therefore, and shall deliver to Beneficiary such policies along with evidence of premium payment as long as the Note(s) secured hereby remains unpaid. If Grantor fails to purchase such insurance, pay the premiums therefore or deliver said policies with mortgagee clause satisfactory to Beneficiary attached thereto, along with evidence of payment of premiums thereon, then Beneficiary, at his option, may purchase such insurance. Such amounts paid by Beneficiary shall be added to the Note(s) secured by this Deed of Trust, and shall be due and payable upon demand by Grantor to Beneficiary.

2. TAXES, ASSESSMENTS, CHARGES. Grantor shall pay all taxes, assessments and charges as may be lawfully levied against said premises within thirty (30) days after the same shall become due. In the event that Grantor fails to so pay all taxes, assessments and charges as herein required, the Beneficiary, at this option, may pay the same and the amounts so paid shall be added to the Note(s) secured by this Deed of Trust, and shall be due and payable upon demand by Grantor to Beneficiary.

3. PARTIAL RELEASE. Grantor shall not be entitled to the partial release of any of the above described property unless a specific provision providing therefore is included in this Deed of Trust. In the event a partial release provision is included in the Deed of Trust. Grantor must strictly comply with the terms thereof. Notwithstanding anything herein contained. Grantor shall not be entitled to any release of property unless Grantor is not in default and is in full compliance with all of the terms and provisions of the Note(s) this Deed of Trust, and any other instrument that may be securing said Note(s).

4. WASTE. The Grantor convenants that he will keep the premises herein conveyed in as good order, repair and condition as they are now, reasonable wear and tear excepted, and that he will not commit or permit any waste.

5. WARRANTIES. Grantor convenants with Trustee and Beneficiary that he is seized of the premises in fee simple, has the right to convey the same in fee simple, that title is marketable and free and clear of all encumbrances, and that he will warrant and defend the title against the lawful claims of all persons whomsoever, except for the exception hereinafter stated. Title to the property hereinabove describe is subject to the following exceptions:

6. CONVEYANCE, ACCELERATION: If Grantor sells, conveys, transfers, assigns or disposes of the hereinabove-described real property or any part thereof or interest therein, by any means or method, whether voluntary or involuntary, without the written consent of Beneficiary, then at the option of Beneficiary and without notice to Grantor, all sums of money secured hereby, both principal and interest, shall immediately become due and payable and in default, notwithstanding anything herein or in the Note(s) secured hereby to the contrary.

7. SUBSTITUTION OF TRUSTEE. Grantor and Trustee convenant and agree to and with Beneficiary that in case the said Trustee, or any successor trustee, shall die, become incapable of acting, renounce his trust, or for other similar or dissimilar reason become unacceptable to the holder of the Note(s), then the holder of the Note(s) may appoint , in writing, a Trustee to take the place of the Trustee: and upon the probate and registration of the same, the trustee thus appointed shall succeed to all the rights, powers, and duties of the Trustee.

8. CIVIL ACTION. In the event that the Trustee is named as a party to any civil actions as Trustee in this Deed of Trust, the Trustee shall be entitled to employ an attorney at law, including himself if he is a licensed attorney, to represent him in said action and the reasonable attorney's fees of the Trustee in such action shall be paid by Beneficiary and charged to the Note(s) and secured by this Deed to Trust.

9. PRIOR LIENS. Default under the terms of any instrument secured by lien to which this deed to trust is subordinate shall constitute default hereunder.

IN WITNESS WHEREOF, the Grantor has hereunto set his hand and seal, or if corporate, has caused this instrument to be signed in its corporate name by its duly authorized officers and its seal to be hereunto affixed by authority of its Board of Directors, the day and year first above written.

(Corporate Name)

_____

By: _____

_____President

ATTEST: _____

_____Secretary (Corporate Seal)

Use Black Ink Only

_____ (SEAL)

_____ (SEAL)

_____ (SEAL)

_____ (SEAL)

SEAL-STAMP

STATE OF NORTH CAROLINA, COUNTY OF _____

I, _____ a notary public of said county do hereby certify _____

that _____

Grantor, personally appeared before me this day and acknowledged that execution of the foregoing instrument. Witness my hand and official stamp or seal, this_____ day of_____, 20_____.

My commission expires: _____ Notary Public

SEAL-STAMP

STATE OF NORTH CAROLINA, COUNTY OF _____

I, _____ a Notary Public of the County and State aforesaid,

certify that _____ personally came before me this day and acknowledged

that _____ he is _____ Secretary of _____ a North

Carolina corporation, and that by authority duly given and as the act of the corporation, the foregoing instrument was signed

in its name by its _____ President, sealed with its corporate seal and attested by _____

_____ as its _____ Secretary.

Witness my hand and official stamp or seal, this _____ day of _____, 20_____.

My commission expires: _____ Notary Public

The foregoing Certificate(s) of _____

is/are certified to be correct. This instrument and this certificate are duly registered at the date and time and in the Book and Page shown on the first page hereof

_____ REGISTER OF DEEDS FOR _____ COUNTY

By: _____ Deputy/Assistant - Register of Deeds

Mortgages on the property that are recorded take precedence over any previously obtained mortgages that have not been recorded. In the event that the buyer fails to repay any of the loans, the lenders are paid in the order the mortgages were recorded. Thus, if a bank issues a loan on a piece of property and immediately records the note (or mortgages), this loan will take precedence over all loans recorded later. In some states, however, the first mortgage always takes precedence over a second or subsequent mortgage regardless of which is recorded first.

Check with the county recorder's office to determine our state's requirements and list them in the State Specific Information box.

STATE SPECIFIC INFORMATION

In the state of _____, mortgages/deeds of trust are/are not recorded in the Office of the _____.

The order of precedence for loans against the property is as follows:

1. _____

2. _____

3. _____

EASEMENTS ✦

An **easement** is a nonownership interest in land that entitles its owner to a limited use of another's property. The most common easements are for utility companies to install telephone lines, electric poles, or underground equipment. Some easements involve a right of way across another's property, as in the case of land located on a golf course or public beach. Sometimes an owner whose land is not accessible from the public road will have an easement over the adjoining property for a driveway. Remember, though, that although an easement enables a property owner to use a portion of another's land, the easement owner does not actually own the land where the easement is located.

Most easements are created by a deed. Since easements constitute an interest in land, they must be in writing and signed by the owner of the property. An easement by necessity is an exception to the writing requirement. Such an easement is created when someone sells a portion of a tract that is not accessible except by passing over another lot in the tract (such property is said to be "landlocked"). Easements by necessity are justified by the intention of the parties and the public policy requirement of access to one's property. For example, suppose William sold the front and back portions of a tract of land to separate buyers, but only the front portion had access to a public road. An easement by necessity would be created for the purchaser of the rear portion of the land. Even though an easement by necessity does not have to be in writing, a prospective buyer should examine the property

easement a nonownership interest in land that gives its owner the right to the limited use of land owned by another.

carefully and request that any necessary easement be written to prevent possible legal problems with future owners of the property where the easement is. An easement by necessity ends when the necessity ceases. Therefore, if a new road provides access to previously inaccessible land, the easement would end.

NUISANCE

A nuisance is an invasion of a person's interest in the use and enjoyment of her property. A private nuisance affects only close neighbors, while a public nuisance affects the general public. For instance, if your neighbor plays her radio so loud that you cannot sleep at night, the loud music would constitute a private nuisance, while a chemical plant emitting pollutants would probably constitute a public nuisance. Most states have passed statutes that protect the public from many forms of nuisance. City ordinances may prohibit residential property from being used for purposes that are noisy or offensive to neighbors. Thus, the neighbor's loud music may violate a municipal ordinance, and a call to the local police department might be helpful if talking to the neighbor does not solve the problem.

LEASES AND RENTAL AGREEMENTS

A **lease** is a contract for the use of land or buildings, but not for their ownership. The lessor (the person who owners the property and rents it to someone else) is called the landlord, and the lessee (the person who rents the property from the landlord) is called the tenant. The tenant pays rent to the landlord for the use of the property.

Written Leases

The Statute of Frauds requires that all interests in land for one year or more must be in writing. Therefore, all leases or rental agreements for a year or more must be in writing and signed by both the landlord and the tenant. It is also advisable to put shorter term leases in writing to protect both parties' interest. The more specifically the rights and responsibilities of both parties are spelled out in the lease, the less likely there will be misunderstandings about the terms. The lease should include the following:

1. The names of the landlord and tenant. The landlord should require that the names of all tenants who occupy the premises be listed
2. The lease term—inclusive date
3. The amount of the rent and when it is due
4. Which party is responsible for utilities and insurance
5. Whether the tenant may sublease the property. Most landlords prefer to prohibit subleases.
6. Persons other than the tenant who may live on the property

lease written rental agreement between a landlord and tenant granting the tenant the right to possession of the property for terms prescribed in the lease.

7. The legal obligations of the tenant and landlord and the recourse each has for a breach of the lease terms. For instance, what is the landlord's recourse if the tenant does not pay rent? Are late payments subject to a flat fee, or is interest charged? If the latter, what is the interest rate?

8. Other fees charged, such as cleaning fees or a deposit. The landlord should be aware that any amounts deposited and not used are refundable to the tenant. While the tenant may be charged for damages to the premises, she may not be charged for ordinary wear and tear.

9. Which party is responsible for repairs to the premises. Some state statutes cover this area.

10. What the rented premises include, such as storage areas and/or garage space

11. The landlord's right to enter the premises. Most states forbid a landlord to enter rented areas unless an emergency exist; other states allow entry by the landlord if it is specified in the lease.

Standardized leases are available on computer disk and in form books. Form leases where you merely fill in the blanks may be purchased in a stationery store. However, some attorneys prefer to use the standardized lease as a starting point and add their own clauses to suit the individual client's situation. Whenever a lease is prepared, the clauses should be written so that the particular client receives the maximum amount of protection. A sample lease is shown in Exhibit 13-4.

Oral Rental Agreements

Some landlords do not require a written agreement for a month-to-month rental. In this case, the tenant occupies the premises on a monthly basis and may be asked to leave with a month's notice. Rent is paid once a month. The tenant only has a right to occupy the premises for a month at a time. Other periodic tenancies may exist for various terms of less than a year, such as a week, three months, or six months.

Eviction or Unlawful Detainer

Landlords who wish to evict a tenant must use a summary eviction proceeding in some states and unlawful detainer in others. The basic procedures are similar, and the end result is the same—the tenant must vacate the premises. Tenants may be evicted for violating the terms of the lease agreement or for failing to pay rent.

Summary Eviction. With the summary eviction proceeding, certain forms must be completed and filed with the court. The forms must specify the reasons for the **eviction**. After the forms are filed, the tenant must be served with the documents and has a set period of time in which to file an appearance. If no appearance is forthcoming from the tenant or the tenant appears but is unable to show why he should not be evicted, a court officer carries out the eviction proceeding.

eviction formal proceeding by an owner of leased property to remove tenants.

EXHIBIT 13-4 Sample Lease

THIS LEASE, made this_____day of_____ ,
between _____ , hereinafter called Owner,
and _____ , hereinafter call the Tenant:

    WITNESSETH: Owner does hereby lease and rent unto Tenant and Tenant does hereby take as tenant under the Owner the following property: _____
_____ , to be used
by Tenant during the term only of _____ months, beginning
_____ , and ending _____ ,
inclusive.

    IN CONSIDERATION WHEREOF, and of the covenants hereinafter expressed, it is covenanted and agreed as follows:

    1. Tenant agrees to pay to Owner, as rent for said premises, the sum of $ _____ per _____ , payable in advance.

    2. Tenant shall not permit any unlawful or immoral practice to be committed on the premises, or to so occupy the premises as to constitute a nuisance.

    3. Tenant shall not have the right or power to sublet the premises or any part thereof, or to transfer or assign this lease, without the written consent of Owner.

    4. Tenant has examined the premises, is satisfied with the physical condition, and his taking possession is conclusive evidence of receipt of them in good order and repair, and Tenant agrees that no representation as to condition of repair has been made.

    5. If the leased premises shall be abandoned or become vacant during the term of this lease, then in such case Owner shall have the right at his option, to take possession of the leased premises, re-enter the leased premises, and annul and terminate this lease.

    6. During the period of his tenancy, Tenant agrees to maintain this property in as good state as he finds it, reasonable wear and tear excepted; and will have repaired, at his expense, any damage done to the water, gas, and electrical fixtures; replace all broken glass and burned out grates; keep sinks, lavatories, commodes, and sewer lines open; repair any plumbing or heating equipment that may be damaged by his negligence; replace all lost or broken keys.

    7. In the event the leased premises are rendered untenantable by fire, rain, wind, or other cause beyond the control of Tenant, or are condemned and ordered torn down by the properly constituted authorities of the State, County, or City, then in either of these events the lease shall cease and terminate as of the date of such destruction.

    8. Owner shall not be held liable for any injury or damage whatsoever which may arise on account of any defect in the building or premises, or for rain, wind, or other causes, all claims for such injury or damage being hereby expressly waived by Tenant.

    9. Owner in person or by agent shall have the right at all reasonable times to enter the leased premises and inspect the same and to show the same to prospective tenants or purchasers. Owner may make such repairs and alterations as may be deemed by Owner necessary to the preservation of the leased premises or the buildings, but Owner is not required to do any repairing upon the premises leased unless so agreed in writing in this lease.

    10. Tenant shall deposit the sum of $ _____ as a security deposit, which deposit will be refunded to Tenant upon tenant vacating the property at the expiration of the Lease. Owner shall not

continued

Exhibit 13-4   *continued*

refund the security deposit in the event Tenant vacates prior to the expiration of the Lease. Owner shall deduct from the security deposit any amount necessary to clean or repair the property. Owner may also retain the security deposit and apply it to any unpaid rent.

    11. Other conditions: _____

_____

_____

_____

_____

_____

_____

    12. Should Tenant fail to pay the rent or any part thereof, as the same becomes due, or violates any other term or condition of this lease, Owner shall then have the right, at his option, to re-enter the leased premises and terminate the lease; such re-entry shall not bar the right of recovery of rent or damages for breach of covenants, nor shall the receipt of rent after conditions broken or be deemed a waiver of forfeiture. And in order to entitle Owner to re-enter it shall not be necessary to give notice of rent being due and unpaid or of other conditions broken to make demands for rent, the execution of this lease being signed by the parties hereto being sufficient notice of the rent being due and demand for the same.

    IN WITNESS WHEREOF, the parties hereto have hereunto set their signatures and seals, the day and year first above written.

_____	_____
Tenant (date signed)	Owner (date signed)
_____	_____
Tenant (date signed)	Owner (date signed)

Unlawful Detainer. **Unlawful detainer** is a more complex system of evicting tenants that is used in California and other states. It requires that the tenant first be served a Three-Day Notice to Pay Rent or Quit (see Exhibit 13-5). If no response is forthcoming from the tenant within three days, then the landlord's attorney prepares a Complaint for Unlawful Detainer, which is served on the tenant and filed with the court, along with a Summons for Unlawful Detainer. The landlord must sign a verification for the complaint, which may be either a form or a pleading. All individuals occupying the premises must be served. The damages requested in the complaint will consist of possession of the premises, past-due rent, attorney fees, and in some cases, treble damages (three times the actual damages). To collect treble damages, the landlord must prove malicious willfulness on the part of the tenant.

The tenant must reply to the complaint within five days of personal service. Note that this date differs considerably from the thirty-day requirement for other complaints.

If the tenant fails to respond, then the landlord can enter a default judgment. If the tenant responds by filing an answer within the allotted time, a court hearing will be held where each party can present his side. Then the court will issue a ruling.

In the case of a default judgment, or if the landlord prevails in court, the court will issue (1) a judgment for the amount of rent due and (2) a Writ of Possession in favor of the landlord. The sheriff will serve the tenant with Writ of Execution for Possession of Real Property. If the tenant does not vacate the premises within five days, the sheriff may physically remove the tenant and his possessions from the premises. Tenants remaining unlawfully in the premises are called tenants in sufferance. Exhibit 13-6 illustrates the steps in the eviction process using unlawful detainer.

Find out what procedure is used for eviction in your own state, and describe it in the State Specific Information box.

STATE SPECIFIC INFORMATION

The following procedure is used for eviction in the state of _____.

_____

_____

_____

_____

_____

_____

_____

unlawful detainer
eviction process used in some states when the tenant stays beyond the time she has a right to occupy the property or she has breached the terms of the lease.

EXHIBIT 13-5 Three-Day Notice to Pay Rent or Quit

3-DAY NOTICE

To Pay Rent or Quit

TO _____

TENANT(S) IN POSSESSION OF THE PREMISES AT

_____

(Street Address)

City of _____ , County of _____ , California

YOU ARE HEREBY NOTIFIED that the rent on the above-described premises occupied by you, in the amount of $ _____ , for the period from _____ to _____ , is now due and payable.

YOU ARE HEREBY REQUIRED to pay the said rent within THREE (3) days from the date of service on you of this notice or to vacate and surrender possession of the premises. In the event you fail to do so, legal proceedings will be instituted against you to recover possession of the premises, declare the forfeiture of the rental agreement or lease under which you occupy the premises, and recover rents, damages, and costs of suit.

DATE:_____   _____

OWNER/MANAGER

EXHIBIT 13-6   The Steps in the Eviction Process Using Unlawful Detainer

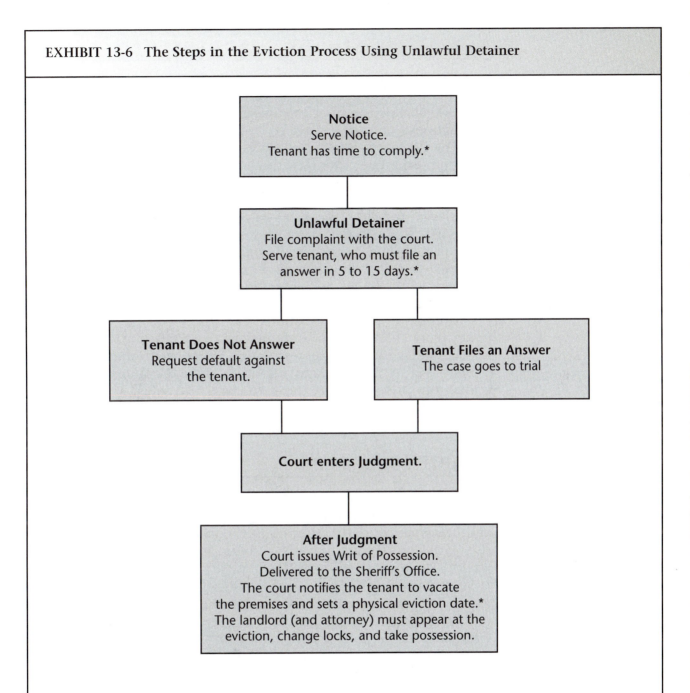

Notice
Serve Notice.
Tenant has time to comply.*

Unlawful Detainer
File complaint with the court.
Serve tenant, who must file an
answer in 5 to 15 days.*

Tenant Does Not Answer
Request default against
the tenant.

Tenant Files an Answer
The case goes to trial

Court enters Judgment.

After Judgment
Court issues Writ of Possession.
Delivered to the Sheriff's Office.
The court notifies the tenant to vacate
the premises and sets a physical eviction date.*
The landlord (and attorney) must appear at the
eviction, change locks, and take possession.

* A fee is required

Note: The eviction may be delayed by documents filed in court by the tenant.

ETHICS and ETIQUETTE

Paralegals often assist the attorney in the preparation of documents for real estate transactions. Most states require that the paralegal must be directly supervised by the attorney in these situations.

The rules vary among the states as to whether paralegals may attend real estate closings without the attorney being present. In general, paralegals may not be responsible for any real estate closing without the attorney's direct supervision. Some states, however, do allow the paralegal to attend the closing for the client if the attorney has reviewed all closing documents and the paralegal has been formally trained in the law and procedures related to real estate closings. The paralegal may not give legal advice to the client at these closings, and the client must first consent to the paralegal's representation.

Conflict of interest situations may arise when the same attorney represents the buyer and the seller in a real estate transaction. Some states allow this representation, and others forbid it. While many real estate sales run smoothly, there are many problems that can arise between the buyer and the seller. It is usually advisable for each party to have his own attorney in these cases.

CHAPTER SUMMARY ✦

The law of real property includes both the transfer of property and landlord/tenant relationships. Real property includes land, buildings, and items permanently attached to the land. Personal property consists of objects that are movable and not permanently attached to the ground.

Most property is owned in fee simple, which signifies absolute ownership. Property may be owned with others as tenants in common or joint tenancy. Spouses may hold property as community property, tenancy by the entirety, joint tenancy, or tenancy in common.

Condominiums and cooperatives are subject to special restrictions. A condominium owner owns the area inside the boundaries of the condominium unit and shares the use of the common areas with the other condominium owners. A cooperative owner owns a share of stock represented by a unit within the complex.

A transfer of real property begins with the location of a real estate agent and the preparation of a listing agreement. Once the seller has accepted an offer, a real estate sales contract is prepared. A title insurance company will determine title to the property and check to make sure there are no liens or encumbrances on it. At the closing (or escrow) a new deed will transfer title to the new owners.

Most purchasers do not pay cash for the property but obtain loans from banks or other lending institutions. The loan is known as a mortgage or deed of trust, depending on the state where the property is located.

Easements constitute nonownership interest in property. They entitle the easement owner to have limited use of another's property.

Leases and rental agreements for a year or more must be in writing. For the protection of both the landlord and the tenant, it is advisable to have all leases and rental agreements in writing regardless of the term. In the event that the tenant breaches the agreement or fails to pay rent, eviction proceedings may be instituted.

✦ KEY TERMS

closing	joint tenancy
community property	lease
condominium	legal title
cooperative	listing agreement
counteroffer	offer
deposit	personal property
easement	quitclaim deed
equitable interest	real property
escrow	tenancy in common
eviction	title insurance policy
fee simple	unlawful detainer
fixture	warranty deed
grant deed	

✦ SELF TEST

Indicate whether the following statements are true (T) or False (F).

_____ 1. Real property includes land and other items permanently attached to the land.

_____ 2. If you live in your car, it is considered to be real property.

_____ 3. Fixtures in a building are personal property.

_____ 4. Personal property is readily transportable from one location to another.

_____ 5. A light fixture permanently affixed to the ceiling of your home is real property.

Circle the correct answer for the following questions:

1. The following items are examples of real property:
   a. land, houses, in-ground swimming pools.
   b. portable microwave ovens, coffee grinders, houses.
   c. a chopped-down tree, a dog, a camper.
   d. none of the above.

2. The following items are personal property:
   a. a car.
   b. a truck.
   c. a camper.
   d. a and b.
   e. all of the above.

3. Absolute ownership of property is called
   a. fee tail.
   b. tenancy.
   c. fee simple.
   d. life estate.

4. Shared ownership in property is called
   a. tenancy in common.
   b. joint tenancy.
   c. community property.
   d. tenancy by the entirety.
   e. all of the above.

5. Individual ownership of a unit within a larger complex is known as a _____ form of ownership.
   a. cooperative
   b. condominium
   c. apartment
   d. tenancy

Fill-in-the-blanks.

1. A _____ owner owns a share of stock represented by an apartment unit.

2. An agreement with a real estate agent for the sale of property is known as the
   _____.

3. A(n) _____ or history of the property's ownership is provided to the buyer with the results of the search.

4. Transfer of ownership of property occurs at the _____.

5. The _____ transfers title from the seller to the buyer.

✦ REVIEW QUESTIONS

1. What is the difference between a condominium and a cooperative? Discuss the advantages and disadvantages of each.

2. What is a closing? An escrow?

3. What are the advantages of a written lease or rental agreement?

4. Describe the steps in the unlawful detainer eviction process.

✦ NOTEBOOK PROJECTS

1. Proofread and retype the cover sheet for the closing document shown in Exhibit 13-7. When retyping the cover sheet, add the names of counsel. The following information is pertinent: National Bank $22,000,000 mortgage loan to Marketing Investments, Inc. Closing date: October 1, 2006. Parties to the action include our office as counsel to the lender and James Roberts as counsel to the borrower. The remainder of the parties are the same as those shown in the Closing Agenda.

EXHIBIT 13-7   A Closing Agenda

CLOSING AGENDA

NATIONAL BANK
$22,000,000 MORTGAGE LOAN

TO

MARKING, INC.

Closing Date: October I, 2006

Parties and Miscellaneous Definitions:

B&K	Bells, Lender
Borrower	Marking, Inc.
HS&M	XXX, Counsel to Borrower
P&C	Point & Click, Lender's New York Local Counsel
Premises	Leap Hotel
222 Main Street
Atlanta, GA
Seller	Leap Hotel
Title Company	First U.S. Title Insurance Company

ATTORNEY NAME HERE

2. Using the facts provided here, prepare a lease using the format in Exhibit 13-7.

Client:	Lynne Paltrow
Tenant:	Ronald and Kirsten Shapiro
Rent:	$1,000 per month
Address of property:	45 Sunset Drive; Your Town, Your State
Deposit:	$1,000 plus one extra month's rent (the last month's rent)
Lease term:	January 1, 2005, for one year
Rent payable:	First day of each month

3. Assume the tenants in Project 2 have not paid their rent for the past two months. It is now June 1, 2005, and our client (Lynne Paltrow, the landlord) wants to initiate eviction proceedings against the tenants. Prepare a Complaint for Unlawful Detainer and a Summons for Unlawful Detainer.

4. Locate a real estate document from the records in the courthouse or the county recorder's office by using the owners' names. Do this project for the property in which you live. Make a copy of the latest deed (deed of trust, warranty deed, grant deed, etc.) for that property.

5. List the steps required to transfer real property in your state and describe what happens at each stage.

6. What would you do in each of the following situations?

   a. Your next-door neighbor plays loud music late at night. You have asked her to turn the volume down, but she has ignored your request.

   b. A client, who is a tenant, complains that the roof of her apartment is leaking and that the landlord refuses to do anything about it. The attorney asks you to get more information about the problem. Where would you start?

   c. Our client lives next door to a toxic waste dump. He tells you that individuals in the neighborhood have been getting sick from the fumes. The attorney asks you to do some factual research on the problem. What is the first thing you would do?

7. Research landlord-tenant laws through your state bar association, the state's attorney general's office, or a computerized legal research system is available to you. Summarize the basic requirements for evicting a tenant in your state in a memo to the instructor.

CONTRACTS

CHAPTER OUTCOMES ◆

As a result of studying this chapter, the student will learn:

- The elements of a valid contract
- The characteristics of bilateral, unilateral, express and implied contracts
- The ways in which contracts may be breached, and remedies for a breach of contract
- The steps in drafting a contact

AN INTRODUCTION TO CONTRACTS ◆

A **contract** is a legally enforceable agreement between two or more parties. This section examines the elements of a contract, what is needed to make a valid contract, and what makes a contract void. Bilateral, unilateral, express, and implied contracts will be discussed, as will quasi-contracts. The importance of the Statute of Frauds, the Parol Evidence Rule, and the Uniform Commercial Code will be examined.

Elements of a Contract

The elements of a contract are the offer, the acceptance, and consideration. The **offer** is the manifestation by one party (the **offeror**) of the intention to enter into a contract. An offer may be as simple as the words, "I offer to sell you my car if you will pay me $400." The **acceptance** of the offer by the **offeree** is required for the contract to be valid. The third element of the contract (**consideration**) creates a bargained-for exchange. Each party gives up something of value and receives something of value in exchange. In the example, the offeror gives up his car and the offeree gives up $400. The offeror receives $400 and the offeree receives the car.

Valid and Void Contracts

A contract can be **valid** (legally enforceable) only if it is formed for a legal purpose. Thus, an individual may not enforce a gambling debt in the courts of most states because gambling is illegal. The gambling contract is considered **void** (not legally enforceable) at the outset.

contract a legally enforceable agreement between two or more parties; consists of an offer, acceptance, and consideration.

offer the manifestation by the offeror of the intention to enter into a contract.

offeror the party who makes an offer to another party to enter into a contract.

acceptance an assent by the person to whom an offer has been made to enter into a contract.

offeree the party to whom an offer to enter into a contract is made; the party who accepts the offer.

consideration the bargained-for exchange created by a contract. Each party gives up and receives something of value as consideration.

valid having legal efficacy or force; having been executed in the proper manner.

void having no legal force or effect.

Contracts made by minors are void and therefore not enforceable. In some states, however, if a minor makes a contract for the necessities of life (food, clothing, or shelter), the contract is enforceable in a court of law. In many states, the minor may enforce a contract even though the contract may not be enforced against the minor.

Intent of the Parties

Even if all of the elements of a contract are present, a contract will not exist unless the parties actually intended to enter into one. For instance, if you jokingly tell your friend that you will sell her your house for $5 and she accepts the offer, no contract would exist because neither party intended that there would be a contract.

Contractual Ability

In order to enter into a valid contract, the parties must have the capacity to do so. As discussed above, minors lack the ability to enter into a valid contract except in those states that allow them to enter into contracts for the necessities of life, including food, clothing, or shelter.

One must also possess the mental capacity to enter into a valid contract. That is, she must know what the contract is and that she will be bound by it. Mental capacity is often difficult to define and can provide a basis for a lawsuit for either enforcement of the contract against the individual claiming lack of mental capacity or the basis for a lawsuit by one who is claiming mental incapacity.

Bilateral Contracts

Most contracts are bilateral in that each party to the contract promises to do or not do something. The **bilateral contract** is created at the exchange of mutual promises by the parties. For instance, if Jane and John both sign a contract where Jane promises to sell her car to John and John promises to pay $5,000 for the car, the contract is created upon the mutual exchange of promises (the signing of the contract). Once the promises are exchanged, the contractual obligation is present. If Jane then refuses to sell the car to John, he may establish a suit for breach of contract.

bilateral contract
a contract in which the contracting parties are bound to fulfill obligations reciprocally toward each other; a contract involving mutual promises between the parties.

A writing is not necessarily required for a bilateral contract to be valid, except for those instances discussed later under the Statute of Frauds. If Jane promises to sell her bicycle to John and John promises to pay her $200 for the bicycle, a valid bilateral contract is created upon the exchange of promises. If she refuses to sell him the bicycle, then she may be liable for breach of contract. Note, however, that in this situation, even though Jane has breached the contract, it would probably cost John more to institute a lawsuit against her than the $200 he would have paid for the bicycle.

Unilateral Contracts

In order to create a **unilateral contract**, one party makes a promise, which is exchanged for the act itself. Instead of being a promise for a promise as in a bilateral contract, it is a promise for an act. For instance, you might tell your neighbor that you will pay him $150 if he mows your lawn. He does not promise to mow your lawn, but if he does mow it, then a contract is created at the time of the completion of the mowing, and he receives $150 upon completion of the job. If he does not mow the lawn, then there is no contract, unlike the bilateral contract where the contract would have been created if it had been based on a mutual exchange of promises.

It is easy to recognize the difficulties inherent in determining whether a contract is bilateral or unilateral. The court looks on the intentions of the parties to determine which type of contract exists.

Express or Implied-in-Fact Contracts

An **express contract** is created by both parties specifically expressing, in words or writing, their intentions. Both parties reach an explicit agreement, to which they mutually assent, and openly state the terms of their contractual arrangement. As will be discussed later in the chapter, however, certain types of contracts must be in writing to satisfy the Statute of Frauds.

In an **implied-in-fact** contract, the mutual assent of the parties is not manifested in words but in the actions of the parties. When a customer goes into a store and picks out a dress, the implication is that she will pay for the dress at the cash register. This contract is implied by the actions of the parties.

Quasi-Contracts

Quasi-contracts (also known as implied-in-law contracts) are reserved for situations where an actual contract was not created but it would be unfair not to enforce the agreement. The courts will enforce these agreements with its equitable powers to prevent unjust enrichment and foster fairness to both parties.

These circumstances are generally based on one individual performing an act expecting some type of payment even though no contract exists between the parties. The courts will provide an equitable remedy to prevent the unjust enrichment of the person who benefited from the actions of the aggrieved individual. To deal with these situations, the courts use a device called quasi-contract, which is essentially a legal fiction that allows a person to receive payment even though there is no contract because to deny payment would be unjust.

To prevail in a suit in quasi-contract, the injured party must prove that the other party unjustly benefited from her actions, even though a mutual benefit was anticipated. In the classic example of a quasi-contract case, an elderly individual tells his young granddaughter that, if she will move into his home and take care of him, he will leave her

unilateral contract
a contract in which one party makes a promise and the other party performs some act.

express contract
an actual oral or written agreement between the parties.

implied-in-fact contract
a contract that is inferred from the conduct of the parties.

quasi-contract a legal fiction that allows a person to receive payment in a situation where there is, in fact, no contract but where circumstances are such that to deny payment would result in the unjust enrichment of the other party.

certain property in his will. The granddaughter relies on her grandfather's statement, sells her own home, and moves in and takes care of him until his death. However, he does not leave the property to her. She could sue her grandfather's estate in a quasi-contract action in equity even though no contract existed between the parties. The court would likely award damages based on the reasonable value of the services she provided.

Contract Wording

The wording of an oral contract may be very simple, such as:

- "I promise to sell you my guitar if you will pay me $200." (statement by seller)
- "I accept your offer of your guitar for my $200." (statement by buyer)

Exhibit 14-1 shows an example of a formal written contract.

Statute of Frauds an English statute, adopted with variations by all the states, that requires certain types of contracts to be in writing.

STATUTE OF FRAUDS ✦

The **Statute of Frauds** is a direct descendant of our ties to the common law of England and specifies that certain contracts must be in writing to be valid. Although different states have adopted different versions

---

EXHIBIT 14-1   Formal Written Contract

This contract entered into this 20th day of September, 2005, between LENORE BISHOP of 24222 Poplar Avenue, in the City of Memphis, County of Shelby, and State of Tennessee and JOSEPH M. YARDLEY of 111 Electric Avenue, in the City of Cordova, County of Shelby, and State of Tennessee, consists of the following terms:

LENORE BISHOP agrees to sell JOSEPH M. YARDLEY her 2005 Toyota truck, Tennessee license number "XBB111," for the sum of $12,000, payable upon receipt of the truck.

IN WITNESS WHEREOF, the parties have hereby executed this contract on the 20th day of September, 2005, at Memphis, Tennessee.

_____
LENORE BISHOP, Seller

_____
JOSEPH M. YARDLEY, Buyer

of this statute, it is most commonly applied to the following types of contracts:

1. Contracts for the sale of goods with a value of more than $500 (the amount may vary in a few states)
2. Contracts for an interest in real property (including a sale or lease)
3. Contracts in consideration of marriage (the "marriage contract" or prenuptial agreement)
4. Contracts that cannot be performed in one year (such as employment contracts for more than a year or leases for more than a year)
5. Promises to pay another's debts.

Because these contracts must be in writing, if the parties perform on the terms of an oral contract in one of these categories, they cannot then sue the other party because the contract was oral. Some states will not allow a suit if the contract has been partially performed. For instance, if the Toyota truck in Exhibit 14-1 had been sold via an oral contract and the buyer had used the truck for several months, he could not then sue the seller based on the oral contract. Once the contract is performed (or partially performed in some states), the other party (not the one who performed) cannot seek to invalidate it later. Nor can the party sue for nonperformance.

List the types of contracts that must be writing in your state to satisfy the Statute of Frauds in the State Specific Information box.

STATE SPECIFIC INFORMATION

STATE SPECIFIC INFORMATION BOX FOR THE STATE OF _____.

In order to satisfy the Statute of Frauds, the following contracts must be in writing:

1. _____
_____
2. _____
_____
3. _____
_____
4. _____
_____
5. _____
_____
6. _____
_____

Covenants and Conditions

The covenants of a contract form the essence of the contractual terms. More specifically, a **covenant** is the actual promise made by each party to the contract; the covenants create the terms of the contract. In Exhibit 14-1, the covenants involve the paying of $12,000 by one party and the giving up of the truck by the other party. The covenants create the contractual terms for both parties. If one party does not perform as promised, then the other party is not required to perform his side of the agreement. For example, if the seller does not provide the truck, then the buyer is not required to pay the $12,000. The seller in this case has **breached the contract** (failed to fulfill the promises made in the contract).

In addition to covenants, a contract may include conditions. A **condition** is an event that creates a duty to perform on one or both parties. Conditions govern the timing of the performance of the contract and are of three types.

1. Conditions precedent
2. Conditions concurrent
3. Conditions subsequent

The names indicate the point in time when the conditions occur.

A **condition precedent** is a condition that must occur before the contract will be performed. For example, the following words in a contract create a condition precedent:

> I promise to sell you my house for $250,000 if the house I am purchasing is completed by the signing of the deed.

Here the condition precedent is the completion of the purchased house. The contract may not be enforceable until the condition has occurred. Therefore, if the house being purchased has not been completed by the time the deed is to be signed, there is no contract.

Most employment contracts include examples of conditions precedent. For example, the following contract language establishes a condition precedent:

> I, GREGORY ALVAREZ, agree to work as a paralegal for the RACHEL AVERY, ESQ. law firm for $2,500 per month, payable on the first day of each month.

In this case, Mr. Alvarez must work for Ms. Avery for one month prior to receiving her $2,500 per month salary.

The most common type of condition is the **condition concurrent**, which creates an obligation on both parties at the time the contract is performed. For instance, the following contract wording creates conditions concurrent:

> I, SUSAN WOOD, agree to sell JENNIE KEAN my 2003 Ferrari automobile for $200,000, upon delivery.

Susan agrees to surrender the car to Jennie at the time that Jennie delivers the $200,000 to her. If the money is not delivered, the car will not be given up.

covenant the actual promise made by each party to a contract. The covenants create the terms of the contract.

breach a contract to fail to perform any promise that forms the whole or a substandard part of a contract.

condition an event that creates a duty to perform on one or both parties.

condition precedent a condition that must occur before the contract will be performed.

As another example, Bill goes to the local coffee house and buys a cup of cappuccino. He pays the store clerk and receives the coffee at the same time. The promise and the act transpire concurrently.

A **condition subsequent** occurs "after the fact," that is, after the contract has been performed. If this type of condition occurs, it relieves the parties of their previous performance. For example, suppose you order merchandise from a catalog that states that if you are dissatisfied for any reason, you may return the merchandise for a full refund. If you subsequently return that merchandise, the catalog company is obligated to refund the purchase price. The basic terms of the contract were that the company would send you the merchandise and that you would pay for it. The condition subsequent was created by the company's statement that the merchandise could be returned for a full refund. Your dissatisfaction with the merchandise relieved you of your obligations under the contract. If the company did not have this refund policy and you did not pay for the merchandise, you would have breached the contract.

Parol Evidence Rule

During negotiations for a contract, individuals may make oral agreements before the contract is finally written. Under the **Parol Evidence Rule**, all previous oral agreements merge in the writing, and the written contract cannot be changed by any oral evidence unless the party can prove that mistake, duress, or fraud occurred when the written contract was being prepared. Therefore, the attorney should advise clients that any oral agreements made between the parties should be included in the written contract.

Uniform Commercial Code

The **Uniform Commercial Code (UCC)** establishes regulations for commercial transactions. Both parties must deal with each other fairly and in good faith. They must perform on their contracts in a timely fashion. They are also required to follow the customs of the industry and the community in which the contract is made, unless the custom is illegal or unsafe. For instance, suppose that the Service Department of a car dealer keeps your automobile overnight in an unlocked lot and does not lock the car. If your car is stolen, the dealer may not defend the theft by stating that it is the "custom" to leave cars unlocked in open parking lots. This custom is clearly unsafe.

Each state has adopted its own version of the UCC. Therefore, you should check your own state's statutes to determine the specific rules governing contracts in your state. The following are examples of some specific provisions of the UCC.

Sale of Goods. Contracts for the sale of goods valued at more than $500 are governed by the UCC (Article II) and must be in writing. Contracts between merchants are also governed by this article.

condition concurrent a condition that occurs at the same time as the contract is performed and creates an obligation on both parties.

condition subsequent a condition that occurs after the contract has been performed and relieves the parties of their previous performance.

Parol Evidence Rule a rule that holds that when a contract is written, all previous oral agreements merge in the writing and that the written contract cannot be changed by any oral evidence unless there is proof of mistake, duress, or fraud in the writing of the contract.

Uniform Commercial Code (UCC) a set of regulations for commercial transactions that have been adopted, with variations, by all the states.

Goods are anything that is "movable" and include such things as merchandise, food, minerals, crops, oil, gas, and electricity.

Other provisions of the UCC hold the manufacturer and the seller **strictly liable** for any injuries caused to the buyer by a product that is defective. In other words, the plaintiff need only prove that the product was defective and caused her injuries in order to prevail in a lawsuit against the manufacturer or the seller. For example, Alex Gallardo purchased a bottle of juice from Gloria's Grocery. The bottle exploded, injuring Alex. He may sue both the manufacturer and the store for his injuries.

Contracts Involving Merchants. Since the UCC is liberally construed, the definition of a **merchant** is very broad. Therefore, not only is the person who regularly deals in goods of this type (an individual who purchases and sells this type of merchandise on an ongoing basis) considered to be a merchant, but anyone who holds himself out as having specific skills related to the product is also included. Therefore, a collector of vintage automobiles may be considered a "merchant" under this provision if she has particular knowledge of the value of these automobiles.

For example, Stephanie Daniels is a collector of vintage automobiles and belongs to the Vintage Car Club. She has been buying and selling these cars for five years and currently owns four classic automobiles. She agrees to sell one of her cars to Michael Nicholson. In this situation, Stephanie would be considered a merchant under the UCC. If Michael is subsequently injured as a result of a defect in the automobile, he may sue her for damages, and she may be held strictly liable for his injuries.

Check your state's statutes to determine the specific rules governing contracts under the UCC in your state and add them to the State Specific Information box.

goods anything that is movable; may include merchandise, food, minerals, crops, oil, gas, electricity, and the like.

strictly liable the condition of being legally responsible without regard to fault. Thus, if a product is defective and causes injury, the manufacturer and seller are held responsible even if they were not negligent.

merchant an individual who is engaged in the purchase and sale of merchandise on an ongoing basis.

STATE SPECIFIC INFORMATION

The rules governing contract under the UCC in _____ are as follows:

_____

_____

_____

_____

_____

_____

_____

Warranties

Warranties create guarantees in relation to the goods being purchased. Under the UCC, certain warranties may be implied. These implied warranties include (1) an implied warranty of merchantability and (2) an implied warranty of fitness for a particular purpose.

Under an **implied warranty of merchantability**, the seller is guaranteeing to the buyer that the item purchased is fit for the ordinary purpose of that particular product. If the buyer and the seller discuss how the buyer intends to use the product and the seller implies that the product is suitable (or fit) for that purpose, then the seller is making an **implied warranty of fitness** for a particular purpose.

For instance, Greta Diaz purchases a lawnmower from Carlos Salmon Hardware Store. If she makes no specific inquiries about the lawnmower, then only the implied warranty of merchantability applies. However, if she asks the seller whether the lawnmower will cut grass that is five inches tall and he assures her that it will, then he has made an implied warranty of fitness for a particular purpose. The seller is guaranteeing that that particular lawnmower will cut grass that is five inches tall.

As another example, Adam Lavasani goes to Wendy Crew's Shoe Store to purchase shoes for her son to use for Little League baseball. The salesperson tells Adam that these shoes are the type used in that league and says specifically that the team coaches have given him this information. However, the shoes do not have cleats, and Adam's son is not allowed to wear them for his baseball game. Wendy Crew's Shoe Store has breached the warranty of fitness for a particular purpose because the salesperson knew of the use to which the shoes would be put and deliberately misled the customer in order to sell the shoes.

This example also involves a breach of an **express warranty** because the seller specifically told the buyer that the shoes could be used for a particular purpose. Express warranties are created by an explicit statement in the contract itself. In this case, an oral contract was made for the sale of shoes. The salesperson explicitly told the buyer that the shoes could be used for the boy's baseball games.

Express warranties may also be made in writing or in a catalog description. For instance, Francine Stinson purchased a dress from Annette's catalog. The description of the dress stated that it was "machine washable." When the dress arrived, however, the label said "dry clean only." Thus, the express warranty in the catalog was breached.

Breach of Contract

If one of the parties to a contract fails to perform his obligations under the contract, the innocent party has an immediate cause of action for **breach of contract**. If a substantial portion of the contract has not been performed, a **substantial breach** has occurred. The plaintiff may sue to **rescind** (cancel) the contract or for **specific performance** to force the defendant to perform on the contract.

warranty a guarantee that goods are as promised.

implied warranty of merchantability a guarantee by the seller that a purchased item is fit to be used for the ordinary purpose of that particular item.

implied warranty of fitness for a particular purpose a guarantee by a seller that a purchased item is suitable to be used for a specified purpose.

express warranty an explicit guarantee included in a contract.

breach of contract the failure to perform any major part of a contract.

substantial breach the failure to perform a substantial portion of a contract.

rescind to cancel a contract and restore the parties to the positions they would have held if there had been no contract.

specific performance doing what was promised in a contract.

Damages for **rescission** (cancellation of the contract) will amount to the monetary loss suffered by the plaintiff. In a suit for specific performance, the defendant will be required to perform his portion of the contract. In some cases, if the plaintiff has suffered other damages as a result of the defendant's lack of performance, she may sue for both specific performance and **money damages**. In most cases, however, the plaintiff may sue for either rescission of the contract and receive her money back or for specific performance and force the defendant to perform.

Suppose Toni Alvarado hires a contractor to build a room onto her house. The contractor finishes half of the room and leaves. Toni will sue for specific performance on the contract and force the contractor to complete the room. But suppose adding the room required the walls of her house to be removed and she cannot live there while the work is being done. The courts would likely award Teresa damages on the contract for her living expenses while the house was uninhabitable.

In the entertainment industry, suits for specific performance may be filed against actors who fail to show up for filming or fail to play the part called for in the contract. Other examples where specific performance would be sought include contracts for the sale of real property and contracts for the purchase of unique property, such as art objects or antiques.

DRAFTING CONTRACTS

To draft a contract properly, you must have a clear understanding of the wishes of both parties involved. Discuss the contractual terms thoroughly with the client to make sure you know exactly what the client wants. Sample contracts clauses can be found in form books and transactional guides. Computer software packages also offer sample clauses. Always check contracts that have been previously prepared in your law office to determine both the format and the sample clauses used. Do not rely too heavily on forms, however, because your client's contract may be different from earlier contracts. The following list provides examples of clauses that are likely to appear in a contract:

1. *Parties to the Contract.* The first paragraph will contain the proper names of the parties to the contract, along with the date the contract is signed. For example:

   AGREEMENT made between MARY MARTINEZ (hereinafter referred to as "Buyer") and ANN ARMSTRONG (hereinafter referred to as "Seller") this 20th day of May, 2005, at Portland, Oregon.

2. *Consideration.* This paragraph constitutes the essence of the contract. It says what the parties are giving and receiving under the terms of the contract. For example:

rescission the act of canceling or abrogating a contract.

money damages a monetary amount awarded as compensation for injuries.

In consideration of the sum of Four Thousand Dollars ($4,000), Buyer agrees to purchase from the Seller her 2002 Honda Civic automobile, #XYZ 123.

3. *Time of Performance.*   Some contracts may indicate a future time at which the contract will be performed. Suppose that the parties in our example had agreed to pay the $4,000 and deliver the automobile on November 1. In that case, a clause such as the following would be included:

Buyer agrees to pay the $4,000 to Seller on November 1, 2006, on which date the Seller will deliver the automobile to the Buyer's residence at 1111 Main Street, in the City of Medford, Oregon.

4. *Signature Clause.*   A standard signature clause will have a line for the buyer's signature and a line for the seller's signature as follows:

_____

MARY MARTINEZ
Buyer

_____

ANN ARMSTRONG
Seller

Other clauses that might also be included in a contract include the following:

1. Conditions (as described earlier in the chapter)
2. UCC Information. Some states have special forms that are utilized for all UCC contracts. Check your own state's rules in this regard.
3. Special Warranties
4. Special Terms, such as installment payments or loan information.

ETHICS and ETIQUETTE

Paralegals are often called upon to draft contracts for clients. The attorney must be responsible for the final product and must review the contract before the client signs it.

If the lawsuit involves a breach of contract action, the paralegal must be certain to remind the attorney of the statute of limitations for this type of action. If the case is not filed before the statute runs, then the client may be barred from filing the action at a later date.

CHAPTER SUMMARY   ◆

To be a valid contract, its elements must include an offer, an acceptance, and consideration. Some contracts must be in writing to satisfy the Statute of Frauds. Contracts that are void may never be made valid.

Contracts may be either express or implied. Express contracts explicitly state their terms within the contract. Implied contracts are based on the intent and performance of the parties.

Certain contracts are covered by the Uniform Commercial Code and must be written. Express and implied warranties are inherent in these contracts.

Specific clauses are required to make a valid contract. The following items must be included: the parties, the date, the consideration, and the parties' signatures.

◆ KEY TERMS

acceptance

bilateral contract

breach a contract

breach of contract

condition

condition concurrent

condition precedent

condition subsequent

consideration

contract

covenant

express contract

express warranty

goods

implied-in-fact contract

implied warranty of fitness for a
   particular purpose

Implied warranty of merchantability

merchant

money damages

offer

offeree

offeror

Parol Evidence Rule

quasi-contract

rescind

rescission

specific performance

Statute of Frauds

strictly liable

substantial breach

Uniform Commercial Code (UCC)

unilateral contract

valid

void

warranty

◆ SELF TEST

Indicate whether the following statements are true (T) or false (F).

_____ 1. A contract is a legally enforceable agreement between parties.

_____ 2. The offeree makes an offer to the offeror of the intention to enter into a contract.

_____ 3. In order for a contract to be valid, the offer must be accepted.

_____ 4. Contracts may be formed for both legal and illegal purposes.

_____ 5. A minor's contracts are usually not enforceable.

Circle the correct answer for the following questions:

1. The elements of a contract are
   a. the offer.
   b. the acceptance.
   c. the consideration.
   d. all of the above.

2. Consideration has been defined as
   a. the manifestation of one party to enter into a contract.
   b. the offeree's acceptance.
   c. the bargained-for exchange.
   d. both (a) and (b).
   e. all of the above.

3. Void contracts include
   a. illegal contracts.
   b. implied contracts.
   c. contracts made by minors.
   d. (a) and (b).
   e. (a) and (c).

4. A contract that requires each party to the contract to promise to do or not to do an act is
   a. a bilateral contract.
   b. a unilateral contract.
   c. an express contract.
   d. an implied contract.

5. In a/an _____ contract, the promise is exchanged for the act itself.
   a. bilateral
   b. unilateral
   c. implied
   d. express

Fill-in-the-blanks.

1. In order to satisfy the _____, some contracts must be in writing.

2. The essence of the contractual terms is known as _____ .

3. The _____ establishes regulations for commercial transactions.

4. Courts provide an equitable remedy if an individual performs an act expecting to be paid even though no contract exists between the parties. This is called a/an _____ _____ .

5. Contracts in which the mutual assent of the parties is not manifested in words but in the actions of the parties are _____ .

✦ REVIEW QUESTIONS

1. What are the elements of a contract? Define each element.

2. What is the difference between express contracts, implied contracts, and quasi-contracts?

3. Are contracts made by minors legal? Explain the circumstances under which such contracts are enforceable.

4. What are the remedies for breach of contract?

5. Define the three types of conditions and discuss the circumstances under which each is used.

✦ NOTEBOOK PROJECTS

 1. Proofread and revise the Contract for Landscaping in Exhibit 14-2.

 2. Draft a simple contract between Marina Martin and Linda Johnson. Marina is selling her 1993 Jaguar XJS to Linda for the sum of $15,000. The automobile will be delivered on November 15 of this year and will be paid for at that time.

 3. Write a contract with your instructor about reading the chapter, answering the questions, and completing any other projects required. Include a time line of when these items will be completed.

 4. Go to the law library on your campus, or the local law library, and find a blank contract form or format for your state under its adaptation of the Uniform Commercial Code.

EXHIBIT 14-2   Contract for Landscaping

Courtesy: of Vicky B. Alexandra

Contrakt for Landscapping

THIS contract, made and enterred in to this _____ day of _____ , 200 ___, by and betwean the CONNOR INVESTMANT CORORATION, a corporation organized and existing under and by virtue of the laws of the State of NY and having its offise and principle place of business at 3611 Gimore Ave., Utica, Oneida Co, NY, here in after refered to as the "Corporation", and Terrance W. Kroft, Jr., d/b/a Kroft contracting, of 231 Templeton Avenue, Utica, NY, hear in after referred to as the "Contractor",

WITNESSETH:

Wereas, the Corporation has agreed to hire the contractor and the Contractor has agreed to perform certain work, labor and services and furnish materials for the Corporation relative to certian landscapping and grading at premices hereinafter discribed and persuant to the plans, drawings and specivacations submitted therefore.

NOW, THEREFORE, in consideratioon of there mutuel promises and covanants set forth herein the partys agreed as follows:

1.   The Contracter shall provide all materials and laber for a landscaping project at 7887 Skyway Blvd., Utica, Oneida Co.,
New York. The Contractor shall bee responsable for the carrying out and the completion of said project in accordence witht he specifacations set out in the attach drawings, which have been prepared by Robert Urban, refered too herein as the Landscape Architect. All work shall be done in the mannor set fourth in the grading plan and specifications tharein.

2.   The work on this contrakt shall began on or about the _____ day of _____ , 200 ___, and will be
completted on or abut the _____ dy of _____ , 200 ___,

3.   The agreed up on complension for the work and materials is Five Thousand Seven Hundred and no/100ths Dollars ($5,700)   Payment shall be maid to the contractor in accordence with the following schedule:

(A)   The Corporation shall pay to the Contractor the some of Twenty-seven Hundred ($2,700) Dollars up on the exacution of this contract.

(B)   The remaining balance of Three thousand and no/100ths Dollars ($3,000.00) shall be pay to the Contractor upon completion of all work discribed here under. Final payment shall e with-held untill all work has been inspected and approved by the Landscap Architact.

C.   Additionall or extraordinery expenses or changes to the original plans and specifacations must be submitted to the Corporation and approved by the Landscape Architect prier to incuring such costs. Any bils for such extraordinary expenses shall be submitted, in duplicate, to the Landscape Archiect for his approval.

4.   The entire contract between the partys is contained in this agreement. A copy of the drawings and specifications are attach hereto and marked Exhibit A and incorporated by referance as though more fuly set forth here in.

5.   All materials and equipment necessery to completing this project shall be provided by the Contractor, in accordance with the specification set fourth in the drawings hearin. All work shall be

continued

Exhibit 14-2 *continued*

comleted to confirm with sanderd building practice and the materials used shall be new. The quality of workmanship shall be first class.

6. Contractor shall provide Landscape Architect with a propose schedule of construction showing such ifnormation as required by him to make proper inspections.

This contract shall be binding upon the party and upon there hiers, successors, executers, administraters and assigns.

IN WITNESS whereof, the partys here to have set there hands and seals the day and year first above writing.

(SEAL)   Conner Investment Corp.

                                      By _____
                                      Richard Collins, Vice President

                                      _____
                                      Terrance W. Croft, Jr. d/b/a
                                      Kroft Contracting

STATE OF NEW YORK)
                                      SS.:
County of Oneida   )

On this _____ day of _____ , 200 ___ , before me came RICHARD CONNOR, to me known, who, being by me dully swore, did depose and say that he resides in Utica, NY; that he is the Vice President of CONNOR INVESTMENT CORPORATION the corporation discribed in, and which eacuted the forgoing instrument; that he knows the seal of said corporation; that the seal affixed o said intrument is such corporate seel; that it was affix by order of the Board of Directors of said corporation; and that he signed his name theirto by like order.

                                      _____

                                      Notary republic

STATE OF NEW YORK)
                          ss.:
COUNTY OF ONEIDA)

On this _____ day of _____ , 200 ___ , before me came TERRENCE W. CROFT, Jr., to me known and known to me to be the same person described in and who eacuted the forgoing instrucment and he dully acknowlledged to me that he exacuted the same.

                          _____
                          Notery Public

EMPLOYMENT AS A LEGAL ASSISTANT OR PARALEGAL

CHAPTER OUTCOMES

As a result of studying this chapter, the student will learn:

- How to prepare a winning resume
- How to write a successful cover letter
- How to prepare for and conduct an employment interview
- How to compose a follow-up letter for an interview

A WINNING RESUME

Preparing a winning resume takes time and effort. Since many employers will be screening hundreds of applicants, you must make sure that your resume stands out from the crowd.

The purpose of a resume is to enable you to get an interview for the position. When you prepare a resume, you are attempting to make a sale. Instead of a product, you are selling yourself. Therefore, you want to use persuasive words that will convince the prospective employer to "buy the product" (hire you).

Your resume should be one or two pages in length. Make sure it does not contain any typographical errors, misspelled words, or grammatical errors. Proofread your resume carefully. Do not depend on the "spell check" on your computer because it will not find misspellings that are actually other words (for example, *there* for *their* or *principal* for *principle*).

Law firms are very conservative. Therefore, use white or another neutral shade such as beige or gray for the paper. Never use bright-colored paper or colored printing.

If you do not feel comfortable preparing your own resume, it may be beneficial to hire a professional resume-writing service. These companies may be proficient in preparing winning resumes. Be sure to do some research before hiring the company, however. Ask to speak to former customers and discuss the services they asked the company to perform and the results they obtained.

The most common format for a resume is chronological. All items are listed in reverse chronological order with the most recent first. Exhibit 15-1 shows an example of a **chronological resume**. If you have changed jobs often, you may prefer a **functional resume**, which

chronological resume a resume with education and experience listed in reverse chronological order.

functional resume a resume that groups skills into functions.

EXHIBIT 15-1   A Chronological Resume

Jamie Paige

100 State Street
Anytown, US 11111
Telephone: (123) 456-7890
Email: jamie.paige@anytown.net

EDUCATION

Paralegal Studies Institute, Phoenix, AZ, June 2006
Civil Practice Certificate
ABA-approved Paralegal Program with emphasis in Civil Litigation
Member: Student Paralegal Association

Local University, Anytown, US, May 2005
B.A. in English, GPA: 3.8/4.0

SKILLS

- Speak, read, and write Spanish and Italian.
- Microsoft Office XP, Wordperfect 11.
- Westlaw Training Certificate.

EXPERIENCE

- **Receptionist**, Local Law Firm, Inc.
  Greeted clients and visitors; assisted legal secretaries with overflow typing; telephone contacts.
  4 years full-time; 4 years part-time while in college.

- **Paralegal Intern**, State Attorney General's Office
  Case management, document production, summarized depositions, prepared pleadings and
  legal documents. 1 year part-time.

PROFESSIONAL ASSOCIATIONS

Phoenix Paralegal Association
National Association of Legal Assistants

SEMINARS

Phoenix Bar Association Seminar on the Fast Track Rules in Civil Litigation

groups positions together by the skills they involve without giving the chronological sequence (see Exhibit 15-2).

Before you begin to prepare your resume, list your previous and present positions along with the duties and responsibilities each position involved. Try to relate those duties to the paralegal or legal assistant position for which you are applying. For instance, if you were formerly a bookkeeper, you might use words like "well organized" or "attention to detail" in describing your duties. Rewrite each duty you have performed in terms of skills required by the legal profession. Be realistic about your accomplishments. Employers will realize when you are magnifying your previous responsibilities.

After you have rewritten all of your previous duties and responsibilities, it is time to prepare the resume. It will include the following sections:

- *Heading* The heading should include your name, address, and telephone number. You will need an answering machine or voice mail to take messages at the number listed. Include your business telephone number only if you have a private telephone at work.

EXHIBIT 15-2   A Functional Resume

LEE KRUGER

1234 Any Street
Your Town, Your State ZIPCODE

EDUCATION

Your Local University, Your Town, Your State, June 2005. BS Degree in English.
GPA: 3.8.

Paralegal Studies Institute, Phoenix, Arizona, June 2006. ABA-approved
Paralegal program with emphasis in Civil Litigation. Civil Practice Certificate.

SKILLS
- Speak, read, and write Japanese.
- Wordperfect 11, Microsoft Word XP.
- Westlaw Training Certificate.

EXPERIENCE

Legal secretarial and research positons in law firms and corporations;
prepared documents and pleadings; case management; document
production; discovery preparation; trial preparation—5 years.

The message on your answering machine or voice mail should be professional. Prospective employers do not appreciate personal messages such as jokes, songs, or messages from children. State your name, say that you are not available to take the call, and indicate when you will be able to return the call. Remember that if the caller does not like your message, you may not get the interview.

- *Objective.*   Some texts on resume writing suggest that you state your objective. If you do, however, you will have to change it whenever you apply for a different position. Therefore, this section is optional.

- *Education.*   Only college-level education should be listed. In addition to the year you graduated, the degree, and the name and address of the college, list any honors received or special courses completed that would be valuable to the prospective employer. Indicate whether your paralegal program is ABA approved. If your grade point average (GPA) is 3.5 or above, mention this. The college you attended most recently should be listed first.

- *Special Skills.*   If you have skills that would be valuable in a law office, they should be set apart under this category. List the following information here:

  1. Bilingual (and language)
  2. Computer skills and software usage
  3. Special legal knowledge
  4. Writing skills
  5. Knowledge of machines (dictation, etc.)

- *Employment.*   Your work experience should be listed in reverse chronological order (most recent jobs first). Be sure to include any field work or internship experiences. Describe your duties and responsibilities in terms of the position for which you are applying. Try not to leave large gaps in employment.

- *Professional Organizations.*   List any professional organizations of which you are a member. Do not include religious organizations or affiliations. Do not list organizations that would reveal your age, such as the American Association of Retired Persons (AARP).

- *Professional Seminars.*   If you have attended continuing legal education seminars list name and date, and include a short description.

- *Volunteer Experience.*   If you have not held paying positions but have completed responsible volunteer work assignments, describe these jobs in a separate category or under Employment History with "Volunteer" indicated.

• *References.* The resume should mention that references are available on request. Contact at least three professionals who know you and are familiar with your work. Ask if they will allow you to use their names as references for employment. Ask former employers, doctors, lawyers, and former instructors. Your supervisor at your Internship Site would make an excellent reference. Prepare a separate sheet of references that includes names, addresses, and telephone numbers to bring to the interview.

THE COVER LETTER

A **cover letter** should accompany each resume. Employers expect to read a letter with your resume. Focus on the individual position for which you are applying and summarize the attributes and accomplishments that make you uniquely qualified for this position. Keep the letter brief, preferably two or three paragraphs.

A different cover letter should be sent with each resume. Never send a mass-produced letter that is designed to be used as an all-purpose letter for all situations. Each letter should be addressed to a named individual. If you are not sure of the name, call the law office and ask the full name and title of the individual who is responsible for screening resumes. Use the person's title in the inside address.

Let the reader know in the letter that you have done some research on the firm. Look the firm up in the **Martindale-Hubbell National Legal Directory** (a national directory of attorneys) for your area. Try to find information about recent cases handled by the firm. Let the reader know that you want this position. At the end of the letter, say that you are looking forward to an interview. Exhibit 15-3 shows a sample cover letter.

JOB FOLDER

Create a **job folder** or a notebook that lists all positions for which you apply. Keep track of all letters, follow-up telephone calls, research about the firm, and interviews. Make a cover sheet like the one in Exhibit 15-4 to catalog all inquiries. If you have a personal computer, you may wish to set up tracking system on your calendar.

Keep the folder next to the telephone so that when a prospective employer calls to set up an interview, you can instantly find the information about the firm in your folder.

WHERE TO LOOK FOR A POSITION

Besides the local newspaper, many other resources are available. If your locality has a legal newspaper, read it daily for prospective employment.

cover letter the letter that accompanies a resume.

Martindale-Hubbell National Legal Directory a national directory of attorneys.

job folder a summary of positions applied for.

EXHIBIT 15-3   A Sample Cover Letter

555 Your Street
Your Town, State ZIP
Today's date

John L. Burns, Esq.
Vice President, Law
Legal Corporation
111 Main Street
Phoenix, AZ 96301

Dear Mr. Burns:

You may recall that we met at the Phoenix Bar Association Seminar on Civil Litigation on March 25. At that time you suggested that I contact you upon my graduation.

In June, I received my paralegal certificate from the ABA-approved paralegal program at the Phoenix Institute for Paralegal Studies. During this period I spent a year as a student intern in the State Attorney General's Office with responsibilities in civil litigation, including document discovery, legal research, case management, and deposition summaries.

I have used both Wordperfect and Westlaw during school and at the Attorney General's Office. I also have experience with many legal software packages, such as LAW and LEGAL. A copy of my resume, listing my education and experience, is enclosed.

May I come in for an interview to discuss my qualifications further? Please call me at 444-1111 to arrange an interview.

Very truly yours,

John L. Washburn

JLW:ja
Enc.

EXHIBIT 15-4   A Job File

Name and address of firm:

Contact Person & Title:

_____

_____

_____   Telephone:_____

DATE OF FIRST CONTACT:

RESUME SENT:

FOLLOW-UP CONTACT:

DATE OF INTERVIEW:
    Name of Interviewer:

THANK YOU LETTER:

FOLLOW-UP CONTACT:

SECOND INTERVIEW:
    Interviewer:

THANK YOU LETTER SENT:

JOB OFFER:

BACKGROUND OF FIRM FROM MARTINDALE-HUBBELL:

    Area of law:

    Size of firm:

    Major cases:

    Major clients:

    Other pertinent information:

Law Firms

Use the Martindale-Hubbell National Legal Directory to find law firms in your locality. Apply to those that are the size you want and that specialize in an area that interests you. This directory is an outstanding source for obtaining information about law firms, such as their size, names of attorneys, schools they attended, type of law practiced, professional affiliations, and other personal information. Some firms list their major clients.

Large Cases

Read the local and legal newspapers to keep track of large cases, that are being litigated. Apply to those firms because they may need additional employees for these cases.

Government Offices

Positions may be available in federal, state, and county government offices.

Federal Government. To apply for a position with the federal government, complete a Standard Form 171, which is similar to an employment application. Obtain the form from your local federal Office of Personnel Management (OPM). Make several copies of the form, with the specific position left blank. Then you can type in the position whenever you apply for an opening. A separate form must be completed for each position sought. By completing all information except the position desired, you will not have to complete a new form each time you apply for a position.

Before completing the form, obtain a copy of the Hiring Standards for each type of position from the Office of Personnel Management. Use these standards in your application so that it reflects the qualifications required for the positions you desire. Doing this also helps alleviate the need to complete a separate form for every position for which you apply.

To obtain additional information about positions in the federal government, contact the local office or write to the following address:

Office of Personnel Management
Room 5L45
1900 E Street, NW
Washington, DC 20415

State and County Governments. Many state and county departments employ paralegals and legal assistants in the criminal area in prosecution and defense. Paralegals assist in preparing cases for trial, do legal research, find and prepare witnesses for trial, and investigate cases. Legal assistants may also assist in case preparation and do factual investigation to assist the attorney and paralegal.

On the defense side, usually called the Public Defender, paralegals and legal assistants interview the accused and conduct background investigations. The Prosecutor (or District Attorney) may require the investigation of prior convictions, legal research, case preparation, and factual investigation.

County governments may employ paralegals and legal secretaries in a variety of departments. The Department of Consumer Affairs helps consumers with problems with merchants, landlords, tenants, and other organizations. The County Counsel handles lawsuits against the county.

Corporations

Go to your local library to obtain a copy of **Standard and Poor's Register of Corporations**, which lists corporate offices, officers, and their addresses. Call corporations that are located in your area to learn whether they hire paralegals or legal assistants. If one of the corporate officers listed is "General Counsel" or "Vice President, Law," the corporation will have an in-house Legal Department that you can contact.

Professional Organizations

Networking with other professionals in your field is the best way to obtain a position. Join your local professional organization as a student member, attend the meetings, and network.

If you have already joined an organization, you will have obtained many business cards of individuals you met at the meetings. Write to each of them, reminding them of your meeting and inquiring about openings at their firms.

Some professional organizations have job banks for members. Members can send resumes to the job bank. Prospective employers who contact the organization are sent (or faxed) copies of resumes that match their requirements. These firms may not advertise their positions in the newspaper.

Agencies

A number of agencies are available for providing help in obtaining temporary legal positions. You may find them in a local telephone book or on the Internet. Two Web sites are:

> http://theaffiliates.com
> http://legaltemps.com

Seminars

Attend seminars of the local bar associations and other professional organizations in the legal field. Network with the attorneys at the seminars and let them know you are about to graduate. Bring copies of your resume and business cards to distribute at the seminar.

Standard and Poor's Register of Corporations a national directory of corporations.

Volunteer Work

Government agencies, nonprofit organizations, and legal aid offices welcome volunteers to help with their legal work. Some courts also allow students to volunteer in the clerk's office or in the courtroom.

Advertising

Some people have obtained positions by placing advertisements in the local legal newspaper under "Positions Wanted." If there is a legal newspaper in your locality, ask about the cost of these advertisements. Call some telephone numbers in prior ads to learn if the individuals obtained results. If you place an ad, list any attributes or skills that make you unique and set you apart from other candidates. Be sure to include your telephone number.

Mass Mailings

Try to send out between ten and twenty resumes each week. If you are applying to firms in the Martindale-Hubbell Directory, start at the A's and fill out a 3 × 5 card for each firm in your area to which you will apply. Write the name, address, and telephone number of the firm. Call to ask who does the hiring and send that person a cover letter and resume. If you are interested in working in a corporation, follow the same procedure using Standard and Poor's Directory.

Some prospective applicants have found it effective to suggest that they will volunteer their time for a short period before actually being hired. In this way, the employer can learn that you would be a valuable employee.

Keep a comprehensive file of all firms to whom you send resumes. Keep responses in the file, along with interview information.

Follow-Up

Follow up all letters with a telephone call. Ask if your resume was received and whether the firm has any questions to ask or would like to schedule an interview. Be persistent but don't be a nuisance.

Informational Interviews

If a firm where you would like to work does not have any openings, try to arrange an informational interview with the hiring authority. Say that you would like to spend fifteen to twenty minutes of the person's time discussing a future career in the organization.

PREPARING FOR THE INTERVIEW   ✦

An interview is a form of two-way communication. Not only does the employer want to get information about you, but you must get information about the organization as well. The interview gives you the opportunity to learn whether this is a firm where you want to work. Therefore, you should make up a list of questions before the interview.

Write out answers to standard interview questions prior to the interview. You may find these questions on the Internet or in books related to the job interview process.

Research the firm where the interview is being conducted to determine the type of law practiced, the size, specialty areas, and any other pertinent information. This information is available at:

http://www.martindale.com	Martindale-Hubbell Legal Directory
http://www.attorneyfind.com	West Legal Directory

Practice the interview with a friend or in front of a mirror. Note any distracting or annoying mannerisms. Learn your questions from memory so that you don't have to refer to notes at the interview.

How to Dress

Dress conservatively. A woman should wear a neutral-colored suit, minimal makeup and jewelry, and neutral shoes and hose. A man should wear a dark suit, white shirt, conservative tie, polished shoes, and long socks. Clothing should be color coordinated in muted tones. Do not chew gum or smoke. Carry a small briefcase with extra copies of your resume, a list of references, letters of recommendation from your references, writing samples, and a list of questions.

A few days before the interview, check the clothes you plan to wear to be sure they are clean and pressed. Polish your shoes. Try your clothes on to be sure they fit properly. Lay your clothes out the night before the interview.

Punctuality

You must arrive at the interview site on time. One attorney I know will not conduct an interview if the individual arrives more than five minutes late. If you are not familiar with the traffic patterns or location, do a "dry run" from your home to the interview site at the same time of day your interview is scheduled. Check to see where you can park, especially if you are driving to a large metropolitan area.

If you do not know the location, ask the receptionist or the interviewer for directions and parking information when you arrange the interview. Do not ask if the firm will validate your parking, however.

THE INTERVIEW ITSELF ✦

Try to arrive at the interview site about fifteen minutes early. Make a stop to check your clothes and appearance.

When you arrive at the office, give the receptionist your name and say you have an appointment with the interviewer. Be friendly but professional. If you must wait, choose a chair that is easy to get up from. Don't sink into a comfortable sofa that requires you to struggle to stand up.

In most cases, the interviewer will walk out to the reception area to greet you. Stand, introduce yourself, and shake hands firmly. Smile and establish eye contact.

If you must complete an application, write neatly and legibly using black ink. Use your resume as a reference source for dates and names.

When you enter the interviewer's office, sit in the chair indicated; if none is suggested, sit across from the desk. Be sure that you maintain eye contact and answer questions directly. Display self-confidence when discussing your accomplishments, skills, and education. Although you should be proud of your background and achievements, do not appear arrogant. Let the interviewer complete that portion of the interview before asking your questions. Never interrupt the interviewer during the interview.

Be prepared to answer questions about your resume, such as former employment, education, and skills. Open-ended questions like "Tell me about yourself" should be expected.

Prohibited Questions

Because of the Civil Rights Act, Title VII, employers may not ask about certain areas that may appear to be discriminatory. Questions about age, height, weight, marital status, children, ethnic background, religion, and other personal matters are not allowed.

Your Questions

Ask specific questions about any aspect of the position that is important to you. Do not ask questions that have already been answered. Do not ask questions about bonuses, salary, and overtime, unless they are major considerations in accepting a position.

Request a tour of the office and pay particular attention to the location of your prospective office. The size and decor of your office usually provide valuable information about the firm's opinion of your position. Compare your office with other offices in the firm.

ETHICS and ETIQUETTE

When the legal secretary or paralegal is seeking a position in a law firm, she must be completely honest and accurate about her education and experience. Potential conflict of interest situations must be explained. For instance, if you worked at a firm whose client was involved in a lawsuit against one of the potential employer attorney's clients, you should inform the attorney at your employment interview.

Follow-Up

After the interview, prepare an evaluation of the firm and the position for your file. Write a thank you letter to the interviewer stressing your desire to work for the firm. Emphasize some of your attributes that would be of value to the firm.

CHAPTER SUMMARY ✦

Winning resumes create a competitive edge in the employment marketplace. Most prospective employers like the resume to be no more than two pages in length. The resume is an opportunity to convince an organization to hire you; hence, persuasive words should be utilized. The resume should include a heading, objective, education, special skills, previous employment history, and professional organizations or seminars attended. Volunteer experience related to the legal profession may be included. A cover letter written specifically for each position should accompany the resume.

The interview is a critical stage of the job search process. The individual should be well prepared and dress professionally. After the interview, a follow-up letter should be written thanking the interviewer. Special attributes suited to this position should be emphasized.

✦ KEY TERMS

chronological resume	job folder
cover letter	Martindale-Hubbell National Legal Directory
functional resume	Standard and Poor's Register of Corporations

✦ NOTEBOOK PROJECTS

1. List your previous jobs and your duties at each. Reword the duties for your resume.

2. Prepare a resume for yourself using the format shown in Exhibit 15-1 or 15-2.

3. Prepare a cover letter to accompany your resume. Choose a law firm from the local legal directory or Martindale-Hubbell and address the letter to the hiring authority for that firm.

4. Prepare a list of questions that you would ask at an employment interview.

5. Research interview questions through an Internet job source site and write out answers to five questions.

6. Research a law firm where you would like to work using one of the directories discussed above. Determine its legal specialties, size, firm type, and services. Write a report of your findings emphasizing your reasons for choosing this firm.

Useful Web Sites

Federal Government Agencies/Organizations

Central Intelligence Agency (CIA)	**http://www.odci.gov/cia/**
Department of Justice	**http://www.usdoj.gov**
Department of Transportation	**http://www.dot.gov/**
Federal Aviation Administration	**http://www.faa.gov/**
Federal Bureau of Investigation (FBI)	**http://www.fbi.gov/**
National Transportation Safety Board	**http://www.ntsb.gov/aviation/aviation.htm**
Securities and Exchange Commission (SEC)	**http://www.sec.gov/**
State Department	**http://www.state.gov/index.html**

Finding Law Firms or Legal Organizations

FindLaw	**http://www.findlaw.com**
West Legal Directory	**http://www.lawoffice.com/**
Attorney Locator Service	**http://www.attorneyfind.com/**
Martindale-Hubbell Legal Directory of Attorneys	**http://www.martindale.com**

Legal Employment Center

Hieros Gamos	**http://www.hg.org/employment.html**

Professional Organizations

American Bar Association	**http://www.abanet.org/**
National Association of Legal Assistants	**http://www.nala.org**
National Association of Legal Professionals	**http://www.nals.org**
National Federation of Paralegal Associations	**http://www.paralegals.org**

State Government Offices

http://www.findlaw.com/

GLOSSARY

A

acceptance an assent by the person to whom an offer has been made to enter into a contract.

administrator individual appointed to administer an estate when the decedent did not have a will or did not name an executor in the will.

adoption a legal proceeding where adoptive parents become the legal parents of an adopted child. The birth parents give up all legal rights and responsibilities for the child.

advice an opinion given to clients by their lawyers and meant to assist in determining correct action or conduct.

agency adoption the adoption of a child through a public or private agency.

aided and abetted assisted someone in committing a crime; knowledge of unlawful purpose with intent to commit, encourage, or facilitate commission of the crime by act or advice.

American Bar Association the largest voluntary organization of lawyers in the country.

Annual Report a yearly report issued by a corporation describing the past year's activities.

annulment the act of making a marriage void; also called nullity.

answer the first pleading by the defendant in a lawsuit responding to the charges and demands of the plaintiff's complaint.

appellant the individual or entity that appeals a case.

appellee the individual or entity against whom the appellant appeals; the opposing party to the appeal.

arraignment the step in the criminal justice process when the defendant is brought before a judge to hear the charges and enter a plea.

arson the intentional burning of another's home or building.

Articles of Incorporation first document in corporate formation. Lists the name, purpose, agent for process, stock structure, and duration of the corporation.

assault attempted battery.

attorney lawyer; a person licensed to practice law.

authentication a formal act that certifies that a document is correct so that it may be admitted into evidence; evidence proving a document is what it purports to be.

B

bankruptcy a procedure by which a person is relieved of his debts once he has placed all property and money under the court's supervision.

battery harmful or offensive touching of another without consent.

bequest a gift of personal property by will; sometimes used to describe any property given in a will.

Best Evidence Rule a rule that requires that when a document is admitted into evidence at trial, either the original must be used or the attorney must show why it is not available.

beyond a reasonable doubt the standard of proof in criminal cases; a higher standard than the preponderance of the evidence standard used in civil cases.

bilateral contract a contract in which the contracting parties are bound to fulfill obligations reciprocally toward each other; a contract involving mutual promises between the parties.

billable hours those hours spent working on a client's case that will be billed to the client.

Board of Directors the individuals who oversee the running of a corporation.

breach a contract to fail to perform any promise that forms the whole or a substandard part of a contract.

breach of contract the failure to perform any major part of a contract.

burglary the unlawful entry of a building belonging to another with the intent to commit a felony inside the building

Bylaws rules that govern the day-to-day operations of the corporation.

C

challenges for cause dismissal of prospective jurors where bias or prejudice can be shown.

Chapter 7 bankruptcy a type of bankruptcy handled under Chapter 7 of the Federal Bankruptcy Act; the bankrupt's property is distributed among creditors who file and prove their claims and the individual may keep some personal property.

Chapter 11 bankruptcy a bankruptcy for business reorganizations short of full bankruptcy.

Chapter 13 bankruptcy a bankruptcy for individuals with standard incomes who wish to adjust debts.

chronological resume a resume with education and experience listed in reverse chronological order.

close corporation a corporation formed by a small number of people who manage and control business.

closing a formal proceeding held in a lawyer's office where property documents and property are transferred from the seller to the buyer.

closing argument the summary of the case each attorney presents to the jury at the end of the trial.

cohabitation living together without a marriage contract and without the intent to enter a common-law marriage.

cohabitation agreement an agreement made between a couple who live together that sets out how their property is to be divided if the relationship ends.

common-law marriage when a man and woman agree to enter a marital relationship and live together as if married but never go through a formal marriage ceremony.

community property property acquired during the marriage that is not a gift or inheritance. The concept applies only in community property states. Property may be acquired by either spouse and is owned by both spouses equally.

complaint the first main paper filed in a civil lawsuit; it includes, among other things, a statement of the wrong or harm done to the plaintiff by the defendant, a request for specific help from the court, and an explanation why the court has the power to do what the plaintiff wants.

condition an event that creates a duty to perform on one or both parties.

condition concurrent a condition that occurs at the same time as the contract is performed and creates an obligation on both parties.

condition precedent a condition that must occur before the contract will be performed.

condition subsequent a condition that occurs after the contract has been performed and relieves the parties of their previous performance.

condominium ownership of a unit within a multiple-unit building.

condoning misconduct when one spouse is aware of the other's misconduct and accepts it.

confidentiality the requirement that a lawyer, or anyone working for a lawyer, not disclose information received from a client.

connivance when one spouse lures the other into misconduct.

Consent and Agreement in adoption proceedings, the forms in which the adopting parents obtain the approval of the biological parents.

consideration the bargained-for exchange created by a contract. Each party gives up and receives something of value as consideration.

consolidation the process in which two corporations dissolve and then join together to form a third corporation.

contingency fees a percentage of the award received in a civil case that is paid to the attorney for his or her fee.

contract a legally enforceable agreement between two or more parties; consists of an offer, acceptance, and consideration.

cooperative similar to a condominium except that the unit is represented by a share of stock.

corporation business entity existing separate and apart from its owner.

counteroffer a higher price named by a seller after a would-be buyer has made an offer.

court forms forms used for some of the documents that are filed with the courts; generally published by the courts and available on their Web pages.

covenant the actual promise made by each party to a contract. The covenants create the terms of the contract.

cover letter the letter that accompanies a resume.

creditor individual or entity to whom the debtor owes money.

cross-complaint a claim brought by one defendant against another or by a defendant against a plaintiff based on the same subject matter as the plaintiff's lawsuit.

cross-examination the questioning of a witness by the opposing attorney.

D

debtor individual or entity that owes money and initiates a bankruptcy proceeding.

decree in adoption proceedings, a form issued by the court that states that the child may be adopted and indicates the child's new name.

demurrer a legal pleading that states that the other side's argument does not give them a legal argument that can be upheld in court.

deposit money given by a buyer to a seller as a pledge or down payment when an offer to purchase property is made; also called a binder or earnest money deposit.

derivative suit a suit by shareholders against a corporation.

devise gift of real property by will.

direct examination the questioning of a witness by the attorney who called that witness.

dissolution 1. The term used for no-fault divorce in many states. 2. Terminating the existence of a corporation; can be voluntary or involuntary.

divorce adversary proceeding to end a marriage.

docket a list of cases, usually with file numbers, scheduled for trial in a court; a list of specific actions taken in a court.

document (word) processing programs programs that allow the legal assistant or paralegal to assist in writing, editing, revising, and printing pleadings, legal documents, correspondence, and research memoranda.

double jeopardy being tried for the same crime twice when a verdict was reached in the first trial.

E

easement a nonownership interest in land that gives its owner the right to the limited use of land owned by another.

e-mail electronic mail.

embezzlement taking property that is lawfully in one's possession with the intent to steal.

equitable interest an ownership interest that does not entitle one to possession of the property, which occurs at the transfer of the deed when the owner obtains a legal interest in the property.

escrow the time period during which a title search is conducted on property; extends up to the time the property is transferred from the seller to the buyer; used in some states instead of a closing.

estate the property a decedent owned at death.

eviction formal proceeding by an owner of leased property to remove tenants.

Examination of Judgment Debtor a formal court hearing where the defendant appears to answer questions about her assets.

executor an individual named in a will who is responsible for administering the provisions of the will and distributing the property after the maker of the will dies; the executor is responsible for handling the decedent's affairs, including paying bills of the estate.

executory contracts contracts in which the terms have not yet been carried out and may depend on a future event.

express contract an actual oral or written agreement between the parties.

express warranty an explicit guarantee included in a contract.

F

fee simple absolute ownership of property.

felony a serious crime punishable by incarceration in a state prison for more than one year.

Felony Murder Rule a doctrine that holds that if a death occurs during the commission of a serious felony, all defendants who were involved may be convicted of first-degree murder, regardless of which defendant actually caused the death.

Final Decree Nunc Pro Tunc a final dissolution of a marriage that is filed after the appropriate time for filing a final decree, but is effective as of the time the dissolution would have taken place if the final decree had been filed in a timely manner.

fixture an item of personal property that is permanently attached to land or to a building is such a way that it becomes part of the real property.

franchise the right to market a company's goods or services in a particular territory. After purchasing the franchise from a franchise organization, an individual owns the business and leases the equipment and facilities from the parent organization.

functional resume a resume that groups skills into functions.

G

garnishment a procedure that enables a creditor to obtain a percentage of the defendant's wages for payment of debt owed.

general jurisdiction court that may hear any kind of case brought before it except for those cases that must be brought in federal court. They may be called superior courts, circuit courts, or county courts.

general partners individuals who invest money in the business and are involved in its day-to-day operations.

goods anything that is movable; may include merchandise, food, minerals, crops, oil, gas, electricity, and the like.

grant deed deed in which the seller guarantees that she has title to the property and the right to convey it and that the property is free of encumbrances except any that have previously been disclosed to the buyer.

grounds for divorce reasons the state allows a couple to obtain a divorce.

guardian ad litem a guardian appointed by a court to take care of the interests of a person who cannot legally take care of him- or herself in a lawsuit involving that person.

H

holographic will handwritten will entirely in the writer's handwriting.

homicide the unlawful killing of another without justification.

hourly fees a set amount per hour that the attorney who works on a case charges the client.

I

implied warranty of merchantability a guarantee by the seller that a purchased item is fit to be used for the ordinary purpose of that particular item.

implied warranty of fitness for a particular purpose a guarantee by a seller that a purchased item is suitable to be used for a specified purpose.

implied-in-fact contract a contract that is inferred from the conduct of the parties.

in rem jurisdiction jurisdiction is obtained over property that is the subject of the lawsuit and is located in that state.

indecent exposure the intentional exposure of private parts of the body in public.

independent adoption an adoption that is not carried out through an agency; usually carried out though an attorney who acts as a middleperson between the biological mother and the adoptive parents.

infraction a minor offense, such as a traffic violation, that is punishable by fine.

Injunction a judge's order to a person to do or to refrain from doing a particular thing.

involuntary dissolution the termination of a corporation against the will of the director; must be initiated by the state, but shareholders or creditors may petition to begin dissolution proceedings.

J

job folder a summary of positions applied for.

joint tenancy ownership of an undivided interest in property by two or more owners with a right of survivorship.

judgment the decision in a civil case; may include money damages.

jurisdiction the geographical area within which a court or a public official has the right and power to operate. Also, the power of a particular court to hear a case.

jury instructions the instructions the judge gives to the jury before deliberations to explain the law the jury should apply.

K

kidnapping the transportation of an individual from one place to another against his will.

L

larceny taking and carrying away another's property with the intent to steal.

lease written rental agreement between a landlord and tenant granting the tenant the right to possession of the property for terms prescribed in the lease.

legal title right to possession of property; transferred through a deed.

letters testamentary forms approved by the probate court that authorize an executor to administer the estate.

limited jurisdiction courts that have the authority to hear certain types of cases. For instance, some courts have the authority to hear only family matters, probate matters, or cases where there is a limited amount of money in dispute.

limited partners individuals who invest capital in the business without management responsibility or personal liability.

listing agreement an agreement made with a real estate agent when property is put up for sale; sets out the agent's commission, the length of the agreement, and the rights and responsibilities of the parties.

M

mail merge an element of most word processing programs that enables the user to generate form letters, envelopes, mailing labels, registers, and mass e-mail and fax circulation.

Marital Settlement Agreement an agreement made by a married couple contemplating divorce that sets forth the manner in which property is to be divided.

marriage the legal union of a man and woman as husband and wife.

Martindale-Hubbell National Legal Directory a national directory of attorneys.

mayhem the purposeful and permanent disfigurement of another.

mental impairment mental defect.

merchant an individual who is engaged in the purchase and sale of merchandise on an ongoing basis.

merger the process in which one corporation takes over another corporation.

Miller v. California the case in which the U.S. Supreme Court defined obscenity.

Miranda v. Arizona the case in which the U.S. Supreme Court set out the rights of the accused during interrogation by the police. The rights are known as the *Miranda* rights.

misdemeanor a minor crime punishable by incarceration in a county jail for up to one year.

money damages a monetary amount awarded as compensation for injuries.

N

no-fault divorce a divorce available in many states that requires neither party to prove grounds. Either party desiring a divorce files a petition to commence the action; also called a dissolution.

nolo contendere Latin for "I will not contest it." A plea by which the defendant does not admit guilt, but also does not contest the charges.

nonbillable hours those hours spent working in the law office that cannot be billed directly to the client.

nuncupative will oral will valid in few states.

O

obscenity any material that appeals to the prurient interest, shows offensive sexual conduct as defined by applicable state law, and lacks serious literary, artistic, political, or scientific value.

offer 1. The manifestation by the offeror of the intention to enter into a contract. 2. Proposal or bid to purchase property at a particular price.

offeree the party to whom an offer to enter into a contract is made; the party who accepts the offer.

offeror the party who makes an offer to another party to enter into a contract.

opening statement the introduction to the facts of the case each attorney presents to the jury at the beginning of the trial.

Order to Show Cause (OSC) a preliminary hearing in a dissolution action where the court issues temporary orders on such matters as support and child custody.

P

palimony support paid to one party after a relationship ends based on an implied contract between the couple while they lived together.

paralegal/legal assistant individual who does law-related work for attorneys, government agencies, and corporations; must work under attorney supervision.

Parol Evidence Rule a rule that holds that when a contract is written, all previous oral agreements merge in the writing and that the written contract cannot be changed by any oral evidence unless there is proof of mistake, duress, or fraud in the writing of the contract.

partnership an association of two or more individuals who have joined tighter to operate a business for profit.

peremptory challenges dismissal of prospective jurors without having to give a reason; may not be used to exclude jurors solely on the basis of race or ethnic background.

personal jurisdiction (in personam jurisdiction) means personal jurisdiction over these particular parties. This means that the court has the power or authority over the individuals in the case, and particularly the defendant.

personal property items that are not attached to land or buildings are movable or easily transportable from one location to another.

petition the form filed to initiate a no-fault divorce or dissolution; also the form filed to initiate an adoption.

plea bargaining pleading guilty to a lesser offense with less jail time than the offense that was originally charged.

preliminary hearing a hearing in court to determine whether enough evidence exists to hold the defendant for trial.

prenuptial agreement an agreement made in contemplation of marriage that delineates the separate property of each party and sets out how property acquired during marriage will divided if the couple separate.

preponderance of the evidence the burden of proof in civil suits. It means that the event in question is more likely than not to have happened in that manner.

probable cause a reasonable ground for believing that a person has committed a crime.

probate the court procedure used to validate a will, appoint a personal representative, and distribute property.

professional corporation a corporation formed by professionals, such as doctors or lawyers.

project fees attorney's fees that are set based on the work the attorney performs, such as writing a will or preparing a trust agreement.

prostitution the provision of sexual favors in exchange for money.

Q

quasi in rem jurisdiction jurisdiction is obtained if the defendant owns property in that state, even if the property is not the subject of the lawsuit. However, in that case, the judgment must be collected from the property in the state.

quasi-community property property in another state that would be community property if located in the state where the couple reside.

quasi-contract a legal fiction that allows a person to receive payment in a situation where there is, in fact, no contract but where circumstances are such that to deny payment would result in the unjust enrichment of the other party.

quitclaim deed deed in which the seller conveys any interest that he may have in the property; least advantageous type of deed; often used to clear title to property.

R

rape a forcible sexual attack; sexual intercourse without consent.

real property includes land and things permanently attached to the land.

recidivism the return to prison of an individual who was previously incarcerated; individual sometimes known as habitual offender.

recrimination when both parties to a divorce have committed the same misconduct.

rescind to cancel a contract and restore the parties to the positions they would have held if there had been no contract.

rescission the act of canceling or abrogating a contract.

retainer fees fees paid at the outset of the case by the client for use only in that particular case.

robbery taking another's property from her person by threat or force.

S

self-proving clause clause in a will before the witness signatures that eliminates the need for the witnesses to sign a proof of subscribing witness form to attest to the fact that the will was signed by the decedent in the presence of the witness.

separate property property acquired before marriage or during marriage through gift or inheritance. The concept applies only in community property states.

shareholders owners of a corporation.

Shepardize use a Shepard's case citator to trace the history of a case after it is decided.

sole proprietorship unincorporated business, usually owned by one person.

Special Circumstances Rule a rule that holds that if a victim dies during the commission of a serious felony, as specified by statute, the defendant may receive the death penalty if he committed the felony, if he aided or abetted its commission with the intent to kill, or if he aided or abetted with reckless indifference to human life and was a major participant in the crime.

specific performance doing what was promised in a contract.

Standard and Poor's Register of Corporations a national directory of corporations.

Statute of Frauds an English statute, adopted with variations by all the states, that requires certain types of contracts to be in writing.

Statute of Limitations a law that sets a maximum amount of time after something happens for it to be taken to court.

statutory fees attorney fees set by statute, such as for the probate of an estate.

statutory rape the rape of a minor.

stepparent adoption the adoption by one spouse of the other spouse's child or children from a former marriage.

strictly liable the condition of being legally responsible without regard to fault. Thus, if a product is defective and causes injury, the manufacturer and seller are held responsible even if they were not negligent.

Subchapter S corporation a corporation that is limited to twenty-five shareholders and to domestic operations; may offer significant tax advantages because the income and losses are reported on the owner's personal income tax returns. In size and structure, it is similar to a close corporation.

subject matter jurisdiction the case must be the kind of case this particular court hears in order for the court to have subject matter jurisdiction over this particular case.

substantial breach the failure to perform a substantial portion of a contract.

summons a notice delivered by a sheriff or other authorized person informing a person of a lawsuit against him; it tells the person to be in court at a certain time or risk losing the suit without being present.

T

tenancy in common joint ownership of property with no right of survivorship.

testator the person who makes a will.

tickler file a reminder system to keep track of deadlines; similar to a calendar, with notations each day about what needs to be done that day.

time sheet a system to keep track of the time spent working on each case; used to bill clients.

title insurance policy policy issued by a title insurance company that insures that the buyer of property is receiving a clear title.

trustee independent party appointed by the court in a bankruptcy proceeding for the purpose of liquidating the assets and distributing funds to creditors.

U

ultra vires acts acts outside the scope of the corporation's powers as set out in the Articles of Incorporation.

Uniform Commercial Code (UCC) a set of regulations for commercial transactions that has been adopted, with variations, by all the states.

unilateral contract a contract in which one party makes a promise and the other party performs some act.

unlawful detainer eviction process used in some states when the tenant stays beyond the time she has a right to occupy the property or she has breached the terms of the lease.

V

valid having legal efficacy or force; having been executed in the proper manner.

venue the local area where a case may be tried. A court system may have jurisdiction to take a case in a wide geographical area, but the proper venue for the case may be one place within that area for the convenience of the parties.

verdict the decision reached by a jury in a criminal case as to whether the defendant is guilty or not guilty; must be unanimous in most states.

void having no legal force or effect.

void marriage a marriage that is not legal; includes marriages between close relatives and bigamous relationships.

voidable capable of being adjudged void, but may also be made legal by taking certain steps.

voidable marriage a marriage that may be voided by one of the parties or may be made legal on the occurrence of certain events.

voir dire the process in which the judge and attorneys select a jury.

voluntary dissolution the termination of a corporation by the shareholders or the directors who act willingly and are not being forced to terminate by the state or creditors.

W

warrant an order issued by a magistrate authorizing the police to make an arrest, conduct a search, or carry out other procedures as part of the criminal justice process.

warranty a guarantee that goods are as promised.

warranty deed deed in which the seller guarantees that he holds full and complete ownership in the property and that the property is free of encumbrances unless specifically noted in the deed.

will a document in which a person tells how his property is to be handed out after death.

word processing (document processing) program that enables you to use the computer to support the preparation of correspondence and documents.

writ of attachment a writ of execution.

writ of certiorari a writ from the higher court asking the lower court for the record of the case; similar to an appeal but one which the higher court is not required to take for decision.

writ of execution a writ filed against assets of the debtor to enable a creditor to satisfy a judgment. The assets may be sold to pay the debt.

INDEX